GAYLORD
R

Encyclopedia of

MULTICULTURALISM

Encyclopedia of

MULTICULTURALISM

Volume 4

Daniel Ken Inouye – Mythology, American Indian

Editor

SUSAN AUERBACH

Marshall Cavendish
New York • London • Toronto

Published By
Marshall Cavendish Corporation
2415 Jerusalem Avenue
P.O. Box 587
North Bellmore, New York 11710
United States of America

∞ The paper in these volumes conforms to the American National Standard for Permanence of Paper for Printed Library Materials, Z39.48-1984.

Library of Congress Cataloging-in-Publication Data

Encyclopedia of multiculturalism / editor, Susan Auerbach.
  p. cm.
  Includes bibliographical references (p. 1767) and index.
  Contents: v. 1. A. Philip Randolph Institute–Business and corporate enterprise; v. 2. Mother Cabrini–Estonian Americans; v. 3. Ethnic and minority group names–Inner city; v. 4. Daniel Ken Inouye–Mythology, American Indian; v. 5. Names and name changes–Six Nations; v. 6. Slavery–Zoot-suit riots.
  ISBN 1-85435-670-4 (set : alk. paper). — ISBN 1-85435-674-7 (v. 4 : alk. paper)
  1. Pluralism (Social sciences)—United States—Encyclopedias. 2. Multiculturalism—United States—Encyclopedias. 3. Ethnology—United States—Encyclopedias. 4. United States—Ethnic relations—Encyclopedias. 5. United States—Race relations—Encyclopedias.
I. Auerbach, Susan, 1956-   .
E184.A1E58   1993
306.4′46′0973—dc20

93-23405
CIP
AC

Second Printing

PRINTED IN THE UNITED STATES OF AMERICA

Contents

Encyclopedia of
MULTICULTURALISM

Inouye, Daniel Ken (b. Sept. 7, 1924, Honolulu, Hawaii): Japanese American politician. Inouye first distinguished himself as a soldier in World War II, earning several decorations and losing his arm in battle. After

Daniel Inouye was elected to the U.S. Senate from Hawaii. (Library of Congress)

receiving his J.D. from George Washington University in 1952, Inouye became an assistant public prosecutor in Honolulu and then went into private practice. He served in the Hawaiian territorial legislature from 1954 to 1959; after statehood, he was elected as the first Representative from Hawaii and the first Japanese American to serve in Congress. He was elected to the U.S. Senate in 1963 and became well known a decade later as a member of the Select Committee investigating the Watergate scandal. He opposed American involvement in the Vietnam conflict and has been active in Democratic Party politics. He is the author of the autobiography *Journey to Washington* (1967).

Integration. *See* **Segregation, desegregation, and integration—historical overview** *or* **—definitions**

Intergroup relations: The United States is a multicultural nation representing the descendants of many diverse racial, ethnic, religious, and other cultural groups from all parts of the world. The way that groups have interacted has varied according to the social conditions that were present, such as exploitation, prejudice, and discrimination.

Several factors should be considered when seeking to understand intergroup relations. The first is the way that the groups came into contact: through voluntary migration (as in the immigration of Europeans seeking religious freedom), involuntary migration (as in the importation of African slaves), or invasion and conquest (as in the European seizing of American Indian lands).

A second factor involves the numerical size and geographic distribution of groups. If one group is larger than another, the economic and political relations will be unequal. A large group concentrated in a certain area might be perceived as more of a threat than a dispersed group with few members.

The last factor concerns social perceptions of cultural and physical differences. When a group is viewed positively, differences are not noticed. When a group is viewed negatively, even minor differences may become barriers to their acceptance. For example, African Americans have been historically oppressed because of socially defined differences. Although there are no longer any legal barriers in the form of JIM CROW LAWS, there is still a great deal of extralegal discrimination. Many African Americans remain disenfranchised from the political and economic system based on presumed physical differences of race. African Americans face higher rates of unemployment, POVERTY, and crime than whites or Latinos. Ostensibly this can be seen as the "fault" of African Americans themselves; however, closer study suggests that the dominant culture has maintained social distance, which breeds PREJUDICE, resulting in discrimination.

Models for relations between the WHITE ANGLO-SAXON PROTESTANT (WASP) majority and various minority groups in the United States have ranged from the extremes of ASSIMILATION to extermination over the past five hundred years. In the second half of the twentieth century, federal, state, and local governments, as well as schools, religious organizations, corporations, and labor unions, began to seek ways to improve intergroup relations. Indeed, intercultural relations, as it is called, became a field of academic study and professional expertise. At the same time,

Fires burn out of control during the Los Angeles riots in 1992. People of diverse backgrounds took part in the disturbances, which further strained intergroup relations. (AP/Wide World Photos)

focus shifted beyond the DOMINANT CULTURE to conflicts between minority groups, as in councils that sponsored dialogue on AFRICAN AMERICAN–KOREAN AMERICAN RELATIONS.

Assimilation. Though it has been controversial with some Americans, assimilation is one of the more benign ways that groups interact with each other. Assimilation is the process of lessening differences between groups to the point that minority group members are accepted by the dominant group as full members of society. As sociologists have noted, assimilation is a complex process of many stages; for example, a group can adopt aspects of the culture of the dominant group (ACCULTURATION) yet never be able to marry members of the dominant group. Most scholars agree that for complete assimilation to occur, the assimilating group must be seen as socially indistinguishable. Intergroup relationships must be those of a primary group, that is, intimate, face-to-face, and personal. If interactions are impersonal and formal, then the group will not assimilate totally but remain outsiders.

speak English and take up the values of Anglo American culture such as individualism, hard work, and thrift.

The VIETNAMESE AMERICANS are a recent example of an immigrant group successfully assimilating into American society. They first arrived in the United States as refugees in the mid-1970's, with most having faced numerous difficulties during the VIETNAM WAR. The majority came with few financial resources, yet despite initial language and cultural barriers they assimilated quickly into American society, sending their children to college and working as professionals or in highly skilled jobs. Some non-Vietnamese Americans helped to sponsor and orient the newcomers, paving

This conference on diversity in the Midwest aimed for greater understanding between various groups. (James L. Shaffer)

The United States has been the destination for many groups of immigrants who were escaping poverty or oppression in their homelands. The first European immigrants to what is now the eastern United States were from England. The national groups that followed ultimately adopted the English-derived culture. To be considered a "real" American, it was important to

the way for this adjustment. Other long-settled Americans, however, resented the rapid rise of the Vietnamese. For example, fishermen in Texas complained that Vietnamese fishermen were depleting the resources along the Gulf Coast; poor relations led to several violent incidents in the 1970's.

In the early 1900's, it was assumed that immigrants

would assimilate through Anglo-conformity and Americanization (becoming more like majority WASP Americans) or through melting their differences into a common identity. The MELTING POT THEORY of assimilation

blindly the culture of another group. They saw assimilation at best as paternalistic and at worst as racist.

Pluralism. CULTURAL PLURALISM is a form of intergroup contact in which each group recognizes the

Under cultural pluralism, children of different backgrounds are encouraged to respect their differences (Chicago, Ill.). (Jim and Mary Whitmer)

counters the idea of Anglo-conformity, since it assumes that all the different groups that migrated to the United States contributed to forming a new, unique American culture. This idea proposes that each group has some cultural element that is worthy of adoption in this intermingling of ideas and customs. The idealistic concept of the melting pot is dependent on people forgetting their prejudices. A major criticism of the melting pot model is that it did not create a new social structure or identity, only additions to Anglo American social structure and identity.

With the rise of the CIVIL RIGHTS MOVEMENT and the ETHNIC HERITAGE REVIVAL in the 1960's and 1970's, the idea of assimilation fell out of favor with many Americans. They were not willing to adopt

validity of the norms, values, and traditions of each other. Ideally, two different groups find themselves living next to each other but yet are equal in political and economic power. Intermarriage is discouraged but not expressly prohibited. Pluralism differs from assimilation in allowing people to keep their culture without any pressure to adopt the culture of the host society.

American society has long had ethnic enclaves that were permitted to use their language and practice their own culture and religion while participating in the mainstream culture. The Chinatowns and Little Havanas of urban areas, both of which maintain strong cultural traditions, are just two examples of cultural pluralism at work in the contemporary United States. The prevalence of ethnic shops, restaurants, and festivals in these neighborhoods is an indication that both Chinese and Cuban cultures are to be valued and maintained. Other communities, such as the AMISH, have very little contact with the mainstream, but their unique lifestyle is to a greater or lesser extent tolerated by those around them.

A negative interpretation of pluralism suggests that either the majority or minority cultures (or both) are ethnocentric and do not wish to interact. The same charge of divisiveness and separatism has been leveled at advocates of MULTICULTURALISM.

Colonialism. COLONIALISM is a negative form of intergroup relations based on RACISM in which the dominant group controls the political and economic structures in society while exploiting native groups. Through its military conquests, the United States has absorbed many different peoples of the world. The legacy of American colonialism has brought such diverse people as Samoans, Guamanians, Hawaiians, Puerto Ricans, and Filipinos into the United States.

Within the United States, there may also be internal colonialism. This situation results when the colonial power is in the same geographic territory as the colonized people, imposing a legal and political system which serves the interests of the colonizer and discriminates against the colonized. During the U.S. conquest and colonization of the northern territories of Mexico, for example, the MEXICAN AMERICAN people systematically lost control over their land as a result of a biased legal system. Even in areas where Mexican Americans are the numerical majority, such as the Rio Grande Valley in southern Texas, the land remains mostly in the hands of the small Anglo minority.

The colonizer's view of the colonized group as inferior may lead to certain types of exploitation. It is easier to exploit the labor of a conquered people such as the Indians during the mission period if their basic needs are not considered important. This might also explain why Mexican and Mexican American farmworkers have often been denied fair wages, safe and sanitary working conditions, and health benefits.

Expulsion. Expulsion is the forced removal of a group of people from their land. Since its inception as a nation, the United States has used this method in dealing with American Indians. One of the most unjust actions of the U.S. government was the removal and relocation of American Indians from the Southeast to the western territories during the 1830's. Since many of the American Indians died along the way as a result

of exposure and exhaustion, this dark passage in intergroup relations is known as the "TRAIL OF TEARS."

Later, American Indians were routinely expelled to the least desirable areas of the United States, where they were forced to live on RESERVATIONS. Since reservations are in isolated areas, few other Americans come into contact with Indians and know about the abysmal conditions that are found there.

Expulsion can also be temporary, as in the case of the Japanese Americans who were forced to leave their homes in 1942 for internment camps in the American wasteland. Although many of the Japanese Americans had been ideal citizens, they were expelled from the West Coast out of fear they would assist Japan in its war with the United States. The Japanese Americans' internment only ended in 1945 when they were no longer seen as an internal threat. As with other expulsions, the government had revoked the rights of a minority group.

Extermination. The ultimate option for dealing with intergroup problems is the annihilation of the subordinate group. While the United States has never had an official policy of extermination, American Indian peoples have been the victims of mass exterminations by Anglo Americans in their "taming" of the wild West. For example, the massacre at WOUNDED KNEE, South Dakota, in 1890, in which about 370 Indian men, women, and children were murdered by U.S. soldiers, suggests that members of the subordinate group were seen as nonhuman and expendable.

Improving Intergroup Relations. In the past, Anglo domination and the need for Anglo-conformity by minority groups was never questioned. With the growth of various racial, ethnic, and other civil rights movements since the 1950's and 1960's, however, government, business, and community leaders have begun to see the need for intergroup sensitivity, tolerance, and understanding. For example, many states and cities established human relations councils in the 1960's and 1970's to provide a forum for addressing these issues and continuing problems such as DISCRIMINATION or HATE CRIMES. Schools, prisons, and other institutions set up training programs to make people more aware of RACISM as well as intergroup similarities and differences. The government began to hire intercultural relations experts to help address the problems faced by American Indians and other ethnic minorities.

The need for multicultural awareness also has practical implications. It is good business not to offend the people with whom you do business. For example, the Frito Lay Company was forced to change an advertising campaign that offended Mexican Americans by perpetuating the stereotype of the Mexican bandido or bandit. The advertising executives were not bigots, just ignorant of the cultural sensibilities of Mexican Americans. Similar misunderstandings have resulted in some corporations and agencies wanting to train their employees to be culturally sensitive. Police departments in large cities now employ intercultural relations experts who educate officers in the culture of minority groups in order to avoid conflicts. Such training has also proved useful as the community within the workplace becomes more diverse with AFFIRMATIVE ACTION and the presence of new immigrants.

Intergroup relations are quite complex. The way different groups relate may lead to peaceful coexistence or conflict. This area remains one of the great challenges of the multicultural United States, where few groups live in isolation.

SUGGESTED READINGS. For more information on assimilation in the United States, see Milton M. Gordon's *Human Nature, Class, and Ethnicity* (1978) and J. Milton Yinger's "Assimilation in the United States: The Mexican-Americans," in *Mexican-Americans in Comparative Perspective* (1985), edited by Walker Connor. Robert Blauner's *Racial Oppression in America* (1972) applies colonial theory to explain the minority experience in the United States. Edward Murguia provides an excellent comparison of assimilation, pluralism, and colonialism in reference to the Mexican Americans with *Assimilation, Colonialism, and the Mexican American People* (1989). For a comprehensive source on intergroup relations, see Harry H. L. Kitano's *Race Relations* (4th ed., 1991).—*Ramón S. Guerra*

Intermarriage: People intermarry when they choose husbands or wives with racial, ethnic, or religious backgrounds that are different from their own. The practice has been atypical but has become increasingly more common in the United States, traditionally a "MELTING POT" of peoples with diverse cultural origins. Several factors have led to a rise in intermarriage since World War II. These include increased global contacts, a rise in ethnic populations, and—especially since the 1960's—more interracial interaction with INTEGRATION and greater personal freedom for young Americans making decisions about marriage. Nevertheless, the "color line" has never been crossed casually in the United States.

Throughout human history, intermarriage has been a common means of preventing inbreeding, broadening genetic variety, and advancing evolution. It has also been a choice made by couples for very personal reasons. Yet there are certain predictable problems that may arise in mixed marriages. People tend to prefer their own cultural and religious values, regarding their peers as normal and viewing outsiders with suspicion and often dislike. Internal conflicts may arise over child rearing and other issues, and the couples and their children are apt to encounter social disapproval

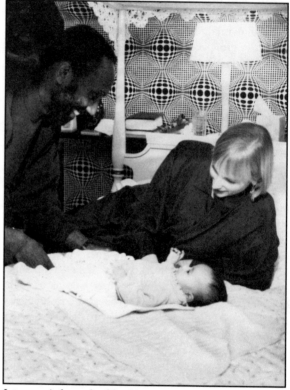

Intermarried couples like this one in Austin, Tex., may have to overcome cultural differences in child rearing. (Don Franklin)

in forms ranging from incidental to severe.

Definitions. Various terms describe different kinds of intermarriage. A marriage to someone outside one's race may be called "interracial" or "biracial." The terms "intercultural," "bicultural," "interethnic," and "biethnic" also occur, but are less clearly defined since the terms "race," "culture," and "ethnic group" are used loosely and are not identical. ("Race" generally describes genetic makeup, "culture" describes group living patterns, and "ethnicity" may apply to either or both.)

In the domain of religion, strong pressures have been exerted by the JEWISH and ROMAN CATHOLIC faiths and by various Protestant churches and sects to marry within one's faith. An "interfaith" marriage, joining people of different religions, goes against this expectation.

The strongly negative term "miscegenation" means mixing of the races, especially marriage or sex between a white person and someone of another race. Traditional disapproval of miscegenation in America can still be sensed in such pejorative terms as "half-breed" or "mulatto" for a racially mixed child, who once might also have been called a "quadroon" (one-quarter black) or "octoroon" (one-eighth black), depending on the percentage of nonwhite ancestry. Since American society in earlier days favored whiteness, any mixing with "colored" races has often seemed a taint. President Thomas Jefferson, who himself is reputed to have had a black slave as a mistress, spoke of a "clearing of the blood" that occurred when racially mixed persons married whites over several successive generations. Though a one-sixteenth portion of "colored blood" was sometimes regarded as legally insignificant, any appearance of racial mixture has tended to give a person minority status in the United States.

A consanguineous marriage (one "with the same blood") is a direct opposite of a "mixed marriage." Consanguinity occurs between people descended from the same ancestor, or within the same family group. Extreme cases—such as marriage between brother and sister—are socially taboo, but marriage within one's blood group, broadly defined, has been common, especially in the past. By contrast, an "exogamous" marriage is defined broadly as one "outside of a specific group, especially as required by custom or law." Some groups, such as the AMISH and GYPSIES, have strict codes prohibiting such marriage.

History. The history of the West involved the mingling of native European peoples and their conquerors—first Romans, and later the invading northern Germanic tribes who ranged southward and westward. In England these were the Anglo-Saxons, who subdued and intermarried with the native Celts.

European settlers coming to the New World after 1492 sometimes had children with American Indian women, creating racial mixtures that still characterize some Central and South American populations and parts of the American Southwest. The famous marriage of the American Indian princess POCAHONTAS in Virginia to the English colonist John Rolfe in 1614 helped bring peace between Indians and whites. The lack of white women on the American western frontier also encouraged some intermarriage between European Americans and American Indians. The racial mixing that occurred between white American settlers and African Americans before the CIVIL WAR was usually extramarital, since antimiscegenation laws made black-white marriages illegal in most places. Nevertheless, a significant amount of sexual activity did occur between white masters and black slave women, producing many slaves with racially mixed ancestry. Alex HALEY's famous book *Roots: The Saga of an American Family* (1976), based on his family history, dramatizes such patterns of mixed relations.

Before World War II, American intermarriage usually occurred between white people of diverse European cultural backgrounds. Many American soldiers returned home after 1945 with European "war brides," thanks to the provisions of the WAR BRIDES ACT. The pattern persisted during the American occupation of Japan, the KOREAN WAR, and VIETNAM WAR as military men married Asian women and brought them home to live. The multiracial makeup of the population in Hawaii, which became a state in 1959, made it a unique model of multiculturalism. After about 1960, a new wave of Latino immigrants from Cuba, Mexico, Puerto Rico, and elsewhere brought an infusion of cultural diversity into the mainland United States that tended to accelerate the number of biracial or bicultural marriages, especially in California, Florida, the Southwest, and large American cities. Changes in immigration legislation after 1965 also brought larger numbers of Asians, Africans, and Caribbean peoples to the country.

According to standard reference works, there were 310,000 intermarried couples in the United States in 1970, and 719,000 in 1983. The pattern of black-white marriages increased proportionally: In 1970, there were 65,000 such couples; in 1980, there were 167,000; and in 1991, there were 231,000. Still, this last figure accounted for only 0.4 percent of all married couples in the United States. Among black-white couples, most were composed of black husbands and white wives rather than the reverse (156,000 of the 231,000 black-white couples in 1991).

The long world history of interfaith marriages might be told as a series of instances in which children went against their parents' wishes by marrying outside their religions. In traditional Western societies, clear separations and frequent enmities have existed among the three major religious groups: Protestants, Catholics, and Jews. Thus "crossing the line" often violated social and parental expectations, even in the United States, which has nominally advocated religious tolerance. Catholics and Jews were widely stigmatized

A Brooklyn Japanese American/English American couple share an embrace after exchanging wedding vows. (Hazel Hankin)

as suspect newcomers, at least until the mid-1900's; their position as minority groups subject to prejudice and discrimination further complicated prospects for intermarriage with Protestants. Jews, as victims of ANTI-SEMITISM and persecution, have traditionally been concerned about their group's survival and have preferred to maintain their own separate cultural and religious identity from generation to generation.

Interracial and Intercultural Marriages. The most easily noticed intermarriages are biracial ones, where physical differences between mates sometimes provoke stares on the street, or worse. Until surprisingly late, such marriages were often illegal. Antimiscegenation laws existed in more than half of the states in 1955, sometimes making a black-white marriage a

felony; eighteen states still had such laws in 1964. In 1967 the U.S. Supreme Court declared all such laws to be violations of the FOURTEENTH AMENDMENT and therefore unconstitutional. This long history of illegality has helped to make black-white marriages seem unusual and unpopular, even after 1967. Racially mixed couples have often encountered hostility in the form of HOUSING DISCRIMINATION and even HATE CRIMES in some areas.

In parts of the country with large Latino and Asian populations, other patterns of intermarriage prevailed. Like African Americans, these minorities had long been marginalized and excluded from mainstream American society. With the growth of the CUBAN AMERICAN and MEXICAN AMERICAN middle class, however, and the large numbers of Asian Americans entering academia and scientific fields, opportunities for intergroup contact with white Americans became more frequent. Some European Americans persisted in anti-Japanese prejudice because of that country's role in World War II, but younger people were generally more open-minded.

During the late twentieth century, MULTICULTURALISM became fashionable, especially in "POLITICALLY CORRECT" circles, on college campuses, and in the media. Rather than emphasizing ASSIMILATION into a common culture with one language, tradition, and value system, Americans tried to learn to tolerate diversity and see virtues in different ethnic patterns. The impact of this movement on biracial families was complex: The "new ethnicity" encouraged tolerance but also drew sharper division lines between ethnic subgroups and their cultural patterns. The political idealism of the 1960's that advocated a color-blind society seemed impractical, and some culturally mixed families—finding it increasingly difficult to keep dual allegiances to two conflicting cultures—were pressed to choose one over the other in order to establish familial and psychic stability.

Though many biracial and bicultural families work well, they may face special problems. Family members may feel they do not fit securely into any culture. Children may be ridiculed at school for being different. Contrasting patterns of upbringing, values, and taste may add to the normal strains of everyday living.

Interfaith Marriages. Donald J. Bogue's *The Population of the United States: Historical Trends and Future Projections* (1985) reports that all religious subgroups in the United States show a strong tendency toward "within-religion marriage" and that even nonbelievers tend to marry nonbelievers. Still, interfaith marriages were becoming "very common," with the percentage being highest among Jewish Americans and Catholics. Whereas only 5 percent of Jews married outside the faith until the 1960's, that proportion had increased to 30 to 40 percent by the 1990's. Intermarriage particularly concerns Jews and Catholics, who fear that their already small numbers will be further diminished by children who no longer identify with the faith. A further complication for CONSERVATIVE and ORTHODOX JEWS is that they do not consider the children of non-Jewish women to be officially Jewish.

In 1977 about one in ten Protestant husbands married a non-Protestant wife. If the Protestant subgroups are considered, the rate of interfaith marriages increases substantially. About one in ten METHODIST husbands, for example, married a BAPTIST wife in 1977. The belief systems and social norms of Protestant churches vary widely—from radical to reactionary—and disagreements can occur in mixed Protestant marriages over such matters as drinking, dancing, child rearing, and doctrine.

Since religious faith not only provides social and moral values but also helps define routine behavior, couples who do not share a common faith must work out compromises on many points. These may include deciding which church or synagogue to attend, which Sabbath to recognize, and which holidays to observe. Common solutions include one partner's "giving in" and adopting the other's faith, often under pressure from in-laws and family members. Other couples try to respect both religious traditions, allowing their children free choice when they reach adolescence. The Catholic church in particular expects a Catholic upbringing for children of interfaith couples.

SUGGESTED READINGS. Many books discuss intermarriage from sociological, psychological, or religious perspectives. General sources include *Intermarriage: Interfaith, Interracial, Interethnic* (1964) by Albert I. Gordon, a Jewish rabbi. Collections of essays on the subject include *The Blending American: Patterns of Intermarriage* (1972), edited by Milton L. Barron, a social scientist; *Interracial Marriage: Expectations and Realities* (1973), edited by Irving R. Stuart and Lawrence E. Abt; and *Adjustment in Intercultural Marriage* (1977), edited by Wen-Shing Tseng and others, which focuses on the racially mixed situation in Hawaii. Guidebooks to help couples in interfaith marriages include James Albert Pike's *If You Marry Out-side Your Faith: Counsel on Mixed Marriages* (1954) and Egon Mayer's *Love and Tradition: Marriage Between Jews and Christians* (1985). Fernando Henriques' *Children of Conflict: A Study of Interracial Sex and Marriage* (1975) traces the history of miscegenation in the United States and abroad.—*Roy Neil Graves*

International Council of Women: International meeting of leading women's rights organizations. The council met in Washington, D.C., in 1888 to commemorate the fortieth anniversary of the historic SENECA FALLS CONVENTION and to create a coalition for women's political rights. While the idea for the meeting came from the National Women's Suffrage Association, the council eventually included fifty-five other major women's organizations and representatives from Europe, India, and Canada. One result of the council was the unification of the two U.S. branches of the suffrage movement in the National American Woman Suffrage Association in 1890.

International Ladies Garment Workers Union (ILGWU): Pioneering labor organization formed in 1900. Though originally set up for skilled male workers in the garment trade, women soon became the mainstay of the union. It supported the New York shirtwaist makers strike in 1909 and received a boost in membership. Despite success unionizing women, only one woman had a position on the union's executive board before World War I. Membership declined during the GREAT DEPRESSION of the 1930's, then soared to eight thousand by the 1940's. Three-quarters of the members were women, including African Americans, Asians, and Hispanics. The ILGWU continues to win benefits for its diverse members. Many consider the ILGWU label in clothing to be a mark of both workers' rights and product quality.

International Longshoremen's and Warehousemen's Union (ILWU): Some sixty years after its founding in 1933, the ILWU had approximately sixty-five thousand members organized in seventy-eight autonomous local unions. The union is mainly concerned with four major industries of the West Coast and Hawaii: shipping, warehousing, distribution, and the growth and processing of sugar and pineapple. As a result of a merger, the union also represents some fishermen and cannery workers in Alaska, Washington, and Southern California. An independent, voluntary association of working men and women, the union bargains collectively on behalf of its members' needs for improved wages, hours, and conditions of employment.

International Woman's Year (1977): Year of events sponsored by the U.S. government to create a policy agenda for women. Activities culminated in a national conference in Houston, Texas, in November, 1977. The two thousand delegates and approximately sixteen thousand observers reflected the diversity of women and their interests. Feminists made up the majority of participants, but groups opposed to ABORTION and the EQUAL RIGHTS AMENDMENT (ERA) were also present. The conference resolutions, presented to President Jimmy Carter in a report entitled *The Spirit of Houston*, sought federal support for the ERA, reproductive freedom, child care,

Internment. *See* **Japanese American internment**

Inuits: Homogenous, uniquely adaptive, and circumpolar native culture spanning four areas: Siberia, Alaska, Canada, and Greenland. The terms "Inuit" and "Eskimo" both describe the same people. Inuit means simply "the people"; Eskimo is derived from an Algonquian word for "eaters of meat" and is considered derogatory by some Inuits. Waves of migrating Inuit populations spread eastward from the Bering Strait over the past three thousand years. The distinguishing features of Inuit life are arctic residence, major dependence on seasonal maritime harvests, use of large open-skin boats and the kayak, rich diversity of natural resources, and a symbolic dualist worldview based on the dichotomy between land and ocean.

Alaskan Inuit family (circa 1886). (Library of Congress)

an end to violence against women and children, the protection of rights of sexual preference, and legislative action on the problem of POVERTY among women.

In the Inuits' world, the state of the ocean changes according to the seasons. When it is frozen, Inuit hunters may travel by dogsled or snowmobile dozens of miles out onto the ice for game or driftwood, or to engage in sealing at breathing holes. In spring and summer, the walrus-skin umiak is used to hunt the baleen whale; the small waterproof kayak is used for lesser catches. Polar bear, caribou, small fur-bearing animals, and migratory birds supplement the food supply. Great herds of caribou pass seasonally at narrow crossing points; the meat contains less of the necessary fat. Inuits also fish for salmon, whitefish, and lake trout.

Ingenious Inuit technology uses driftwood, stone, skin, bone, ivory, snow, and ice for needs varying from caches, weapons, tools, lamps, and pots to clothing, tents, boats, and sleds. Traditionally, Alaskan Inuits lived in semisubterranean sod-covered houses, while Greenlanders built homes of stone. In northeastern Canada, snow igloos provided temporary winter quarters.

The work of women was crucial for the survival of all in the Arctic. Women and girls sewed hunting outfits with waterproof gut and fabricated sealskin boots that stayed warm and dry. They butchered and stored carcasses, cooked whale meat and fish, gathered berries, kept house, and reared the children. Men were concerned with house building, hunting, fishing, travel, tool making, ivory carving, and the ceremonial cycle.

The Inuit bilateral kinship system is flexible, and it resembles European-American kinship structure; descent and inheritance are reckoned through both father and mother. The most prominent aspect of Inuit social organization is the seasonal shift between camps and the alternation between a large population group and splinter groups.

A unique aspect of Inuit society is the importance of partnerships and alliances unrelated by blood or marriage. Men inherited trading partnerships, joking relationships, and namesake mates. They forged bonds through wife exchange or sharing the same woman, through dance partnerships, and boat-crew membership. This widened the interpersonal support network of partners and provided economic assistance in time of need.

Today Inuits run art cooperatives marketing ivory and soapstone carvings, baleen baskets, dance masks, fur mittens and bootees. Inuit corporations administer the Land Claims Settlement (finalized in 1971) and invest income from oil leases. Present-day Inuits work in canneries and at fire fighting. They are also active in the National Guard, the distant early warning line, post office, and schools.

The Yupiks of the Alaskan southwest have their own newspaper and television station, and Yupik is taught in the schools there. Half of Alaskan Inuits live in Anchorage or Fairbanks. They often attend college, many choosing business administration. In Alaska, Canada, and Greenland, Inuits send elected representatives to local, state, and national government.

Suggested Readings. Recommended reading includes Nelson Graburn's *Circumpolar Peoples* (1973), Asen Balikci's *The Netsilik Eskimo* (1970), Bryan and Cherry Alexander's *The Eskimos* (1991), and *The Eskimos* (1988) by Ernest S. Burch, Jr.

Iranian Americans: Iran lies at the northern edge of the Persian Gulf and the Gulf of Oman, bounded to the west by Turkey and Iraq, to the north by Armenia, Azerbaijan, Turkmenistan, and the Caspian Sea, and to the east by Pakistan and Afghanistan. This Middle Eastern country has ruled over and been dominated by countries with radically diverse customs, languages, and religions. Iranian Americans reflect this ethnic and religious diversity; Persian-speaking Muslims, Jews, Armenians, Baha'is, Assyrians, and Zoroastrians are all part of Iranian culture in the United States. The largest U.S. Iranian community is located in California where, according to the Census of 1990, more than 57 percent of Iranian immigrants have settled.

Iranian Americans represent a relatively recent pres-

Iranian Americans protest against the treatment of Iranians by the Iranian government. (Frances M. Roberts)

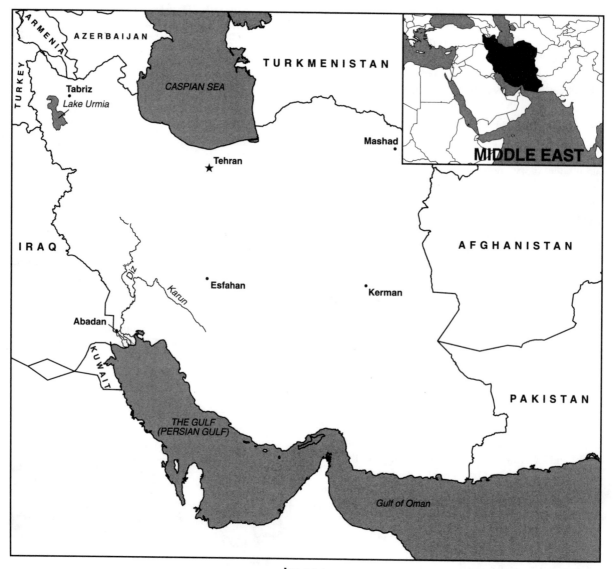

IRAN

ence in the United States. Economic inducements, educational opportunities, and politics have been the primary factors fueling Iranian immigration to the United States, which rose steadily during the second half of the twentieth century. The 1978-1979 revolution in Iran, which toppled the Shah and led to the rise of the Muslim fundamentalist Khomeini regime, was responsible for the largest exodus of Iranians. University educations and political upheaval brought primarily educated, well-financed Iranian men to American shores, many of whom were followed by family members who fled the revolution.

Their proficiency in English and strong business skills have enabled Iranian Americans to create a significant market force. Iranian American-owned businesses include banks, bookstores, and fast-food restaurants. Nearly 1,600 businesses are listed in the nationally distributed *Iranian Yellow Pages*. Despite economic success in the United States, many Iranian Americans continue to confront anti-Iranian prejudice and stereotypes spurred by the 1979-1981 hostage crisis, in which American hostages were held by militants in Iran. Like other ethnic groups, Iranian Americans have formed cultural and social organizations to maintain communal ties, where they celebrate holidays and festivals such as Noruz (Persian New Year).

Iraqi Americans: Few Iraqis have immigrated to the United States, apart from a small number that arrived after World War II. Those that have follow the immigration patterns of other Arab newcomers. They generally retain their religious identity, most often Islam, although a few are Christian. They do not cluster in enclaves, but they do tend to settle in cities, close to professional jobs. Iraqi Americans maintain their Arab identity and culture through strong ties to their families and their mosques.

The land that is now the country of Iraq was originally called Mesopotamia, a Greek word that means the land "between the rivers" of the Tigris and the Euphrates. This area was part of the Fertile Crescent, an arc of arable land that stretches between the Persian Gulf and the Mediterranean Sea. The Sumerians founded one of the world's earliest civilizations here about six thousand years ago. They invented cuneiform writing on clay tablets, some of which still exist today.

Semitic tribes from the Arabian desert soon conquered the Sumerians and established their capital at Akkad, which later became known as Babylon. The most famous Semitic king was Hammurabi, who lived in the early sixteenth century B.C.E. A copy of Hammurabi's Code, the set of laws for which he is best known, was discovered in Iran early in the twentieth century.

In about 1600 B.C.E., the Babylonian kingdom was overrun by the Hittites from Asia Minor and by the Kassites. The Hittites withdrew, but the Kassites ruled Mesopotamia for the next five hundred years.

The land that became Iraq is located in the middle of western Asia. Consequently, it has served as a crossroads for invading countries. Subsequent conquerers included the Assyrians, Persians, Greeks, Romans, and the Arab MUSLIMS. The Muslims invaded in the seventh century, just after the death of Muhammad. Soon after, Islam fragmented. One powerful group of Arabs, the Abbasids, moved the capital of Islam to Bagdad in 750. For five hundred years, civilization in Bagdad flourished, especially under the rule of Harun al-Rashid and his son in the years from 786 to 833.

Two Mongol invasions, one by Hulagu in 1258 and another by Timur in 1393, left the land and its essential system of canals devastated. It never regained its former glory. Turkey soon conquered the country and ruled it as part of the Ottoman Empire until World War I, when it was liberated by the British.

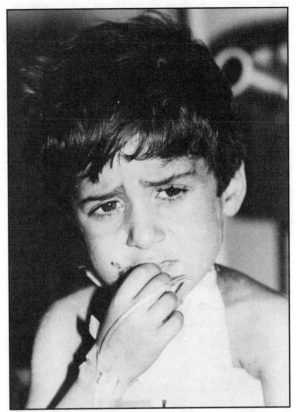

The Kurds of Iraq, like this mustard gas victim, have received harsh treatment from government forces, prompting immigration to the United States and Europe. (AP/Wide World Photos)

In 1920, the League of Nations authorized Britain to prepare Iraq for independent statehood. Iraq achieved independence in 1932 under King Faisal I, originally from Syria. After Faisal's death and that of his son, Iraq fell into political disarray.

The United States and Britain used Iraq as a passageway to Russia during World War II. A left-wing revolution allied Iraq with the Soviet Union in 1958. The Baath Arab Socialist Party came to power ten years later, setting the stage for Saddam Hussein to become president of Iraq in 1979.

Iraq is internally divided between two groups of Muslims, the Sunnis, who usually make up the ruling class, and the more radical Shiites. Iraq also has a substantial minority of Kurds, a tribe that has lived in the mountains in the northern part of the country for three thousand years. The Kurds have struggled for centuries against the Turks and later the Iraqi government to establish an independent homeland.

Irish American women: In the 1840's, after the potato famines had ravaged rural Ireland, enormous numbers of single Irish women, as well as mothers and young girls, left their homeland for the United States. As a group, these women constituted the majority of one of the oldest and most successfully integrated groups of immigrants in the United States. Their reasons for leaving, their values, and the ways they adapted made Irish

Like her immigrant ancestors before her, this Irish American telephone repairer is a strong, independent woman. (Hazel Hankin)

women a unique element in American cultural history.

Post-famine Ireland offered little promise for most rural Irish women. Early marriages, large families, and farming of small, subdivided family plots, which had previously characterized the rural Irish, became obsolete. Family property was transferred to one son and a dowry was often available for only one daughter. Under these conditions, marriage was either deferred or forfeited as economically unfeasible. Young Irish women found few alternatives but to travel abroad to seek employment. Millions migrated to the United States along female family lines—sisters bringing sisters, aunts helping nieces.

Irish women were the only sizable group of immigrants who traveled in female clusters. Upon arrival, most unmarried women sought positions as live-in domestics, an occupation shunned by other groups. The mandatory single life was not unduly burdensome, since their culture did not promote marriage as the only desirable status a woman could attain.

These women generally married Irish spouses for cultural as well as religious considerations. Irish wives were considered the dominant, unifying force in the family structure. In the face of domestic violence, alcoholism, desertion by their husbands, and early widowhood caused by industrial accidents, Irish-born women drew upon their own resourcefulness to meet the challenge of being the family breadwinner. When domestic service was not an option, Irish-born women raising families sought employment wherever they could find it, frequently as laborers in textile mills. Some, such as Mary Harris "Mother" Jones, became leaders in the nation's fledgling labor unions.

Family solidarity and relentless faith in Catholicism were fundamental to Irish women, whose social circles were their church and neighborhood. Their dedication to these fundamental values nurtured an enduring ethnic identity for following generations.

First-generation Irish American women succeeded in their focused struggle for financial security and social standing. They saw their children advance as professionals—predominantly teachers, nurses, politicians, and labor leaders. These "lace curtain" Irish left the tenements for better, but decidedly Irish, neighborhoods.

Despite their independence and assertiveness in the marketplace, most Irish American women resisted the ideology of the feminist movement of the late nineteenth century as an affront to their Catholic faith and as a threat to family stability.

Irish American women of the twentieth century have prospered and diversified politically, socially, and professionally (U.S. Supreme Court Justice Sandra Day O'Connor, artist Georgia O'Keeffe, and actor Maureen O'Hara being only a few prominent examples). They have also experienced a renewed ethnic pride, evidenced by the wealth of social organizations in the United States perpetuating the language, history, and traditions of Ireland. In some measure, they still remain daughters of Erin.

Suggested Readings. Robert E. Kennedy provides

a study of Irish women's lives in the late nineteenth and early twentieth centuries in *The Irish: Emigration, Marriage, and Fertility* (1973). Other excellent sources are *Erin's Daughters* (1983) by Hasia Diner and *Ourselves Alone* (1989) by Janet Nolan. *Models for Movers* (1990) by Ide O'Carroll presents individual accounts of Irish women who have emigrated.

Irish Americans: The history of Ireland is a melancholy one, but it has created a strong people. The country was first invaded and conquered in 1169 by the Norman knights of Henry II of England. Ireland remained a troubled and only partially controlled land for the next

remained under the control of the native Celtic lords. The subjugation of the Irish people continued over the next two hundred years as English control was challenged by sporadic Irish rebellions and uprisings. The English attempted to establish tight control with the Act of Union in 1800. Ireland was no longer to have its own parliament or government; all government agencies were moved to London, and Ireland became a colony of England.

Later political movements attempted to provide the Irish with greater control of their lives, culminating in a war between the English forces and the native Irish. This was resolved in 1921 by a treaty creating the

Irish policeman chats with New Yorkers. (Library of Congress)

four hundred years. During the reign of Elizabeth I, Catholic Ireland endured the forced settlement of English and Scottish Protestants; only the west of Ireland

Irish Free State in the south and keeping the six counties of Northern Ireland under British control. The history of Northern Ireland since the 1970's has been indelibly marked by "the troubles" that have polarized the Catholic and Protestant communities. Decades of terrorism by the Irish Republican Army (IRA) have failed to make those counties a part of the Irish Republic.

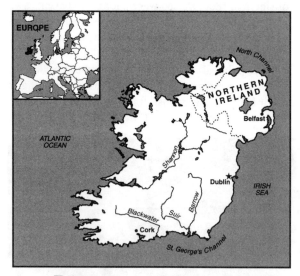

REPUBLIC OF IRELAND

Immigration. Irish immigration to the United States began as early as the seventeenth century. By the eighteenth century, there were more than forty thousand Irish immigrants in the United States. A single event, the Potato Famine of the 1840's, however, led to the largest migration of Irish across the Atlantic. Most Irish peasants at that time lived on small plots of land and depended for subsistence on the potato crop. When the potato blight ruined this most important crop in 1840, hundreds of thousands of Irish were displaced from their land, unable to pay rent; as many or more starved to death. The English, then in control of Ireland, provided very little relief for the Irish crop disaster; their belief in laissez-faire economics prevented any meaningful intervention. In desperation, the Irish began their great migration to the United States. From 1845 to 1854, some 1.5 million Irish emigrated to the promised land. Another 1.5 million arrived between 1855 and 1870.

The Irish who arrived during this period were primarily rural people, mostly farmers. In the United States, however, Irish farmers gravitated to the emerging American cities rather than the rural areas. Cities such as Boston, New York, Chicago, and Philadelphia experienced a huge influx of Irish immigrants. The newcomers arrived in such great numbers over a short period that they often disrupted established social and political institutions.

The number of immigrants gradually decreased but continued through the twentieth century as a result of the limited economic opportunities found in Ireland.

Politics and Community Life. The earliest Irish organizations in the United States were established to aid new immigrants. The newcomers faced prejudice and discrimination from established Americans, who attempted to block Irish social advancement. Want ads often included the phrase, "No Irish Need Apply." Mutual assistance societies were formed in nearly every important American city to help fellow Irish survive and get ahead in American life.

Soon assistance groups led to political and social clubs, including the notorious TAMMANY HALL in New York. Irish political leaders made sure that all of their fellow Irish Americans were registered to vote and began to win control of precincts and wards in large American cities, especially Boston and New York. By 1900, there were Irish mayors in New York City; Chicago; Boston; and St. Paul, Minnesota. The Irish seemed to have a genius for politics. They could bring together a coalition of Irish and other ethnic groups and then seize control from the primarily English, Protestant settlers of earlier centuries.

Irish Americans have been a mainstay of the Democratic Party since the mid-1800's. They became senators and governors of states such as New York, Massachusetts, and Illinois. Al Smith, whose father immigrated from Ireland, ran for United States president in 1928 but was defeated by the prejudice of a large portion of the electorate. Finally, in 1960, an Irish American CATHOLIC, John F. Kennedy, was elected president. The Irish had gone from poor and unwelcome immigrants to the highest office in the country. Since that time, Irish Americans, such as former House Speaker Thomas "Tip" O'Neill, have continued to hold high political office.

Religion. The Irish have greatly influenced the history and development of American Catholicism. They were the earliest large group of Catholics to immigrate. The upper reaches of the clergy have been controlled by Irish bishops and cardinals since the nineteenth century. The early Irish Catholic prelates, especially Cardinal Gibbons, stressed Americanization; Irish settlers were to drop their allegiance to their home country and become Americans. Thus the church became a major force in promoting Irish Catholic ASSIMILATION.

Irish American Catholicism is marked by a Jansenist strain that differs from the Catholicism of Latin countries such as Italy and Spain. This was inherited directly from the church in Ireland, although it originated in France. Jansenism stresses a rigid and puritanical view of sexuality. Sex was seen as something that was dirty, and virginity was encouraged and enforced. There was no significant sex education in Irish Catholic schools or homes. Ignorance was considered better than forbidden knowledge. The Irish tended to overlook such "sins" as gambling and drinking, but they condemned and ostracized those who had sex before marriage or extramarital affairs.

One of the achievements of Irish American Catholicism is a PAROCHIAL SCHOOL system that has flourished for over a century. Catholic schools were originally established to protect young Catholics from the influence of the Protestant-controlled public schools and to teach the precepts of Catholicism. These schools ranged from the elementary grades to prestigious colleges and universities, such as Georgetown, Notre Dame, and Catholic universities.

Catholicism has thrived in many Irish American cities and neighborhoods. The control of pastors and bishops, however, waned in the late twentieth century as churches and Catholic schools lost membership or closed. As more Irish Americans have moved from the city to the suburbs, the political and religious unity that they enjoyed in their urban ethnic enclaves has declined. Today it is often hard to distinguish Irish Catholics from other groups in America.

Cultural Contributions. Irish Americans have made their mark in nearly every area of American culture. Their contributions in literature have been perhaps the most outstanding. Eugene O'Neill, one of the most important American playwrights, deals extensively with the Irish American experience, especially in *Long Day's Journey into Night* (1956), his finest play. Novelist F. Scott Fitzgerald is admired for *The Great Gatsby* (1925), in which an outsider attempts to crash the barriers of the establishment. Gatsby is not identified as an Irishman, but his struggle evokes the yearning of many Irish Americans to become part of the establishment elite.

The novelist who portrayed the Irish American experience most directly was James T. Farrell. His Studs Lonigan trilogy (1932-1935) is an intriguing study of the Irish in the United States. Set in Chicago, Farrell's novels focus on the Irish American family, male camaraderie, and men's fear of women and sexuality.

Other Irish American writers who have drawn on their ethnic background include short story writer J. F. Powers and novelist Edwin O'Connor.

Other areas in which the Irish contributed to the culture of the United States are in the theater, films, and sports. There were many prominent Irish actors in the American theater, beginning in the late nineteenth century. Most notable of these was George M. Cohan, an actor, singer, songwriter, and producer who created a theatrical empire in the early 1900's. His songs and plays celebrated the qualities of the American Irish, reinforcing the image of their charming and warm side.

Later, such Irish actors as James Cagney, Pat O'Brien, Spencer Tracy, and Maureen O'Hara enriched American films. These actors also presented a different side of the ethnic group's image: the tough, no-nonsense Irishman, even the Irish American criminal or gang leader. The work of James Cagney, for example, is far from the sentimentalities of Cohan. Prominent among their roles were the Irish American priests played by O'Brien, Tracy, and later Bing Crosby. The Irish American priest became a benign figure. The creation of sympathetic Irish American characters on stage and screen further aided Irish assimilation.

The Irish were especially prominent in sports in the early 1900's. Figures such as John L. Sullivan, the Irish American heavyweight champion, reinforced another stereotype: that of the strong American Irishman who was prone to fight at the drop of a hat. Irish boxers and baseball and football players remained prominent until they were displaced by other ethnic groups, such as the Italians, the Poles, and the African Americans.

The Irish Americans have not been well known in the fine arts, although there have been a few important Irish artists such as Georgia O'KEEFFE. Thousands of American Irish, however, played important roles in the American public school system and, perhaps even more so, in the parochial schools that were created in nearly every city and town in the United States.

SUGGESTED READINGS. The most complete popular account of the Irish in the United States is *The American Irish* (1963) by William V. Shannon. It is especially good on Irish American political development. A more academic study is *The Irish Diaspora in America* (1976) by Lawrence J. McCaffrey, which gives a full account of the patterns of Irish immigration and of the Irish role in the development of the American

Catholic church. Marjorie R. Fallows' *Irish Americans: Identity and Assimilation* (1979) is a clearly written study of the Irish for the general reader which contains detailed portraits of Irish American communities.—*James Sullivan*

Iroquois League: Political alliance made up of the Senecas, Cayugas, Onondagas, Oneidas, Mohawks, and

IROQUOIS TERRITORY

later, the Tuscaroras. Originally formed by their desire to stand together against invasion of their lands, the league resolved disputes and promoted peace between the tribes. The difference between the Iroquois League and other Indian federations was their effective adoption of a centralized government structure that used the "ritual of condolence" to stress peace. Despite the league's attempt at neutrality, there was a division within the league during the AMERICAN REVOLUTION. The Oneidas and Tuscaroras sided with the American cause, while the other tribes fought for the British. When 4,000 Americans defeated the tribes near present-day Elmira, New York, in 1779, the Iroquois League came to an end. After the war ended, the remaining tribes that had not fled to Canada or the western frontier were forced to live on RESERVATIONS.

Israeli Americans: The relatively young state of Israel was established as a political entity in 1948, chiefly to serve as a homeland for JEWS after the HOLOCAUST. Comprising a land area approximately the size of New

Jersey, Israel lies on the eastern shore of the Mediterranean Sea and is bordered on its other sides by Lebanon, Syria, Jordan, the Red Sea, and Egypt.

After the founding of Israel, the country became known as a place of massive immigration rather than emigration. In the first two decades of Israel's existence, however, approximately 300,000 Israelis relocated to the United States. Some moved to the United States to join relatives; some who had suffered in the Holocaust and were receiving restitution payments from Germany used the extra money to start their lives over in "the land of opportunity"; many left purely because of "push" factors—namely, the hardship and austerity of life in Israel.

With the 1970's came a major wave of migration from Israel to the United States that continued into the 1990's. Though reliable statistics vary, it is estimated that somewhere between 100,000 to 400,000

Salute to Israel parade, New York City. (Richard B. Levine)

Israelis arrived during this time. Factors motivating them include repeated wars and the threat of future wars with Israel's Arab neighbors; high taxes in Israel; greater educational and career opportunities in the

United States; and the relative familiarity of American culture.

Israelis in the United States have faced contempt from a large number of American Jews who believe that the continued growth of Israel is crucial for the survival of the Jewish religion, culture, and traditions. The Israeli government frowns upon Jewish emigration from Israel as well.

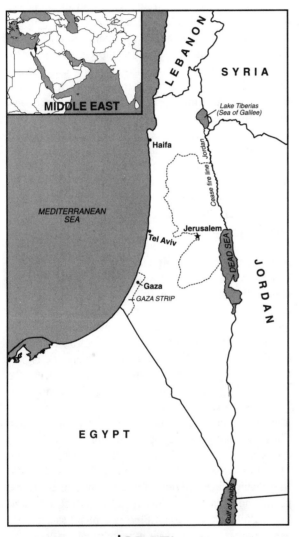

ISRAEL

The majority of Israeli immigrants have settled among the already large Jewish populations of New York City and Los Angeles. Most are well educated and middle-class or affluent, with fewer than 4 percent employed as blue-collar workers. Israeli Americans and Jewish Americans have established Hebrew newspapers and journals, as well as Hebrew broadcasts on local television channels and radio stations; some Israeli Americans speak Hebrew in their homes. Their connection to Israel remains strong: The majority have traveled to Israel several times since emigrating.

Among Israeli contributions to American life are Middle Eastern food specialties such as falafel and hummus, which have become readily available in the United States, and Israeli folk dancing, which has long been popular among Jewish Americans.

Issei: First-generation Japanese immigrants; that is, those born in Japan. In practice, the term is used mostly for those who immigrated before World War II. Issei were fluent speakers and writers of Japanese, and most retained Japanese citizenship. Their children, born in the

Mrs. Noguchi, an Issei, proudly displays photos of her grandson and great-grandson. (National Japanese American Historical Society)

United States and therefore American citizens, are Nisei. Issei wanted their children to retain their Japanese heritage, but most Nisei resisted. Within the Japanese American community, Issei held great influence and power prior to World War II. After the war, most of the power transferred to the Nisei.

Italian Americans: Italian American history began in the early colonial period, although the massive emigration of Italians to the United States did not occur until the late nineteenth and early twentieth centuries. Because of their identifiable names and their choice to retain their cultural identity, Italian Americans did not

ITALY

easily ASSIMILATE into the American "MELTING POT." Like other ethnic minorities, they endured considerable PREJUDICE and DISCRIMINATION, an experience which left scars on successive generations.

Immigration. The Italian Christopher Columbus is credited with the European discovery of America, although he sailed under the Spanish flag. Italian immigration to the territory of the present-day United States can be traced to the Spanish colonies in the sixteenth century. In the British colonies before the revolution, and in the young American republic, several Italians were prominent in political life. Foremost among them was Filippo Mazzei, a friend of Thomas Jefferson and political philosopher, whose sentiments were reflected in the Declaration of Independence. At this time, the dominant American culture was defined by immigrants from Northern Europe and the British Isles;

Italians were too few to have a major impact on American customs.

From 1820 to 1989, Italians accounted for 10 percent of all immigrants to the United States. The major wave of Italian immigration occurred between 1880 and 1920, when more than five million Italians arrived, the majority from the rural south of Italy. A series of agricultural crises precipitated the initial immigration. Later immigrants came in diminishing numbers to join relatives or find riches. In the 1980's, it was estimated that twelve to twenty million Americans of Italian ancestry lived in the United States.

Italian American immigrants and their descendants overcame the obstacles of comparatively late arrival in America, discrimination, and painful STEREOTYPES to become one of the more successful immigrant groups in the United States.

The Immigrant Experience. Problems began for the new immigrants in the ships en route to America. Poor sanitary conditions contaminated immigrants with infections and life-threatening diseases such as cholera. After arrival, life in the crowded, dirty, and disease-ridden tenements was a far cry from the America of their dreams. They faced discrimination from the northern European immigrants who preceded them, as well as from long-settled Americans. Italians stood out among the fair northern Europeans because of their distinctive names and olive complexions. They were hired for undesirable jobs at low wages.

Italians settled in small towns, as well as big cities, but the Italian American immigrant experience is perhaps best reflected in the cities of the Northeast. To cushion themselves against the rapid transition to American urban life, Italians created colonies of fellow immigrants from the same region in large cities. These communities attempted to replicate the Italian life, culture, food, and customs they had left behind. The most famous such enclaves are New York's Little Italy, which has provided the background for films, plays, and even opera; Chicago's Near West Side; and South Philadelphia (South Philly), which has survived as an Italian enclave in an ethnically and racially diverse city.

Even the ROMAN CATHOLIC church, one of few familiar institutions, did not always give Italian immigrants a warm welcome. The American church was dominated by the Irish, and although the faith was the same, religious practices and customs differed considerably. Italians formed predominantly Italian Catholic parishes where native customs, such as the celebration

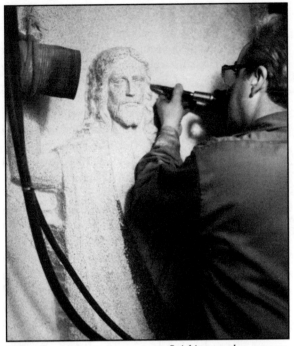

Italian American stonecutter puts finishing touches on a religious carving in Barre, Vermont. (Smithsonian Institution)

of the feast days of their favorite saints, could be continued.

Within a generation or two, Italians recognized that EDUCATION was the vehicle to success and adopted the American dream for their children. Parents worked long hours to send their children to college and professional schools. Within a few generations, Italian Americans came to be seen as an ambitious and hardworking people who produced doctors, lawyers, teachers, and businesspeople, to succeed the laborers, skilled workers, and small grocers of earlier generations.

The single most important institution among Italian Americans was the family (*la famiglia*), both nuclear and extended. Italian families were fiercely close, making many sacrifices for their members. Italian Americans tended to marry within their own community to perpetuate their customs. Conscious that they were different and not fully accepted by the dominant society, Italians maintained a degree of separateness for a long time.

Stereotypes. Despite the group's progress over time, it suffered from stereotypes. American films and television perpetuated the stereotype of the barely literate Italian American peasant or laborer who could barely speak English or who in later generations spoke an Italian American dialect from "da Bronx." Italians were subjected for decades to derogatory nicknames. Although prejudice gradually declined, the Italians did not receive full acceptance as Americans until the late 1900's, a time of substantial new waves of immigration from Asia and Latin America.

Another stereotype, even harder to shake, was the gangster image. The Mafia, an Italian secret society engaged in criminal activity, was transplanted to the United States during the mass immigration period. Although the Mafia was a small group, its reputation tainted Italian Americans as a whole. Italian gangsters were prominently featured in American films in the 1930's because of the notoriety of Al Capone and his generation. In the 1960's, *The Untouchables* on television highlighted criminals with Italian surnames, and in the 1970's, the film *The Godfather* (1972) immortalized the Mafia image. Subsequent films have kept the stereotype alive.

Achievements and Contributions. Italian Americans have made notable contributions to American science, arts, food, sports, education, and public life. In popular music, Frank Sinatra, Tony Bennett, Perry Como, Frankie Avalon, Connie Francis, and Vic Damone are among the internationally known performers, while Henry Mancini is an important composer. Gian-Carlo Menotti and John Corigliano are noted Italian American classical composers. Ezio Pinza thrilled audiences in opera and on Broadway, while Mario Lanza influenced a generation of singers through his films. There are also many orchestral musicians of Italian origin, as well as lesser-known actors and singers.

In theater and film, Italian Americans have established a solid reputation with talented actors such as Al Pacino, Robert DeNiro, Anne Bancroft, and Nicolas Cage, and with personalities such as Sylvester Stallone and the controversial Madonna (Madonna Louise Ciccone)—not to mention the king of silent films, Rudolph Valentino. Francis Ford Coppola, Frank Capra, Vincente Minnelli, and Martin Scorsese are among the great film directors of the twentieth century.

In contemporary America, Italians play an active role in public life. This, however, was a hard-won gain. For a long time, Italians could not break into big-city politics. Fiorello La Guardia, the legendary mayor of New York (from 1934 to 1945), was the first to win a highly visible public office. Other well-known Italian American politicians have included Governor John Pastore of Rhode Island, Governor

Mario Cuomo of New York, and Representative Geraldine Ferraro, the first woman to run for vice president in one of the two major parties. Associate Justice Antonin Scalia was the first Italian American to serve on the Supreme Court. Lee Iacocca of Chrysler Corporation and Amadeo Giannini, founder of Bank of America, may be the best-known Italian American business executives.

Italian American writers include Mario Puzo, Jerre

Italian Americans have played an important role in sports, most notably baseball and boxing. Famous Italian American athletes include a number of New York Yankees such as the legendary Joe DiMaggio, Billy Martin, Phil Rizzuto, and Yogi Berra. More recently, Frank Viola, Tom Candiotti, Mike Pagliarulo, Tony LaRussa, Tommy Lasorda and Lou Piniella have been well-known players and managers. Italian boxing champions included Rocky Graziano and Rocky Marciano, and Mario Andretti is a superstar in auto racing.

Italian American cuisine has had a strong impact on American cooking. Pizza, a dish imported from the Naples region, has become a staple. Spaghetti and meatballs has given way to many varieties of pasta as health-conscious Americans realize the nutritional value of complex carbohydrates. The benefits of the traditional Italian diet of vegetables, fruits, complex carbohydrates, and olive oil have gained recognition in the American quest for a healthier, longer life.

SUGGESTED READINGS. A few general books recommended for further reading are Luciano J. Iorizzo and Salvatore Mondello's history, *Italian Americans* (1980); J. Philip Di Franco's *The Italian American Experience* (1988) for younger readers; and the anthology

Italian Immigration to the United States: 1830-1980

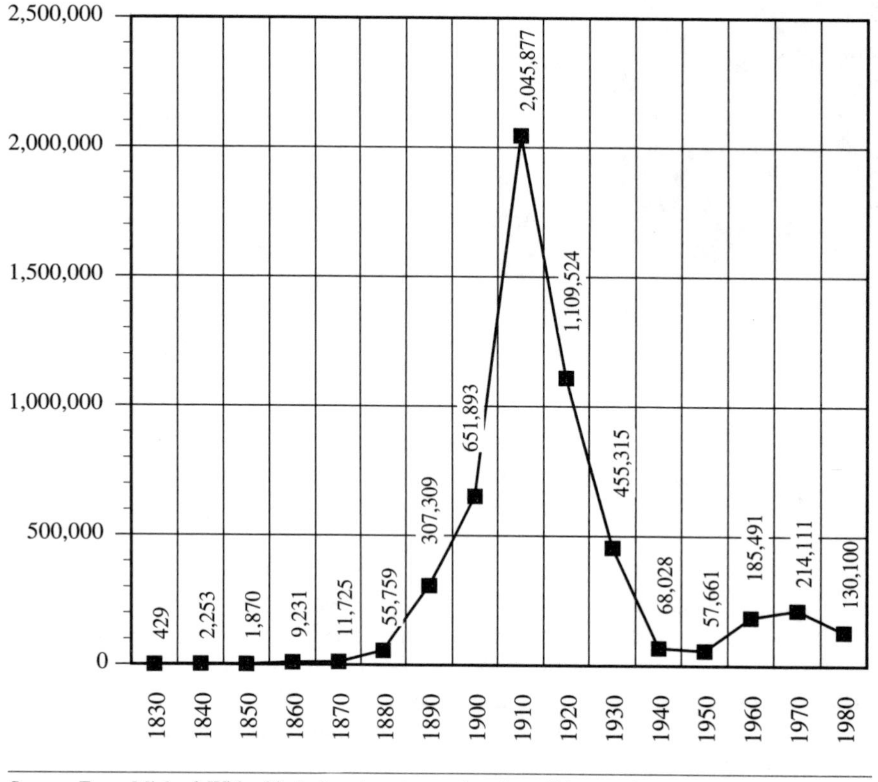

Data points:
- 1830: 429
- 1840: 2,253
- 1850: 1,870
- 1860: 9,231
- 1870: 11,725
- 1880: 55,759
- 1890: 307,309
- 1900: 651,893
- 1910: 2,045,877
- 1920: 1,109,524
- 1930: 455,315
- 1940: 68,028
- 1950: 57,661
- 1960: 185,491
- 1970: 214,111
- 1980: 130,100

Source: From Michael Witkoski, *Italian Americans*. American Voices series, p. 43. Vero Beach, Fla.: Rourke Corp., 1991.

Mangione, and Barbara Grizzuti Harrison. In higher education, perhaps the best-known Italian American is G. Barlett Giamatti of Yale University and baseball fame. In religion, Mother Frances Cabrini was the first American canonized as a saint by the Roman Catholic church.

The Italian Experience in the United States (1970), edited by Silvano M. Tomasi and Madeline Engel. Among memoirs that capture the flavor of Italian American life is Jerre Mangione's *Mount Allegro* (1981).—*Norma Corigliano Noonan*

J

Jackson, Jesse Louis (b. Oct. 8, 1941, Greenville, S.C.): African American political leader. Jackson emerged as a civil rights leader during the 1960's and was a Democratic candidate for president in 1984 and 1988. His supporters were organized as the RAINBOW COALITION. A Baptist minister, he first worked with Martin Luther KING, Jr., and various civil rights organizations in the South and later in Chicago. In 1970 he formed People United to Save Humanity (PUSH), a group working to help the poor gain political and economic power. He urged blacks to help themselves, and to vote. In 1971 Jackson ran against Richard Daley for mayor of Chicago and lost. In 1988, his speech at the Democratic National Convention and his presidential campaign slogan, "Keep Hope Alive," inspired the nation. In the 1980's and early 1990's, he was a vocal advocate for human rights not only in the United States but also on missions to trouble spots overseas.

Jamaican Americans: Jamaica, which has a population of over two million, is by far the most populous of the English-speaking West Indian islands. It is also the English-speaking island with the highest number of migrants to the United States. While English-speaking Caribbean peoples began to migrate to the United States

Civil rights leader and politician Jesse Jackson speaking to reporters in 1990. (AP/Wide World Photos)

and Canada in the early nineteenth century, the bulk of Jamaicans and other West Indian migrants came after 1900, especially between 1911 and 1924.

Jamaican migrants differed from other Caribbean migrants—such as Dominicans, Cubans, and Haitians—with respect to their history, language, and culture. Many early Jamaican migrants were middle-class professionals and were of mixed black/white heritage. Over 90 percent of all Jamaican migrants to the United States were literate.

Population estimates for Jamaican Americans vary considerably. It is believed that there are more than 300,000 Jamaicans in the United States and Canada. This figure, however, does not take into account substantial illegal immigration.

Major concentrations of Jamaican migrants are to be found in New York City (mainly in the boroughs of Brooklyn, the Bronx, and Queens), Chicago, Miami, Los Angeles, San Francisco, Washington, D.C., and Boston, as well as Quebec and Toronto in Canada. Jamaicans may also be found in smaller and medium-sized towns in the West and Midwest.

History. Jamaica was first sighted by Christopher

JAMAICA

Columbus in 1494 on his second voyage to the New World. The island occupies an area of 4,400 square miles and is the third largest island of the Greater Antilles (after Cuba and Hispaniola) and the largest island of the Commonwealth Caribbean. The island has a varied topography. The highest area is that of the Blue Mountains.

Jamaican American dancer giving a demonstration; many Jamaican Americans prefer to maintain cultural ties rather than assimilate totally into American culture. (Claire Rydell)

The population of Jamaica is predominantly composed of the descendants of slaves brought to the Caribbean from the African coast. There is also a small elite population (mostly whites of European heritage) and a sizable middle-class population who claim to be of mixed black/white heritage. Elites are concentrated in the major city of Kingston (the capital), and larger towns such as Ocho Rios and Montego Bay. In addition, there are also considerable numbers of Asians (Chinese and Indians), Portuguese, Syrians, and Lebanese as well as white Europeans and Americans (many of whom came to Jamaica during the twentieth century). Some white Jamaicans have had families on the island for more than two hundred years. There are a number of isolated Maroon settlements in the Cockpit Country. These seven thousand descendants of runaway slaves have had a substantial impact on the life and character of the island.

Immigration. The majority of Jamaicans say that they migrated to the United States and Canada for a combination of economic and social reasons. Since the end of the nineteenth century there have simply been too many Jamaicans with too few opportunities to earn a decent living in their homeland. Land is unevenly distributed on the island, and there are too few jobs outside the agricultural sector. After World War I, much available land was consolidated in the hands of a few local planters, absentee landowners, and foreign corporations. By 1935, for example, over half the island of Jamaica was held under fourteen hundred titles of over a thousand acres each. Hurricanes between 1920 and 1921 further damaged the agricultural economy and provided additional incentives for Jamaicans to migrate. The growth of industry following World War II—chiefly in bauxite, construction, and tourism—has not generated sufficient new jobs: unemployment has remained at over 25 percent. Moreover, the stronger American economy and the promise of a "better life" has continued to draw Jamaicans to the United States. Migrants frequently encourage family members, neighbors, and friends to join them in the United States.

Jamaican migration represents different regions of the island and various races and social classes. Like other Caribbean migrants, large numbers of educated professionals have migrated as well as poor, unskilled peasants. White Jamaicans of European and Asian ancestry have also immigrated to the United States.

Black and white Jamaicans have made significant contributions to American intellectual and political life. Marcus GARVEY (1887-1940), a Jamaican immigrant, was a major figure in shaping West Indian politics in the United States as well as influencing relations between West Indians and African Americans.

Garvey's Universal Negro Improvement Association (UNIA) did a great deal to foster racial unity, self-reliance, and black pride. Garvey also formed the Black Star Line, a steamship company to transport blacks between the United States, the Caribbean, and Africa. Although his "back to Africa" movement received considerable public attention, Garvey's major focus was on the formation and promotion of black enterprises.

Jamaican migrants aim neither for total assimilation into American society and culture nor for a return to Jamaica when and if the economic situation changes for the better. On the other hand, Jamaicans maintain frequent contact with friends and relatives in Jamaica, and—like other British West Indians—take great pains to differentiate themselves from "native" American blacks. Relations between "native" American-born blacks and Jamaican migrants are often strained because members of both groups see themselves in direct competition for available jobs and housing. Most primary associations are with fellow Jamaicans of the same social class. There are a number of Pan-West Indian organizations such as cricket clubs and literary societies whose memberships transcend islands of origin. Jamaicans in the United States have also exhibited a strong attachment to the British royal family, a loyalty that tends to separate them from American blacks as well as whites.

Religious Life. A distinguishing feature of Jamaican culture is the intensity of their religious beliefs. Most Jamaicans are Protestants; about 8 percent attend Roman Catholic churches. Various Muslim, Jewish, and spiritualist groups are also present. Many Jamaicans belong to Fundamentalist and Pentecostal groups and attend African-derived religious ceremonies such as Revival Zion, Kuminia, and Pocomania. Religious affiliations in the United States and Canada closely parallel those in Jamaica. In New York City and Toronto, for example, there appears to be a marked preference for worship in predominantly West Indian congregations.

Rastafari, an indigenous religious movement that has its origins in Kingston, Jamaica, constitutes roughly 5 percent of the Jamaican population. Rasta is a complex, highly individualistic religion that combines selected elements from Protestantism and various *ganja* (marijuana)-inspired apocalyptic visions to provide a unique blend of Caribbean and European beliefs and rituals. Its founders and leaders, each working in isolation from the others, came to the con-

clusion that Haile Selassie, then enthroned as Ethiopian emperor, was the "Lion of Judah" who would lead blacks back to the Promised land—Africa. Rasta has come to play a dominant role in Jamaican political life and has become a world religion of immense significance. With no seminaries to enforce orthodoxy, there may be as many variants of Rasta as there are adherents to the religion. There are many variants of Rasta in American urban centers, and a growing number of Rasta adherents are non-Jamaican African or European Americans.

SUGGESTED READINGS. Among the best introductions to the island of Jamaica and Jamaican culture remains Clinton V. Black's *The Story of Jamaica from Prehistory to the Present* (1965). On Jamaican religion, see Joseph Owens' *Dread: The Rastafarians of Jamaica* (1976) as well as Anita M. Waters' *Race, Class, and Political Symbols: Rastafari and Reggae in Jamaican Politics* (1985). For an introduction to the West Indian experience in the United States, see Miriam Klevan's *The West Indian Americans* (1990). See Nancy Foner's essay "The Jamaicans: Race and Ethnicity Among Migrants in New York City" in her edited collection, *New Immigrants in New York* (1987).—*Stephen D. Glazier*

Japan-bashing: Blaming of Japan for the faltering U.S. economy. In the 1980's, a growing antipathy in the United States toward the nation of Japan developed into a cultural phenomenon that the Western media termed "Japan-bashing." This antagonism grew out of Western economic insecurity, but was exacerbated by underlying racist elements as shown in a lingering distrust of the Japanese as enemies in World War II.

As Japan experienced rapid economic growth through the 1960's and 1970's, it imported fewer products made in the United States. At the same time, the American trade deficit was expanding. While the American automobile industry, for example, moved further into domestic and international decline, Japanese automobiles sold in record numbers in the American consumer market, closely followed by high-volume sales for Japanese electronic products.

Calls from beleaguered U.S. industries to "buy American" went largely unheeded; Japanese products not only were competitively priced, but also were perceived as being of higher quality than their American counterparts. By 1985, the U.S. trade deficit with Japan was at $40 billion and steadily climbing. The Japanese were widely perceived as callously indifferent to both economic fair play and the plight of a long-standing postwar ally. After initially responding to diplomatic pressures to limit auto exports to the United States in the early 1980's, the Japanese increased those exports by 24 percent when the quotas were lifted in 1985. American popular opinion began to suspect far more than healthy international trade competition was at stake.

The belief began to grow in American journalistic and economic circles that Japan's Ministry for International Trade and Industry had as its principal mission the economic domination of the world. In 1989, the purchase of Columbia Pictures by the Japanese Sony Corporation and the acquiring by Mitsubishi Estates of a controlling interest in the Rockefeller Group (including an American landmark, Rockefeller Center in New York City) indicated to some that the mission had expanded beyond economic control to include cultural domination.

In the early 1990's, popular opinion was further incensed by Japan's refusal to commit troops to the allied effort in the Persian Gulf War. Japan was continuing to adhere, as Secretary of State James Baker termed it in 1991, to a policy of "checkbook diplomacy," when many westerners believed it should have been taking a more active role in international politics. Negative feelings were also stirred when, as the United States commemorated the fiftieth anniversary of the attack on Pearl Harbor in 1991, the Japanese government offered a statement of regret but stopped short of a direct apology.

The "bashing" of Japan, however, was also recognized by many American commentators, including Japanese Americans, as a resort to finding a scapegoat for American economic woes. Mitigating facts were frequently overlooked. The expanding American trade deficit, for example, was not confined to Japan, but was worldwide. Likewise, even through the 1980's, when Japan's economic motives were under suspicion, it bought more U.S. goods each year than any other nation except Canada.

SUGGESTED READINGS. Michael Crichton's popular novel *Rising Sun* (1992) is sometimes cited as an example of Japan-bashing; the book occasioned considerable controversy when it was published. As a former ambassador to Japan, Edwin O. Reischauer, in *My Life Between Japan and America* (1986), offers interesting insights into cultural differences and commonalities. The basis for the racial antagonism is effectively examined in Charles G. Cleaver's *Japanese and Americans: Cultural Parallels and Paradoxes* (1976), as is

the basis for commercial conflict in Lester C. Thurow's *Head to Head: The Coming Economic Battle Among Japan, Europe, and America* (1992).

Japanese American Citizens League (JACL): Organization formed in 1930 by second-generation Japanese American professionals and businessmen. They believed that the best way to achieve economic success in the face of anti-Japanese feelings was to demonstrate super-patriotism and loyalty to America. The JACL did not publicly criticize discrimination, but worked quietly and forcefully to change discriminatory laws. During World War II, the league urged cooperation with the government to bring an end to the internment of Japanese Americans. The league was active in the late 1980's to get redress and greater reparations from the government for those who had been interned.

Japanese American internment (1942-1945): Detention of Japanese Americans in remote relocation camps, allegedly in order to prevent their collusion with Japan, with which the United States was at war. On December 8, 1941, one day after Japan bombed the United States naval base at Pearl Harbor in the Hawaiian Islands, the United States declared war against Japan. Another kind of war was subsequently declared against the more than 120,000 persons of Japanese ancestry then living on the U.S. mainland. The first-generation Japanese immigrants in the United States, known as Issei, were ineli-

INTERNMENT CAMPS WITH CAPACITY

Source: Adapted from Frederick S. Rolater and Jeanette Baker Rolater, *Japanese Americans*. American Voices series, p. 17. Vero Beach, Fla.: Rourke Corp., 1991.

Signs with "instructions" on how to leave their homes marked the beginning of the internment of Japanese Americans. (National Archives)

gible for citizenship; however, their children, the Nisei, were U.S. citizens by birth.

Arrests and Removal. At the time of World War II, approximately two-thirds of all people of Japanese ancestry on the mainland were citizens, and about 90 percent lived on the West Coast. Within days after declaring war on Japan, the Federal Bureau of Investigation (FBI) arrested more than two thousand Japanese, supposedly for engaging in activities "dangerous to the public peace and safety." It must be assumed that these arrests were primarily designed to relieve public fears during wartime, since no indictment for espionage or sabotage was ever sought against any Japanese resident or citizen of the United States. The arrests did serve to strip the Japanese community of

its most effective leadership in a time of crisis. The government announced as security measures various restrictions to be placed on "alien enemies." Travel was restricted; bank accounts were frozen; a number of items were declared contraband for Japanese; and searches were authorized for their homes. By law, these measures were to apply only to foreign-born Japanese who were noncitizens (Issei), but in reality, they were applied indiscriminately against all persons of Japanese heritage.

Upon declaration of war, the U.S. president has virtually absolute power over "alien enemies." A little more than two months later, President Franklin Roosevelt issued Executive Order 9066, granting the Secretary of War power to establish certain military

Barracks in the camps (Manzanar is pictured) were divided into six rooms; each family, unless very large, was assigned one room. (National Japanese American Historical Society)

zones "from which any or all persons may be excluded" as deemed necessary. As a result of this order and widespread fear of the Japanese, more than 110,000 Japanese and Japanese Americans were subject to curfew and then removed from their homes on the West Coast in early 1942 under the guise of "military necessity." "Removal orders" were issued in stages, each involving approximately a thousand persons. Most groups were given only one week to prepare for removal. The "evacuees," as they were called, were instructed to report to a specified assembly center, bringing with them only what they could carry. All other property had to be hastily disposed of, regardless of the loss.

The Japanese were held temporarily in makeshift assembly centers such as race tracks and fair grounds and finally dispersed to ten "relocation centers" in Arizona, Arkansas, California, Colorado, Idaho, Wyoming, and Utah. There they were held for two to three years under armed guard, even though the majority were American citizens who had committed no crime.

Camp Conditions. The camps, managed by the War Relocation Authority (WRA), were constructed in remote areas, selected because they were isolated, easily

secured, and posed no threat to neighbors. Camp climates were often extreme contrasts for those of West Coast origin. For example, in the Wyoming camp, winter temperatures sometimes dropped to -30 degrees; at the other extreme, summer temperatures in one Arizona camp were known to reach 130 degrees.

Most of the camps were not ready for occupancy when the internees arrived. In some cases, Japanese laborers were made to build fences for their own imprisonment and help to finish the building of barracks, schools, hospitals, mess halls, and other common facilities. Living quarters were very much the same from one camp to another. The barracks were of military design, intended for the temporary housing of soldiers, not for families and certainly not for the young, the old, or the infirm. Rooms were furnished with only heating stoves and sleeping cots. Any other furniture was made by residents from scrap lumber or purchased by mail order.

Barracks were divided into six rooms, usually 20 feet by 20 feet. Families, unless very large, were usually assigned only one room. Buildings were grouped into blocks, composed generally of 250 to 300 people (in family units) per block. Most centers contained thirty blocks or more. Each block comprised two rows of six or seven barracks with a mess hall, recreation room, laundry, and bathroom in between. No running water was provided in the barracks. Cooking in the rooms was forbidden. Families were to eat, bathe, wash clothing, use the toilet, and play in communal areas.

Japanese Americans in Hayward, Calif., waiting for the bus that will take them to the Tanforon Assembly Center. (National Archives)

The physical facilities and organization of the camps reflected a total disregard for Japanese culture, especially for family life and privacy. Obviously, the physical properties of the camps made privacy impossible. Even toilets in the communal baths were lined up in a row with no partitions between. It fell to the internees themselves to provide some privacy. They found scraps of lumber, pieces of cloth, even cardboard boxes to partition the toilets against this indignity.

Americanization Efforts. Once in the camps, every effort was made to "Americanize" the Japanese; indeed, there were few opportunities for the internees to maintain their native culture. Before they were forcibly removed from their homes, the Issei had gone through a kind of cultural divestment to escape the

suspicion associated with all things Japanese and to present themselves as loyal Americans. Long cherished artifacts associated with Japan were destroyed: flags, books, letters, clothing, and other family keepsakes. Institutional structures as basic as those of the family, work, and religion were undermined, and roles learned earlier no longer applied. The impact was felt in every aspect of life but was perhaps most severe on the family.

There were almost thirty thousand Japanese American (Nisei) young people of school age interned. All camps eventually built and minimally equipped schools. Initially, classes were held in any kind of makeshift facility. Most of the teachers and all of the administrators were Caucasians and were properly certified, although their turn-over rate was high. The basic philosophy of the curriculum was the teaching of the American way of life. Students were not allowed to speak Japanese. Many U.S. holidays and only a few Japanese ones were celebrated. Classroom instruction, regardless of the subject, was laced with heavy mixtures of American history and lessons in democracy. The contradiction of teaching democracy to involuntarily interned citizens escaped neither students nor teachers.

Other examples of Americanization can be seen in the activities sponsored for the entire camp population. There were English classes for all. For the women, there were classes on baking, cooking, and weaving. For young people, there were numerous athletic and scouting programs. Each camp provided church services and opportunities for worship; however, there was a shortage of Buddhist priests—only two to serve more than eight thousand residents in one camp. Unquestionably, and no doubt intentionally, the culture of the camps was more American than Japanese.

The camps were really prisons structured on the basis of two races and two classes of people: appointed personnel (known as APs), and "residents" or "evacuees." The APs were all white people of European descent, and the internees were all Japanese or Japanese Americans. This reinforced some internees' resentment of the racism that they felt was behind their removal.

Assessing the Camps' Advantages. Former internees and social scientists have written extensively about the internment (with varying degrees of subjectivity) and about the advantages and disadvantages of that experience for those involved. Even the harshest critics acknowledge that some positive consequences resulted

The living quarters of the Takemoto family at the Manzanar, Calif., internment camp. (National Japanese American Historical Society)

from the camp experience. There is some level of agreement on three "advantages," although for each there appears to be an accompanying disadvantage. First, the camps have been credited with expanding the social world and opportunities for Japanese Americans by providing some of the opportunities and experiences of a small, homogeneous community. Residents could participate in limited community organization, internal political activity, and leadership without competition from a dominant group. There were also selected cultural and social events and even regulated business enterprises in the form of cooperatives offering goods and services within the camp. Young internees had their first opportunity to compete and to lead in sports, scholastic, and other pursuits simply because of the absence of members of the dominant group. Some Nisei got their first white-collar jobs working for the WRA doing routine office work and processing papers and supplies. Nevertheless, they worked at exploitation wages compared with Appointed Personnel doing the same tasks.

A second advantage often cited in conjunction with the camp experience is that it was conducive to group unity. The internment had a built-in leveling effect because all members of the Japanese community were treated the same. The most serious divisions within the camps were often between generations of Issei and Nisei. The WRA tended to exacerbate these differences because of its preference for dealing with the more Americanized, English-speaking Nisei. Even

with this generational difference, however, traditional Japanese culture demanded respect for and loyalty to one's elders, and the Nisei were never unmindful of this aspect of their heritage.

Finally, some credit the camp experience with Americanizing the Japanese population, thus contributing to their success after release. It is doubtful whether this process was as successful in a prison-like environment as it would have been in the free setting of a public school. In retrospect, some Nisei have suggested that prior to internment they were well on their way to becoming thoroughly American and that their Japanese heritage was actually reinforced because of their anger over the internment.

Primarily, however, the notable success of Japanese Americans after the war must be attributed to the

Internees, called "evacuees," were only allowed to take possessions they could carry. (National Archives)

strength of the Japanese family and ethnic community. One dynamic that apparently worked for the Japanese recovery was the combined, complementary, and sometimes conflicting interests and cultural orientations of the Issei and Nisei. These two generations provided a unique form of biculturalism, a balance of restraint and action that helped the Japanese regain control of their lives, families, and communities after internment. Bill Hosokawa, one-time president of the JAPANESE AMERICAN CITIZENS LEAGUE, in calling attention to the many accomplishments of the Nisei generation, said, "We have overcome."

Reassessing the Internment. Many concerned

Americans wonder why the government decided to intern a people charged with no crime who were permitted no hearing or trial. They puzzle over how American citizens, their parents, and grandparents—once welcomed in the United States for their labor—came to be regarded as "alien enemies." The initial list of internal enemies during World War II included not only Japanese, but Germans and Italians as well. Some Germans and Italians were arrested or moved from strategic military areas, but they were not evicted or arrested on the basis of group membership alone. The decision to intern all Japanese, while justified as a "military necessity," can be fully explained only by racism and the fact that the Japanese as a group were easily identifiable because of racial characteristics and easily contained because of their concentration in a relatively small geographic area.

The case of the Japanese in Hawaii seems to support the idea that racism was the underlying cause of the official and unofficial treatment of the Japanese population on the mainland. Surely if the Japanese were a security threat, their presence would have been most ominous in Hawaii immediately after the attack on Pearl Harbor. Although Japanese people made up more than 35 percent of the state's population, no massive or severe measures of control were exercised there in comparison to those on the mainland. In fact, fewer than two thousand Japanese were taken into custody in Hawaii for the duration of the war. The explanation for this apparent discrepancy was that race relations were much better in ethnically mixed Hawaii than on the West Coast, where the Japanese and the Chinese had once been labeled the "yellow peril" and excluded by various immigration laws. The shameful internment of Japanese and Japanese Americans must finally be attributed to racism, fear, and rejection of a people different from the Eurocentric dominant culture of the day.

In 1981, the U.S. government set up the Commission on Wartime Relocation and Internment of Civilians in response to the lobbying of Japanese American groups concerned about injustices during World War II. The result was an official apology from the government for the violation of the civil rights of Japanese Americans and the awarding by Congress of funds as reparations for interned Japanese Americans.

SUGGESTED READINGS. See *Personal Justice Denied* (2 vols., 1983) by the Commission on Wartime Relocation and Internment of Civilians for their report. Roger Daniels offers historical background in *The De-cision to Relocate the Japanese Americans* (1986). A number of books provide more personal views of the internment, notably *Beyond Words: Images from America's Concentration Camps* (1988) *by Deborah Gesensway and Mindy Roseman, Repairing America* (1988) by William Hohri, *Years of Infamy* (1976) by Michi Weglyn, and *Lest We Forget* (1992) by Joyce E. Williams and Alice M. Coleman.—*Joyce E. Williams*

Japanese American internment—reparations: Payments made to compensate Japanese Americans for loss of income and civil liberties while interned by the U.S. government during World War II. Public Law 100-383,

President Ronald Reagan (seated) signed the bill authorizing reparations and formally apologizing to internees on Aug. 10, 1988. (AP/Wide World Photos)

which authorized the payments, was passed on August 10, 1988, after an official government investigation on the internment and increased agitation by Japanese American activist groups.

In 1942, while the United States was at war with Japan, President Franklin Roosevelt authorized the military to take "appropriate" measures to ensure the safety of the West Coast. Military and other officials suspected that Japanese Americans had disloyal contacts with the enemy that could lead to sabotage and espionage. General J. L. DeWitt of the Western Defense Command first imposed a curfew on people of Japanese descent on the West Coast, and then excluded them from certain areas. Approximately

112,000 Japanese Americans, including some 70,000 U.S. citizens, were forced to leave their homes and businesses and report to assembly centers. They were held in detention at the centers and later taken to remote relocation camps, where most were compelled to stay until the end of the war.

The U.S. Supreme Court upheld the legality of the curfew and the exclusion orders in HIRABAYASHI V. UNITED STATES (1943) and KOREMATSU V. UNITED STATES (1944), respectively. Yet long after the war and the release of the detainees, many younger Japanese Americans believed that internment had been a violation of their constitutional rights. The cause was of particular concern to American-born Nisei (second-generation) and Sansei (third-generation) Japanese Americans who had been influenced by the ideas and tactics of the CIVIL RIGHTS MOVEMENT and peace activism in the 1960's and 1970's. Through organizations such as the JAPANESE AMERICAN CITIZENS LEAGUE, these activists tried to win both the attention of politicians and the press, and the support of older Issei (first-generation) survivors of the internment. Many Issei were at first reluctant to open old wounds and demand government compensation. Eventually, however, seventy-five witnesses testified to the injurious effects of the internment before a congressional panel known as the Commission on Wartime Relocation and Internment of Civilians.

The commission, established in 1981, issued recommendations that led to the introduction of a reparations bill in the U.S. House of Representatives in January, 1987. After compromises with the Senate, President Ronald Reagan signed the bill into law about a year and a half later. The law, which includes a formal apology to internees from the government, set up a trust fund of $1.25 billion in reparations to be paid over ten years. Each of the 60,000 former internees who were still living was to receive a tax-free payment of twenty thousand dollars. Each person had up to eighteen months to decide whether or not to accept the money. The acceptance of reparations was considered final settlement of any claim that person might make against the government. If a victim was deceased, the money was to go to a surviving spouse or, in equal shares, to all children living at home at the time of payment. Otherwise the money was to stay in the trust fund. The law also provided $21.4 million in compensation to ALEUTS evacuated in 1942 from the Aleutian and Pribilof Islands off Alaska.

SUGGESTED READINGS. For an account of the investigation that led to reparations, see Personal Justice Denied (2 vols., 1983), the report of the U.S. Commission on Wartime Relocation and Internment of Civilians. Good sources for background on internment are *Justice at War* (1983) and *Justice Delayed: The Record of the Japanese American Internment Cases* (1989) by Peter Irons; Roger Daniels' *Concentration Camps U.S.A.: Japanese Americans and World War II* (1971); and *Prejudice, War, and the Constitution: Japanese American Evacuation and Resettlement* (1954).

Japanese Americans: According to the U.S. Census of 1990, there were 848,000 people of Japanese ancestry in the United States, making them the third-largest Asian American group. They were concentrated mostly in California, Hawaii, Washington, New York, and Illinois. In spite of widespread discrimination against them during their early period of settlement and especially during World War II, Japanese Americans were highly assimilated and successful by the late twentieth century. At the same time, they maintain an ethnic identity and ethnic

JAPAN

cultural institutions that are among the strongest in American multicultural society.

Historical Background. Ancient Japanese society was based on the cultivation of rice, but it was not a simple society; the social organization was highly stratified. By the year 300, a Japanese writing system was established, using in part the well-developed character system of the Chinese language.

During the Asuka period (593-710), the Japanese imperial line, claiming descent from the sun goddess, was established. Buddhism was introduced into Japan, and in 645 the Taika Reform ("great change") led to moving the capital to Naniwa, near Osaka. A complex system of centralized, patrimonial rule and land redistribution characterized the brief Nara period. The Heian period (794-1185) was noted for its artistic developments, such as the literary masterpiece *The Tale of Genji*. Present-day Kyoto became the capital, and long-imitated elements of Chinese society were adapted to form a truly Japanese national culture.

The military government established at Kamakura in 1185 was overthrown in 1333, precipitating two centuries of turbulence in the Muromachi period. In spite of the general instability, a number of Buddhist sects spread and Christianity was introduced in 1549. During the brief Azuchi-Momoyama period (1568-1600), Japan experienced its first direct contact with European civilization through traders and Catholic missionaries.

The Japan "opened" by Commodore Matthew Perry was closed during the Tokugawa period (1600-1868). Many samurai left the farms to live in the towns of their feudal lords, stimulating a widespread growth of cities. Many commoners received an education rooted in Confucian precepts. By the nineteenth century, scholars began to find new meaning in early Japanese works, and Shinto ideologies, indigenously Japanese, were revived. The shogunate fell in 1868, when the Emperor Meiji ascended the throne.

While the revival of an emperorship seemed a return to the past, the Meiji period (1868-1912) is associated with reform and Japan's emergence as a modern state. Feudalism was abolished, prefectures were established, and commoners were given new privileges. By 1889, an imperial rule was institutionalized that lasted until its replacement in 1947.

The Sino-Japanese War in 1894, centered on Japanese relations with Korea and China, interrupted domestic progress. Although militarily successful, Japan was still regarded as having second-class status. "Great power" status came with the Russo-Japanese war, which, although immensely costly in terms of men and money, heightened the prestige of the emperor Meiji until his death in 1912.

Many Japanese regard the period of Emperor Taisho's reign (1912-1926) to be crucially important as a time of introduction to participatory democracy.

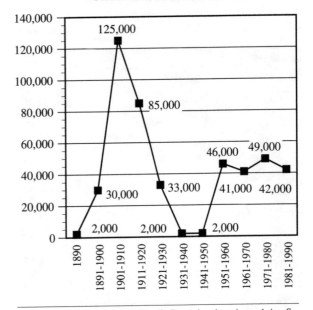

Japanese Immigration to the United States and Hawaii: 1890-1990

Source: Data are from Tricia Knoll, *Becoming American: Asian Sojourners, Immigrants, and Refugees in the Western United States.* Pp. 308-309. Portland, Oreg.: Coast to Coast Books, 1982.

The emperor's son, the Crown Prince Hirohito, was named regent in 1921. This era saw the declaration of World War I, in which Japan sided with Great Britain. Meanwhile, Japan moved to further its interests in East Asia, as seen in the Twenty-one Demands it presented to China in 1915. World War I provided an economic boom which ended with the end of the war. Growing tensions in foreign relations culminated in the "Manchuria incident" of 1931, Japan's withdrawal from the League of Nations, and the China War.

Deteriorating Japanese-American relations in the 1930's culminated in a surprise Japanese air attack on Pearl Harbor, Hawaii, on December 7, 1941. The following day, the United States declared war on Japan, an action that would have devastating effects for both civilians in Japan and Japanese Americans in the western United States. World War II ended on August 14, 1945, following tragic American atomic bomb attacks on Hiroshima and Nagasaki. The period between 1945 and 1952, when Japan was under an American-dominated occupation, was a time of demilitarization, war crime trials, and extensive reform.

Japan's postwar history is one of phenomenal economic recovery and social change, based in part on a strong educational system and political shifts. Post-

occupation Japan has been preoccupied with such issues as foreign policy, United States presence in the
form of military bases, and trade considerations.

Immigration. Japanese immigration began in 1868,
when 148 contract laborers landed in Hawaii to work

Celebrations such as the summer bon odori *dance festival
are popular in Japanese American communities.* (V. E.
Horne, Unicorn Stock Photos)

on sugar plantations. The Meiji era's push for industrialization was especially difficult economically for
agricultural workers, and the opportunity to go to Hawaii, where sugar plantation work was flourishing and
the Chinese workers' contracts were running out, provided ample incentive to immigrate. In 1869, more
than twenty immigrants from the Wakamatsu area of
Japan arrived in San Francisco, California, and attempted to grow tea and produce silk at Gold Hill,
near Sacramento. This group was sent to test the
United States as a place for political refuge. Drought
conditions, however, soon ended their work. A grave
marker near Gold Hill today provides a reminder of
that venture.

Further large-scale emigration from Japan did not
occur until 1885, when emigration restrictions were
relaxed. Responding to promotional campaigns, some
immigrants signed contracts with the Hawaiian gov-

ernment for transportation, jobs, food, and shelter,
largely to replace those workers lost through the CHI-
NESE EXCLUSION ACT of 1882. Others came directly
to the mainland United States. At first most immigrants were young, single male farmers with a middle
school education. They tended to view themselves as
temporary sojourners.

Discrimination was a major problem for these early
immigrants. For example, first-generation (Issei) Japanese were declared ineligible for citizenship. The second major wave of American nativism, which targeted
the Japanese for anti-immigrant sentiment, flourished
from 1870 to 1882. Various discriminatory factors
peaked between 1905 and 1924. One of the most notable cases occurred in 1906, when the school board
in San Francisco voted to segregate Japanese schoolchildren.

In 1908, Japan and the United States signed the
GENTLEMEN'S AGREEMENT specifying immigration
conditions that forbade the arrival of Japanese laborers
but allowed a small amount of other Japanese immigration. Thereafter, immigration of "picture brides" for
male immigrants took place. This helped to create and
stabilize Japanese American families. Many used savings to establish businesses in the United States, and
their presence was considered advantageous because
it provided an inexpensive labor force.

Between 1868 and 1924, some 270,000 Japanese
migrated to the United States before the IMMIGRATION
ACT OF 1924 barred further immigration. The early
immigrants engaged primarily in agriculture, railroad
construction, mining, and lumber-related work. The
vast majority settled in California and Hawaii; by
1930, more than thirty-five thousand Japanese immigrants and their children inhabited Los Angeles, and
large groups settled in San Francisco and San Jose.
Over time, major communities developed in the Seattle area of Washington as well as in Illinois and New
York.

The fact that while Americans and Japanese Americans were largely isolated from each other tended to
fuel anti-Japanese PREJUDICE. A fear of INTERMAR-
RIAGE and ethnic dilution may have added to the
prevalent attitude of NATIVISM. For their part, the Japanese Americans tended to seek their own ethnic community, in which they could find familiarity and
safety.

Between the 1920's and the 1940's, settlement and
community development were emphasized. This was
a time of gradual transition in the Japanese American

community, as the first generation of immigrants grew older and a sizable population of second-generation Japanese Americans, the Nisei, came of age. The Nisei were less fluent in the Japanese language than their Issei parents. As they reached adulthood, they found that unfavorable economic conditions and continued racial discrimination kept them from getting jobs commensurate with their education. Unlike their parents, however, the Nisei could vote, and they began to use electoral power to advance their goals.

Internment and Postwar Community Life. After the United States declared war on Japan in December, 1941, more than 120,000 Japanese Americans in the West were relocated in remote internment camps. This was reportedly done to prevent disloyal acts by those who might have contact with an enemy during wartime. The relocation orders issued by the government applied equally to everyone of Japanese background, including U.S. citizens. In addition to the loss of jobs, property, and savings, the ethnically oriented economy provided by the Japanese American workers was lost, as many were dispersed to the Midwest and East Coast. A number of western Japanese American communities were destroyed, and profound psychological consequences accompanied this displacement. The Japanese American internment was to prove central in forming a distinct ethnic identity later in the century and in fomenting civil rights activism within the community. Not until 1976 did the U.S. government, through President Gerald Ford, formally acknowledge that the evacuation of Japanese Americans during World War II was wrong and that the Japanese Americans had been and were loyal Americans.

Nisei soldiers, notably the 442ND REGIMENTAL COMBAT TEAM and the 100th Battalion, were some of the most frequently decorated units during World War II.

Recent generations of Japanese Americans have faced less hostility and prejudice than their forebears. (Robert Fried)

These soldiers proved their loyalty and patriotism to their native country, the United States. Thirty thousand soldiers who served in this war were Japanese Americans, and about six thousand studied Japanese and other Asian languages in order to be translators, interpreters, and interrogators during the war.

After the war, Japanese American civilians struggled to rebuild their lives. Contrary to predictions that the Japanese were "unassimilable," many persons, especially Nisei in the East, made their way up the ladder of success in professions and managerial positions. There were some Issei-Nisei generational struggles, but gradually stability was established. Postwar Japanese Americans demonstrated amazing adaptability.

In religious matters, many viewed adopting Christianity as a means of becoming American. Their tolerance for all theologies and their concept of religion as ethical behavior appeared to have been brought with the Issei to the United States, along with BUDDHIST and SHINTO practices. Between Nisei and Sansei (third-generation Japanese Americans), discontinuity in religious preference was noticeable; however, intergenerational groups maintained social relationships without severe problems.

The Japanese community exercised effective social control over themselves. Juvenile delinquency and crime rates were generally lower than the norm of the larger community. Nisei students studied diligently during school hours and studied Japanese after school. Traditional Japanese values such as family cohesion and honor were inculcated at the same time that adaptation to new ways was taking place.

Especially among Hawaiian Japanese Americans, some Japanese customs were retained, while others were dropped. The New Year celebration, for example, diminished, while the summertime *bon odori* (*bon* dances) were as popular as ever. This festival, observed in midsummer, was to welcome ancestors' spirits return to earth and to bid them farewell at their departure. Especially since World War II, the tea ceremony, flower arranging, and the martial arts have attracted many non-Japanese students.

For years, numerous Japanese American organizations of four major types had sprung up: church-related, political, ethnic, and sports-related. The earliest was the Japanese Gospel Society, formed in San Francisco in 1877. The Japanese Association of America, founded at the end of the nineteenth century, assisted new immigrants, fought the exclusion movement, and supported economic, social, and educational programs. The JAPANESE AMERICAN CITIZENS LEAGUE, founded in 1930, was especially concerned with representing the interests of American-born Japanese Americans and promoting their acceptance into American life. In addition to these organizations that were primarily concerned with civil rights, such mainstream organizations as the AMERICAN LEGION and the Optimist Club organized Japanese American chapters. A number of communities had Saturday schools for teaching children Japanese language and culture.

Japanese communities sprang up and flourished in a number of major U.S. cities. Today, more than 60 percent of Japanese Americans live on the West Coast in San Francisco, Sacramento, San Jose, Los Angeles, Seattle, and Vancouver. Other large communities may be found in Chicago, Houston, Dallas, and New York.

Cultural Contributions. Japanese Americans made cultural contributions to American society for years without high visibility. By the 1970's, however, there was an increasing awareness of the impact of the Japanese American culture and presence in the United States. To a great extent, Japanese American expertise in particular occupations reflects cultural characteristics that individuals have brought to those jobs and which, collectively, have affected all Americans.

As early as 1915, Japanese American expertise in agricultural and floricultural pursuits was abundantly evident. The Japanese concepts of harmony with nature, of keen attention to detail, and of seeking perfection at any task made possible phenomenal success. By 1941, land that Japanese Americans had enriched brought $280 per acre, compared to $38 for other West Coast farmland. Societies for bonsai and flower arranging enthusiasts have flourished because of Japanese American influence.

Nisei and Sansei who used their considerable skill and their appreciation of simplicity, harmony, and fitting detail must also be acknowledged in the area of landscaping and architectural design. Similar qualities are also evident in Japanese American cuisine. From noodles to sushi, Japanese culinary arts have found their place in the United States, and fine Japanese ethnic restaurants are scattered throughout the country.

Japanese Americans, like their ancestors, have retained a strong sense of the value of education and of working for success. Thus, as second- and third-generation Japanese Americans have benefited from their forebears' battle against prejudice and discrimination, they have become well-represented in professions and occupations requiring advanced education, such as medicine and scientific research. The impact of Japanese Americans is also evident in many areas of business, sometimes in concert with companies based in Japan. For example, Japanese styles of providing hospitality and comfort, elegant understatement in design, and culinary expertise have boosted the hotel industry. While it is difficult to assess an exact ratio of Japanese involvement from abroad to Japanese American presence in the United States, clearly, Nisei and Sansei Japanese Americans have contributed to a growing appreciation of the Japanese culture.

The cultural impact of Japanese Americans in religion has been considerable. Not only in Hawaii, but also on the mainland, Buddhists have grown from only a handful to well over a million adherents, including converts, and Buddhism has joined numerous other religions and religious sects that are a part of multicultural American society. In Hawaii, many funerals follow Buddhist tradition, and some of the traditional holidays and festivals are widely celebrated.

The combination of effective social control, students' diligent attention to their studies, and parental emphasis on a close-knit family and family honor resulted, by and large, in success in the social and business world. Thus, Japanese Americans are prominent members of the so-called "model minority" that has risen above discrimination and disadvantage.

Individual Japanese Americans have been impressive in their achievements. In politics, Daniel INOUYE of Hawaii became U.S. senator; in addition, by the early 1990's there had been two Japanese American congressmen, two California state assemblymen, more than thirty elected city officials, and nearly twenty judges of Japanese descent, including Masato Dai. Misaji Marumote was the first Nisei justice of the Supreme Court of Hawaii; Patsy Takemoto Mink was the first woman Nisei lawyer in Hawaii; she was elected to the U.S. House of Representatives in 1964. Jimmie Sakamoto was a noted boxer and publisher; Seiji OZAWA became the conductor of the San Francisco and Boston symphony orchestras. Dennis Ogawa, of the American studies department of the University of Hawaii, is one of dozens of distinguished educators. George SHIMA (Kinji Ushijima), an entrepreneur, was "Potato King" of California. Not only loyal citizens, these and many other Japanese Americans have also proved themselves to be productive and successful Americans.

SUGGESTED READINGS. Sheila Hamanaka provides a thoroughly researched account of the Japanese Ameri-

Seiji Ozawa, renowned symphony conductor. (AP/Wide World Photos)

can experience in *The Journey: Japanese Americans, Racism, and Renewal* (1990). *Nisei: The Quiet Americans* (1969) by Bill Hosokawa traces the history of the second-generation Japanese in the United States. Gene N. Levine and Colbert Rhodes's *The Japanese American Community: A Three-Generation Study* (1981) compares and contrasts the experiences of Japanese Issei, Nisei, and Sansei. Mike Masaoka collaborates with Bill Hosokawa in *They Call Me Moses Masaoka: An American Saga* (1987) to trace the problems and the successes of Japanese Americans.—*Victoria Price*

Japanese Americans and dual citizenship: The situation of a second-generation Japanese American (Nisei) being considered a citizen of both the United States and Japan. Until the 1920's, Japanese law stipulated that anyone with a Japanese father was a citizen of Japan. American law considers anyone born in the United States to be an American citizen. Those Americans who did not like the Japanese felt that no one who also held Japanese citizenship could really be a loyal citizen of the United States. In 1924, after years of pressure, the Japanese government revoked Japanese citizenship for second-generation Japanese Americans. Despite this change, dual citizenship remained a sensitive issue for Japanese Americans, particularly when their loyalty was questioned during World War II.

Japanese Federation of Labor: Labor federation established in Hawaii in 1919. It was the first umbrella organization to represent the interests of laborers on all of the islands of Hawaii. In 1920, the Japanese Federation of Labor and the Filipino Federation of Labor negotiated with the Hawaiian Sugar Planters' Association (HSPA) for higher wages, but had no success. The Filipino workers went on strike, and the Japanese workers reluctantly followed suit. In response, the HSPA evicted twelve thousand workers from plantation housing. Most of those evicted were members of the Japanese Federation of Labor.

Japanese language: Japanese symbols are written vertically in columns and are usually read from top to bottom and from right to left. They are of two types, Kanji (literally, "Chinese writing") and Kana. Kanji are Chinese ideographs, introduced into Japan in the sixth century, which are used primarily for nouns and verb stems; in ideographic writing, a symbol stands for an entire word or concept. As in the Chinese written language, Kanji are stylized pictures that may require only one stroke or as many as twenty-five strokes. There are nearly fifty thousand Kanji in the Japanese writing system, but since 1946, Japanese high school students have been required to master a standardized set of about two thousand. Kanji may be read either in their original Chinese pronunciation or as the Japanese words that correspond to the Chinese meanings.

Kana is a syllabic system in which symbols designate syllables. There are two sets of Kana that a Japanese student must master, each numbering forty-eight signs. Kana are also derived from Chinese ideographs, but they are used for verb endings, adjectives, adverbs, and prepositions. Also, many words not of Japanese origin, especially English words, are written in roman letters, which are also taught in the Japanese school system. Thus, a single sentence in Japanese may be composed of Kanji, representing main roots and concepts; Kana, to indicate modifiers and word inflections; and words with roman spellings, if appropriate.

As is typical, this small Japanese American business has signs in both the Japanese and English languages. (National Archives)

The oldest written materials in Japan are written in Chinese. For example, the earliest surviving code of law (from the year 701) and the first history of Japan (712) were both written in Chinese, which was introduced in the third century. Gradually, Chinese ideographs were used to write Japanese words. There were difficulties, however, in using Chinese symbols derived from a largely monosyllabic and uninflected language for Japanese words that are typically polysyllabic and highly inflected. Thus, beginning in the ninth and tenth centuries, Japanese scholars began to develop new symbols (Kana) derived from Chinese to signify Japanese syllables and inflections. While several competing systems resulted from this time period, two emerged as the most widely accepted. These are hiragana, which uses stylized and simplified versions of Kanji signs, and Katakana, which selects one element of a complex Kanji sign and uses it to symbolize a particular Japanese syllable. Hiragana and Katakana were standardized in the nineteenth century, but many regional and individual variants are still used.

In addition to being a means of communication, Japanese writing has also been developed in Japan as an art form, known as *sho-do*, or brush-writing. A *sho-do* composition consists of Japanese symbols produced by ink and brush in an aesthetically pleasing manner on plain parchment. *Sho-do* was also introduced from China and is believed to have been used in Japan since the sixth century.

SUGGESTED READINGS. The history of the Japanese language is well described in Edwin O. Reischauer's *Japan: The Story of a Nation* (1990). The place of language in modern Japan is discussed in *Hidden Differences: Doing Business with the Japanese* (1987) by Edward T. Hall and Mildred Reed Hall. More technical descriptions of Japanese may be found in Susumu Kuno's *The Structure of the Japanese Language* (1973) and Roy A. Miller's *Japanese and the Other Altaic Languages* (1971).

Japantowns: Areas within larger cities that include Japanese American-owned shops, restaurants, hotels, travel agencies, and other businesses, as well as cultural organizations. These areas are easily recognized by the written Japanese characters on many of the buildings, storefronts, and signs. In the United States there are only two cities that still have areas known as Japantowns: Los Angeles' "Little Tokyo" and San Francisco's "Japantown," both near downtown. New York City, Chicago, Seattle, and cities in Hawaii have fairly large Japanese communities but no specific neighborhoods called Japantowns.

Japantowns grew out of a response to a hostile social environment. In the early 1900's, when the first

Performances such as those of this taiko (drum group) in Seattle, Wash., help maintain identity and tradition in Japanese American communities. (V. E. Horne, Unicorn Stock Photos)

generation of Japanese immigrants (Issei) arrived in the United States, they sought and found security within their own ethnic enclaves. Regarding themselves as sojourners, they came to the United States in search of financial security and planned to return to Japan once they became financially secure. First, they settled in Hawaii where they worked on plantations; later, many moved to the mainland. The early Japanese found work as laborers and farmhands in California and the Pacific Northwest region. Although they significantly contributed to the region's economic development, the Issei encountered PREJUDICE, DISCRIMINATION, and occasional violence. This was especially the case when they moved to cities, seeking employment and housing. Denied opportunities in the public and private workforce, most Japanese Americans sought self-employment. In some cities a separate Japanese district of hotels, boarding houses, restaurants, laundries, pool halls, and stores grew to meet the needs of these new immigrants. These urban enclaves became known as Japantowns or *Nihonmachi* (Little Tokyos).

In Japantowns, Japanese Americans could feel safe and comfortable among their compatriots while escaping racial discrimination from white businessmen. They could also easily find work and a place to live, while continuing to speak their language and maintain ethnic ties.

Since 1915 the proportion of Japanese Americans living in Japanese American neighborhoods has steadily declined. In an effort to combat widespread prejudice and discrimination, the JAPANESE AMERICAN CITIZENS LEAGUE (JACL) consisting of second-generation Japanese Americans (Nisei) urged its members to follow a path of economic success through individual enterprise, friendship with other Americans, and ASSIMILATION into American culture during the 1930's and 1940's. JAPANESE AMERICAN INTERNMENT during World War II disrupted the way of life in Japantowns; in Los Angeles, for example, African Americans typically took over Japanese American businesses. As Japanese Americans became better off financially, social CLASS and not ETHNICITY determined residential patterns. As more tolerant social conditions developed following the *BROWN V. BOARD OF EDUCATION* decision in 1954, the CIVIL RIGHTS ACT OF 1964, and the IMMIGRATION AND NATIONALITY ACT OF 1965, there was a further shift out of Japanese American communities into typically Anglo neighborhoods.

By the 1980's and 1990's, Japantowns were thriving

business and cultural centers but not primarily residential areas. An exception is special housing projects for older Americans in Little Tokyo, which has also become popular with Japanese tourists and temporary Japanese residents of Los Angeles. The neighborhood profited from investment by major corporations in Japan and strong Japanese American community support. It boasts an impressive Japanese American Community and Cultural Center with a large theater, office building, exhibit space, and open plaza for cultural events, and a new Japanese American National Museum housed in a converted BUDDHIST temple.

SUGGESTED READINGS. An excellent study of Japanese American communities is provided in Gene Levine and Colbert Rhodes's *The Japanese American Community: A Three-Generation Study* (1981) and Darrel Montero's *Japanese Americans: Changing Patterns of Ethnic Affiliation Over Three Generations* (1980). A thorough historical account of Japanese Americans is provided in Ronald Takaki's *Strangers from a Different Shore: A History of Asian Americans* (1989); Roger Daniel's *Asian America: Chinese and Japanese in the United States Since 1850* (1988); and Robert Wilson and Bill Hosokawa's *East to America: A History of the Japanese in the United States* (1980).

Jazz music: Musical style that originally evolved in the United States in the early twentieth century as a result of the blending of two great musical traditions: those of West Africa and Europe. The African tradition contributed various rhythmic elements and a distinctive vocal approach to playing melodic material that featured the use of "bent" notes that did not exist in the Western musical system. These notes could be played easily on instruments such as the clarinet, the trumpet, the trombone, and the guitar—instruments that were available to African Americans. The European tradition contributed musical forms (such as song forms and dance forms) and harmonic structures over which both composed and improvised melodies could be played.

The drum was the foundation of African music (particularly because the gods were thought to speak through drums), and much of the distinctive sound of the music that came to be called jazz is the result of attempts by African American musicians to reproduce drum patterns on melodic instruments. Because drums were used by Africans to communicate, African American slaves were, in most cases, forbidden to play drums. It was not until the end of the CIVIL WAR in 1865 that African Americans were able to use drums in a relatively unrestricted manner.

After the war, the former slaves were free to travel if they chose. Thus, musicians were able to develop new rhythmic patterns because of the increased interaction with musicians of different cultures. Much of this occurred in the Mississippi Delta and in cities along the river, such as Memphis and New Orleans.

Religious music had a strong influence on the development of jazz. The singing of SPIRITUALS by African Americans may date back to 1800; the music of black churches also included the ring-shout, the song-sermon, the jubilee, and the gospel song. In the ring-shout, which comes from West Africa, people dance in a circle and create a song that has a leader-chorus form with much repetition, focusing on rhythms rather than melody.

The minstrel shows that were popular in the United States during the last half of the nineteenth century helped spread the influence of African American music. Horace Weston, Billy Kersands, and the Bohee brothers were all famous African American performers. Many of them toured Europe with Haverly's Colored Minstrels. By the beginning of the twentieth century, many early jazzmen had toured with the minstrel shows, many of which actually featured European American entertainers in "blackface" who often made fun of African Americans through their stereotypical portrayals.

Another formative influence on jazz was ragtime, which achieved its highest popularity from approximately 1896 to 1917. Unlike spirituals and the BLUES, ragtime was melodic and cheerful. It represented a blending of West African and European musical elements, with more European influence than any of the other forerunners of jazz. Ragtime originated in the Midwest and was performed by both white and black musicians. The undisputed master, however, was Scott JOPLIN, who had a rich classical background. Ragtime contained many elements of the French quadrille and the melodic patterns of European music.

Jazz historians tend to agree that the original forms of jazz were beginning about 1900, and the period from 1900 until the start of World War I saw much experimentation. One of the motivating factors behind the early development of jazz in New Orleans, a major center for this music, was the large number of secret societies and fraternal organizations which laid the foundation for the brass bands that started there. These brass bands became a major part of the African American funeral in New Orleans. On the way to the funeral,

Jazz trumpeter Louis Armstrong the great star of jazz. (AP/Wide World Photos)

the band would perform hymns. On the way home, however, the music took on a completely different format, characterized by syncopated beats and a livelier mode.

Just as there is no way to establish a precise time and place where jazz "began," there is no one person who can be credited with first playing jazz. Among the early influential New Orleans musicians who are considered jazz players were Buddy Bolden, a trumpeter whose horn could be heard "clear across Lake

Pontchartrain," Edward "Kid" Ory, and Louis ARM-STRONG, who became the first international jazz star. One often-cited factor in the growth of jazz in New Orleans was the need for music in the more lavish houses of prostitution in Storyville, the city's red-light district. Prostitution was legal in Storyville until 1917. Even lowly bawdy houses often employed a piano player; one of them, Ferdinand "Jelly Roll" Morton, was very influential in the development of jazz. Even before Storyville closed in 1917, jazz musicians had begun to migrate up the Mississippi to St. Louis and, especially, Chicago. A Chicago jazz style emerged that was subtly different from the jazz played in New Orleans. (In later years, other regional styles would develop and be given such tags as New York jazz and West Coast jazz.)

The 1930's was the decade of swing, which featured big bands playing carefully crafted arrangements; swing music was popular through the 1940's. Although the clarinetist and bandleader dubbed the "King of Swing" was a white musician named Benny Goodman, an African American named Fletcher Henderson was instrumental in developing the swing style in the 1920's before Goodman made it popular. In the 1930's, Henderson became Goodman's chief arranger.

Pianist Thelonius Monk, a major figure in the bebop genre of jazz. (AP/Wide World Photos)

African American bandleaders Count BASIE and Duke ELLINGTON were also immensely popular. Ellington's repertoire was more eclectic than Basie's blues-based approach. Ellington pulled on numerous musical traditions, occasionally writing compositions that used Middle Eastern and Latin American motifs.

By the 1940's, a new style known as bebop, or simply bop, had emerged. Bebop featured smaller combos and was favored by a new generation of musicians who saw much of the big-band music as clichéd. Bebop placed strong emphasis on improvisation. Among the leading bebop players were Dizzie Gillespie, Charlie "Bird" PARKER, Thelonius Monk, and Bud Powell.

Miles Davis, a trailblazer in both the cool jazz and fusion styles. (AP/Wide World Photos)

A typical bebop combo consists of piano, bass, drums, alto or tenor saxophone (or both), and trumpet. Each musician is expected to play solos. New variations soon evolved from bebop; among them were hard bop, as typified by the music of Sonny Rollins and Clifford Brown, and free jazz, as played by Ornette Coleman and the enormously influential John COLTRANE. Free jazz pieces would sometimes contain atonal sections; whole songs might even be composed spontaneously. The 1950's saw the emergence of cool jazz. The name most associated with this style is trumpeter Miles Davis, but other players included Stan Getz and Dave Brubeck.

Beginning in the late 1960's, a style known as fusion became popular; it combines jazz improvisation with rock rhythm patterns. Opinion is divided on whether fusion can truly be considered jazz; nevertheless, many jazz greats pioneered the genre of fusion. Among them were Miles Davis, Wayne Shorter, and Josef Zawinul (the latter two cofounded the group Weather Report). Many international influences, from Latin to Asian Indian music, have strongly influenced fusion styles.

Although jazz is generally considered predominantly an African American musical form, and rightly so, other cultures have long been playing jazz and participating in its development. The influence of Latin music has been felt in jazz since the early years. Dizzie Gillespie, at the height of his fame in the 1940's, cowrote a song entitled "Manteca" with Cuban drummer Chano Pozo; its Latin rhythm created a sensation. A genre known as Afro-Cuban music, featuring Caribbean rhythms and percussion instruments such as conga drums, became popular in the 1950's. Exponents of Latin jazz have included Cal Tjader, Laurindo Almeida, and Tito Puente. Brazilian music, notably the samba style, exerted a strong influence in the 1960's.

The European classical tradition has also been important; in particular, a style sometimes called third stream music, evolving in the 1950's, was a hybrid of the jazz and classical traditions. Japanese American pianist and bandleader Toshiko Akiyoshi has recorded and toured widely with her award-winning big band. The fusion group Hiroshima, composed of Japanese Americans, combines fusion music with Japanese elements such as the koto, a traditional string instrument, and taiko drumming.

Audiences and musicians the world over have responded to the multicultural sounds of jazz. Most European countries have their own local jazz communities. One of the most renowned jazz festivals, in fact, takes place annually in Montreux, Switzerland. Another is held in Pori, Finland. American jazz bands travel to other countries to perform, but jazz bands from other countries increasingly come to play in the United States as well.

SUGGESTED READINGS. Innumerable sources exist on jazz, from historical surveys to detailed biographies of musicians. See Gunther Schuller's multivolume *The History of Jazz*; the first volume, *Early Jazz: Its Roots and Musical Development*, was published in 1968. Frank Tirro's *Jazz: A History* (1977) is a useful overview. Other good general sources include Leonard Feather's *The Encyclopedia of Jazz* (1960) and *From Satchmo to Miles* (1984) and Nat Hentoff's *Jazz Is* (1984).—*Bruce M. Mitchell*

Jehovah's Witnesses: Premillennial American religious movement founded in the 1870's by Charles Taze Russell. This organization represents perhaps the most intense form of premillennial thinking to gain currency among Christian believers in the United States and, later, the world. Premillenialism is a biblical interpretation that prophesies the imminent return of Jesus and an apocalyptic end to the current evil age in a horrific battle called Armageddon, and, thereafter, the establishment of a thousand-year period (the millennium) characterized by Christian peace and righteousness. These ideas were already at work in the religious imagination of Americans in the nineteenth century, primarily among Adventist Christians.

During a time of personal spiritual despair in the early 1870's, Charles Taze Russell (1852-1916), met an Adventist minister who reignited his faith with a premillennial spark. A convenient point to date the beginning of the Jehovah's Witness movement is 1879, the year Russell published his first issue of *Watch Tower*. Adherents were known variously as the Millennial Dawnists, International Bible Students, the Watch Tower Bible and Tract Society, Russellites, and Rutherfordites. The group's extreme views on the nature of their evil age and the impending apocalypse put the organization at odds with the DOMINANT CULTURE. Russell taught that Satan had infiltrated secular government and the churches, and that neither institution should be tolerated. He also claimed that the present age would end in 1914 and that in a forthcoming battle, called Armageddon in the Bible, Jesus would return to lead an army of true Christians against Satanic forces. After Satan was vanquished, Russell preached, 144,000 elect people would live in heaven; average servants of the Jehovah God would enjoy a peaceful life on Earth; and everyone else, especially people belonging to any other Christian denomination, would lie in their graves forever (Russell denied the existence of hell).

When Jesus did not return in 1914, Russell, after a careful reexamination of Scripture, claimed that Christ actually had returned "in spirit," a prelude to his imminent physical reappearance. This explanation satisfied believers, and the religious organization continued to grow steadily.

After Russell died in 1916, his successor, Joseph Franklin ("Judge") Rutherford, popularized the slogan "Millions now living will never die" and introduced the name "Jehovah's Witnesses" for his followers in 1931. Moving out from "kingdom halls," every member was called upon to spend several hours each week "witnessing," or proclaiming their message of salvation. The group's attacks on the "satanic" establishment brought them notoriety and persecution. Witnesses found themselves in court for refusing to salute the American flag or register for the draft, and they were often harassed with petty municipal charges such as disturbing the peace or peddling without a permit. Witnesses have also faced problems in American schools for their beliefs, including the nonobservance of holidays and birthdays. Because Jehovah's Witnesses have separated themselves theologically and institutionally from the dominant culture, the organization has historically provided an oasis of tolerance and acceptance for believers regardless of race, ethnicity, gender, or economic status.

SUGGESTED READINGS. For comprehensive historical accounts of the movement, see James Beckford's *The Trumpet of Prophecy* (1975), James Penton's *Apocalypse Delayed* (1985), Marley Cole's *Jehovah's Witnesses* (1955), and Herbert H. Stroup's *The Jehovah's Witnesses* (1945).

Jen, Gish: (Lillian Jen; b. 1955, New York, N.Y.): Chinese American writer. Born Lillian, Jen took the name Gish as a teenager in honor of actress Lillian Gish. After graduating from Harvard University, she worked in publishing and then traveled to China to explore her heritage. She attended business school briefly, leaving to pursue creative writing at the Iowa Writers' Workshop. Influenced by Jewish American writers, Jen had stories published in *The New Yorker, The Atlantic Monthly,* and the anthology *Best American Short Stories of 1988. Typical American*, her acclaimed 1991 debut novel, describes a Chinese American family's pursuit of the American Dream. Jen has received fellowships from the National Endowment for the Arts and the Bunting Institute.

Jewish American–African American relations. *See* **African American–Jewish American relations**

Jewish American communities: In 1991-1992 there were 5,798,000 American Jews, composing less than 3 percent of the total U.S. population of 248,710,000.

Jewish communities tended to cluster in urban and suburban areas in the Northeast, Southeast, Midwest, and West. The key communities in 1991 were those in New York (1,664,000, with 1,450,000 in New York City); California (923,000, with 600,000 in Los Angeles and 200,000 in the Bay Area); Florida (593,000, with at least 250,000 in Miami); Pennsylvania (330,000, with 250,000 in Philadelphia); Illinois (257,000, with 248,000 in Chicago); Massachusetts (275,000, with 228,000 in Boston); Michigan (107,000, with 94,000 in Detroit); Washington, D.C. (165,000); Georgia (74,000, with 67,000 in Atlanta); and Maryland (211,000, with 94,500 in Baltimore).

New York City. The large-scale influx of European Jewish immigrants to New York in the latter half of the nineteenth century virtually created the modern American Jewish community. By 1992, New York

Chinese American author Gish Jen, whose first novel, published in 1991, is entitled Typical American. *(AP/Wide World Photos)*

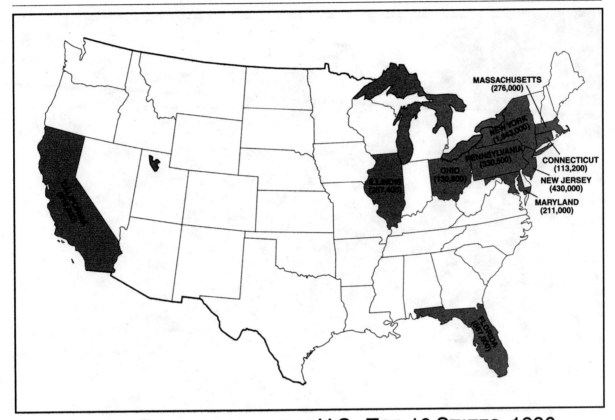

JEWISH POPULATION IN THE U.S., TOP 10 STATES, 1990

Source: Data are from U.S. Bureau of the Census, *Current Population Reports*, series P-25, no. 1044.

City had more Jews than any single city in Jewish history. It is a microcosm of diverse waves of immigration, among them the SEPHARDIC JEWS from England, Holland, the Balkans, and the Mediterranean; the GERMAN JEWS who came after 1848; and the massive wave of EASTERN EUROPEAN JEWS who came from the early 1880's through the 1920's.

In 1972, 1,836,000 Jews lived in the five boroughs of Greater New York: Manhattan, Brooklyn, the Bronx, Queens, and Richmond (Staten Island). Sizable communities had also developed in the adjacent suburban counties of Nassau, Suffolk, and Worchester. Of the five boroughs, Brooklyn had the largest Jewish population, estimated at 760,000, including many adherents of Orthodox Judaism. Queens, the gateway suburb to Long Island, witnessed a rapid Jewish population growth—at the expense of the once-dominant Irish and German communities—with a population in 1972 of 420,000. The downtown borough of Manhattan was still the focal point of the New York and national Jewish community. The Jews of the other four boroughs as well as of suburban Long Island, northern

New Jersey, Westchester, and Rockland counties—commuted to Manhattan daily for work. Manhattan continues to serve as the headquarters for every citywide Jewish organization and, more important, of virtually all national Jewish agencies.

Jews have played a prominent role in the city's politics, businesses, educational institutions, and cultural life throughout the twentieth century. The old-family Protestant elite turned the politics of the city over to the Jews, the Irish, the Italians, the Germans, and the African Americans. Two prominent American Jews, Abraham Beam and Edward Koch, served as the city's mayor during the 1970's and 1980's. Numerous Jewish politicians from New York influenced state and national politics, among them Herbert Lehman as governor and senator, Jacob K. Javits as senator, and Bella ABZUG as a congresswoman. In the early 1900's, Jews were active in the GARMENT INDUSTRY and the American LABOR MOVEMENT, especially on the city's Lower East Side.

Jews were generally associated with liberal causes and viewpoints. Yet in the 1980's, the community be-

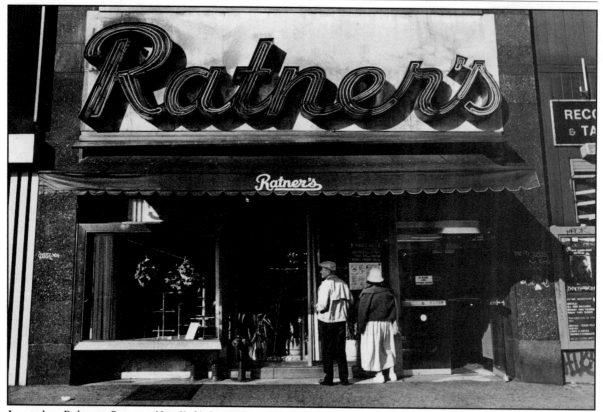

Located on Delancey Street on New York's Lower East Side, long a Jewish enclave, Ratner's has been a local eatery, meeting place, and landmark since 1905. (Kim Iacono)

came a flashpoint for crises in AFRICAN AMERICAN-JEWISH AMERICAN RELATIONS, especially in Brooklyn neighborhoods where Orthodox Jews and blacks lived in close proximity. In 1993, the community was still reassessing its role and attempting to repair the damage of violence in the Crown Heights neighborhood in 1991, in which both a black child and a Jewish yeshiva student were killed.

The New York City Jewish community underwent profound demographic transformations from 1972 to 1991. It witnessed a significant decline, especially in the middle-class suburban regions of Nassau, Worchester, and the borough of Queens. The population loss is partly attributable to the pattern of the elderly segments of the Jewish population relocating to Florida for their retirement years; they have not been replaced in sufficient numbers by young persons. Conversely, there was a Jewish population increase of nearly 15 percent in Manhattan during the 1980's. Whereas 1,836,000 Jews lived in the five boroughs in 1972, only 1,450,000 did so in 1991.

Los Angeles. When the U.S. Census of 1850 was taken in Los Angeles, only eight Jews were recorded, all bachelors who lived in their stores at the city's center. By 1880, several hundred Jews had arrived from Prussian Poland, Germany, Austria/Hungary, Saxony, and France.

At the beginning of the twentieth century, large numbers of eastern European Jews began to arrive in Los Angeles. By 1920, the Jewish population of Los Angeles reached forty thousand out of a total population of 576,000. The major Jewish neighborhoods before the 1930's were around Temple Street downtown, Boyle Heights to the east, and the Central Avenue district to the south.

The Los Angeles Jewish population grew considerably after World War II when thousands of war veterans and HOLOCAUST survivors moved to the city. By 1948, there were as many as 250,000 Jews in Los Angeles, many of them in the middle-class Fairfax district, where Yiddish was often heard on the streets. The midwestern United States was another important area of origin: Nearly 40 percent of Los Angeles Jewry during the 1950's came from Chicago. By 1967, more than 450,000 Jews lived in the city and its suburbs, notably the San Fernando Valley. Los Angeles and its environs had emerged as the second largest Jewish community in the United States after New York City.

The rapid Jewish population increases resulted in a proliferation of synagogues, an expanded Jewish Federation Council of Greater Los Angeles, and the setting up of major branches of prominent national Jewish organizations such as B'NAI B'RITH, the AMERICAN JEWISH COMMITTEE, the ANTI-DEFAMATION LEAGUE, the American-Israel Public Affairs Committee, and the American Jewish Congress. After the 1940's, important Jewish institutions for higher learning were established, including the University of Judaism, Hebrew Union College, and the West Coast's Yeshiva University as well as the Simon Wiesenthal Center for Holocaust Research. Jewish elementary and secondary day schools also proliferated after the 1960's, as did synagogues with the explosion of the Orthodox community in the 1970's and 1980's. The city remains one of the country's most diverse Jewish communities, ethnically and religiously, with institutions for every subgroup, including congregations for gay Jews and deaf Jews.

Whereas in New York City the Jews were important in the art, music, and theater worlds, their counterparts in Los Angeles were instrumental in promoting the motion picture industry. Film distributors and exhibitors such as Marcus Loew, Adolph Zukor, William Fox, Carl Laemmle, Lewis Selznick, Samuel Goldwyn, and Louis B. Mayer flocked to the suburb of Hollywood. The advent of talking pictures was sparked by the Warner brothers, who produced *The Jazz Singer* (1927) about a Jewish cantor. The biggest Jewish businesses in town, however, were construction, financing, and real estate. Jewish companies built some of the large suburban areas and surrounding cities such as Lakewood, La Mirada, Panorama City, and Santa Susana.

In the 1970's, the Jewish population continued to grow with immigrants arriving from Israel, the Soviet Union, and Iran. In 1992, of the 923,000 Jews in California, as many as 600,000 lived in Los Angeles.

In urban Jewish American neighborhoods, one can always find a gathering place to discuss the day's events. Pictured is New York's Ahearn Park (Samuel Dickstein Plaza). (Kim Iacono)

The Los Angeles riots of 1992 forced this influential community, which had long been active in liberal Democratic politics, to reassess its role in a city of rapidly shifting demographics and increasing ethnic balkanization. During the 1950's and 1960's, Jewish and African Americans in Los Angeles had united to fight for civil rights and social justice. It was from these bonds that Los Angeles' most enduring modern political alliance formed, bringing together activist African Americans from the inner city and progressive Jews from the Westside and San Fernando Valley. Their coalition propelled African American Tom BRADLEY into the mayor's office for five consecutive terms from 1973 to 1993. Because of strong Jewish and African American ties, many synagogues raised relief funds in the days following the 1992 riots; visited riot-torn areas to sweep up rubble and distribute food; and took part in interfaith demonstrations for racial harmony. The Jewish community leadership has also taken measures in the past decade to reach out to other ethnic communities, such as Latino and Korean Americans.

Chicago. Unlike the early Jewish settlers of colonial New York, who were mainly Sephardic, those who first settled in Chicago were German-speaking Ashkenazic Jews of central European descent. By 1860, there were approximately 1,500 Jews in Chicago, most of whom lived around Lake and Wells Streets, where they owned clothing and dry goods stores. By 1870, the Chicago Jewish community was enlarged by further immigration from Russia, Poland, Romania, and Lithuania and had spread to Van Buren Street, Polk Street, the Chicago River, and Lake Michigan. The great fires of 1871 and 1874 destroyed most of the homes and businesses of the Chicago Jewish community, as well as many of their synagogues. This prompted Jews to resettle farther away from downtown, as in the South Shore and Kenwood-Hyde Park districts.

The German-speaking Jews coexisted well with their non-Jewish counterparts. They read German newspapers, attended German theaters, and belonged to German organizations. They founded the Michael Reese Hospital on the South Side in 1880, which served until 1990 as one of the main health centers in Illinois, and the Chicago Home for the Jewish Aged in 1893.

When large numbers of eastern European Jews began to arrive in Chicago during the final quarter of the nineteenth century, they created ghettos such as the Maxwell Street area. The German Jews, on the other hand, were more ethnically integrated, established, and accepted. By 1900, Chicago's Jewish population reached eighty thousand, of whom more than fifty thousand were eastern Europeans. Many of these immigrants from eastern Europe worked in the sweatshops of the garment industry and in cigar-making factories. Others were peddlers, tailors, kosher butchers, bakers, and small merchants or artisans. In 1930, 275,000 Jews lived in Chicago, with 80 percent of them from Eastern Europe. Second-generation Jews began to ASSIMILATE, moving out of the old neighborhoods to Grand Boulevard, Washington Park, and Englewood.

The Chicago community swelled in the post-World War II era with the arrival of refugees from former Nazi-occupied Europe. Some of these Jews migrated to Los Angeles in the 1950's. In the late 1950's and early 1960's, the community saw a decline in population and institutions as the racial composition of the Hyde Park and Lawndale area changed and increasing numbers of Jews migrated to the northern suburbs. Areas such as Lincolnwood, Skokie, Niles, Morton Grove, Evanston, Wilmette, Winnetka, Deerfield, Northbrook, Glencoe, and Highland Park remained key Jewish suburbs in the 1990's.

The Jewish population of the Chicago metropolitan area stood at 275,000 in 1975. This number had dwindled to 248,000 in 1991 because of a low birthrate, movement to the Sunbelt states, assimilation owing to INTERMARRIAGE, and the slowing of immigration.

SUGGESTED READINGS. For general demographic trends and a first-hand account of the Jews of New York City, see the *American Jewish Year Book* for the years 1972-1992 and Harry Golden's *The Greatest Jewish City in the World* (1972). The best and most reliable sources for Los Angeles are Max Vorspan's and Lloyd P. Gartner's *History of the Jews in Los Angeles* (1970) and *The Jews of Los Angeles: Urban Pioneers* (1981), edited by Norton B. Stern. Bob Sipchen wrote an important analysis of the Los Angeles riots and their aftermath in relation to the Jews in *The Los Angeles Times*, October 16, 1992, p. A1. On Chicago Jewry, see Irving Cutler's "The Jews of Chicago: From Shtetl to Suburb," in *Ethnic Chicago* (1981), edited by Peter d'A. Jones and Melvin G. Holli, and *History of the Jews of Chicago* (1924), edited by Hyman L. Meites. For information on other major American Jewish communities, see Robert A. Rockaway's *The Jews of Detroit* (1986); Steven Feldman's *Guide to Jewish Boston and New England* (1986); David Altshuler's *The Jews of Washington, D.C.* (1985); and Lloyd P. Gartner's *History of the Jews of Cleveland* (1978).—*Michael M. Laskier*

Jewish American women: A variety of perspectives have shaped the role and experience of Jewish women. The ancient Israelites, a patriarchal society, sharply limited the role of women. The rabbinic view during the centuries following the Roman conquest of Judea (70 C.E.) continued in a similar vein. Attitudes in the latter portion of the twentieth century are decidedly more liberal, particularly in Conservative and Reform Judaism.

Ancient attitudes reflect the biblical perspective: Woman was created after man as a helpmate, and her chief function was the production of children. A woman could be sold as payment for a debt. Her religious functions were likewise of secondary importance. Nevertheless, she did have a say in choosing her marriage partner, and her legal status was the same as that of a man.

The rabbinic view during the talmudic period can be summarized in the prayer in which the man thanks

Liberal and feminist Bella Abzug was among the Jewish American women who broke with tradition by entering politics. Abzug served in the U.S. Congress from 1971 to 1976. (AP/Wide World Photos)

God that he was not born a woman. Though the context can be easily misinterpreted, the thanks were for being required to carry out religious obligations such as study of the Torah—strictly the man's duty. Women were praised for encouraging study in their sons, not in themselves, and were barred from formal Jewish education.

The liberal, modern view had its roots in the Reform movement, and the Jewish Haskalah, or Enlightenment, in the eighteenth and nineteenth centuries. In Reform, and to a lesser extent Conservative, Judaism women are considered religiously equal. They are entitled to participate fully in religious services, and at least within Reform Judaism, may be ordained as rabbis. In both Reform and many Conservative synagogues, women count toward the minyan, the minimum of ten adults needed for a service. The Orthodox view continues to relegate woman to a less involved status, although their Jewish education is now encouraged.

Upholding Jewish tradition within the home continues to be within the purview of the woman. In addition to maintaining a Jewish home, her traditional duties include the lighting of Sabbath candles. The Jewish identity of a child passes through the mother, not the father. Jewish women have also long been active as professionals and volunteers in Jewish social welfare

Jewish women, while active in intellectual pursuits and social causes, also fulfill traditional roles. (Hazel Hankin)

and educational organizations.

The 1970's saw the rise of Jewish feminism and Jewish women's spirituality groups as part of the Jewish renewal movement. Women began challenging male domination of Jewish life and researching Jewish women's history. They also created new rituals for female life passages such as first menstruation and baby naming. Rosh Chodesh celebrations, which welcome the new moon and thus the new month, have also become popular. Leading the way in much of this exploration are a new generation of women rabbis.

SUGGESTED READINGS. A historical perspective on Jewish women is found in the *Encyclopedia Judaica* (1972), edited by Cecil Roth. Isaac Bashevis Singer's "Yentl, the Yeshiva Boy" (1962) is a delightful fictional account of a woman wishing to study the Talmud in nineteenth century Europe. Tamar Frankiel, in *The Voice of Sarah* (1990), provides a feminist view of Orthodox Judaism. Attitudes toward the education of Jewish women is one of the topics in *The Jewish Woman: New Perspectives* (1976), edited by Elizabeth Koltun.

Jewish Americans: Though the Jewish population of the United States has never represented more than 2 to 3 percent of the country's total population, Jews have played a significant role in all aspects of American culture. Jews have always placed a strong emphasis on education. Particularly in the twentieth century, large numbers of American Jews became college educated. The result was the extensive contributions and prominence attained by Jews in professional and cultural areas, far in excess of their proportion of the population. For example, by 1970, approximately 10 percent of the faculty in American colleges was Jewish. Jewish scientists participated in many of the most important discoveries and developments in American technology. As musicians and writers, large numbers attained notable distinction. Many immigrants and children of immigrants entered the entertainment field, playing leading roles in the development of the motion picture industry. Such prominence belies the simple beginnings of American Jews but says much about the availability of opportunity in the United States.

The first Jewish immigrants were primarily SEP-HARDIC JEWS from Spain and Portugal. This group remained in the majority until the German immigration of the 1830's and 1840's. After 1890, a large influx of EASTERN EUROPEAN JEWS permanently changed the character of the community.

Prerevolutionary Period. The first Jewish immigration into the United States dates to 1654, when twenty-three refugees from Portuguese Brazil settled in what was then Dutch New Amsterdam (New York).

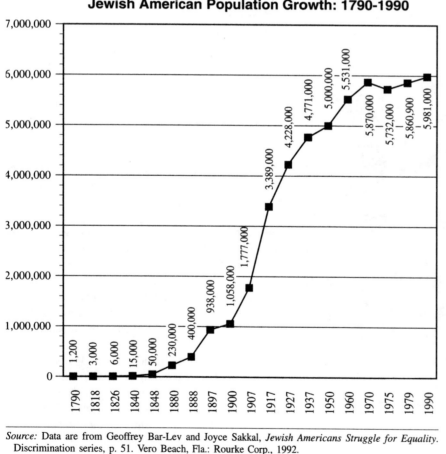

Jewish American Population Growth: 1790-1990

Source: Data are from Geoffrey Bar-Lev and Joyce Sakkal, *Jewish Americans Struggle for Equality.* Discrimination series, p. 51. Vero Beach, Fla.: Rourke Corp., 1992.

Their original destination was either Jamaica or Cuba, but the Spanish refused them permission to settle there. By the time the ship reached New Amsterdam, the passengers were out of money and low on supplies. Like many refugees who would arrive over the next three centuries, these Jews simply had nowhere else to go. New Amsterdam governor Peter Stuyvesant initially refused to grant them residency because of a fear of economic competition. The owners of the Dutch West India company, which employed Stuyvesant, bowed to Jewish backers in their native Amsterdam and forced Stuyvesant to accept the new immigrants. Ironically, the Jewish community became a mercantile success and, with burgeoning opportunities elsewhere, actually began to disperse.

Over the course of the next century, Jewish communities became established along the entire Atlantic seaboard and as far inland as Montreal. By the start of the AMERICAN REVOLUTION, the Jewish population had reached about 2,500. Most were retailers: merchants, tailors, bakers, and small shopkeepers. Many of these persons maintained little in the way of religious practice, eventually becoming assimilated into the larger population. By the mid-1700's, synagogues existed in only five American cities. The identification of Jewish life with the city, its culture, and economy, was not to change significantly over the years.

Settlement of the German Jews. The population of American Jews exhibited its first major expansion beginning about 1850. It had doubled between 1825 and 1850, reaching approximately 18,000 by 1850. Between 1850 and the beginning of the Civil War in 1861, the population ballooned to 150,000. A large number, though by no means all, of these Jews emigrated from German lands. About half came from Bavaria. Many others came from Bohemia, Moravia, or from parts of what had been Poland.

Their reasons for coming to the United States varied. Not surprisingly, these were related to the political and economic conditions abroad. Large numbers of political refugees fled failed revolutions in central Europe. Economic hardships also drove thousands of GERMAN JEWS to American shores. Unlike their Gentile counterparts, however, who were often illiterate German farmers, even the poorest Jewish immigrants usually had been taught to read. Thus, they arrived with strong potential for success. Jewish cultural contributions during this period were primarily confined to the music field, as they had been in Germany. One exception was the poet Emma Lazarus, known primarily for her inscription on the Statue of Liberty.

Eastern European Immigration: 1880-1925. By 1880, the American Jewish population had risen to approximately 280,000. Between 1880 and 1925, nearly 2,400,000 Jews came to the United States, raising the total Jewish population to 4,500,000. The vast majority of this migration came from the lands of Russia in eastern Europe. Lack of economic opportunity for a burgeoning Jewish population, excluded from the cities, forced the poor to emigrate. Others were driven by fear of pogroms and religious persecution. Most eastern European Jews were young people under age forty-five, and most settled in the large cities.

Unlike the German Jews who had arrived earlier, the later arrivals had few immediate plans to ASSIMILATE. They carried their religious practices and culture with them into the GHETTOS of the city along with their own Yiddish language. A social and cultural right developed between Jewish immigrants of the "old"

New York's Eldridge Street Synagogue was the first synagogue built by eastern European Jewish immigrants. (Kim Iacono)

and "new" waves. For example, German Jews tended to be the founders and directors of a host of Jewish organizations formed to educate, Americanize, and otherwise help the newcomers.

In the major cities, the Yiddish theater flourished. Large numbers of Jewish immigrants entered the vaudeville circuit, with George Burns, Al Jolson, and Fanny Brice among the most famous. It is estimated that by 1910, approximately 60 percent of the vaudeville houses in the ten largest cities were Jewish-owned.

Among those who recognized the potential of the early motion picture industry were large numbers of Jewish entrepreneurs. Harry Cohn, Samuel Goldwyn, Louis B. Mayer, David O. Selznick, and the Warner brothers all became successful in the early days of Hollywood. Others such as Robert Levy, owner of Reol Productions, an early attempt to produce films for the black audience, were less successful. Many did rise from the tenements of New York to the glitter of Hollywood. The poverty of the American Jewish ghetto bred its share of gangs and criminals. Some people, such as Eddie Cantor and Phil Silvers, overcame these beginnings while others, such as Arnold Rothstein, died as they had lived—at the hands of other crime figures.

Children of eastern European immigrants were quick to find a time-honored means of escape from the ghetto: sports. Many took to boxing, producing a large number of professional champions in the period between 1910 and 1925. The Lower East Side in New York City produced Abe Attell, Benny Leonard, and Barney Ross, among others. Basketball was to provide another popular outlet for Jewish athletes in the cities.

The large wave of Jewish immigration around the turn of the century created an audience for the "great Jewish novel." Henry Harland, though not a Jew, wrote a number of popular books on Jewish subjects under the pseudonym Sidney Luska. Gradually, Jewish writers such as Mary Antin, Ludwig Lewisohn, and Charles Reznikoff began to depict American Jewish life as it existed during this period in memoirs and novels.

The horrors of World War I, followed by the Bolshevik revolution and Russian Civil War, created millions more refugees, many of whom were Jewish. At the same time, American fear of the Bolsheviks, some of whom were Jewish, coupled with intense isolationism and NATIVISM, served to limit the number of immigrants allowed into the United States during the

1920's. By the beginning of the GREAT DEPRESSION in 1929, Jewish immigration had effectively ceased.

Rosalyn S. Yalow was awarded the Nobel Prize in 1977 for her work developing the technique of radioimmunoassay. (The Nobel Foundation)

Most Jewish east European immigrants were relatively young; about 80 percent were between the ages of fifteen and forty-five. Men typically made the initial journey, with the rest of the family eventually following. Unlike the German Jews, these later immigrants settled in the industrial cities: New York, Chicago, Philadelphia, Boston, and Cleveland. Many became associated with the LABOR MOVEMENT. In the mid-1920's, for example, some 80,000 families belonged to the Arbeter Ring (Workmen's Circle), which provided sick and death benefits for its members and took part in an extensive Yiddish cultural environment with Yiddish newspapers, choruses, theaters, and "folk" schools.

In New York City between 1885 and 1914, more than 150 Yiddish publications were available, twenty of them daily newspapers. The *Jewish Daily Forward* became the largest Yiddish newspaper in the world. A large number of immigrant societies were formed based on the members' town of origin (landsmannschaften). Here, too, could be found both camaraderie and benefits.

Education was foremost in the minds of immigrant parents, and support for quality public schools and colleges was strong. This was supplemented by afternoon Hebrew schools, with an emphasis on religious training, which became established early in the twentieth century.

Anti-Semitism and Discrimination. Jewish immigrants were well aware that, despite the image of the United States as the "golden land," discrimination existed. Their new home was a land of Gentiles, not all of whom welcomed this influx from eastern Europe. The German Jews enjoyed easier adjustment. Their numbers were fewer, and they were much more likely to integrate into society, often losing Jewish identity in the process. The hatred of groups such as the KU KLUX KLAN after the Civil War was less directed at Jews than at African Americans. This changed, however, with the enormous influx of eastern European immigrants after 1880. Their "Jewishness" was much more obvious, from their dress to their spoken language, Yiddish. Furthermore, the parent generation had little desire to assimilate with the endogenous population, which later put them at odds with their own children.

Despite the massive Nazi propaganda available in the United States during the 1920's, ANTI-SEMITISM bred mostly in the rural areas of the country. The Great Depression particularly hurt those areas, and the Jews often made for a convenient SCAPEGOAT. Though there was little support for this attitude in mainstream Christian churches, anti-Semitic preachers such as Father Charles Coughlin of Royal Oak, Michigan, railed against "New York Jews" to industrial workers, many of whom had lost their jobs.

Before World War II, American Jews were affected by various forms of religious discrimination such as immigration QUOTAS, college admission quotas, RESTRICTIVE COVENANTS in housing, and banning from certain professions and social organizations.

Immigration and the Effects of World War II. The destruction of the German economy in the 1920's and 1930's resulted in the rise to power of Adolf Hitler and the Nazis. In his book *Mein Kampf (1925-1927),* Hitler made no secret of his desire to eliminate Jewry from Europe. With the invasion of Poland in September, 1939, Hitler put his wishes into large-scale practice. By the end of the war in 1945, six million European Jews had been systematically slaughtered in what is now called the HOLOCAUST.

Some of the survivors made their way to the United States. Between 1945 and 1959, approximately 192,000 Jews arrived, bringing the Jewish population to more than 5 million. Most continued to live in the cities. After the establishment of the state of Israel in 1948, which provided a Jewish homeland for the first time in nearly two thousand years, many European Holocaust survivors settled in Israel instead of the United States.

The Jewish population of the United States remained relatively static in the years after World War II. Though the general population grew from 140 million persons in 1945 to more than 240 million by the 1990's, the Jewish population remained between 5 and 6 million. The reasons were twofold: Jewish families

In Germany, a boycott of Jewish businesses was begun by the Nazis in 1933. The sign urges Germans to defend themselves: "Do not buy from Jews." (National Archives)

were having fewer children, and relatively few immigrants were Jewish. Most postwar Jewish immigrants were survivors from Europe, numbering some 120,000 persons through 1951. Between 1952 and 1970, less than 150,000 Jews entered the United States, mainly from Israel and elsewhere in the Middle East, though some fled Castro's Cuba. With the changes in the Soviet Union during the 1980's, several hundred thousand Russian Jews were able to emigrate to the United States, representing the largest Jewish influx from a single country since the early 1900's. Most Soviet Jewish families settled in the large cities, such as New York and Los Angeles, where they formed ethnic enclaves. Unlike the Russian Jews from earlier generations, these immigrants often had minimal knowledge about Judaism.

Postwar Contributions. In the 1950's, Jewish writers such as Saul Bellow, Bernard Malamud, and Norman Mailer achieved increasing prominence. Though some of these individuals could more properly be de-

E. L. Doctorow, Jewish American novelist, has depicted both Jewish and general American culture and history in his work. (Barbara Walz)

scribed as writers who happened to be Jewish, rather than as Jewish writers, many brought the insights from their backgrounds into their work. Some, such as playwright Arthur Miller (once married to a Jewish actress named Marilyn Monroe), struggled with their Jewishness and the question of conformity in American society. Others, such as novelists Meyer Levin, Philip Roth, and Leon Uris, fully explored Jewish material and themes.

Beginning in the 1950's, Jewish literary critics developed a new form of criticism which analyzed literature in a broad context rather than in isolation. The 1950's and 1960's also saw the start of a genre known as the "Jewish best-seller," which became popular among both Jews and Gentiles. These included novels and stories written by Sam Levenson, Harry Golden, Herman Wouk, Leon Uris, and Chaim Potok.

The Jewish presence in the arts and entertainment industry ran the gamut from the big band sounds of Harry James and Benny Goodman to the classical music performances of Jascha Heifetz and Vladimir Horowitz. The generation coming of age in the 1960's contributed Marvin Hamlisch and Barry Manilow to American music. Groucho Marx, who with his brothers Harpo, Chico, and Zeppo popularized comedy in Depression-era films, continued with a major television show throughout the 1950's. Other popular Jewish motion picture and television actors in the early postwar years included Sammy Davis, Jr., Jack Benny, Milton Berle, and Lauren Bacall, though again the Jewishness of the artist was mostly incidental to the role. The art field saw caricaturist and painter David Levine and artist Saul Steinberg.

Jewish scientists were in the forefront of American technological discoveries and development. The development of the polio vaccines by Jonas Salk and Albert Sabin during the 1950's effectively eliminated a terrible childhood scourge. The awarding of the 1952 Nobel Prize in Physiology or Medicine to Selman Waksman honored the discoverer of the antibiotic streptomycin, one of the new wonder drugs. In 1977, Rosalyn Yalow became only the second woman to be awarded the prize in that same category.

Role in Contemporary Society. As the immigrant memory of American Jews has faded, the Jewish community has become increasingly diverse. Most American Jews are not religiously observant in the sense of following traditional Jewish law. Yet most consider religion important; among American-born Jews, three-fourths are either conservative or reform in their beliefs. Much of the change has resulted from living in a society with no legal restrictions; Jews have become part of the educated American elite. The grandchildren of immigrants have become as mobile as the rest of society. Many have left the cities for the suburbs. Even as it lives the American dream, the Jewish community faces an uncertain future. A low birthrate (less than two children per average family) and increasing rates of intermarriage (nearly one-third of Jews marry outside the faith) have raised concern among community leaders.

Most Jews have remained essentially liberal in their views. Jews in Congress have consistently voted in favor of social programs. In presidential elections in the 1980's, most Jews still voted Democratic. Despite political infighting in Israel and controversy with the Palestinians over land and rights during the 1980's, most American Jews also remain united by their strong support for Israel.

SUGGESTED READINGS. A concise but thorough review of the history of Jews in the United States can be found in the *Encyclopedia Judaica* (1972), edited by Gail Roth and Geoffrey Wigoder. Arthur Hertzberg's *The Jews in America* (1989) provides an excellent history of the immigrant experience, while the five-volume *The Jewish People in America* (5 vols. 1992), edited by Henry L. Feingold, is a broader history of the same subject. *Ellis Island to Ebbets Field* (1992) by Peter Levine discusses the role played by sports in the "Americanization" of the Jewish immigrants. Darryl Lyman's *Great Jews on Stage and Screen* (1944) does the same for the entertainment industry.— Richard Adler

Jewish–Christian relations. *See* **Christian–Jewish relations**

Jewish Defense League: (JDL) Militant Jewish organization. The JDL was founded in New York in 1968 by flamboyant, fanatical Rabbi Meir Kahane. Under the slogan "Never Again" (referring to the HOLOCAUST), the JDL refuses to see Jews submit to persecution and forcefully opposes any incidence of ANTI-SEMITISM. The group has been active in the physical protection of elderly Jews from urban crime and in campaigning for freedom for Soviet Jews. It has also made common cause with ultranationalist, anti-Arab Israelis, sometimes engaging in acts of violence. Because of its tactics and extreme views, the JDL is controversial both within and outside the American Jewish community.

Jewish immigrants: Though Jews were present in the United States as early as the seventeenth century, the majority of Jewish American families trace their ancestry either to the influx of German Jews in the mid-1800's or to the massive immigration of Eastern European Jews around the end of that century.

In the early 1800's, American Jewry was small, probably numbering no more than 6,000 persons. Then, insurrections against the monarchs of central Europe in the 1840's—though in general unsuccessful—upset the status quo, and Jews became a convenient SCAPEGOAT. Wealthier Jews moved from the villages to cities such as Berlin or Vienna. The poorest, with few alternatives, came to the United States.

Some eastern European Jews made a living as peddlers, dealing largely with people who came from their own villages or regions in the Old Country. (Library of Congress)

Many, though not all, came from Germany, especially Bavaria. The largest Jewish population was in Russia, but Russian society remained traditional and Jews there gave little thought to emigration during this period.

By 1860, immigration had swelled the Jewish population in the United States to 150,000, and by 1880, to approximately 280,000. Settlement of these "old" immigrants spanned the continent. A significant portion occurred along the route of the Erie Canal across upstate New York. Other settlements developed along the Mississippi River as Jews became prominent in the commercial and industrial growth in those areas.

As these German Jews became settled, and often successful, a new wave of immigration occurred between 1880 and 1925. Pogroms (massacres) and expulsions in Russia finally made Jewish life untenable. The pogroms of 1881-1882 killed and injured hundreds of Jews. At the same time, the growth in the Jewish population made earning a livelihood increasingly difficult, as Russian government policies excluded many Jews from the cities. Those who had education, money, or family connections remained. Again, it was the poorest who came to the "golden land," the United States.

Between 1880 and 1929, nearly 2,500,000 Jews entered the United States from eastern Europe. Most of these persons settled in the larger cities of the East Coast among "landsmen," persons from their own villages. Largely uneducated, they survived in small trades such as peddling or worked long hours in GARMENT INDUSTRY sweatshops. Speaking a different language, Yiddish, and following different customs, this population of "new" immigrants found it difficult to assimilate into the wealthier, established population of largely German Jews. Many eastern European immigrants were Orthodox Jews, who attempted to maintain a traditional ethnic culture within a very open society. Some of the social divisions between Jews of German background and Jews of eastern European background persist in contemporary American Jewry.

SUGGESTED READINGS. Excellent histories of the period are found in Arthur Hertzberg's *The Jews in America* (1989) and *The Promised Land* (1912) by Mary Antin. *World of Our Fathers* (1976) by Irving Howe describes the life of Jewish immigrants in New York. A discussion of the German Jews can be found in *Encounter with Emancipation* (1984) by Naomi Cohen.

Jewish philanthropy: Jewish philanthropy is based upon the biblical commandment to "love thy neighbor." The concept of *tzedakah*, or charity, is one of the Jew's essential duties. In biblical Israel, a corner of the planted fields was left for the needy, while crops left unpicked were available for those who might otherwise go hungry. The levels of charity were eventually codified by the twelfth century philosopher Maimonides, with an emphasis on anonymity.

Prior to the nineteenth century, charitable activities by Jews in the United States were centered in the synagogue. Activities consisted primarily of aid to transients and other needy individuals, and maintenance of cemeteries. The first organized charitable institution in the United States was the Hebrew Orphan Asylum, organized in 1802 in South Carolina.

Beginning in the mid-1800's, the large number of Jewish immigrants, particularly from Germany, over-

Jewish philanthropists are major benefactors of the City of Hope research hospital. Here Quincy Jones displays the Spirit of Life award presented to him by the City of Hope. (AP/Wide World Photos)

taxed the institutions in place. Jewish charitable organizations expanded. Most communities established a Hebrew Relief Society. Fund-raising and distribution were primarily at the local level, with only rare appeals outside the immediate community.

Large-scale immigration from eastern Europe began in the 1880's. Existing institutions again proved inadequate to handle the tens of thousands of immigrants who came each year. Local Hebrew Relief Societies began to coalesce into federations, with services provided for families, children, hospitals, and settlement houses.

With the end of World War II, the enormous impact of the Holocaust on European Jewry became apparent, and Jewish philanthropy took on an international scope. The United Jewish Appeal (UJA) was founded to aid the survivors of the devastation and to provide a means to establish a Jewish state in Israel. By the 1990's, the UJA became established as the leading private charity in the United States.

During the 1940's and 1950's, Jewish federations and councils underwent extensive mergers, as it became apparent that duplication of appeals and services was self-defeating. Programs were expanded to encompass educational, cultural, social, and recreational concerns.

Jewish philanthropy has expanded beyond the Jewish community. Synagogues frequently serve as shelters for the homeless during periods of less than peak use, such as during Christmas. A response to the problem of hunger in the 1980's was the establishment of Mazon, a national organization which encourages Jews to donate 3 percent of the cost of joyous events, such as weddings, to help feed the needy. As individuals, Jews are also notable for their generous support of civil liberties, human rights, and other liberal organizations and political campaigns.

SUGGESTED READINGS. Discussion of the code of Jewish law can be found in *Introduction to the Code of Maimonides* (1980) by Isadore Twersky. The importance of *tzedakah* is discussed in *Basic Judaism* (1975) by Milton Steinberg. The history of Jewish philanthropy is covered in the *Encyclopedia Judaica* (1973).

Jewish Theological Seminary (New York, N.Y.): Spiritual and educational center of American Conservative Judaism. Founded in New York in 1887, the seminary trains rabbis, cantors, teachers, and synagogue administrators. Its library boasts the largest collection of Jewish books in the world. The school opened its California branch, the University of Judaism, in 1947.

Jews—Conservative: Members of one of four main movements in Judaism, marked by its flexible approach to tradition. The Jewish Conservative movement rose in nineteenth century Germany and developed further in the United States in the early 1900's. Its peak growth occurred in the years after World War II, and by the 1990's it was the largest movement in American Judaism.

Conservative Judaism has been called a "middle way," one holding to Jewish tradition yet acknowledging a concern for progress and growth. It has also been called tradition without orthodoxy in that it attempts to incorporate features of both Orthodox and Reform Judaism. While some critics argue that Conservative Judaism began largely as a reaction to the Reform movement, it has developed its own identity. It seeks, or at least approves of, ways to synthesize traditional observance with modern life, preserving those traditions that provide continuity in Jewish culture. Conservative Judaism advocates an evolving ideology so long as it does not disrupt tradition and remains in accord with Jewish law.

Some Conservative Jews point to the Talmud as a classic example of their stance on evolution and tradition. They see the Talmud as a record of developing ideology and responsible interpretation of the Torah (Jewish scripture and law). Conservative Jews reject fundamentalism, but at the same time insist upon ceremonial observance. For example, they may approve of travel on the Sabbath but only for the purpose of attending services. They may allow large parts of their services to be in the vernacular, but insist that men cover their heads with a yarmulke (skull cap). The extent of flexibility in observance usually depends upon the individual congregation. As a case in point, women were approved for the rabbinate in 1985, but the decision to accept women on the pulpit has been left up to local congregations. Many Conservative synagogues actively involve women in both the liturgy and roles of leadership.

Because of its flexibility, Conservative Judaism has been accused of having no ideology, of being neither Reform nor Orthodox. Conservative Jews, however, are likely to see the lack of a formal statement of ideology as an advantage, an opportunity for each congregation to adapt to its own particular circumstances.

SUGGESTED READINGS. Among the excellent studies of Conservative Judaism are Moshe Davis' *The Emergence of Conservative Judaism* (1963). Joseph Blau's *Modern Varieties of Judaism* (1966) and Gilbert Rosenthal's *Four Paths to One God* (1973) trace the history and ideology of all four major modern Jewish movements. More specialized studies of the Conservative movement include Seymour Siegel's *Conservative Judaism and Jewish Law* (1977), which studies Conservative interpretation of law within their own ideology. For a description of Jewish observance according to Conservative principles, see *A Guide to Jewish Practice* (1978) by Isaac Klein.

Jews, Eastern European. *See* **Eastern European Jews**

Jews, German. *See* **German Jews**

Jews—Orthodox: Members of the most traditional of the four main movements of Judaism. Until the French Revolution, all Jews would probably have been regarded as Orthodox, but in modern times Orthodoxy has developed a self-conscious ideology that, for some, distinguishes it from historical or traditional Judaism. Orthodox Judaism was initially a response to the Jewish Enlightenment (spirit of free, rational inquiry) and Emancipation (freedom from the ghetto) of the late eighteenth and nineteenth centuries in central and eastern Europe. It grew in the United States with the immigration of Orthodox leaders before and after World War II. Appalled at the assimilation they felt characterized Reform Judaism, which was still dominant at the time, the Orthodox established a network of synagogues and yeshivas (religious day schools) to bring American Jews back to the Torah (first five books of the Bible) and Jewish law.

Some ultra-Orthodox Jews prefer to be known as Torah-true, meaning they remain true to Torah regardless of cultural circumstances and consider Jewish law "a way of life." Others, known as the modern Orthodox, obey Jewish law while becoming more integrated into secular, mainstream life and culture. Though Orthodox Judaism remains small compared to Reform and Conservative Judaism, it saw tremendous growth in the late 1900's. This can perhaps be attributed to the high birth rate the movement encourages and the attraction of Hasidism and other ultra-Orthodox sects for previously alienated young Jews.

Orthodox Jews believe that the Torah was supernaturally revealed at Mt. Sinai and is literally true. A Jew's reason for being is anchored in *halakhah* (traditional observance), which is perhaps the essence of Orthodox Judaism. The Torah was given through Moses, and it is intended to govern all aspects of Jewish life. As the law of God, it is not to be judged by people or their laws. It stands, in fact, in judgment of humanity and all social institutions.

Obligation and commandments (*mitzvot*) are important concepts in understanding Orthodox Judaism. For example, a Conservative or Reform Jew may observe the Sabbath for cultural or personal reasons; an Orthodox Jew observes the Sabbath because it is his obligation. An Orthodox Jew is likely to seek employment that makes Sabbath observance possible, regardless of cultural attitude toward the work week. It is the obligation of Orthodox Jews to support *kashrut* (the laws governing kosher food preparation) even, for some, to the extent of refusing invitations to eat in places where Jews cannot observe kashrut. Jewish holiday observance, circumcision, ritual bathing—indeed all aspects of ceremonial law—are obligations.

During Orthodox services, women are generally seated separately from men. They are not counted in the minyan (quorum of ten required for public worship) and may not help conduct services or serve as rabbis.

SUGGESTED READINGS. Bruce Lawrence's *Defenders of God: The Fundamentalists* (1989) and Leon Stitskin's *Studies in Torah Judaism* (1969) are in-depth studies of Orthodox Judaism. Zvi Kurzweil's *The Modern Impulse of Traditional Judaism* (1985) provides a look at how Orthodox Judaism functions in a modern world.

One ultra-Orthodox sect is the Lubavitcher Hasidim. (Richard B. Levine)

Jews—Reconstructionist: Members of the newest and smallest of four main Jewish movements, stressing Jewish culture and humanistic values. It originated in the United States during the 1920's and 1930's, largely under the direct influence of Mordecai M. Kaplan and the indirect influence of the American pragmatist John Dewey. Reconstructionist Judaism is highly democratic, stressing as the basis of Judaism not the traditional congregational unit but a broader, democratic community providing for all the activities and needs of persons within it. Reconstructionism maintains that Judaism is more than a religion; it is an evolving civilization with a common history and culture, shared obligations and relationships, as well as ethics and cultural ideals. Reconstructionism embraces both religious and secular Jews who subscribe to its tenets.

Jewish tradition is valuable to Reconstructionism but only to the degree that it contributes to the maintenance and development of Jewish culture. For example, the Hebrew language is perceived as essential because it is the key to the literature of the culture; one may respect the kosher laws more because they fulfill certain ideals than because they are divine obligations.

Reconstructionist Jews prefer their movement for its stress on the development of a democratic culture, a Judaism without supernatural revelation, without the notion that the Jews are a chosen nation, but with full celebration of many of the traditional customs, ceremonies, and holidays because they contribute to the survival of Jewish culture. Worship and prayer may be quite important to a Reconstructionist Jew but in a subjective way, as an enrichment of social progress or individual growth.

Reconstructionist Judaism provides for significant adjustments in the definition and development of Jewish culture. Unlike traditional Judaism, it recognizes a child as a Jew if his or her father is a Jew even though his or her mother may not be. It is open to intermarriage between Jews and non-Jews within certain guidelines. Women are permitted to initiate and obtain divorces, and they have been admitted to the rabbinate.

SUGGESTED READINGS. Two good studies of Reconstructionist philosophy and practice are Mordecai Kaplan's *Judaism As a Civilization* (1967) and *The Meaning of God in Modern Jewish Religion* (1962). Jacob Neusner's *American Judaism, Adventure in Modernity* (1972) highlights Reconstructionism's response to the modern world, and Marc Lee Raphael's *Profiles in American Judaism* (1984) gives a thorough treatment of Reconstructionism. Jacob Neusner in his book *Death and Birth of Judaism* (1987) provides useful comparisons of Reconstructionism with other modern Jewish movements.

Jews—Reform: Members of one of four main movements in Judaism, marked by its liberal approach. Although some Jews believe that Judaism, by its very nature, has always been reforming, most scholars conclude that the movement known as Reform Judaism began in Germany, largely as a product of the eighteenth century European Enlightenment and renewed interest in progress and reason. The first Reform synagogue was established in Seesen, Westphalia, in 1810. The movement really crystallized in the mid-eighteenth century, however, among German Jews who immigrated en masse to the United States. Their early synagogues, founded on a Protestant church model, included robed rabbis, organ music, greatly increased use of the vernacular (English or German), and a central role for sermons in religious services. Gradually, more ritual and Hebrew prayer were reintroduced into Reform temples.

Reform Judaism is a result of continuing adaptations of traditional practice to modern cultural concerns. Rejecting the idea that Jewish law is binding, the movement holds that each age and culture may make its own distinct contributions to Judaism. Acknowledging the significance of God, Israel, and Torah, it stresses the ethical demands entailed in the concept of God.

Reform Jews are likely to advocate or at least approve of the use of an organ in services; a shortened liturgy; more prayer and teachings in the vernacular; and basic changes in the prayer book such as removal of unedifying phrases or references to rebuilding the temple and restoring animal sacrifice. Reform Jews generally reject or deemphasize the importance of traditional views on the coming of the Messiah, return to the land (Israel), and a restricted role for women. The Reform movement was the first to allow the ordination of women as rabbis, beginning in 1972. Reform Judaism has historically been more open than other movements to the notion of intermarriages between Jews and non-Jews, as well as more welcoming to converts. Reform Judaism is itself constantly reforming.

SUGGESTED READINGS. Eugene Borowitz provides a look at modern Reform practice in *Reform Judaism Today* (1978); while Gunther Plaut traces the history

Unlike Orthodox Jews, who frequent stores like Murray's Kosher House of Prime Meat pictured here, most Reform Jews do not follow kosher dietary laws. (Kim Iacono)

of the movement in *The Growth of Reform Judaism* (1965). Jacob Neusner's *Death and Birth of Judaism* (1987) provides helpful comparisons of the four major contemporary Jewish movements and Marc Lee Raphael's *Profiles in American Judaism* (1984) stresses Reform Judaism in the United States, capturing many of its essential features.

Jews, Russian. *See* **Russian Jews**

Jews, Sephardic. *See* **Sephardic Jews**

Jews and intellectual life: Jews have long played a role in American intellectual, cultural, and political life that is far greater than their proportion of the population. Their contributions became especially prominent after the massive waves of immigration by eastern European Jews in the early 1900's and later by German Jewish émigrés in the 1930's and 1940's. In the postwar period, Jews continued to be well represented in influential literary, scientific, academic, and political circles.

Nineteenth Century Contributions. The Jews who migrated to the United States in the eighteenth and early nineteenth centuries were largely poor, undereducated, and of small-town origin. Only after the American Civil War did the "Gilded Age" foster a new entrepreneurial elite, many of whom were German Jews. Some became generous cultural philanthropists. Otto Kahn regularly covered the Metropolitan Opera's considerable deficits. The Guggenheims came to be celebrated, over several generations, for their literary and academic fellowships and their renowned art museum. Joseph Pulitzer established a chain of newspapers, most notably the *New York World,* committed to exposing public corruption. On his death in 1911, he left bequests founding Columbia University's School of Journalism as well as the annual prizes that bear his name.

In medical research, New York City's Mount Sinai Hospital, opened in 1852 and originally called Jews' Hospital, was to become one of the world's greatest centers for the investigation of both physical and mental ills. In the late nineteenth century, Abraham Jacobi established the nation's first department of pediatrics there; Simon Baruch became the "father of physical medicine" (as well as of presidential adviser Bernard Baruch); Carl Koller pioneered the use of cocaine as a local anesthetic; Béla Schick devised the Schick test for diphtheria; and Nathan Brill, Burrill Crohn, Bernard Sachs, Jacob Churg, Lottie Strauss, and Emanuel Libman provided the classic descriptions of the illnesses and syndromes that bear their names. In other scientific disciplines of the period, Emile Berliner invented the microphone, gramophone, and transformer; Albert Michelson measured the speed of light and became the first American physicist to receive the Nobel Prize; Franz Boas explored cultural anthropology to puncture racist myths and nationalist conceits; and Joseph Jastrow was the first American psychologist to apply Sigmund Freud's theories.

By the eve of World War I, the 3.5 million Jewish Americans had become the largest Jewish community in the world. New York City's 1.6 million Jews had become the nation's fourth "city," surpassed in numbers only by the entire populations of New York, Chicago, and Philadelphia. Between 1890 and 1914, an enormous wave of Jewish immigrants escaped persecution in Russia, Poland, and parts of the Austro-Hungarian Empire. Many shared in the dynamic new socialist-revolutionary ideologies sweeping through eastern and central Europe. The most impressive

The work of brilliant Jewish physicist Albert Einstein was central to twentieth century science. (AP/Wide World Photos)

Jewish radical of the era was Morris Hillquit, who became Eugene V. Debs's trusted lieutenant as the most intellectual leader among American Socialists. Yiddish- language journalism, prose, poetry, and theater all achieved distinction.

The Interwar Period. The Jewish community's greatest legal scholar was Louis Brandeis, whom President Woodrow Wilson nominated for the Supreme Court in 1916. Brandeis' liberalism aroused fierce opposition to his confirmation from large corporations, former president William Howard Taft, and Senator Henry Cabot Lodge; hate mail from anti-Semites inundated the Senate Judiciary Committee. Nevertheless, after a five-month struggle, the Senate confirmed Brandeis by a 47-22 vote. He was to use his enormous prestige to make the cause of Zionism acceptable not only to American Jews but also to many non-Jews.

Ethnic discrimination against Jews became particularly intense from 1914 to the mid-1940's. Throughout

Cynthia Ozick's story "The Shawl" (1981) depicts the horror of a Nazi concentration camp. (Julius Ozick)

adopted Jewish quotas by the mid-1930's.

In medical schools, the quotas became all but exclusionary. In 1923, Jewish enrollment at Columbia's College of Physicians and Surgeons was 50 percent; by 1939, it had dropped to 6 percent. Law schools were equally strict. Such legal mandarins as Harlan Stone, who would become Chief Justice of the United States, deplored the infusion of Jews into their genteel enclave.

In the interwar period, Jewish scholars were systematically denied appointments in most colleges and universities. Through the 1920's, fewer than one hundred Jewish professors had appointments in American faculties of arts and sciences. Ludwig Lewisohn, a brilliant literary critic and novelist, found academic doors shut to him. Cultural and literary critic Lionel Trilling was told by the chair of Columbia's English Department that it was unwilling to keep on "a Freudian, a Marxist and a Jew"; only the intervention of the university's president saved his position. Only by sheer tenacity and talent and industry did many Jews

Novelist Saul Bellow, celebrated author of Herzog *(1969), who often chronicles the American Jewish experience.* (The Nobel Foundation)

the United States, RESTRICTIVE COVENANTS excluded Jews from attractive residential housing and suburban towns, clubs, and resorts. The literary image of the Jew was often that of an aggressive businessman with little understanding of American cultural values. Distinguished novelists such as Edith Wharton, Thomas Wolfe, Willa Cather, Ernest Hemingway, and F. Scott Fitzgerald portrayed Jews unfavorably as coarse, abusive, often corrupt, and physically repulsive. The ANTI-SEMITISM of Henry Adams, as well as of poets T. S. Eliot and Ezra Pound, became notorious.

The mounting phalanx of anti-Semites did not stop at the doors of academe. By 1919 Jews made up 13 percent of Yale's student body, 20 percent of Harvard's and Brown's, and 40 percent of Columbia's. The response to this rising proportion of Jewish students was the imposition of admissions QUOTAS by administrators. By 1928 the proportion of Jews admitted to Harvard's freshman class dropped to 10 percent; by the 1930's at Yale to 8 percent; and at Princeton, Dartmouth, and Swarthmore to between 3 and 5 percent. Virtually all private higher educational institutions had become achievers in their careers.

In the 1930's a number of gifted Jewish writers made their reputations. Prominent among them were Anzia Yezierska, who wrote of immigrants struggling in an alien culture; Daniel Fuchs, whose Williamsburg trilogy is set in cheerless slums; Henry Roth, whose novel *Call It Sleep* (1934) renders the cruelty of ghetto life in an unforgiving New York; Michael Gold, whose *Jews Without Money* (1930) stresses class struggle in a harshly proletarian setting; Meyer Levin, who conveyed the gritty reality of second-generational Jewish life in *The Old Bunch* (1937); Nathanael West, who wrote searingly satirical fiction that scanted Jewish characters; and Budd Schulberg, son of a film studio head, whose *What Makes Sammy Run?* (1941) is a merciless dissection of a Jewish hustler in Hollywood.

In the GREAT DEPRESSION of the 1930's, radicalism flowered as it rarely does in the United States. Many young Jews, witnessing the rise of Nazism and Fascism in Europe and experiencing racial and religious discrimination in their own country, espoused progressive movements, though comparatively few joined the COMMUNIST PARTY outright. In 1934 Philip Rahv and William Phillips founded the *Partisan Review*. Its stance was at first hard to the left, but after the Hitler-Stalin Pact of 1939 it became the most important journal for liberal non-Communist critics, scholars, and fiction writers, publishing work by Trilling, Delmore Schwartz, Meyer Shapiro, Sidney Hook, Saul Bellow, and other leading intellectuals. Many of them had risen from humble homes on New York's Lower East Side, as did the brilliant jurist Felix Frankfurter. After a splendid record at Harvard Law School as both student and then professor, Frankfurter became one of President Franklin Roosevelt's most influential advisers, securing key assignments in the NEW DEAL for many of his protégés. In the theater, the 1930's most gifted playwrights were also Jewish: Clifford Odets (*Waiting for Lefty, Awake and Sing*), Elmer Rice (*The Adding Machine*), and Lillian HELLMAN (*The Little Foxes*).

Émigré Intellectuals. The waves of Jewish refugees who fled central Europe in the 1930's may well have constituted the most talented tide ever to wash ashore in the United States. The reception of many of these newcomers was less than heartening, even among American Jews. Such assimilated luminaries as the distinguished journalist Walter Lippmann preferred to ignore their presence out of fear that they might increase anti-Semitism in the United States. Yet these

Microbiologist Selman Waksman developed the antibiotic streptomycin. (The Nobel Foundation)

outcasts included many of the world's most renowned scholars, musicians, philosophers, psychoanalysts, and, above all, scientists.

The story of the nuclear research projects that led to the world's first atomic explosions in 1945 is well known. Instrumental in prompting President Roosevelt to authorize a uranium program were two native Jews, Lewis Strauss and I. I. Rabi, and four immigrants: Enrico Fermi, Leo Szilard, Eugene Wigner, and Albert Einstein, who had moved to the United States in 1933. An extraordinary group of Hungarian Jewish geniuses joined the Los Alamos nuclear project: Theodor von Karman, Georg von Hevesy, Michael Polanyi, John von Neumann, and Edward Teller. The laboratory's superb director was the native-born J. Robert Oppenheimer.

Two Jewish-founded institutions of learning, Princeton's Institute for Advanced Study and New York's New School for Social Research, provided teaching and research opportunities for many distinguished Jewish scholars. The New School became a university in exile for nearly one hundred refugee intellectuals.

Various University of California campuses also gave appointments to European Jewish academics, many of whom were able to continue distinguished careers.

In chemistry, Peter Debye, Kasimir Fajans, James Frank, Walter Loewe, Otto Loewi, Otto Meyerhof, and Gustav Neuberg brought about a revolution in their field. Konrad Bloch, Hendrick Dam, Fritz Lipman, and David Nachmansohn made splendid contributions in biochemistry, molecular biology, and neurology. Witold Hurewicz, Jerzy Neyman, and Stanislaw Ulam promoted advances in mathematical set theory and topology. Franz Neumann, Hans Kohn, and Peter Gay became leading historians, while Erwin Panofsky, Walter Friedlander, and Jacob Rosenberg did notable work in art history. Oscar Morgenstern, Fritz Machlup, Jakob Marschak, and Albert Hirschman excelled in economic game theory, econometrics, and Third World economics. Lewis Coser, Paul Lazarsfeld, Hans Morgenthau, and Leo Strauss were giants in political science.

While nineteenth century Americans had often gone abroad to complete their educations, now European educators, mostly Jewish, had immigrated to the United States to complete the education of young Americans.

The Postwar Period. From the late 1940's to the mid-1950's, a miasma of suspicion, fueled largely by the demagogic Senator Joseph McCarthy, brought academic faculties under attack as "subversive." Some Jewish professors were driven off campuses by accusations of communism, and Oppenheimer, despite his wartime services, was stripped of his security clearance. In spite of MCCARTHYISM, however, no major anti-semitic political movement took hold. The six million Jews slaughtered in Adolf Hitler's HOLO-CAUST, as well as Joseph Stalin's anti-Jewish purges, made discrimination against Jews increasingly disreputable.

A mood of egalitarianism took over. When the G.I. Bill encouraged a vast influx of veterans into the universities, the growing demand for instructors opened up new teaching slots for Jews. Admission restrictions of Jewish students eased considerably. By 1973, 58 percent of Jewish graduate students were enrolled in the nation's top ten most respected graduate schools, and Jews constituted 34 percent of their sociology, 28 percent of their economics, and 24 percent of their political science faculties. In 1985 the journal *The Public Interest* cited thirty-two Jews in its list of the seventy most eminent intellectuals in the United States. Among university administrators, Jews from the 1970's on became presidents of the universities of Chicago, Pennsylvania, Columbia, Princeton, Dartmouth, and Yale, as well as of smaller colleges.

Hannah ARENDT emerged in the 1950's as the most renowned of German Jewish émigré political thinkers, *The Origins of Totalitarianism* (1951) being a classic analysis. Psychiatry was almost wholly dominated by Jews, with Erik Erikson, Bruno Bettelheim, and Erich Fromm making particularly outstanding contributions. In the medical sciences, one statistic is startling: By 1992, of fifty-five American Nobel laureates in the field, twenty were Jews. New York Jewish intellectuals were notable in editing, publishing, and writing. For example, Norman Cousins headed the *Saturday Review of Literature* from 1940 to 1970; Irving Howe edited the social-democratic *Dissent* from 1954 to his death in 1993; *Commentary,* launched by the AMERI-CAN JEWISH COMMITTEE, sought out conservative contributors; and *Tikkun,* created to counteract *Commentary,* sought out liberals. *The New York Review of Books,* founded in 1963 by Robert Silvers and Barbara Epstein, became the most influential of American intellectual publications.

Jewish writers have been prominent in American fiction since World War II. Space permits only a listing of the more prominent names: Saul Bellow, Norman Mailer, J. D. Salinger, Joseph Heller, Bernard Malamud, Edward Louis Wallant, Philip Roth, E. L. Doctorow, Cynthia Ozick. Isaac Bashevis Singer was a special case, since he wrote in Yiddish yet resided in the United States from the 1930's until his death in 1991. Both Bellow and Singer won Nobel Prizes. Famous Jewish dramatists include Arthur Miller, Neil Simon, David Mamet, and Tony Kushner.

Jews remained politically active in the postwar period. While the vast majority of intellectuals voted Democratic and were liberal on such issues as abortion and equal rights, a minority veered to a more cautious pragmatism, if not outright conservatism, in the 1970's and 1980's, among them Norman Podhoretz, Seymour Lipset, Nathan Glazer, and Irving Kristol. The philosopher Sidney Hook and economist Milton Friedman were perhaps the leading advocates of this stance. The New Left, by contrast, was spearheaded by Jews such as Herbert Marcuse, Noam Chomsky, Paul Goodman, and Howard Zinn. Jews were also usually the most widely publicized leaders of student activism in the 1960's on college campuses, as with Columbia's Mark Rudd and Berkeley's Bettina Aptheker. Contemporary American feminism was pioneered by such Jews as Betty FRIEDAN and Gloria STEINEM, while Rosalyn Yalow became the first American woman to win the Nobel Prize for medicine.

Altogether, the history of Jews in the United States has been an extraordinarily successful one, providing a significant testing ground for American ideals— especially the goal of apportioning rewards according to individual merit as opposed to hereditary privilege or ethnic identity.

SUGGESTED READINGS. Anthony Heilbut's *Exiled in Paradise: German Refugee Artists and Intellectuals in America from the 1930's to the Present* (1982) is a gracefully written, comprehensive chronicle of the odyssey of a superbly gifted group. Irving Howe's *A Margin of Hope: An Intellectual Autobiography* (1982) is a valuable memoir by an eminent scholar-critic who was at home in the Jewish, political, and literary worlds. The best single historical volume is *A History of the Jews in America* (1992) by Howard Sachar. Alan M. Wald's *The New York Intellectuals* (1987) is a study of the rise and decline of the mostly

Jewish, anti-Stalinist Left from the 1930's through the 1980's.—*Gerhard Brand*

Jim Crow laws: A series of laws designed to maintain a rigid form of racial SEGREGATION. Shortly after 1877, when federal troops were being withdrawn from RECONSTRUCTION duties in the Southern states following the CIVIL WAR, the municipal and state governments of the former Confederacy began to enact laws that created separate facilities and institutions for African Americans and whites. Although a phenomenon predominantly identified with the South, these statutes were not unknown in some border and northern states. In the South, they continued to exist well into the twentieth century, until widespread public protest culminated in the CIVIL RIGHTS LEGISLATION of the early 1960's and brought about their timely end. "Jim Crow" comes from "Jump Jim Crow," an 1828 minstrel routine. It was used as a collective racial epithet for African Americans as early as 1838, and the phrase "Jim Crow law" first appeared in print in 1904.

The restrictions incorporated by these laws covered

Among the signs carried in the mammoth 1963 March on Washington were those reading "No U.S. Dough to Help Jim Crow grow." (Library of Congress)

almost every element of daily life. Separate and poorly maintained facilities and accommodations in restaurants, hotels, theaters, passenger trains, trolley cars and buses, parks, churches, schools, and public restrooms were commonplace realities in the lives of African American citizens.

The first significant challenge to Jim Crow laws came in 1896 in the infamous PLESSY V. FERGUSON case. In 1892, Homer Plessy, a man who was seven-eighths Caucasian and one-eighth African American, was ordered to leave a railroad car designated for whites only and to take his seat in the Jim Crow car. When he refused to do so, he was arrested and charged with violating Louisiana's "separate car" law. Plessy sued, arguing that the separate car law violated constitutional rights guaranteed by the THIRTEENTH and FOURTEENTH AMENDMENTS. Four years later, the case was heard by the U.S. Supreme Court. The court, in a 7-2 decision, upheld the Louisiana law, declaring that separation did not necessarily mean an abrogation of equality. This decision established a legal precedent for the doctrine of "separate but equal" in all matters relating to socialization and public interaction between whites and African Americans, reinforcing Jim Crow laws for more than half a century.

The doctrine of "separate but equal" was particularly oppressive in the area of public education. Educational facilities funded collectively by white and African American taxpayers were invariably separate but notoriously unequal, particularly in the southern states. Court challenges to such patent inequality were continually refuted by the precedent set in Plessy v. Ferguson. In 1950, the NAACP Legal Defense and Education Fund, led by Thurgood MARSHALL, decided to mount a challenge to its constitutionality. An amalgam of five school segregation cases came to the Supreme Court in 1953, under the title BROWN V. BOARD OF EDUCATION. On May 17, 1954, the Court reversed itself in the Plessy case, declaring by unanimous decision that "in the field of public education the doctrine of 'separate but equal' has no place."

Although deprived of its legal strength, the Jim Crow mentality refused to die, and the controversy turned violent in the late 1950's and 1960's. African American resistance, such as the 1960 Woolworth lunch counter sit-in in Greensboro, North Carolina, sparked a wave of similar SIT-INS across the South, many of them marked by state and locally condoned violence. Finally, Congress put the official power of the federal government behind the Supreme Court's

1954 decision when it passed the comprehensive CIVIL RIGHTS ACT OF 1964, effectively ending the era of Jim Crow laws.

SUGGESTED READINGS. Leonard P. Stevens' brief but compelling *Equal!: The Case of Integration vs. Jim Crow* (1976) is highly recommended. For thoroughness and scholarly detail, see Neil R. McMillen's *Dark Journey: Black Mississippians in the Age of Jim Crow* (1989). For an interesting perspective prior to the 1960's, see C. Vann Woodward's *The Strange Career of Jim Crow* (1957).—*Richard Keenan*

Jobs program. *See* **Comprehensive Employment and Training Act of 1973**

Johnson, Albert (Mar. 5, 1869, Springfield, Ill.—Jan. 17, 1957, American Lake, Wash.): Editor and politician. Johnson began his career in publishing, serving in editorial posts on the *New Haven Register, The Washington Post*, and the *Tacoma News* from 1896 to 1906. He was elected to the U.S. House of Representatives from Washington State in 1912 and became chairman of the Committee on Immigration and Naturalization in 1919. In that position, he introduced and championed the IMMIGRATION ACT OF 1924, also called the Johnson Act, which responded to growing American XENOPHOBIA by severely restricted immigration, forbidding entry to all new arrivals except family members of resident aliens.

Johnson, Earvin "Magic" (b. Aug. 14, 1959, Lansing, Mich.): African American basketball star. After leading Michigan State to the 1979 National Collegiate Athletic Association (NCAA) championship, six-foot, nine-inch guard Magic Johnson turned professional as the number-one draft pick of the Los Angeles Lakers of the National Basketball Association (NBA). Johnson's astonishing ball-handling and playmaking skills made him the centerpiece of the Laker dynasty of the 1980's, and he led the team to five NBA titles in a nine-year period. In 1987, 1989, and 1990, he was named the league's most valuable player. In 1991, still one of the game's top players, Johnson announced that he had been infected with the acquired immune deficiency syndrome (AIDS) virus and was retiring from basketball to become an advocate for AIDS research. Nevertheless, Johnson played in the 1992 NBA All-Star Game as an honorary selection and won the game's most valuable player award. He won a gold medal as a member of the U.S. "Dream Team" in the 1992 Olympics before making a brief comeback effort with the Lakers before the 1992-

Magic Johnson (right) in 1990 game against the Chicago Bulls, trying to maneuver around Michael Jordan. (AP/Wide World Photos)

1993 season. He retired again in November, 1992, because of the controversy his presence was bringing to the court.

Johnson, James Weldon (June 17, 1871, Jacksonville, Fla.—June 26, 1938, Wiscasset, Maine): African American author, scholar, and lawyer. Johnson was a leading black poet, literary critic, and novelist of the pre-Harlem Renaissance generation. Author of "Lift Every Voice and Sing" (1900), the "Negro national hymn," Johnson is well known for his book of poems titled *God's Trombones* (1927), one of several collections. He took degrees from Atlanta University and Columbia, and became a lawyer, diplomat, and executive secretary (1920-1936) of the NATIONAL ASSOCIATION FOR THE ADVANCEMENT OF COLORED PEOPLE (NAACP). After 1930 he taught writing and literature at FISK UNIVERSITY.

Jokes, ethnic. *See* **Ethnic jokes**

Jones, James Earl (b. Jan. 17, 1931, Arkabutla, Miss.): African American actor. A powerful presence on stage and screen, Jones's performance in *The Great White Hope* in 1969 was a breakthrough for black actors. Jones grew up in Michigan and, after graduating from college and serving in the military, studied theater in New York City. He made his off-Broadway debut in 1957. He has since appeared in more than thirty plays and received many awards for acting. Jones has done numerous films, including *Dr. Strangelove* (1964) and *Conan the Barbarian* (1982). A serious actor, he costarred in the acclaimed Broadway version of *Othello* (1982) and portrayed writer Alex HALEY in the television sequel to *Roots.*

Jones, Quincy (b. Mar. 14, 1933, Chicago, Ill.): African American composer, arranger, and producer. Winner of twenty Grammy awards and a four-time Oscar nominee, Jones has composed, arranged, and produced music for many great singers and bands. He has written more than thirty-three film scores, including music for *The Wiz* (1978), *In Cold Blood* (1967), and *The Color Purple* (1985). He got his start in a band at age fifteen with Ray CHARLES in Seattle, then traveled with jazz artist Lionel Hampton in Europe and studied at Berklee College of Music in Boston. Jones joined Mercury Records in 1961 and was its first black vice-president. He produced the

James Earl Jones (right) appearing in 1987 in August Wilson's play Fences. (AP/Wide World Photos)

album and video *We Are the World* (1985) and Michael Jackson's best-selling *Thriller* (1982). He has used his talents and influence to help many fellow blacks succeed in the music industry.

Jones Act (1916): Legislation important in ending "Americanization" policies in the Philippines and paving the way for independence for the archipelago. The United States had taken possession of the Philippines during the SPANISH-AMERICAN WAR in 1898 and between 1900 and 1913 had attempted to restructure its government and society. Francis Burton Harrison, appointed governor general of the Philippines by President Woodrow Wilson in 1913, worked to reverse this trend by transferring responsibility in the government and civil service to Filipinos. The Jones Act was a significant move toward this end in that it established an elected senate as the upper house of the Philippine legislature and extended the vote to all male citizens over twenty-one who could read and write. The act also stated that the United States sought to recognize Philippine independence "as soon as a stable government can be established therein."

Joplin, Scott (Nov. 24, 1868, Texarkana, Tex.—Apr. 1, 1917, New York, N.Y.): African American composer. Joplin was a self-taught musician who became the "king of ragtime." He began his career as a piano player in the cafes, honkytonks, and brothels of St. Louis and other Missouri towns (1885-1895). In 1896 he began playing at the Maple Leaf Club in Sedalia, Missouri. Late in the 1890's, when he published some piano pieces, his "Maple Leaf Rag" became famous. The folk opera *Treemonisha* (1911) was his most ambitious work. In 1909, he moved to New York City, where he died in a mental institution. Joplin's reputation gained new life when "The Entertainer" (1902) was used as theme music in the motion picture *The Sting* (1973).

Jordan, Barbara Charlene (b. Feb. 21, 1936, Houston, Tex.): African American lawyer and politician. After earning a law degree, Jordan set up practice in her mother's kitchen in an attempt to lower attorney fees for her clients. She got involved in politics through voter registration drives for African Americans, as well as other volunteer work. In 1973 she was elected to Congress from the Eighteenth District in Texas. During her terms she was elected president pro-tempore of the House and served as chair of the Labor and Management Commission and the Urban Affairs Commission. After

serving three terms, Jordan stepped down and returned to a local law practice and a teaching position at the University of Texas.

Jordan, Michael (b. Feb. 17, 1963, Brooklyn, N.Y.): African American basketball star. The National Basketball Association's most valuable player in 1988, 1991, and 1992 and the second NBA player to score more than three thousand points in a single season (1986-1987), Jordan excelled as a collegiate player at the University of North Carolina before turning professional with the Chicago Bulls. A six-foot, six-inch guard renowned for his spectacular slam dunks, Jordan led the Bulls to NBA championships in 1991, 1992, and 1993 and won a gold medal as a member of the U.S. "Dream Team" at the 1992 Barcelona Olympics.

Michael Jordan celebrating the Chicago Bulls' win over the Portland Trail Blazers in the 1992 NBA finals. (AP/Wide World Photos)

Jordanian Americans: The Hashemite Kingdom of Jordan was created as an autonomous caliphate, called Transjordan, in 1921. It achieved independence from Britain as a monarchy in 1946. Jordan lies just to the east

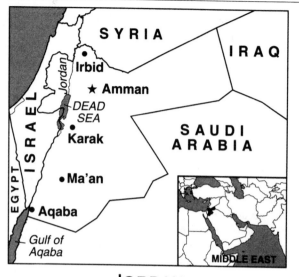

JORDAN

of Israel. It is surrounded on its other borders by Syria, Iraq, and Saudi Arabia.

Jordan is an Arab country that is 98 percent Sunni MUSLIM. Its chief conflict is with Israel, which lies on the opposite bank of the Jordan River. In the 1948 Arab-Israeli war, Jordan gained the West Bank territory and the old city of Jerusalem, which lie across the river. In the 1967 war, Israel recaptured all this land and caused Arabs who had been living on the West Bank to stream into Jordan.

Jordan itself has become a land of immigrants, or rather, refugees. Arabs from neighboring states involved in war flee to Jordan and live in camps. Large numbers arrived after the 1967 Arab-Israeli war. Approximately 700,000 Kuwaitis fled to Jordan after Iraq invaded Kuwait in 1990. Many refugees in Jordan refuse to settle permanently because they insist on their right to return to their homelands; some of them have lived in camps for decades.

Jordan is an arid land with few resources—it has never been able to support its own population without outside aid. The Bedouins, nomads who once inhabited the eastern desert of the country, have been part of an extensive migration from rural to urban areas that has strained the resources of the cities.

Very few Jordanians came to the United States before 1965. In that year, the IMMIGRATION AND NATIONALITY ACT was ratified with a clause stating a preference for professionals. This law induced educated Jordanians to emigrate. In fact, from 1965 to 1976, all Arab countries experienced a serious "braindrain." This problem eased a bit in the 1980's in Jordan, when employment opportunities improved there.

Jordanian Americans are culturally indistinguishable from other Arab immigrants. They are generally well educated and live in cities near their professional jobs. They tend to retain their religion, which is usually Islam. Jordanian Americans maintain their Arab identity and culture through strong ties to their families and their mosques.

Joseph, Chief [Heinmot Tooyalakekt] (c. 1840, Lapwai Preserve, northeastern Oreg.—Sept. 21, 1904, Colville Indian Reservation, Wash.): Chief of a band of Nez Perce Indians who peacefully resisted a fraudulent land cession extracted from the Nez Perce (1863) during the Gold Rush. This eventually led to an uprising in 1877. In what is often called the strangest of the Indian wars and a heroic, fighting retreat, Chief Joseph and several hundred Nez Perce undertook a 1,300-mile retreat to Canada but were forced to surrender to General Nelson A. Miles only thirty miles from their goal. Chief Joseph spent the rest of his life on the Colville Reservation in eastern Washington, striving to improve the conditions of his people.

Journalism, ethnic. *See* **Ethnic journalism**

Journalists and journalism: Journalism, according to the dictionary, is the collection and editing of news for

Benjamin Franklin bought the Pennsylvania Gazette *in 1722; he also published the first foreign-language colonial newspaper, the* Philadelphia Zeitung. *(Library of Congress)*

Political caricatures, such as this from 1832, animated early journalism in the United States. (N.Y. Historical Society)

presentation through the media. Although news has been collected and circulated for centuries, publication dedicated to providing news for mass consumption is barely two hundred years old. Men and women who wrote for newspapers were, before the penny press revolution of the 1830's, printers, editors, or anonymous writers, interested in commerce or in promoting social or political change. Until the 1820's, very little press was dedicated to ethnic minorities or women.

Until well into the twentieth century, newspapers and magazines in various forms were the primary vehicles for journalists. Since the development and common acceptance of radio and television news programs, journalism as a profession includes all those who write, edit, publish, or broadcast news.

The Colonial Press. The American press began with the September 25, 1690, sole issue of Benjamin Harris' *Publik Occurrences, Both Foreign and Domestick* in Boston. Four days after its publication, the three-page paper was suppressed by the colonial government. Fourteen years later, John Campbell began America's first continuous newspaper, the Boston *Newsletter*, which he composed from news garnered from foreign newspapers, gossip, and the mails. His paper, approved in advance by colonial authorities, carried little local news and no editorials. The notion of a free press would wait until the U.S. Constitution provided the first official guarantee.

After printing America's second newspaper, the Boston *Gazette*, in 1719, James Franklin left to start his own newspaper, the *New England Courant*, with backing from members of the Hell-fire Club, a Boston tavern discussion group. Unlike its predecessors, the *Courant* editorialized, and soon Franklin was in trouble for criticizing Cotton Mather's advocacy of vaccination for smallpox. Franklin spent much of his career in trouble with Boston authorities and eventually moved to Rhode Island to start that colony's first newspaper. Besides demonstrating that newspapers could be more than mundane official organs, Franklin also provided the first opportunity for a woman to be involved in printing an American newspaper. Ann Franklin, his wife, assumed ownership of the Rhode Island *Gazette* following his death in 1735 and later began the Newport *Mercury*. Four other women were involved in newspapers before 1765: Anna Zenger in New York, Elizabeth Timothy in South Carolina, and editors Sarah and Mary Katherine Goddard in Providence, Rhode Island. After 1765, women were commonly involved in the printing business.

Benjamin Franklin followed his brother James into the printing business as his apprentice at age twelve. In 1722, he achieved considerable success in Philadelphia, buying the *Pennsylvania Gazette* after destroying its owner and publisher, Samuel Keimer, with a series of satirical articles. Unlike his brother, Ben was careful not to aggravate colonial authorities. He was appointed postmaster and used the position to suppress his competition and enrich himself. Franklin's long career included two American firsts: He started the foreign-language press with the Philadelphia *Zeitung* in 1739 and began the first colonial magazine, the *General Magazine*, in 1741. Both enterprises failed, but their successors flourished.

The Revolution and the Party Press. By 1765, when the ferment for revolution had become public, there were twenty-four newspapers in America. By 1775, the number had doubled, primarily because newspapers were the most efficient way to spread discontent with British rule.

The Stamp Act of 1765, which taxed newsprint and all other paper in the Colonies, proved to be the catalyst for a free press. Samuel Adams, Thomas Paine, and others railed against what they called unfair taxation. American demands for a free press centered on the right to publish a single point of view, free from government control and taxation. Printer/editors on both sides saw their presses shattered and their offices burned in the name of liberty. Most historians credit the patriot press—often in the form of letters and pamphlets printed anonymously or over pseudonyms—with fomenting the American Revolution and with keeping revolutionary zeal high enough to convince the British to surrender.

After the war, newspapers continued in the tradition of partisanship, and for almost fifty years the nation's major newspapers were primarily party organs. John Fenno's *The Gazette of the United States*, established in 1789, was soon joined by numerous other Federalist newspapers. The Republicans, led by Thomas Jefferson and James Madison, established a press of their own, including the short-lived but prominent *National Gazette*, published by Philip Freneau, and Samuel Harrison Smith's *National Intelligencer*.

The partisan press reached its peak in the Jacksonian era, flourishing not only in major cities but in most towns and villages as well. Andrew Jackson, whose election in 1828 marked the beginning of modern presidential politics, had three official newspapers: Amos Kendall's *Argus of Western America* in Kentucky, Duff Green's *United States Telegraph* in Washington, D.C., and Francis Blair's Washington *Globe*. These papers helped Democrat Jackson win the presidency and promoted his programs once he was elected. Newspapers remained politicized for years.

As important as the party press was, the price of newspapers and the method of distribution limited readership to the elite. Newspapers commonly sold for six cents an issue, but only through subscription. Common citizens, whose wages averaged eighty-five cents a day, could not afford to buy newspapers; African Americans, American Indians, and the poor had no forum in the press.

Abolition and the Sectional Press. The abolitionist press began with Charles Osborn's *Philanthropist* in Ohio in 1817, followed by Elijah Embree's *Manumission Intellengicer* in Tennessee and Benjamin Lundy's influential *Genius of Universal Emancipation*. Antislavery newspapers, including William Lloyd Garrison's *Liberator*, suffered low circulation, persecution, censorship, and disagreement within the ABOLITIONIST MOVEMENT over the disposition of freed slaves. Few abolitionist newspapers lasted for more than a few years or managed circulation beyond three thousand. Lewis Tappan's *National Era*, which ran Harriet Beecher Stowe's *Uncle Tom's Cabin* in 1852-1853 in installments, reached a circulation of twenty-five thousand, and *The Liberator* lasted thirty-five

Abolitionist Frederick Douglass established the North Star *in 1847.* (Library of Congress)

years, but they were the exceptions.

In 1827, Samuel Cornish and John Russwurm established the first black newspaper, *Freedom's Journal*, in New York City. Other black newspapers joined the abolitionist movement, most of them established because African Americans had no voice in the white press. In 1847, the most famous black spokesperson of the period, Frederick Douglass, established the *North Star* (later renamed the *Frederick Douglass Paper*) and wrote eloquent attacks on slavery until publication was suspended in 1860. Religious organizations sponsored several black newspapers, including the *Christian Recorder*, also established in 1847, which survives as the longest continually published black newspaper in the country. Most black newspapers, like their white abolitionist counterparts, advocated nonviolence and citizenship for African Americans and lasted for only a few years.

Other minorities established newspapers as well. In 1828, the *Cherokee Phoenix* became the first American Indian newspaper, lasting until pressure from the Georgia legislature and federal removal of the Cherokee to Oklahoma ended its publication. The second American Indian newspaper, the *Shawnee Sun*, begun in Kansas in 1835, met the same fate.

Reporters Ed Bradley (left) and Diane Sawyer, here with CBS anchor Dan Rather in Moscow in 1987, typify the increasing presence of women and minorities in broadcast journalism. (AP/Wide World Photos)

During the second half of the nineteenth century, most frontier towns had newspapers. In 1850, there were fewer than ten newspapers west of the Mississippi River; by 1900, there were seven hundred. Editors promoted their communities, believed in freedom of the press, and promoted education and culture. They frequently attacked competing newspapers, rarely exhibited objectivity, and often reflected the RACISM, particularly against African Americans and American Indians, that was rampant at the time. Except for a growing number of foreign-language newspapers, primarily German, Norwegian, and Spanish, minorities had little voice. A few editors, such as Minnesota's Jane Swisshelm, who campaigned for abolition, for women's rights, and against Indians, refused to be either intimidated or bought out, but most others were captives of their patrons.

The Penny Press. The arrival of the penny press in 1833 signaled a revolution in American journalism. The growth of a democratic market economy, advanced printing technology, and a growing spirit of individualism in business and politics provided the impetus for a cheap press. Newspapers that once depended largely on the sale of subscriptions now used advertising to pay for printing costs and circulation to establish advertising rates, and news replaced partisan causes as the mainstay of journalism.

Benjamin Day established the first penny newspaper, the New York *Sun*, in 1833. Two years later, James Gordon Bennet founded the New York *Herald*, the greatest of the penny papers, and dozens of others followed. The penny press established modern journalism. A wide readership demanded facts, and news had to be current. Newspapers sent correspondents to

Katherine Graham assumed control of The Washington Post *in 1963, becoming president and chief executive officer.* (AP/Wide World Photos)

Washington, D.C., and to foreign capitals, and competition for news and readers became the order of the day. The one-person newspaper was gone except in small towns. News became big business.

Journalism in the Twentieth Century. News as big business did not mean that presentation of facts had to be objective. During the last years of the nineteenth century and the first twenty years of the twentieth, businessmen such as William Randolph Hearst and Joseph Pulitzer dominated the national press. News-

paper chains grew and circulation, not objective news stories, was most important. Reporters were, to a great extent, entertainers, and their news stories reflected their sense of the dramatic.

During the first years of the twentieth century, such writers as Lincoln Steffens, Ida Tarbell, and Upton Sinclair, the so-called muckrakers, wrote popular articles to expose corruption in government and industry. Few of the writers concerned themselves with racial inequality or civil rights. Ray Stannard Baker and

William Walling encouraged the Progressives to champion the cause of African Americans, but there was little true reform. Despite the massive influx of immigrants, fair treatment of minorities in the American press had to wait until the 1950's.

During the period between 1914 and 1945, the United States was involved in two wars and a world depression. Interest in minority concerns and objective treatment of minorities faded before the patriotic zeal of anti-German and anti-Japanese sentiment. The

Latino television journalist Geraldo Rivera hosting a 1989 program on firearms. (AP/Wide World Photos)

inaccuracies, propaganda, and blatant lies contained in the world's newspapers, however, led to the acceptance of accuracy and objectivity that now characterizes American journalism. Even so, it was not until the Supreme Court declared segregation in schools to be unconstitutional in BROWN V. BOARD OF EDUCATION in 1954 that the civil rights of minorities and, ultimately, women, seriously involved the American press.

By then electronic journalism had entered the fray. Radio news began to supplant newspapers as the primary mass medium. Within twenty years, television displaced both newspapers and radio. Reporters of color began to appear regularly in newspapers and on television. The issues of equality, civil and human rights, and social justice began to receive more routine coverage.

The Role of Women and Minorities. Before WORLD WAR II, a few women gained notoriety as serious journalists. Dorothy Thompson was published in some two hundred newspapers and appeared on NBC radio in the 1930's and 1940's. Dorothy Kilgallen covered a wide range of stories, Sylvia Porter cracked the financial page, and, with Eleanor ROOSEVELT's help, May Craig, Emma Bugbee, Korena Hickock, and others became press regulars. Helen Thomas began her illustrious career in 1943, and by the 1970's had become the UPI chief White House correspondent.

The war took men from the desks of newspapers, and women took their places. A few went overseas. Photographer/reporter Margaret BOURKE-WHITE covered World War II and the KOREAN WAR, and in 1951 war correspondent Marguerite Higgins became the first woman to win the Pulitzer Prize for foreign correspondence. After the war, most women returned to domestic duties. The 1950's signaled a return to prewar status quo.

The major break for female and minority journalists came after the CIVIL RIGHTS MOVEMENT of the 1960's and resulting AFFIRMATIVE ACTION legislation, but it was a slow process. During the VIETNAM WAR era, such women as Georgette Chapelle, Margaret Kilgore, Liz Trotta, Marguerite Cartwright, and a dozen or so others covered the war, but only a few became well-known. Liz Trotta later joined the White House press corps. By 1974, when Ann Compton became the first female to be named chief White House correspondent, women had effectively broken down the major barriers in print and broadcast journalism. Television network journalists Barbara WALTERS, Leslie Stahl, Nancy Dickerson, and Marlene Sanders were followed in the late 1970's and 1980's by hundreds of women on the local, regional, and national levels.

A few black broadcasters joined the networks as well. Ed Bradley and Bernard Shaw achieved prominence in the 1980's and 1990's, but most minority broadcast journalists work in local and regional markets. The print media, led by the Gannett chain, has integrated its newsrooms, but only a few women, such as Geneva Overholser of the Des Moines *Register*, have become managing editors of major newspapers. Katherine Graham, who inherited *The Washington Post* in 1963, became America's most successful and best-known female publisher. Female publishers in the Gannett and Lee chains represent a small but growing number of women in executive positions in the print and broadcast media, most of whom work in small markets.

Many black journalists continue to work in the black press. Such newspapers as the New York *Amsterdam News*, the *Michigan Chronicle*, and the Chicago *Daily Defender* publish weekly, but their journalists rarely achieve national prominence. Nationally syndicated columnist Tom Giago, who also publishes *Indian Country Today*, the nation's largest American Indian newspaper, is easily the most prominent Indian journalist.

The United States's mass media coverage of minority concerns, although vastly improved since the 1960's, concentrates on the problems of urban blacks and largely ignores Indians, Latinos, and Asian Americans except during periods of violence or tragedy. Improvement is slow, but the free press guarantees contained in the American Constitution are gradually becoming reality.

SUGGESTED READINGS. *The Media in America: A History* (1989), edited by William David Sloan and James G. Stovall, is a comprehensive history of American journalism. Michael Schudson's *Discovering the News: A Social History of American Newspapers* (1978) is an excellent book on the profession. Marion Marzolf's *Up from the Footnote: A History of Women Journalists* (1977) is the best history of women in journalism.—*Stephen G. Sylvester*

Judges: Authoritative decision makers within the third branch of government. They make decisions that significantly affect people's lives. Judges can decide whether injured people will receive compensation or how many years a convicted criminal must serve. Judges may also determine major issues of public policy. American judges have ordered schools to be desegregated, prisons to be built, and mental hospitals to be reformed. They have also determined the extent to which people will enjoy rights to privacy, freedom of speech, freedom of religion, and other civil liberties.

Many people believe that judges simply follow the law by drawing from their special training in law school and their professional experience as lawyers in their rulings. Research has shown, however, that American judges actually use their power to create new legal principles and public policies based on their personal attitudes, values, and policy preferences. Thus, for example, judges who are Democrats frequently decide cases concerning civil liberties differently than judges who are Republicans. Because judges are powerful decision makers and have the ability to shape law and public policy, it is not surprising that through most of American history, judges made decisions that advanced the interests of their own ethnic group and social class. Specifically, the affluent males of English descent who constituted nearly all American judges prior to the early 1900's made many decisions that endorsed DISCRIMINATION against women, African Americans, JAPANESE AMERICANS, CHINESE AMERICANS, MEXICAN AMERICANS, and other groups not represented in the judiciary. Although American judges in 1992 remained over-

whelmingly male, affluent, and of European descent, twentieth century changes in the composition of the judiciary gave decision making power to people who were sensitive to the social conditions facing various minority groups.

Judges Prior to the Mid-twentieth Century. American judges are selected through political processes. Federal judges are nominated by the president and confirmed by the U. S. Senate. Presidents have almost always chosen federal judges from among friends and political supporters within their own political party. This approach generally limits the pool of potential judges to politically active, well-connected lawyers. State judges are usually selected by the voters in elections, but a few states permit governors or legislatures to choose judges. People are often appointed state judges as a reward for their loyal political service to a political party or elected official. In states that elect judges, lawyers who wish to become judges must normally gain the support of a political party. This is true even in those states with nonpartisan elections for judges; political parties are usually working behind the scenes to help their supporters win judicial elections.

Prior to the twentieth century, few people other than affluent males of English descent possessed the necessary political connections for appointment to the federal judiciary. Women did not gain the right to vote nationally until 1920, and they were not permitted to become lawyers in most states until early in the twentieth century. Immigrants from China and Japan faced serious discrimination and had little political power. Immigrants from Italy, Ireland, Poland, and other European countries initially had little political influence, as they had to work hard simply to find jobs and support their families. In the early twentieth century, however, many members of these European groups eventually gained political office with the support of votes from the growing immigrant populations in cities. Thus, some members of these ethnic groups eventually became sufficiently politically active and influential to win judicial appointments.

African Americans were generally excluded from political participation prior to the abolition of SLAVERY. Except for the brief RECONSTRUCTION period (1865-1877), during which federal soldiers occupied the South and ensured that African American men would be permitted to vote, African Americans had little political power before the 1960's. Some African Americans won elections for local justices of the

President Johnson appointed Thurgood Marshall to the Supreme Court in 1967. (AP/Wide World Photos)

Although the American judiciary is overwhelmingly composed of males of European ancestry, representation of other groups is increasing. Pictured are Judge Lillian Sing (left) and attorney Mari J. Matsuda. (National Japanese American Historical Society)

peace, low-level judges who are not lawyers, during Reconstruction. The withdrawal of federal troops in the 1870's, however, permitted Southern whites to use violence against blacks in order to regain complete control of government and the courts. White politicians and judges then instituted new laws excluding African Americans from participating in government and from studying law.

The consequences of the judiciary's lack of ethnic diversity were harsh for certain groups. For example, despite the constitutional guarantee of equal protection for all citizens, in 1896 the U.S. Supreme Court endorsed systematic racial segregation that forced African Americans into inferior schools and housing. A study in the 1940's demonstrated that local judges systematically discriminated against African Americans in civil and criminal cases. Chinese Americans were similarly victimized by discriminatory decisions. During World War II, the U.S. Supreme Court endorsed

the internment of thousands of innocent Japanese Americans in isolated concentration camps based on unfounded fears that they were not loyal to the United States.

Composition of the U.S. Supreme Court. The nation's highest court was composed almost exclusively of Protestant males of northern European descent until early in the twentieth century. In 1916, President Woodrow Wilson nominated Louis Brandeis, a famous Jewish lawyer who had moved to the United States from Germany as a youth. The bitter battle in the Senate over Brandeis' confirmation was fueled by ANTI-SEMITISM. Jews as well as immigrants from Italy, Ireland, Poland, and other eastern and southern European countries had long faced discrimination from established lawyers in the United States when they sought to enter the legal profession. Bar associations created new qualifications, education requirements, and bar examinations in an effort to prevent immigrants from

Louis Brandeis, the first Jewish Supreme Court Justice. (Library of Congress)

gaining social mobility and income as lawyers. Many of the established attorneys who sought to keep the legal profession and judiciary the exclusive domain of men of northern European ancestry also fought against the appointment of the first immigrant Jewish justice to the Supreme Court. Brandeis was finally confirmed and became known as one of the most outstanding justices ever to serve on the Court. His success helped pave the way for the appointment of subsequent Jewish justices (Benjamin Cardozo, 1932; Felix Frankfurter, 1939; Arthur Goldberg, 1962; Abe Fortas, 1965), who faced much less ethnically based opposition.

Considerations of race, ethnicity, and demographic representativeness have influenced several Court appointments as presidents made political statements or curried favor with political constituencies. William Brennan was not the first Irish-Catholic Democrat appointed to the Supreme Court; he was preceded by Pierce Butler in 1922 and Frank Murphy in 1940. Brennan, however, was appointed by Republican President Dwight Eisenhower in 1956 in an explicit effort to gain support from ethnic Democratic voters. In 1967, President Lyndon Johnson attempted to defuse the inevitable opposition to the appointment of an African American justice by appointing Thurgood MARSHALL, a famous lawyer who had superb credentials as a former U.S. Solicitor General and federal appellate judge. President Ronald Reagan sought support from women voters by promising to nominate the first female justice, which he did by appointing Sandra Day O'CONNOR in 1981. Reagan also appointed the first Italian American justice, Antonin Scalia, in 1986 at least partly as a bid for the support of Italian Americans. President George Bush sought support from African American voters by appointing Clarence THOMAS in 1991, thereby insuring that the highest court would not become all-white upon the retirement of Marshall.

Ethnic and Racial Integration in Other Courts. In the first half of the twentieth century, certain European immigrant groups began to overcome barriers that had hindered their entry into the legal profession. Simultaneously, Irish, Italian, and Polish candidates began to win elections in such cities as Boston, New York, Philadelphia, and Chicago. Politicians from other European groups gained success in other cities. When members of these ethnic groups became influential within their local political parties, they were in a position to help lawyers from their own groups to gain appointments or win judicial elections.

Meanwhile, Asian American, Latino, and African American lawyers faced more deeply rooted racial prejudice and had a more difficult time gaining judicial office. The CIVIL RIGHTS MOVEMENT of the 1960's helped to remove barriers to electoral participation and HIGHER EDUCATION, so more members of minority groups had the opportunity to go to law school or enter public life through electoral politics. To become judges, however, these individuals had to be well-connected and politically active. By 1972, there were nearly 208 African American judges in state and federal courts, but two-thirds of them were in only seven northern jurisdictions in which African Americans had gained political power (California, the District of Columbia, Illinois, Michigan, New Jersey, New York, Ohio, and Pennsylvania). Several states, especially in the South, designed election procedures which reduced the chances of minorities being elected judges, such as at-large rather than district elections. The Supreme Court declared some of these election procedures to be unconstitutional.

Although the composition of the judiciary began changing in the 1960's, this did not create equal representation in the judiciary by the 1990's. For example, in the early 1960's, the approximately three hundred judges on state supreme courts throughout the country were all white and males except for three women judges. By 1985, there were four Asian Americans on the Hawaii Supreme Court, reflecting the size and political power of that ethnic group within the state. Twenty-three women and nine African Americans were among the judges on the other forty-nine states' highest courts. Further integration continued in state courts after 1985, as in the election of the first African American justice to the Louisiana Supreme Court in 1992.

In the federal courts, President John F. Kennedy appointed the first black judge in the early 1960's. Except for President Johnson's effort to appoint an African American to the Supreme Court in 1967, no president other than President Jimmy Carter emphasized ethnic diversity in the federal judiciary as a primary goal. During his four-year term (1977-1981), Carter appointed thirty-eight African Americans to federal judgeships—more than all other U.S. presidents combined. Carter's total of sixteen Latino federal judges was nearly matched by President Reagan's appointment of fifteen Latinos during his eight-year tenure (1981-1989). Presidents Bush, Ford, Nixon, and

Sandra Day O'Connor, the first woman appointed to the U.S. Supreme Court, with then Chief Justice Warren Burger. (Library of Congress)

Johnson each appointed a few Latino lawyers to federal judgeships. Similar small numbers of Asian American judges were appointed by Presidents Reagan, Carter, Ford, and Nixon.

Judges with differing backgrounds and political orientations still make different decisions on certain kinds of issues, but the inclusion of diverse groups in the American judiciary has reduced the overt bias and systematic discrimination that characterized judicial decision making for most of American history. Affluent white judges no longer come into contact with members of minority groups only when minorities stand before them accused of a crime or work for them as domestics. Because there are lawyers and judges from nearly every ethnic group who have professional contact with judges at every level of the court system, most judges have become more aware of how discrimination can unfairly influence judicial decisions.

SUGGESTED READINGS. For descriptions of nominees' backgrounds and political considerations affecting appointments to the Supreme Court, see Henry J. Abraham's *Justices and Presidents: A Political History of Appointments to the Supreme Court* (2d ed., 1985).

Articles on the selection of judges are regularly contained in the periodical *Judicature,* including Sheldon Goldman's "The Bush Imprint on the Judiciary," *Judicature* 74 (April, 1991), p. 294, and Henry R. Glick and Craig F. Emmert's "Selection Systems and Judicial Characteristics: The Recruitment of State Supreme Court Judges," *Judicature* 70, no. 4 (1987), pp. 228-235. A sample of African American judges' perspectives on the judicial system is contained in *From the Black Bar: Voices for Equal Justice* (1976), edited by Gilbert Ware.—*Christopher E. Smith*

K

Kachinas: Small, ornamental dolls carved from wood. These dolls represent spirits worshiped by the Pueblo Indians. Meant as toys and religious teaching aids, the dolls are made by men in the ceremonial room, or kiva, and given to young girls within the tribe. The identity represented by the doll is indicated by the elaborate color and ornamentation of the feathers, fabric, and leather. The PUEBLOS believe in and worship the kachinas as divine beings. Altough they are not gods themselves, these spirits act as intermediaries between humans and the divine.

Kadohata, Cynthia (b. 1956, Chicago, Ill.): Japanese American writer. Kadohata studied journalism at the University of Southern California before turning to fiction in the early 1980's. She wrote and submitted a story a month until her "Charlie O" was accepted for publication in *The New Yorker* in 1985. Kadohata studied in the Columbia University graduate writing program, expanding her stories into a novel. Her debut novel, *The*

Cynthia Kadohata brings a Nisei perspective to her futuristic fiction set in the West. (AP/Wide World Photos)

Floating World (1989), portrayed a Japanese American girl coming of age in the Pacific Northwest. It was followed in 1992 by *In the Heart of the Valley*, a story focusing on an Asian American girl in futuristic Los Angeles. Kadohata has received the prestigious Whiting Award and a National Endowment for the Arts Fellowship.

Kansas-Nebraska Act (1854): Act of the United States Congress establishing the Kansas and Nebraska territories. Though the act led to serious conflicts over the issue of slavery, it all started with a railroad.

In the early 1850's, the heaviest concentrations of western settlers were in the central plains and on the West Coast. The nation needed a transcontinental railroad to link these settlers and their commerce to the eastern states.

Several routes had been proposed, but only one line could be built. Because it involved the least amount of uncharted land and American Indian "interference," the southernmost route seemed likely to be chosen. The government even went so far as to make the GADSDEN PURCHASE, paying Mexico $10 million for land through which the line would eventually pass.

Before Congress could approve the southern route, however, Senator Stephen A. Douglas stepped forward with another plan. Not coincidentally, the central route that he proposed passed through land in which he held a financial interest.

Douglas introduced a bill to create the Territory of Nebraska out of the central plains. This would give the federal government authority over the land through which the railroad would pass. Previous efforts to create a federal territory on the plains had been put down by the South because the MISSOURI COMPROMISE of 1820 forbade SLAVERY there. Southerners did not want free territories added to the Union, since this would weaken southern power and influence. To appease the South, Douglas proposed that the new territory should make its own decision regarding slavery in a position known as "popular sovereignty."

As the bill was debated in Congress, it was amended so that consensus could be reached. A new version of the bill explicitly repealed the antislavery portions of the Missouri Compromise. Further, the

Nebraska Territory was divided into Kansas and Nebraska in an effort to make each side feel it could claim a new territory of its own. These attempts at compromise only managed to bring to the surface tensions that had been hidden since 1820 when the Missouri Compromise drew a line dividing slave and free states. Once again, the North and South argued bitterly over the extension of slavery.

On May 25, 1854, the Kansas-Nebraska Act was passed. Its consequences were swift and damaging. The rush by North and South to win control of the new territories led to violence, and the split caused by "Bleeding Kansas" eventually led to the CIVIL WAR. In addition, the new settlement required the removal of American Indians who had signed treaties with the United States granting them the same land.

SUGGESTED READINGS. The most complete looks at the act are *The Nebraska Question, 1852-1854* (1953) by James C. Malin and *The Kansas-Nebraska Bill: Party, Section, and the Coming of the Civil War* (1977) by Gerald W. Wolff. See also the discussions in *Kansas: A Bicentennial History* (1976) by Kenneth S. Davis, and *A House Divided: Sectionalism and Civil War, 1848-1865* (1988) by Richard H. Sewall.

Karenga, Maulana Ron (Ron N. Everett; b. 1941, Md.): African American nationalist, teacher, author. In the 1960's, as a doctoral student newly out of prison, activist Ron Karenga adopted the title "Maulana" (Swahili for "lord") and founded the Los Angeles-based black nationalist movement US. The group advocated upholding black *Kawaida* (custom and tradition), celebrating KWANZAA (a week-long celebration in December), and speaking Swahili. Later Karenga taught at California State University, Stanford University, and the University of Nebraska. As director of the Institute of Pan-African Studies in Los Angeles, he became an authority on black studies. His books include *The Black Aesthetic* (1972), *Afro-American Nationalism* (1976), and *Introduction to Black Studies* (1982).

Keller, Helen (June 27, 1880, Tuscumbia, Ala.—June 1, 1968, Westport, Conn.): Writer, socialist, and early advocate for disabled people. After an illness during infancy, Keller was left blind, deaf, and mute. Her parents hired Anne Sullivan as her teacher. Keller excelled at Radcliffe College, and at age twenty-three wrote *The Story of My Life* (1903). She raised over $2 million from lecturing, which she donated to the American Foundation for the Blind. During college she was involved with

With her remarkable abilities to learn, teach, and inspire, Helen Keller brought new attention to the potential of people who are disabled. (Library of Congress)

socialist organizations, and fought against child labor and capital punishment. Among her works are *The Song of the Stone Wall* (1910) and *Out of the Dark: Essays, Letters, and Addresses on Physical and Social Vision* (1913).

Kelley, Florence (Sept. 12, 1859, Philadelphia, Pa.—Feb. 17, 1932, Philadelphia, Pa.): Social worker and reformer. In 1887 Kelley translated philosopher Friedrich Engels' work *The Condition of the Working Class in England in 1844*. She then worked at Hull House, Jane ADDAMS' settlement house in Chicago, until 1899. As the first woman factory inspector for the state of Illinois, she researched sweatshop conditions. In 1905 she published *Some Ethical Gains Through Legislation* seeking laws that would protect women and children. She was one of the founding members of the NATIONAL ASSOCIATION FOR THE ADVANCEMENT OF COLORED PEOPLE (NAACP) in 1910 and was a delegate to the International Congress of Women for Permanent Peace in 1919.

Kerner Commission and Report: A special advisory group appointed by President Lyndon B. Johnson. The responsibility of the Kerner Commission, officially known as the National Advisory Commission on Civil Disorders, was to study the causes of widespread rioting that swept through many of the major metropolitan centers of the United States during the summer of 1967. Particularly hard hit were Newark, New Jersey, and Detroit, Michigan, where National Guard troops were activated to restore order.

NATIONAL ASSOCIATION FOR THE ADVANCEMENT OF COLORED PEOPLE (NAACP); Katharine Graham Peden, the Kentucky commerce commissioner; and Herbert Jenkins, the chief of police for Atlanta, Georgia. In outlining his charge to the commission, President Johnson asked them to address three basic questions: "What happened?" "Why did it happen?" and "What can be done to prevent it happening again?"

In February, 1968, the commission completed its investigation and issued a 1,400-page report with a

President Lyndon B. Johnson (center) and Govenor Otto Kerner (seated to his right) are surrounded by the members of the National Advisory Commission on Civil Disorders. (Library of Congress)

The commission was appointed on July 27, 1967, with Illinois Governor Otto Kerner designated as chair, and New York City Mayor John V. Lindsay as vicechair. The other members of the eleven-person panel were Democratic Senator Fred Harris of Oklahoma; Republican Senator Edward W. Brooke of Massachusetts; Democratic Congressman James Corman of California; Republican Congressman William M. McCulloch of Ohio; I. W. Abel, the president of the United Steelworkers labor union; Charles Thornton, the president and chairman of the board of Litton Industries; Roy WILKINS, the executive director of the

dire conclusion: "America," in the view of the commission, was moving toward "two societies, one black, one white—separate but unequal." According to the commission, the central culprit was not the result of an organized conspiracy, as some had suspected, but of homegrown white RACISM, a widespread attitude that was essentially responsible for the gradual increase of volatile tensions accumulating in large urban areas since the end of World War II. The poverty-stricken African American GHETTOS of the inner cities were, as the commission saw them, the products of a predominantly racist perspective, created, maintained, and condoned by white society.

In a preface to its recommendations for immediate national action, the commission warned the president and the American people that the necessary remedies would be both drastic and costly. Failing to apply them, however, could result in a continuing polarization of the American community and would run the risk of an irretrievable loss of basic democratic values. In addition to a call for sweeping reforms in federal and local enforcement, media responsibility, housing, and education, four basic remedies were central to the commission's general recommendations: a complete revamping of the welfare system, with the federal government assuming up to 90 percent of the costs; immediate action to create jobs; federal subsidization of on-the-job training for the hard-core unemployed; and a long-range approach to a guaranteed minimum income through a "basic allowance" to individuals and families of the inner cities.

In his response to the report, President Johnson cited certain political realities of the times that he believed precluded the Kerner Commission's recommendations. Johnson thought that it was unrealistic to expect multibillion-dollar appropriations for the inner cities at a time when Congress was funding existing social welfare programs with considerable reluctance. The basis for that reluctance, however, was more fiscal than racial; in addition to the cost of domestic programs, the Vietnam War, at its height in 1968, was draining the nation's resources at the rate of two billion dollars a month. As a result of the impasse, the Kerner Commission's report did not lead to the passage of any major social legislation.

SUGGESTED READINGS. For a general discussion of the 1967 riots, see *Quiet Riots: Race and Poverty in the United States* (1988), edited by Fred R. Harris and Roger W. Wilkins. Irving Herbert Siegel's *The Kerner Commission Report and Economic Policy* (1969) offers a detailed analysis of the report and its immediate impact.

Kibei: Second-generation JAPANESE AMERICANS who were born in the United States in the 1920's and 1930's but sent to Japan for their education. First-generation immigrants (Issei) found it difficult to work as hard as they wanted to without family nearby to help with the children. They also found it difficult to maintain Japanese culture and tradition while their children were living and learning in the United States. Sending children to Japan to live with relatives seemed a good solution for these problems. During World War II, many Kibei returned to Japan rather than fight with the Americans; others became valuable intelligence officers for the United States.

Kim, Jay C. (b. March 27, 1939, Seoul, Korea): First Korean American member of the U.S. House of Representatives. Kim was a successful businessman and the Republican mayor of Diamond Bar, California, before being elected to Congress. During his campaign, he promised to work to reduce taxes and regulations on businesses, to give businesses more incentives to train and hire the unemployed, and to encourage Congress to reduce spending. Kim's constituency was conservative and racially mixed. He had no plans to represent Korean Americans specifically, but hoped his success in business and politics would offer a role model to younger Asian Americans.

King, Billie Jean (Billie Jean Moffitt; b. Nov. 22, 1943, Long Beach, Calif.): Tennis champion. King won her first Wimbledon title at seventeen. She proceeded to win an impressive twenty Wimbledon titles (in singles, doubles, and mixed doubles) between 1961 and 1979. Active in campaigning for equal rights for women in sports, she organized a boycott by women players of the American Lawn Tennis Association, demanding equal prize pay for men and women. In 1973 she beat Bobby Riggs, a former men's Wimbledon champion, thereby proving women's ability to compete against male athletes. In 1975 she established the World Team Tennis League and the Women's Professional Softball League. She also promoted *WomanSport* magazine. King was the first sportswoman to earn $100,000 in one year.

King, Coretta Scott (b. Apr. 27, 1927, Marion, Ala.): African American civil rights leader. The wife of Dr. Martin Luther KING, Jr., and a force in her own right for social change in America, King studied education and music at ANTIOCH COLLEGE and the New England Conservatory. She met Martin in Boston, and their marriage in 1953 began a fifteen-year period during which, as wife and mother, she supported his civil rights campaigns and pastoral work. Her Solidarity Day speech in 1968, two months after Dr. King's assassination, marked her transition into a public figure. Since then she has worked as an author, speaker, and activist, devoting much time to the King Center for Social Change in Atlanta.

Billie Jean King reaches for a shot at Wimbledon in 1978. (AP/Wide World Photos)

Martin Luther King (second from right) stands on the balcony of his Memphis motel the day before he was shot; also shown are (from left) Hosea Williams, Jesse Jackson, and Ralph Abernathy. (AP/World Wide Photos)

King, Martin Luther, Jr. (Jan. 15, 1929, Atlanta, Ga.— Apr. 4, 1968, Memphis, Tenn.): African American minister and leading civil rights activist. While completing his studies at Boston University's School of Theology, King, son of a Baptist minister, became pastor of Dexter Avenue Baptist Church in Montgomery, Alabama, settling there with his wife, Coretta Scott KING, in May, 1954.

King's public career was launched when he gained national prominence for his role in the MONTGOMERY BUS BOYCOTT. In December, 1955, the eloquent preacher was recruited by the NATIONAL ASSOCIATION FOR THE ADVANCEMENT OF COLORED PEOPLE (NAACP) to head a boycott that would defy segregated seating on Montgomery, Alabama, buses. The year-long boycott was a success: On December 20, 1956, desegregated bus service began in the city.

King's plan of action was to keep moral and legal pressure on white society, particularly Congress and the president, to grant blacks civil rights. Since the Eisenhower Administration remained mostly aloof from civil rights, King and other black leaders formed the SOUTHERN CHRISTIAN LEADERSHIP CONFERENCE (SCLC) in August, 1957, to coordinate and expand civil rights activism throughout the South. The SCLC's first major project was a voter registration drive, begun in 1958. King electrified listeners, white and black alike, with his impassioned speeches and roused the American conscience with his references to justice in the Bible and great American documents.

During John F. Kennedy's presidency (1961-1963), King hoped for progress in civil rights, but had to prod the administration to take a strong stand. FREEDOM RIDES, begun in 1961, seized national headlines, especially when their black and white participants were violently attacked; this, in turn, forced the federal government to take action.

Like his role model, Mahatma Gandhi, King espoused nonviolence, a position that would ultimately cost him dearly. He and his followers used mass marches and arrests for civil disobedience to bring about "creative tension," revealing the evils of segregation for all to see. This approach culminated in the

Martin Luther King stirs the nation with his "I Have a Dream" speech at the March on Washington in 1963. (AP/World Wide Photos)

August 28, 1963, MARCH ON WASHINGTON, a high point in King's career. His stirring "I Have a Dream" speech was heard by millions, igniting even more zeal for his cause.

After Kennedy's assassination in 1963, King pressured President Lyndon B. Johnson to throw his support behind a civil rights bill, which had become stalled in Congress. King knew that the CIVIL RIGHTS ACT OF 1964 was no panacea to end racial injustice, but it was a solid start.

After winning the Nobel Peace Prize in late 1964—the youngest person and third black person to do so—King again turned his attention to increasing voter registration among African Americans. He led some 250 marchers down the streets of Selma, Alabama, on Feb-

ruary 1, 1965, and was arrested with them. More marches and demonstrations followed without him, bringing hordes of reporters to Selma. In August, President Johnson signed the VOTING RIGHTS ACT OF 1965, outlawing all literary tests and other voting restrictions. It was another milestone in King's fight for his people and for the larger goal of instilling pride in their race and history.

As the Vietnam War escalated, Johnson's crusade against poverty and racial injustice became sidetracked. King spoke out early and publicly against the war, forging a link between the civil rights and peace movements. He opposed the war not only because of the loss of lives but also because he felt it jeopardized the urgently needed WAR ON POVERTY.

King's leadership gave hope to black youth both during and after his lifetime. (Frances M. Roberts)

Despite criticism from Johnson, the press, and many black colleagues, King persisted, attending a giant antiwar rally at the United Nations in New York in 1967.

In March, 1968, King flew to Memphis, Tennessee, to support black sanitation workers who were on strike for higher wages. King was assassinated in Memphis on April 4, causing an outpouring of grief around the nation and the world. His life and beliefs are commemorated every January in the national celebration of Martin Luther King Day.

SUGGESTED READINGS. Stephen Oates's *Let the Trumpet Sound* (1982) is a well-rounded study of King's life. Lewis V. Baldwin has two books exploring King's life: *There Is a Balm in Gilead* (1991) and *To Make the Wounded Whole* (1992). The former focuses on cultural forces shaping King's personality, thought, and vision, while the latter examines King's legacy and its effects on contemporary black theology and ethics.

King Philip's War (1672-1677): Devastating to the Indians of southern New England, this uprising was against forced conversion to Puritan values and the English settlers' seizure of tribal land. The uprising was started in July of 1675 by Metacom, the son of Massasoit, who was called "King Philip" by the English. The war (also known as Metacom's Rebellion) became one of the costliest and bloodiest battles in colonial history. More than 600 white settlers lost their lives while, among the Wampanoags, the Nipmucks, the Narragansetts, and the Pocumtucks, whole tribes were massacred. Following the death of Metacom in August of 1676, American Indian resistance collapsed, with some supporters escaping to Canada and others being enslaved and transported to the Caribbean.

Kingston, Maxine Hong (b. Oct. 27, 1940, Stockton, Calif.): Chinese American writer. Born to a family of Chinese immigrants, Maxine Hong spoke Chinese at home and learned English in school as a second language. She graduated from the University of California at Berkeley in 1962 and taught English in California and Hawaii from 1965 to 1977. Her first book, *The Woman Warrior* (1976), a collection mixing autobiographical stories with traditional Chinese tales, earned a National Book Critics Circle Award. Kingston devoted herself to her writing, producing stories for magazines and several more books, including *China Men* (1980) and *Tripmaster Monkey: His Fake Book* (1989). She received National Endowment for the Arts and Guggenheim fellowships in 1980-1981, and was proclaimed a Living Treasure of Hawaii.

Kirkpatrick, Jeane J. (Jeane Duane Jordan; b. Nov. 19, 1926, Duncan, Okla.): Politician. Kirkpatrick earned a political science degree from Columbia University in 1950. In 1972 she helped establish the Coalition for a Democratic Majority, representing a branch of the Democratic party marked by neo-conservatism. In 1980 President Ronald Reagan appointed Kirkpatrick as the United States Permanent Representative to the United Nations, where she served until 1985. Her published works include *Political Woman* (1974), *The New Presidential Elite: Men and Women in National Politics*

Former ambassador Jeane Kirkpatrick has the distinction of working with both the Democratic and Republican parties. (Courtesy Jeane Kirkpatrick)

(1976), and *The Reagan Doctrine and U.S. Foreign Policy* (1985). She has also written for *The New Republic, Commentary,* and the *American Political Science Monitor*, as well as scholarly political journals.

Kitano, Harry H. L. (b. Feb. 14, 1926, San Francisco, Calif.): Japanese American sociologist. Kitano was trained at the University of California at Berkeley, receiving his Master of Social Work degree in 1951 and his Ph.D. in 1958. His work has focused on various aspects of the Asian American experience, and his books include *The Child Care Center* (1962) and *Japanese Americans: The Evolution of a Subculture* (1969) as well as coauthored works such as *American Racism: Exploration of the Nature of Prejudice* (1970), and *Japanese Americans, from Relocation to Redress* (1986). With Roger Daniels, he developed the theory of the two-category system of race relations and the concept of subculture. During the 1970's, Kitano established an academic office for AFFIRMATIVE ACTION at the University of California at Los Angeles.

Knights of Labor: First important labor organization in the United States, formed in 1869 by Philadelphia GARMENT INDUSTRY workers. In order to strengthen the trade unionists' position, the Knights opened membership to all workers, both skilled and unskilled. Following a number of successful strikes in the early 1880's, membership rose to 700,000. Knights of Labor legislators enacted laws to prohibit the use of convicts as commercial laborers, to establish a bureau of labor statistics, and to enact labor agreements with European laborers. Following years of internal strife after 1886, the union had essentially disintegrated by 1890. Many of its members joined the rising AMERICAN FEDERATION OF LABOR (AFL) in 1891.

Korean American–African American relations. *See* **African American–Korean American relations**

Korean Americans: Before 1882, Koreans did not travel to the United States. In the preceding centuries, China had dominated Korean policy, and Korea had isolated itself from the rest of the world, earning the name "hermit kingdom." Late in the nineteenth century, however, events combined to promote Korean immigration to American soil.

In 1882, Korea signed a treaty with the United States that allowed trade and travel between the two nations. American missionaries arrived in 1885 and began converting thousands of Koreans to Christianity. The printing of Bibles led the lower classes to learn to read and thus to attain education. Church work gave sheltered, submissive Korean women new freedom and a stronger sense of self-worth, and many Ko-

KOREA

reans gained insight into American ideals such as democracy and opportunity for all. A few dozen students, political refugees, and ginseng merchants even traveled to the United States.

At the same time, China, Russia, and Japan were struggling for control of the weak Korean government. The Japanese finally dominated. Their authority over the Korean nation was harshly enforced. They opened the country to Japanese immigration, confiscated land, and transferred much Korean wealth and business opportunity to the new Japanese residents. They set up a powerful secret police force and made Japanese the language of instruction in the schools. Protest demonstrations in 1919 were met with horrible recriminations. Many Koreans, especially Christians, were killed. About 20,000 were arrested; half of these were tortured, or executed, or both.

Emigration to Hawaii. Hawaiian sugar plantations needed cheap labor, and they had earlier recruited Chinese and Japanese workers. The work, however, was very hard, living conditions were poor, and pay was low. Protesting Japanese workers had orchestrated work stoppages, and the owners hoped Koreans would balance the power of the Japanese. Since Koreans gen-

Small businesses such as corner grocery stores have been a traditional means of livelihood for Korean Americans. (Frances M. Roberts)

erally hated the Japanese, they could be counted on as strikebreakers.

Koreans had powerful impetus for emigrating. Some had lost their land and wealth. A famine, beginning in 1901, threatened many with starvation. Others simply believed that political conditions in their homeland were so harsh that survival was not possible.

A boatload of Koreans arrived in Hawaii in January, 1903, the first 102 of about 7,000 who came in sixty-five crossings before their government stopped the flow in 1905. The Koreans who came to Hawaii were different from the Asian work force already there. They had come for political as well as financial reasons, and their group included educated people and professionals in addition to farmers and artisans. About 40 percent were Christians and about 10 percent were women. While many other Asian workers had come intending only to earn money and return home, Koreans came to stay. They regarded themselves as exiles and felt they could not go home until the Japanese had been driven from Korea.

Plantation work was backbreaking and poorly paid. Workers arose and went to the fields as early as 4:00 or 5:00 A.M., worked all day in the hot sun, and then took turns using what was often the plantation's one bathtub. In the fields, foremen whipped workers for talking or falling behind their team. One former Korean immigrant to Hawaii later recalled receiving sixty-seven cents for each ten-hour day of labor.

Discrimination and Economic Struggle. By 1907, about 1,000 of the Koreans had moved to the mainland United States in search of better economic opportunities for themselves and their families. There they encountered hostility. In 1905, white laborers in San Francisco had formed the Japanese and Korean Exclusion League to keep Asians from taking jobs. On occasion, Korean workers were even attacked by bands of white workers.

The new Korean Americans were threatened by both ASSIMILATION and DISCRIMINATION. While struggling to retain their cultural heritage, they found them-

Korean American families have settled in the suburbs and in smaller cities such as St. Paul, Minn., where these girls live much like their longer settled neighbors. (Cleo Freelance Photo)

selves relegated to jobs as servants, miners, and migrant farm workers. ALIEN LAND LAWS prohibited Asian land ownership; at times, Asian children were kept from attending white schools. California made it illegal for an Asian to testify in court against a white person. Denied citizenship, Asians could not even vote. Most infuriating of all to Koreans, many whites mistook them for Japanese.

Koreans formed communities and family groups wherever they could. Their churches became social mainstays, and women's associations dedicated themselves to preserving Korean culture in the United States. The immigrants also formed political organizations to support the Korean resistance movement across the ocean. Korean immigrants struggling for survival together donated staggering sums of money to this cause, and they produced leaders to formulate strategies to assist in it such as Syngman Rhee (1875-1965), Pak Yong-man (1881-1928), and Ahn Chang-ho (1878-1938).

Koreans often took agricultural work. Performing migrant labor, they planted, picked, and packed crops, following the work from farm to farm and sleeping outdoors or in rough camps. Out of pride and hope for a better life, they worked hard, often for sixteen to twenty hours a day.

Discrimination closed professions and certain well-paying jobs to Koreans, but they could start their own businesses, and many did. Some were able to save money or pool capital through rotating-credit associations. Korean farmers formed corporations, such as the *Hanin Nongop Jusik Hoesa* in Nebraska, to cultivate large crops. Individuals and groups often took poor, infertile land and through labor-intensive farming made it productive. Although immigrant Koreans could not own real estate, they leased it, purchased it in their American-born children's names, or gained use of it through oral agreements. American industrialization and urbanization had created a large market for garden produce, and the new transcontinental railroad, with the invention of the refrigerator car, made it possible to get the perishable produce to market.

By the 1930's, Koreans owned more than sixty businesses in Los Angeles, including shops and trucking firms. Korean farmers were also successful in California. Two Korean farmers, Kim Ho and Kim Hyung-soon, began an orchard business that grew into an empire. The Kim firm developed new varieties of fruit, including the fuzzless "Le Grand" peach now known as the nectarine, and created a vertical business structure to enhance their efficiency. In 1957, the Kims contributed half a million dollars in real estate to establish the Korean Foundation.

Population Growth and New Immigration. The Korean American population grew slowly. In 1920, the U.S. census counted 6,181 Korean Americans, and in 1940 only 8,568. The IMMIGRATION ACT OF 1924 confirmed the Koreans' status as noncitizens, and many remained outside the mainstream of American culture. For the most part, Korean men managed to find Korean wives and formed family units that cherished the KOREAN LANGUAGE and culture.

During WORLD WAR II, Koreans were often mistaken for Japanese and verbally and physically abused.

Syngman Rhee and other Korean leaders had close ties to early Korean immigrants concerned about the political situation in their homeland. (AP/Wide World Photos)

In Hawaii, they were formally classified as enemy aliens and compelled to wear badges identifying them as such. In reality, Korean Americans were strong supporters of the war effort, for through it they hoped to realize their dream of defeating Japan and freeing their homeland. More than one hundred Koreans served in the California Home Guard in a special unit called the Tiger Brigade.

Korea did become an independent nation after World War II, and Syngman Rhee returned home to be elected its first president. Subsequent events in Korea, however, were disappointing. Soviet troops occupied North Korea, and the north's communist government invaded South Korea, which was defended by American troops. The resulting KOREAN WAR lasted three years and resulted in an uneasy stalemate.

After the Korean War, Korean immigration to the United States resumed. Among the first arrivals of this period were 28,000 war brides of American soldiers who had served in Korea. About 10,000 South Korean students enrolled in American universities, and about three-fourths of them stayed. Thousands of Korean orphans were adopted by American families. The greatest increase in Korean immigration followed the IMMIGRATION AND NATIONALITY ACT OF 1965, which opened the doors to large numbers of non-Europeans for the first time. Within a decade, Korean immigration swelled to more than 30,000 per year. Adoption of Korean orphans increased as well. Between 1978 and 1989, about 50,000 of these children and infants became members of American families. By the early 1990's, there were nearly one million Korean Americans.

Modern Korean American Life. Most Korean Americans live in urban centers such as New York, Los Angeles, and Chicago. Most of the adult immigrants are well-educated, and many are professionals such as engineers, doctors, and nurses. Many must accept a difficult period of menial labor while they learn English or make arrangements to reenter their professions. Often Korean medical professionals must work in urban, high-crime areas in order to get jobs. Others start small businesses such as fruit and vegetable markets, often, again, in the inner city. About 40 percent of college-age Korean Americans are enrolled in colleges and universities.

Korean immigrants generally accept difficult working conditions, putting in long hours to gain the capital to better themselves. Their success is itself sometimes a problem, leading to resentment by other ethnic groups. Korean-African American relations have been particularly strained because of tense encounters and cultural differences in the inner city. Korean businesses have been targets for vandalism, boycotts, and crime, especially when other unrest or anger sparks a riot, as in the LOS ANGELES RIOTS of 1992.

Korean Americans are served by numerous community organizations as well as Korean-language newspapers and radio and television programs. Across the

A Korean shopping mall burning in Los Angeles on April 30, 1992, the second day of the civil disturbances there. Many Korean American families were economically ruined by the riots and were left confused and discouraged about their lives in the United States. (AP/Wide World Photos)

nation, there are about two thousand Korean American churches of various denominations, which support their congregations, including new immigrants, socially as well as spiritually. KOREATOWNS have formed in large cities such as Los Angeles, where there are hundreds of Korean shops, offices, and churches along a four-mile stretch of Olympic Boulevard.

Contributions. Individual Korean Americans have distinguished themselves throughout the twentieth century. So Chae-pil, also known as Philip Jaisohn (1866-1951), came to the United States as a political refugee in 1885. He became a physician and one of the first leaders in the Korean independence movement. Younghill Kang (1903-1972) was a successful novelist, authoring *The Grass Roof* (1931), *The Happy Grove* (1933), and *East Goes West* (1937). The works of writer Richard Kim include *The Martyred* (1964), *Lost Names* (1970), and *The Innocent* (1968). Sammy Lee became a physician and a swimmer and diver, winning the gold and bronze medals for diving at the 1948 Olympics. Myung-whun CHUNG is a concert pianist and an internationally respected conductor. The Korean work ethic has made Koreans disproportionately successful in the professions and in business, and Korean engineers and scientists have benefited American corporations.

Korean culture has strongly affected American life. Korean foods, especially the national dish kimchee (hot pickled vegetables) and Korean barbecue, are enjoyed by Americans of diverse backgrounds. Multicultural FESTIVALS in American cities often feature stunning performances of Korean FOLK DANCE and music or the complex arts of the Korean court.

Acculturation. Some new immigrant Koreans have had difficulty adapting to American culture. Their traditionally strong family unit, with its authority centered in the father, sometimes crumbles under stresses caused by overwork and by the new freedom discovered by wives and children. Wife abuse, divorce, and suicide have afflicted Korean American families, and some of their children have fallen victim to drugs, GANGS, and delinquency. Discouraged by riots and conditions for business in the inner city, some Korean Americans returned to Korea in the 1990's.

The yearning for the homeland persists. South Korea has become industrialized, and its economy is growing. Its Gold Star and Samsung electronics and its Hyundai automobiles have found a market in the United States, and its shipyards now build most of the world's supertankers. These new economic conditions,

and the hope that the end of the COLD WAR may bring the reunification of Korea, lure many Koreans back home, even as thousands of new Korean immigrants pour into the United States.

SUGGESTED READINGS. Books providing an overview of the Korean American experience include Bong-youn Choy's *Koreans in America* (1979) and Jodine Mayberry's *Koreans* (1991). For a compelling personal account by a Korean American, see Mary Paik Lee's *Quiet Odyssey: A Pioneer Korean Woman in America* (1990).—*Barbara Glass*

Korean language: Korean is written vertically and is read from top to bottom and in columns from right to left. It is based on an alphabet composed of eighteen consonants, ten simple vowels, and eleven compound vowels; compound vowels are made up of simple vowels combined with an initial "y" or "w" sound. Though generally described as an alphabetic writing system, in which each symbol indicates a sound, Korean is regarded by some as a syllabary, in which each symbol indicates a syllable. Those who favor describing the Korean writing system as a syllabary note that the basic writing unit is a syllable made up of a consonant-vowel-consonant block, rather than a word, as is the case in English. Since the KOREAN WAR (1950-1953), there have been many proposals to write the Korean language in a roman alphabet. Two competing systems of romanization exist, the McCune-Reischauer system, which is widely used by non-Koreans to symbolize Korean words, and the Korean Ministry of Education system, which is more prevalent among Koreans. In addition, Chinese loan words in Korean are often written in Chinese symbols, though they are read with their Korean pronunciations.

The first written language in Korean history was Chinese, which is believed to have been in use by at least the fourth century. Chinese ideographs were eventually borrowed to write Korean words; the resulting system, called Ancient Korean, was in use at least by the tenth century. In the fifteenth century, Sejong, a nationalistic Korean king of the Vi dynasty, ordered his court scholars to develop a new set of symbols for the Korean language. A set of twenty-eight symbols was presented to the king in 1443 and officially adopted in 1446. Originally called *hunmin chongum* or, literally, "correct sounds to teach the people," this new alphabet was resisted by traditional scholars who continued to write court documents and literary works in Ancient Korean. *Hunmin chongum,* or as it came to be known, *han'gul*, ("the common script"), became widely used as a way of writing popular works of poetry called *shijo*. By the twentieth century, *han'gul* had come to replace Ancient Korean as the standard writing system. Through the centuries, the *han'gul* has gone through many alterations as symbols have been added or have gone into disuse. The current set of symbols was officially standardized in 1933.

SUGGESTED READINGS. Both the history and the general characteristics of the written Korean language are described in Andrew C. Nahm's *Korea: Tradition and Transformation* (1988). Additional information may be obtained from *A Handbook of Korea* (6th ed., 1987), prepared by the Korean Overseas Information Service. For a technical discussion of Korean, see the *International Encyclopedia of Linguistics* (1991), edited by William Bright.

Korean War (1950-1953): Limited conflict fought exclusively on the Korean peninsula between U.S.-backed South Korea and Communist North Korea. Though the war did not change political boundaries in Korea, it did bring about greater integration of the U.S. Army. American women served with distinction in nursing positions with mobile hospital units, and many Korean women migrated to the United States as war brides in the wake of the armistice signed in 1953.

Origins. Korea had been broken roughly in half along the 38th parallel at the end of World War II, with Soviet troops accepting Japanese surrender to the north and Americans to the south. Initially there was no intention of a permanent division, but the growing tensions of the COLD WAR led, in 1948, to the creation of the Republic of Korea (ROK) south of the parallel and the Democratic People's Republic of Korea to the north.

Neither the capitalist government of Syngman Rhee in South Korea nor the Communist regime of Kim Il Sung in North Korea was content with the division of the Korean nation, but neither leader was prepared to compromise his ideology to achieve union. Both were belligerent. The United States backed the ROK, but limited military aid largely to small arms to prevent trouble. Rhee's army had some artillery but no armor or antitank weapons. Moscow, on the other hand, provided Kim's army with T-34 tanks, perhaps the best medium tank built during World War II. This disparity meant little, however, as long as a Communist attack seemed certain to provoke a direct U.S. response.

The amphibious landing of U.S. Marines at Inchon was one of the fastest operations on record. (Courtesy U.S. Department of Defense)

American policy concerning the Communist bloc was summed up in the word "containment." This meant keeping Communism within its existing boundaries and waiting for it to collapse economically and politically. The Korean situation seemed to change on January 12, 1950, when Dean Acheson, then U.S. secretary of state, made a speech tracing the line of containment "along the Aleutians to Japan and then . . . to the Ryukyus . . . [and] to the Philippine Islands." Realizing that this did not include Korea, the North Korean People's Army (NKPA) struck across the 38th parallel on June 25, achieving complete surprise and driving ROK forces rapidly to the south. That same day the Security Council of the United Nations (U.N.) called for immediate withdrawal of North Korean troops. On June 27, President Harry S. Truman ordered air and naval support for the ROK Army, and, on June 30, he committed troops. A week later, General Douglas MacArthur became commander of what became a largely American force of U.N. peacekeepers defending South Korea.

Wartime American Attitudes toward Asians. American disdain for Asians in general and Koreans in particular was quickly apparent. Dependents of U.S. diplomatic personnel in Seoul rebelled when one of the ships that was to carry them to safety proved to be Chinese. They chose instead to crowd seven hundred people onto a Norwegian fertilizer ship with bunks for six passengers. The U.S. military proved no more tolerant than these civilians when dealing with the ROK Army. American soldiers regarded their putative allies as incompetent and cowardly, and treated them with scant courtesy. Supplies were not shared and initially ROK military police were simply dismissed. There were even instances of American soldiers shooting Korean civilians for sport.

President Rhee fared little better. Junior officers denied him access to his own country's telegraph system when he wished to send diplomatic cables in part because what he wished to say violated U.S. Army policy concerning press releases. Getting permission for the duly elected President of the Republic of Korea to send messages to allied states took two days and intervention by the U.S. Embassy.

ROK forces did sometimes break and run, particularly early in the war, but so did Americans. During the initial invasion a panic-stricken ROK officer blew up the last bridge over the Han River outside Seoul several hours before the enemy arrived. His action left large numbers of his own forces trapped between the advancing NKPA and killed many civilian refugees who were on the bridge at the time of the explosion. Just as there were incidents of failure, however, there were also successes. A few weeks later, in defending the perimeter around Pusan into which U.N. forces

The Korean War marked great progress in the integration of the army, as seen in this machine gun crew. (National Archives)

had withdrawn, the ROK 1st Division held its own in the bitter week-long defense of Taegu. ROK forces kept pace with Americans in the pursuit of the NKPA after the break-out from the Pusan Perimeter in September, 1950. The ROK 3d Division raced north along the eastern coast, reaching the 38th parallel before American units. Prejudices were little affected by such heroic events, and throughout the war Americans continued to be more disdainful of Koreans than the latter's performance merited.

Desegregation of the Military and the 24th Infantry. The U.S. Army entered the Korean War with internal racial problems of its own. In 1948, President Truman issued an executive order requiring DESEGREGATION of the military. He set up the Fahy Commission to oversee the progress made. Although by January, 1950, the Air Force had integrated more than half of its black personnel, the Army had done little. Not until April, 1950, did the Army even drop its policy of not allowing African Americans to be more than 10 percent of its force. When it did so, black enlistments rose rapidly, and black units were quickly filled beyond capacity. The outbreak of war in Korea resulted in a flood of recruits, both black and white, in unprecedented numbers. This forced integration of basic training (not completed until March of 1951), which occurred without significant problems.

The first American units committed to the conflict in Korea were part of the occupation force still in Japan, and these included the all-black 24th Infantry Regiment. The units coming from Japan in the summer of 1950 had not kept up proper training activities. They were physically out of shape, they had not had maneuvers of more than company size while in Japan (sometimes for several years), and their equipment was inadequate. They had, for instance, few antitank weapons and little ammunition for those available. The units from Japan were sent into the battle to buy time by slowing the enemy advance, bolstering ROK morale, and establishing the U.S./U.N. commitment to defend the Republic of Korea. Although marked by occasions of awesome individual bravery, their performance on the whole was one of the lowest points in U.S. military history. There were several instances in which units fled almost at first contact with the enemy—"bugging out," as the soldiers called it.

For the 24th Infantry, all of the problems of the occupation troops were complicated by the impact of SEGREGATION and DISCRIMINATION. Early harbingers of the CIVIL RIGHTS MOVEMENT, including the execu-

Though U.S. Marines helped to restore peace in places such as Inchon, they did not always treat Korean civilians or military personnel with respect. (Courtesy U.S. Department of Defense)

tive order to desegregate the military, gave them hope for improved circumstances while white resistance led to disillusionment and anger. Unprepared as soldiers and torn about their place in the society that was asking them to risk their lives, the African Americans of the 24th had some problems, though accounts differ as to how serious these were. Eyewitness accounts, including that of a *New York Times* correspondent, indicate that the 24th successfully recaptured the town of Yechon against significant opposition. Captain Charles Bussey was awarded a Silver Star for almost single-handedly stopping a flanking movement by several hundred NKPA troops. Official army accounts either ignore all this or dismiss it as minor. A field

recommendation that Bussey get the Medal of Honor was ignored, and in his memoirs he asserts that a white officer told him that such awards were not appropriate for African Americans. The nation's highest honor did go to Private First Class William Thompson, who died at his machine gun covering his unit's retreat when it was overrun on August 7.

A few days later, however, a Lieutenant Gilchrist refused an order to attack a roadblock. He was subsequently tried by court martial and sentenced to death, though the penalty was reduced by the president to twenty years in prison. The commander of A Company, Leon Gilbert, got a similar sentence for refusing an order to attack near Sangju, where the 24th had taken serious casualties. On July 29th, after a long mortar barrage, the 1st Battalion of the 24th fled. They left behind a company of black combat engineers supported by a field artillery battalion to hold the line for a night, which they did only by a desperate struggle. These and other such incidents left the 24th Infantry with a reputation of "bugging out" that it never was able to shed. General William B. Kean, Commander of the 25th Division, eventually recommended that the 24th be broken up and its men used as replacements in other units because the regiment was "untrustworthy and incapable of carrying out missions expected of an infantry regiment." This was finally done in the summer of 1951.

When considering the performance of African American troops, it must be kept in mind that before the arrival of the 1st Marine Brigade, freshly equipped and trained in the United States, the performance of American units generally was inconsistent. In late July, 1950, when General Walker criticized his units for failing to stop the NKPA, he named the entire 25th Division (which included the 24th Infantry Regiment) and the 1st Cavalry. Thus, memories focused solely on the shortfalls of African American units are selective.

Final Stages of the War. With a defensive perimeter stabilized around the port of Pusan, General Douglas MacArthur turned the momentum of the war with one brilliant, daring, and partly foolhardy stroke: an amphibious landing at Inchon on September 15, 1950. Although Inchon presented enormous difficulties as a landing place, the maneuver was a complete success and with a break-out from the perimeter, the NKPA was driven steadily northward. By the late fall U.N. forces were nearing the Yalu River, the Korean/Chinese border. In late October, a Chinese offensive stopped the advance, but MacArthur dismissed the new threat as minimal. Without securing his flanks or supply lines, he renewed the offensive only to be met by massive Chinese intervention that by the early spring had forced U.N. forces south of the 38th parallel. This resulted in MacArthur openly and privately in diplomatic circles criticizing President Truman's policy of limiting the conflict. On April 11, 1951, Truman relieved the general of command. The war settled into a stalemate along a line in the vicinity of the 38th parallel. While negotiations dragged—the armistice was not signed until July 27, 1953—a bloody war of attrition was waged along the battlefront as the two sides struggled to take and hold strategic points.

Effects of the War on Army Integration. Reports of cowardice among black troops led to charges that African Americans were being made scapegoats for the army's failure. In November, 1950, S. L. A. Marshall, Infantry Operations Analyst for the 8th Army, reported that integration worked and should be extended. MacArthur and other officers disagreed. In January and February, 1951, attorney Thurgood MARSHALL of the NATIONAL ASSOCIATION FOR THE ADVANCEMENT OF COLORED PEOPLE (NAACP) visited Korea to investigate charges of scapegoating. Also in February, an army review suggested that INTEGRATION was a success but expressed concern about allowing large numbers of poorly educated African Americans into the ranks. Black units were significantly overstrength and replacements were sorely needed in Korea, but high ranking officers and Defense Department officials continued to debate the question of integration.

The issue was somewhat resolved over the next six months. Project Clear, an investigation of the progress toward integration in the military conducted by social scientists from Johns Hopkins University, was begun, and General Matthew Ridgeway, MacArthur's replacement, proposed integrating all blacks in his command. It took several months and a preliminary report from Project Clear supporting integration to convince southern politicians such as Richard B. Russell and Carl Vinson, both of Georgia, that military efficiency required mixing of the races. On July 26, 1951, the army said full integration of its forces in Japan, Korea, and Okinawa would be complete by early 1952. Commanders simply moved excess African Americans into previously white units without waiting for orders. Dire predictions proved without foundation, for full integration of the army produced virtually no decline in martial performance.

SUGGESTED READINGS. The best history of the Korean War is Clay Blair's *The Forgotten War: America in Korea, 1950-1953* (1987), the first work to deal effectively with both sides of the racial issues in the war. Joseph C. Goulden's *Korea: The Untold Story of the War* (1982) is more popular in style and not always accurate in accounts of black troops' activities. Concerning the question of integration of the military, Richard M. Dalfiume's *Desegregation of the Armed Forces: Fighting on Two Fronts, 1939-1953* (1969) is excellent. Charles M. Bussey's *Firefight at Yechon: Courage and Racism in the Korean War* (1991), although really a memoir of the author's life through his time in Korea, is an honest and sometimes angry look at the performance of African American soldiers in Korea and their treatment by the establishment.— *Fred R. van Hartsveldt*

Koreatowns: Areas located within larger cities that include Korean American-owned stores, hotels, gas stations, travel agencies, barbershops, insurance companies, restaurants, and nightclubs, as well as churches and cultural organizations. These areas are easily recognized by the written Korean characters on many of the buildings, storefronts, and signs. In Los Angeles, along Olympic Boulevard and Western Avenue; in New York, within Lower Manhattan and Flushing; and in Chicago, between north Clark and Lawrence Streets are areas called Koreatowns.

ism or poverty. Finding limited opportunities in Hawaii, many Koreans moved to the mainland. Korean Americans, like other Asian Americans, turned to self-employment as a way around discrimination in the job market. Eventually Korean Americans organized a rotating credit system (*Kae*) in which members would each contribute money and allow one another to borrow from the fund. In this way Korean Americans were able to rent and lease farmland and later to purchase their own land and businesses.

Before the passage of the IMMIGRATION AND NATIONALITY ACT OF 1965, Korean Americans were so small in number and spread out geographically that they represented a hidden or invisible minority. Since then, in some cities, separate Korean American com-

Parades and ethnic festivities bring out crowds in Koreatowns, where Korean Americans typically do business and celebrate, rather than make their homes. (Frances M. Roberts)

The first Korean immigrants to the United States came to Hawaii in the early 1900's. Forty percent of these immigrants were Christian converts who had been encouraged to come to the United States by missionaries; others had left to escape Japanese imperial-

munities have emerged. These urban enclaves are called Koreatowns.

Koreatowns have become places of work for Korean Americans but not necessarily places of residence. The majority of Korean Americans, partly because of their increasing economic prosperity, now live in suburban areas and have shown no signs of developing residential ethnic neighborhoods of their own. Los Angeles with 150,000 Korean Americans and New York City with 100,000 Korean Americans represent the largest concentrations of Korean Americans in the United States.

Recent Korean immigrants have generally come from the college-educated middle class rather than from the farming and working classes of previous Korean immigrants. For example, 78 percent of Korean greengrocers in New York City hold college degrees, and 70 percent of Los Angeles' Korean American residents hold college degrees, including many relating to the medical professions. Because of the inability to pass English-language tests and medical tests in their areas of specialization and because of discriminatory employment practices, however, many Korean Americans have taken jobs as grocers, hospital orderlies, nurse's assistants, and low-paid factory workers. Most Korean Americans, including recent immigrants, are employed in Korean American-owned businesses, and many such businesses are concentrated in Koreatowns.

Various religious organizations, including Presbyterian, Methodist, and Baptist churches, as well as Buddhist temples and the Unification Church of Reverend Sun Myung MOON, have played a significant role in Korean American social, political, and cultural development. They, too, may be headquartered in Koreatowns along with Korean-language newspapers, movie theaters, social clubs, choirs, and community centers. The role of Los Angeles' Koreatown as a symbolic center of the dispersed community is highlighted during the annual Korea Day parade down its main streets and appearances there by local politicians.

SUGGESTED READINGS. A thorough, but somewhat dated, historical account of Korean Americans from a Korean American perspective is provided in Bong-Youn Choy's *Koreans in America* (1979). An excellent sociological study of Korean Americans that also includes a brief historical overview is Won Moo Hurh and Kwang Chung Kim's *Korean Immigrants in America: A Structural Analysis of Ethnic Confinement and Adhesive Adaptation* (1984). A broader perspective is provided in Ronald Takaki's *Strangers from a Different Shore: A History of Asian Americans* (1989). A brief but unbiased account of Asian Americans is provided in Stanley Karnow and Nancy Yoshihara's *Asian Americans in Transition* (1992).

Korematsu v. United States (1944): U.S. Supreme Court decision concerning whether Japanese American citizens had to obey an order by a military commander to leave their homes and report to an assembly center, the first step in the process of the INTERNMENT of West Coast Japanese Americans during WORLD WAR II.

A Japanese American couple is forced to say good-bye to the family dog on Bainbridge Island, Wash., under the 1942 exclusion orders that the Korematsu case challenged. (National Archives)

After the declaration of war against Japan by the United States, President Franklin Roosevelt issued Executive Order No. 9066 on February 19, 1942, authorizing the military commander of the Western Defense Command to take appropriate measures to ensure the safety of the West Coast. On March 21, 1942, Congress ratified and confirmed Roosevelt's order. General J. L. DEWITT issued Civilian Expulsion Order No. 34, which required all people of Japanese ancestry along the West Coast (around 112,000 persons), including citizens of the United States (around 70,000 persons), to register at assembly centers for relocation.

The Court, in a six-to-three opinion written by Justice Hugo Black, upheld the exclusion of Japanese

Americans from the West Coast. Black said that Fred Korematsu was convicted for remaining in San Leandro, California, after the proper military authorities had decided that there was the gravest imminent danger to the public safety—namely, the threat of espionage and sabotage. The curfew that had been imposed previously had been deemed inadequate. Approximately five thousand citizens had refused to swear unqualified allegiance to the United States and to renounce allegiance to the Emperor of Japan. Several thousand evacuees had requested repatriation to Japan. The exclusion order had been issued on May 3 to take effect after May 9, and Korematsu was still in the area on May 30. Black would look only at the exclusion, not the detention and relocation, and he concluded that Korematsu was excluded not because of hostility to him or his race but because the nation was at war. Military authorities feared invasion and took proper security measures.

There were three dissenting opinions. Justice Owen Roberts found the exclusion a clear violation of the constitutional rights of Japanese Americans and part of an overall plan of forcible detention. The Americans of Japanese ancestry were sent to concentration camps solely because of their ancestry without regard for their citizenship or loyalty. Justice Frank Murphy thought the whole affair was based on RACISM in that it implied that all persons of Japanese ancestry might have a dangerous tendency to commit sabotage or espionage. There was no reliable evidence to support the military's decision, only years of accumulated misinformation, half-truths, and insinuation in his view. Justice Robert Jackson believed that even if the military orders were reasonable or temporary, they were not constitutional. The courts should not be asked to execute a military expedient that has no place in law under the Constitution.

In the 1970's and 1980's, the Korematsu case became well known as an instance of racial injustice, as portrayed by the Japanese American civil rights movement. A government Commission on Wartime Relocation and Internment of Civilians acknowledged broad violation of the constitutional rights of Japanese Americans during World War II. The Korematsu conviction was erased by a federal district court in 1983.

SUGGESTED READINGS. For more information, see the court decision in *United States Reports* (vol. 323, 1945) and a detailed account of the case in Peter Irons' *The Courage of Their Convictions* (1988). The case and the internment issue are viewed in a broad historical context in Ronald Takaki's *Strangers from a Different Shore: A History of Asian Americans* (1989).

Kosher: Dietary rules based on Jewish law and tradition, observed by Orthodox and some other Jews. Used broadly in English to denote anything that is proper or within the law.

In its original biblical usage (Ecclesiastes 10:10, 11:6; Esther 8:5), kosher meant anything that was considered proper. It was not used in connection with food. In the later rabbinic literature, the term was also applied to objects considered ritually correct and faultless, such as properly transcribed scrolls of the Torah (the first five books in the Bible).

A patron at a kosher bakery in New York City enjoys his favorite baked good, potato kugel. (Kim Iacono)

As it is understood in the modern sense, kosher, or *kashrut*, is a collective term pertaining to the preparation and consumption of foods permitted under Jewish law. Specifically, the laws concern themselves with which animals, birds, or fish may be consumed, and in particular, the method by which meat must be prepared. Each law has a biblical basis.

For example, animals that chew their cud and possess cloven hooves such as sheep are permitted (Deuteronomy 14:6). Animals such as pigs that do not exhibit both characteristics are forbidden (Deuteronomy 14:7). Animals must be killed in a quick, humane manner by a specially certified ritual slaughterer or *shochet*. All blood must be removed from the animal, since its consumption is forbidden by biblical law (Leviticus 7:26, 17:10). This is accomplished by salting the meat or roasting it over an open flame.

Kosher dietary laws forbid cooking or eating meat and milk products together (Exodus 23:19, 34:26; Deuteronomy 14:21). In the strictest sense, this requires the use of separate dishes and utensils, and separate sinks or basins for washing—customs still practiced by ORTHODOX JEWS. However, these restrictions do not apply to the milk obtained from a mother's breast while nursing.

Fish are considered kosher if they possess at least one fin and one removable scale (Leviticus 11:9). This makes all shellfish unacceptable for observant Jews. All fruits and vegetables are permitted and may be eaten with either meat or dairy meals. Though the Bible does list birds considered "unclean" (Leviticus 11:13; Deuteronomy 14:12), it does not include a list of those considered proper for consumption. Hence, the modern basis for "kosher" birds is based primarily on tradition. Birds of prey, such as vultures, and their eggs are considered unclean. Opinions as to what is considered kosher differ in various communities. For example, pheasant is considered proper in some areas, but not in others.

The basis for the laws of *kashrut* is unclear. The Torah considers the application of these laws to be associated with the concept of "holiness." *Kashrut* consecrates the act of eating and sets limits on human appetites, thus putting people in better harmony with the universe, according to some modern interpretations. There may also have been hygienic reasons for kosher rules, since many of the forbidden foods or practices are known to be associated with the spread of disease.

SUGGESTED READINGS. An extensive description of *kashrut* may be found in the *Encyclopedia Judaica*, edited by Cecil Roth (1972). More concise summaries and explanations are provided in *The Jewish Book of Why* (1981) and *The Second Jewish Book of Why* (1985) by Alfred Kolatch. The process of "kashering" and a description of kosher foods are also covered in *A Guide to Jewish Religious Practice* (1979) by Isaac Klein.

Ku Klux Klan: Various organizations which employ violence as a means to advance the supremacy of white people have existed in the United States since the Civil War era. The largest and most notable of these organizations is the Ku Klux Klan. The Klan, which was formed shortly after the Civil War, employs violence to terrorize African Americans and thereby prevent them from voting and otherwise fully participating and succeeding in the political, social, and economic mainstream of American society. The Klan's ideology of racial purity, white superiority, and Christian supremacy

Early Klan members, such as these in Mississippi in 1872, were attracted to the group's secrecy, ceremony, and exalted titles as well as its policy of white supremacy. (Library of Congress)

This scene from 1869 shows a Klan nighttime attack on a black family—a tactic used to intimidate African Americans during the reforms of Reconstruction. (Smithsonian Institution)

has also been employed by its members to target people from various other ethnic groups, including Jews, Latinos, and Asian Americans.

Political Ideology. Early members of the Ku Klux Klan sought to use violence against African Americans to enforce their belief in the supremacy of white people. Members of the Klan believe that their organization restored Christian morality and saved the southern states from ruin after northerners and African American politicians gained political office during RECONSTRUCTION (1866-1877). In fact, Klan chapters during the post-Civil War era consisted entirely of small bands of hooded nightriders who whipped and murdered people, both white and African American, who supported civil rights for newly freed slaves.

In the early twentieth century, Klan membership boomed as many whites reacted against the influx of immigrants who moved to the United States from eastern and southern Europe. During this period, Klan ideology moved beyond white supremacy to become closely associated with fundamentalist Protestant Christian beliefs.

Members of the organization believed that they were directed by God to advance the superiority of their ethnic group and oppose other groups' efforts to participate fully in American society. The Klan's animosity was aimed not only at African Americans, but also at Catholics, Jews, and immigrants from Italy and

other southern and central European countries.

Later during the twentieth century, the Ku Klux Klan's search for allies led to affiliations with other supremacist groups, such as the American Nazi Party, that also advocated the moral and intellectual superiority of whites and espoused racial hatred. Since the late nineteenth century, myths about the Klan's success in preserving the morality and racial purity of the white Christians whom God ordained to rule the country remained central to the group's ideology. In order to demonize the groups they despised, Klan leaders frequently alleged that their enemies, especially Jewish Americans, union organizers, and African Americans, were connected to Communist organizations. The organization's ideology romanticized fictitious accounts of the Klan's accomplishments and denied the group's actual history of violence.

Ku Klux Klan chapters have relied heavily on rhetoric and rituals to attract and keep members. The Klan's rhetoric of hate blames other racial and ethnic groups for every social crisis from unemployment and inflation to loosening standards of morality. The Klan primarily attracts less affluent, poorly educated whites who feel disaffected and unsuccessful in American society. By giving nearly every member an exalted title and office in the organization and by involving them in elaborate cross burnings and other ceremonies, the Klan gives relatively powerless people the illusion that

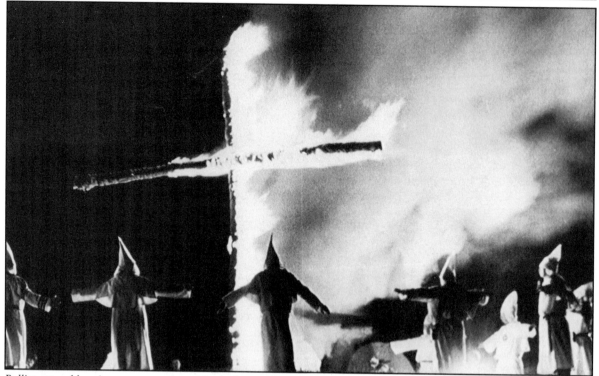

Rallies around burning crosses, such as this one in rural Maine, continued to draw Klan members as late as 1987. (AP/Wide World Photos)

they are important members of a powerful organization ordained by God to return the United States to a glorious, albeit imaginary, past.

Historical Background. The Ku Klux Klan was founded in Pulaski, Tennessee, in December, 1865, by six young Confederate veterans. Originally they formed their secret society as a kind of social club to alleviate their boredom. The young men gave themselves grandiose titles, such as "Grand Cyclops," and amused themselves by donning sheets and galloping through the town at night. They initiated new members with secret oaths and hazing ceremonies.

Initially, the Klansmen engaged in malicious mischief. By wearing white sheets and covering their faces with masks, they attempted to frighten African American families by riding past the families' homes at night and pretending to be ghouls and ghosts. During 1866, new Klan chapters were formed throughout the South and in 1867, a national convention was held in Nashville, Tennessee, that elected former Confederate general Nathan Bedford Forrest as the group's first Imperial Wizard. Mischief turned to violence as armed Klansmen made nighttime visits to African American families to warn them not to exercise their right to vote and to threaten them if they were not

sufficiently deferential to white people. Any African Americans who did not heed these warnings risked being beaten, shot, or hanged if the masked nightriders returned.

The Klan's evolution from mischief to violence reflected the unhappiness felt by many white southerners with the social changes that occurred as a result of the Civil War. Having grown up believing that African Americans were inferior beings who should work for whites as slaves, many former Confederates were outraged to see African Americans gaining the right to vote and, during the post-Civil War era, winning elections to state legislatures and other political offices in the South. Because many whites had participated in nightriding slave patrols designed to capture runaway slaves before the Civil War, the Ku Klux Klan provided an attractive vehicle for resuming night patrols intended to restore white supremacy after the Civil War. The Klansmen also attacked whites who supported civil rights for African Americans.

By 1868, the Klan's widespread use of violence had drawn the attention of government officials. The federal government and state governments controlled by northerners passed laws aimed directly at the Klan. Nightriding and the wearing of masks were prohibited and many crimes were made federal offenses. During the 1870's, organized Klan activities died down. The Klan's initial demise was only partially caused by the government's anti-Klan actions. Disgruntled whites in the South also felt less need to support the Klan's violent methods when the former Confederates regained control of southern state governments in the 1870's and began to enact racial SEGREGATION laws. The Klan's violent tactics were no longer needed to maintain white supremacy because white supremacists controlled state and local governments.

In the early twentieth century, there was a resurgence of interest in the Klan. Many whites were upset at the surge in the immigration of Jews and Catholics. The white supremacist ideology that was popular in the South generated a new set of segregation laws and also fueled a series of gruesome LYNCHINGS in which African Americans were brutally murdered by mobs.

The Klan was reestablished and enjoyed an unprecedented boom in popularity in the aftermath of D. W. Griffith's 1915 motion picture *The Birth of a Nation*, which portrayed the hooded Klansmen as the moralistic saviors of the South who prevented African Americans and northern politicians from ruining the region after the Civil War. As one of the first epic films to be produced in an era of short comedies and melodramas, *The Birth of a Nation* captured national attention. The film's fictitious presentation of southern history came to be accepted and promoted by Klan supporters as an accurate portrayal of events. Thousands of whites were spurred to join the resurgent organization. The growth in membership was also triggered by conservative whites' hostility to immigrants, labor unions, African Americans, politically active women, and others whose egalitarian goals for American society clashed with the Klan's glorified vision of a fictitious past controlled by virtuous white male Protestants.

More than 100,000 people were members of the Ku Klux Klan in 1921, and membership swelled to an estimated 3 million by 1925. Leaders of the Ku Klux Klan's central organization attempted to influence politics by staging marches in Washington, D.C., including one that attracted forty thousand robed Klan members in 1925, and by endorsing specific candidates for elective office. Klan chapters were not limited to the South. There were members in Indiana, California, and other states throughout the country. The Klan gained such respectability for a brief period of time that President Warren Harding joined the or-

ganization in an initiation ceremony held at the White House. The national leaders of the Klan denied that the organization engaged in violent acts, but they could not control the activities of local members. Thus the twentieth century Klansmen continued their tradition of whipping, shooting, and lynching people that they considered to be immoral or traitors to the white race.

Klan membership dipped substantially during the 1930's as its national leaders squabbled with one another and as Americans became preoccupied with the GREAT DEPRESSION. Klan members continued to attack people who supported racial equality and, after World War II, incorporated anti-Communist rhetoric into their denunciations. The Klan experienced a small but violent revival in response to the CIVIL RIGHTS MOVEMENT of the 1950's and 1960's. Klan membership was estimated to be thirty-five to fifty thousand in 1965. Klansmen made headlines for attacking peaceful civil rights marchers and murdering African Americans and whites who worked in the South to register African American voters. Eventually, the Federal Bureau of Investigation (FBI) began to infiltrate the Klan and arrest prominent leaders for engaging in violent anti-civil rights activities.

In the 1970's and 1980's, small Klan chapters continued to exist. Some of the organization's leaders attempted to cultivate an image of respectability, and individual leaders won primary elections and garnered thousands of votes in unsuccessful general election campaigns in California and Louisiana. Some chapters also emphasized paramilitary training for members. Although many activities focused on cross burning rallies and protest marches, there were also violent HATE CRIMES involving Klansmen. For example, Klansmen killed five left-wing activists during a political march in Greensboro, North Carolina, in 1979, and armed Klansmen in Texas harassed Vietnamese American refugee fishermen.

During the 1980's, the Southern Poverty Law Center successfully sued Klan members for the murder of an African American man and thereby seized the Alabama chapter's building and funds for the victim's family. The center sought to limit the violent activities of other Klan leaders by seeking recovery of financial damages on behalf of victims of ethnically motivated violence.

Political Significance. The significance of the Ku Klux Klan for American society has changed during its various phases of development. For a brief period

Modern Klan activities are not limited to the South; this woman takes part in a cross burning in Middletown, Ohio. (AP/Wide World Photos)

in the late 1860's, Klansmen wreaked havoc throughout the South and contributed to efforts to prevent African Americans from exercising their civil rights. The resurgent Klan of the 1920's had several million members whose voting power influenced some politicians to treat it as a respectable organization. The twentieth century Klan also broadened the focus of its animosities to condemn Jewish people, immigrants, progressive women, and labor union organizers. Later, violent activities by Klansmen inadvertently helped to mobilize public support for the CIVIL RIGHTS movement. With only a few thousand members by the late twentieth century, the Klan had less conventional political influence yet remained a dangerous organization because of its emphasis on paramilitary training and its links with American Nazis and other armed white supremacist groups. Moreover, during the late 1980's, the success of former Klan leader David Duke in winning the Republican nomination for governor of Louisiana and his brief attempt at a presidential campaign in 1992 indicated that there remained thousands of potentially disaffected whites who might be willing to overlook the Klan's violent history and support the organization's rhetorical scapegoating of various ethnic and non-Christian groups during eras of economic distress and social conflict.

SUGGESTED READINGS. For a brief history of the Ku Klux Klan and its ideology, see the Southern Poverty Law Center's special report entitled *The Ku Klux Klan: A History of Racism and Violence* (3d ed., 1988). A more extensive history of the organization is presented in Wyn Craig Wade's *The Fiery Cross: The Ku Klux Klan in America* (1987). Other works discuss the Klan during particular eras, such as Arnold S. Rice's *The Ku Klux Klan in American Politics* (1972) concerning the 1920's and Kenneth T. Jackson's *The Ku Klux Klan in the City: 1915-1930* (1967). The Klan's development and activities in specific regions are discussed in such books as *The Invisible Empire in the West* (1992), edited by Shawn Lay.—*Christopher E. Smith*

Kwanzaa (Dec. 26-Jan. 1): African American holiday. Kwanzaa celebrates the history, culture, and aspirations for the future of Americans of African descent. With its origins in the nontribal East African language of Kiswahili, the word *kwanzaa* means "the first" or the "first fruits of the harvest."

Kwanzaa was originated in 1966 by Maulana "Ron" KARENGA, the leader of US, a black nationalist organization (Karenga later became a noted scholar in the field of black studies). The holiday serves to promote the spiritual, cultural, psychological, and physical liberation of African Americans who had been encumbered by superficial values and a debilitating sense of self imposed on them by others.

The celebration recognizes the seven principles of Kwanzaa referred to as Nguzo Saba. Umoja (Unity) means "to strive for and maintain unity in the family, community, nation and race." Kujichagulia (Self-Determination) means "to define ourselves, name ourselves, create for ourselves and speak for ourselves instead of being defined, named, created for and spoken for by others." Ujima (Collective Work and Responsibility) means "to build and maintain our community together and make our sister's and brother's problems our problems and to solve them together." Ujamaa (Cooperative Economics) means "to build and maintain our own stores, shops and other businesses and to profit from them together." Nia (Purpose) means "to make our collective vocation the building and developing of our community in order to restore our people to their traditional greatness." Kuumba (Creativity) means "to do always as much as

Kwaanza celebration with candelabra and harvest fruits, 1992. (Roy Lewis)

we can, in the way we can, in order to leave our community more beautiful and beneficial than we inherited it." Imani (Faith) means "to believe with all our heart in our people, our parents, our teachers, our leaders and the righteousness and victory of our struggle."

At minimum, the celebrant's home is decorated with symbols of the holiday including fruit and vegetables clustered on a place mat; a *kinara* (candle holder) for the *mishumaa saba* (seven candles—three green, one black, and three red); *vibunzi* (ears of corn) for each child hoped for or born into the family; *zawadi* (gifts of a cultural or educational nature, preferably handmade), and a communal unity cup for the pouring of libations. To supplement these symbols, the celebrant may also display the seven principles printed in large letters and the black nationalist flag. The colors of the flag and candles—black, red, and green—hold special significance. Black symbolizes peoples of African descent, red symbolizes the blood historically shed and the continuing struggle of black people to liberate themselves from their oppressors, and green symbol-

izes Africa and the potential for future growth.

Each day one of the candles is lit in remembrance of the seven principles. The celebrant recites the fundamental principle of that day and explicates its importance. One of the highlights of the holiday is the Kwanzaa Karamu—a feast held on the evening of December 31. This usually includes a program that encourages the celebrants to reflect on the past and recommit themselves to an ideology and to activities that strengthen and uplift the African American community.

Suggested Readings. Maulana Karenga provides a thorough account of the origins, symbols, and activities of the holiday in his book *The African American Holiday of Kwanzaa* (1988). Traditions and recipes can be found in Eric V. Coppag's *Kwanzaa: An African-American Celebration of Culture and Cooking* (1991). An easy-to-read history of the holiday and its traditions is Cedric McClester's *Kwanzaa: Everything You Always Wanted to Know but Didn't Know Where to Ask* (1990).

L

Labor Day: American national holiday falling on the first Monday in September. The KNIGHTS OF LABOR initially advocated such a day to recognize the role of "labor"—working people such as machinists, fishermen, factory workers, dock workers, and drivers—in American life by sponsoring a parade on September 5, 1882. More than ten thousand workers attended. Oregon was the first state officially to declare such a holiday. Largely because of the efforts of Matthew Maguire, head of the Machinists Union of Paterson, New Jersey, and Peter J. McGuire, head of the United Brotherhood of Carpenters and Joiners and the Federation of Organized Trades and Labor Unions (which eventually became the AMERICAN FEDERATION OF LABOR), Congress designated a national holiday in 1894.

The celebration of Labor Day evolved from two related events in the late nineteenth century: the violence that grew out of a strike in Chicago and the subsequent adoption of May 1 by socialists as an international workers' holiday. The Federation of Organized Trades and Labor Unions called for a strike on May 1, 1894, to demand an eight-hour workday. The McCormick Reaper Works called in police to put down the strike. When the police killed six strikers, the workers called for a show of support in Haymarket Square for May 3. The otherwise peaceful assembly was marred at the end by a bomb thrown at the police, killing eight of the officers. Several labor leaders, some who had not even been present that day, were tried, convicted, and hanged for inciting a riot.

International labor organizations chose May 1 as their labor day to express solidarity with their fallen American brothers and sisters. It was only after more strikes and further labor strife throughout the United States that the holiday was eventually agreed upon. The U.S. government decided to place the holiday in September primarily to put an end to the more radical labor celebrations being held on May 1, which in 1889 had been officially adopted by socialists as an international socialist workers' holiday.

Subsequently, Labor Day has been celebrated as a day of family and community picnics and political rallies. Traditionally, the Democratic candidate for president begins his campaign in Detroit on this day.

SUGGESTED READINGS. Philip Foner's *May Day: A Short History of the International Workers' Holiday* (1986) describes the history of the holiday from a markedly socialist point of view. *The Folklore of American Holidays* (1987), edited by Hennig Cohen and Tristram Potter Coffin, describes various celebrations and festivals held on Labor Day.

Labor movement: American labor unions remain the United States' largest interest group, despite declining memberships. Unlike their counterparts in other countries they are nonideological and pragmatic, oriented toward improving workers' benefits and working conditions. Contemporary unions tend to be moderate and avoid radical political action. This is in contrast to labor actions of the past, which resulted in violence in incidents such as Chicago's Haymarket Square bombing, the 1890's Homestead steel strike and Pullman railroad strike, and the mine-mill-and-smelter workers strikes of the 1900's.

Historical Background. The KNIGHTS OF LABOR was the first major American labor association, with its orientation toward one big union of skilled, semiskilled, and unskilled workers. It began as a secret society in 1869 but went public in 1878. Membership was open to all who toiled (though lawyers, bankers, and certain other occupations were excluded). It opposed the use of strikes and advocated arbitration of industrial disputes (although some local assemblies of the Knights did conduct strikes). It lost ground in the 1890's to the AMERICAN FEDERATION OF LABOR (AFL), a collection of skilled craft workers headed by cigar maker Samuel Gompers, whose motto was "more." He sought "bread and butter" improvements for the industrial army: an eight-hour day, higher pay, fringe benefits, and restrictions on child labor.

Under the domination of the AFL, the labor movement was essentially a conservative force in domestic and foreign policy. The movement's goal was to secure for labor a greater share of capitalism's material rewards for workers. Unions are viewed by some as a benefit to the capitalist economy because they impose discipline upon the labor force, usually eschewing wildcat strikes. They have challenged the so-called "iron law of wages" (in which wages are determined by supply and demand, with no relation to workers'

Representatives of steel and metal workers union of the AFL in 1917. The federation dominated union organizing in the late 1800's and early 1900's. (Culver Pictures, Inc.)

needs or performance). Their negotiating efforts as well as minimum wage laws, unemployment insurance, Social Security, housing supplements, and family supports have provided the mass purchasing power that has allowed sustained prosperity in the United States. The only time the AFL endorsed a presidential candidate was in 1924 when it backed Robert La-Follette, the candidate of the Progressive Party.

As late as 1913, twenty-five thousand American workers were killed on the job and another 700,000 were seriously injured. Safety equipment and practices seemed, to employers, to be unnecessary expenses, and the courts used the "fellow servant" doctrine to remove any blame from employers. About 150 women and girls lost their lives in the 1911 TRIANGLE SHIRT-WAIST COMPANY FIRE in New York City; windows had been shuttered and doors locked to prevent union organizers from spying and workers from stealing. Conditions and events such as these boosted union membership in the early 1900's.

Labor warfare was fierce in the early days of struggle for recognition. The Colorado National Guard in 1914 attacked and burned a strikers' tent colony at Ludlow, killing eleven women and two children. Eventually the conscience of the American public and the political influence of the unions combined to create a change in atmosphere.

Unions and Legislation. In 1932 Congress passed the Norris-LaGuardia Act. It said that workers could not be forced to sign yellow dog contracts, which stated that they were not and would not become union members, and it attempted to prevent strikes from being broken by court injunctions. In 1935 Congress re-approved labor relations provisions from the 1933 National Industrial Recovery Act, affirming the right to bargain collectively, as the Wagner National Labor Relations Act. It set up a government agency to guarantee the right to collective bargaining and to supervise elections for bargaining representatives. It also forbade companies from engaging in unfair labor practices

Miners have historically worked under extremely dangerous conditions. Here miner's wives rummage for coal during the Anthracite Coal Miner's Strike of 1902. (Library of Congress)

such as threatening workers before a collective bargaining vote, establishing a blacklist, or imposing a union on its workers.

With World War II, full employment, and the almost complete unionization of heavy industry, the pendulum began to swing away from unionism. In 1942 Congress passed the Case Act to prevent strikes against the war manufacturing industries. The 1943 Smith-Connally War Labor Disputes Act required unions to wait thirty days before striking and empowered the president to seize a struck war plant. In 1947 the Taft-Hartley Act outlawed the closed shop (in which only union members could be hired), though it allowed the union shop (in which, after a probationary period, workers had to be in the union to hold their jobs). States, however, could pass "right to work laws," allowing only the open shop (where no preference would be given to union membership). Taft-Hartley also prohibited a set of unfair union practices, such as conducting secondary boycotts (that is, refusing to handle merchandise of companies with strikes) and jurisdictional strikes (by one union against another union). To prevent national emergencies, the president could declare an eighty-day cooling-off period during which the parties would attempt to settle their disagreement and the strike would be suspended.

Evidence of labor racketeering led Congress in 1959 to pass the Landrum-Griffin Labor Management Reporting and Disclosure Act. This enabled union members to exercise more control over their leaders with greater government supervision of union elections and finances. Despite a Democratic president and Congress in 1978, the unions suffered legislative defeat on the issue of further labor law reform.

Minorities in the Unions. As recently as 1944, twenty-two national unions, including the building trades, barred African Americans from membership. Other unions relegated blacks to "auxiliary locals." They were welcomed, however, by the auto, chemical, steel, seafarer, packing house, teamster, service, hotel, and restaurant employee unions. Minorities generally were excluded from the best paying crafts such as machinists, pattern makers, and printing trades. Family connections and word of mouth were often the basis for union memberships, and minority workers were usually outsiders. Larger numbers of African Americans and Latinos would have liked to be union members than were accepted. The highest minority and female participation rates occurred in the larger locals, especially those with more than one thousand members.

One of the early unions open to African Americans was the BROTHERHOOD OF SLEEPING CAR PORTERS, organized by A. Philip RANDOLPH. Also a vice president of the AFL-CIO, Randolph tried to make that organization more effective in promoting integration. This led to a heated exchange with AFL-CIO president George Meany in 1959, and Randolph's censure by the executive council in 1961. By 1963, however, Meany referred to him as "our own Phil Randolph."

By the early 1990's, African Americans made up approximately one-seventh of the membership of the AFL-CIO unions. A coalition of black trade unionists represents twenty-seven local groups with members in seventy-six trade unions. Its purpose is to maximize the strength the influence of black and other minority workers in organized labor. Since the 1955 merger convention, there have generally been one or two black AFL-CIO vice presidents.

Among the sectors of the labor force that are the hardest to organize are agricultural workers and undocumented workers. César CHÁVEZ, leader of the UNITED FARM WORKERS, had some success in organizing mostly Chicano MIGRANT WORKERS and cannery employees in California in the 1970's. His union, founded in 1962, seeks to recognize the dignity and human rights of farm laborers by improving their working conditions and wages. Undocumented immi-

A. Philip Randolph, leading march, struggled to bring more African Americans into both the leadership and membership of unions. (Schomburg Center, NY Public Library)

grants, including many Latinos and Asian Americans, often work long hours under exploitative sweatshop conditions in the GARMENT INDUSTRY without the benefits of union membership.

AMERICAN INDIANS are well represented in the building trades, where they are known for their skill and daring at great heights, as in skyscraper construction. This prominence is partly a result of high Indian participation in the ironworkers' and roofers' unions.

AFL-CIO president Lane Kirkland has worked to create an alliance of workers including blacks, Latinos, and women, as well as older Americans, environmentalists, and consumers to pursue the organization's agenda. A cross section of unions are involved in AFFIRMATIVE ACTION campaigns and other aspects of MULTICULTURALISM in the workplace.

Women in the Unions. Only 14 percent of women workers were unionized in 1990, roughly the same percentage as thirty years before. Yet women constituted 47 percent of the American work force and will

form the majority by the year 2000. While male membership has slipped from 35 percent to about 20 percent of the total male labor force, the female percentage of union membership has risen to 37 percent of the female labor force.

Women were also among the forgotten people in the building of trade unions. Their participation was highest in unions that represented the lower paid occupations and industries such as service employees, clothing workers, hotel and restaurant employees, laundry and dry cleaning, office and professional employees, paper workers, and retail clerks.

Typically, unions with mostly female members had male officers. For example, though 80 percent of the members of the INTERNATIONAL LADIES GARMENT WORKERS UNION (ILGWU) were women, men were disproportionately represented in the leadership. A woman was named to the executive council of the AFL-CIO for the first time in 1980. She was Joyce Miller, a vice president of the Amalgamated Clothing

César Chávez, president of the United Farm Workers, at the beginning of the Salinas lettuce strike in California in 1979. (AP/Wide World Photos)

and Textile Workers Union and president of the Co-alition of Labor Union Women.

The Decline of Unions. At one time about one-third of the U.S. work force was unionized but today only one-sixth of all workers belong to unions. Union membership peaked as a percentage of the work force in 1970, when about one in every four workers belonged to trade unions. Twenty years later the percentage had declined to about 16 percent.

By the late 1900's, trade unions no longer represented the have-nots. American workers had become middle-class and conservative. There was a decline in popular approval of unions. Polls indicated that nonunionists believed that unions increase the risks that companies will go out of business; unions were also thought to stifle individual initiative, fight change, and have leaders who do not represent the views of the rank-and-file members. Whereas only 30 percent of the white nonunion work force in a 1977 survey said they would join a union if one existed in their workplace, 69 percent of nonwhite nonunion workers indicated their interest in unions. This is because members of minorities see themselves as the most vulnerable of workers with the most to gain from union benefits.

Opposition to unions had always been strong in the South and Southwest, where the population was increasing. With the decline in the manufacturing sector, unions were on the defensive. The decline in union density has been smaller in the Rust Belt of the Northeast and Midwest than in the Sunbelt of the South and Southwest. When companies relocate to nonunion areas, union membership suffers. Corporate mergers and acquisition have also hurt unionization. The increase in alien workers, both legal and illegal, has also made unionization more difficult.

Broad economic forces have also affected the labor movement. The level of joblessness regarded as normal in the early 1990's was nearly double what it was in the immediate years after World War II. The United States may be transforming to a labor surplus society. There have been major changes in workplace technology and global trade competition, along with a decline in national productivity. Deregulation policies have eroded the protection many companies and unions once enjoyed. The work force is now better educated, more individualistic, and middle class.

Modern unions have had little interest in organizing younger workers, women, and those in clerical and service occupations. Among the reasons that the pri-

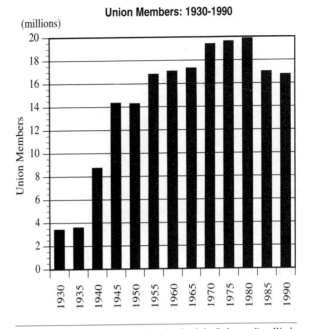

Union Members: 1930-1990

(millions)

Source: From Michael R. Bradley, *On the Job: Safeguarding Workers' Rights.* Human Rights series, p. 26. Vero Beach, Fla.: Rourke Corp., 1992.

vate service sector has been resistant to unionism are the prevalence of smaller, owner-operated businesses; greater personalization of work; extensive employment of youth, part-timers, and women; the educational requirements of many occupations; and the large number of white collar positions. Workers in the new high-technology industries are much less likely to be unionized than workers in the old smokestack industries. This has hurt unions such as the UNITED AUTO WORKERS, the United Steelworkers of America, and the International Association of Machinists and Aerospace Workers. Meanwhile, there were gains in the nontraditional areas of union membership such as migrant farm workers, service workers, and public employees (including police, fire fighting personnel, and TEACHERS). Since 1976, however, the proportion of employees organized in the public sector has fallen. The nation's largest union is the National Education Association, which, like the powerful International Brotherhood of Teamsters, has about two million members.

Labor unions were once the major source of political action group contributions. They now rank fourth. The unions tend to endorse Democrats, but the leadership is not very successful in convincing the membership. Union political activity includes collecting money for campaigns, ringing doorbells, distributing literature, and staffing phone banks to help get out the vote.

In the Reagan-Bush years the National Labor Relations Board and the Supreme Court had a probusiness orientation. President Reagan's appointees to the board were drawn from the ranks of lawyers engaged in fighting unions. (Three-fourths of all American companies hire professional consultants to guide them in keeping out unions.) The crushing of the lengthy air traffic controllers' strike in 1981 sent a signal to the country comparable to the lesson drawn from the 1919 Boston police strike with massive firing of strikers. Many companies were encouraged to take on their unions in the hopes of cutting back on labor's strength. Failure of worker and union solidarity made the position of strikers more vulnerable.

Legislation raising the minimum wage or allowing parental leave has been slow in coming, though in 1988 Congress approved laws requiring companies to give workers sixty days' notice before closing a plant or laying off workers.

SUGGESTED READINGS. A number of academic observers and labor practitioners collaborated in 1986, the one hundredth anniversary of the American Federation of Labor, on the study *Unions in Transition: Entering the Second Century*, edited by Seymour Martin Lipset. Two treatments of the involvement of African Americans in the labor movement are Ray Marshall's *The Negro and Organized Labor* (1965) and Philip S. Foner's *Organized Labor and the Black Worker: 1619-1973* (1974). Foner is also the author of *Women and the American Labor Movement: From Colonial Times to the Eve of World War I* (1979). See also Michael Goldfield's *The Decline of Organized Labor in the United States* (1987) and *The Transformation of American Industrial Relations* (1986) by Thomas A. Kochan, Harry C. Katz, and Robert B. McKersie.—*Martin Gruberg*

Landsmannschaften: Jewish immigrant benevolent societies. Landsmannschaften (derived from the Yiddish word for "fellow countrymen") were organized by Jews who shared the same east European birthplace. Originally religious in nature in the 1800's, they expanded to serve a range of secular purposes in the early twentieth century. They provided comradeship as well as practical assistance in the form of sick benefits, interest-free loans, and burial services. During World War I, the societies organized war relief and lobbied for increased immigration for fellow European Jews. Later, they opposed Nazi ANTI-SEMITISM and offered assistance to refugees of the HOLOCAUST in Israel and the United States.

Language bias—history: Favored status of one language over another, particularly the language of a majority culture over that of a minority culture. Because language and culture are so closely linked in the history of the United States, considerable XENOPHOBIA has often been disguised as legislation to promote the use of English. Such was the effort of the Official English/ENGLISH ONLY MOVEMENT of the 1980's, which attempted to amend the U.S. CONSTITUTION to make English the official language of the United States. The proposed amendment would have prohibited states or municipal governments from requiring the use of languages other than English in order to reach large segments of their populations who were of limited English proficiency.

The American tradition of language bias parallels other historical and political developments. Anti-British sentiment among many colonists led early European immigrants to establish schools with instruction in their native languages. The period of American nationalism, however, subsequently promoted the development of Federal English as distinct from British English. Ethnic schools began to teach in both English and the native European language. Speaking English, however, eventually came to be equated with being a good citizen, and linguistic ASSIMILATION became the goal for many immigrants.

A resurgence of NATIONALISM and NATIVISM in the late nineteenth century led to linguistic legislation as a weapon against particular religious and ethnic groups. For example, the Anti-Chinese Workingman's Party promoted the ratification of California's first English Only provision. Students in American Indian schools were forbidden to use their native languages. With the IMMIGRATION ACT OF 1917, Congress cut off immigration from particular geographic areas and added LITERACY TESTING to immigration requirements in efforts to reduce immigration from southern and eastern Europe. The anti-German sentiment created by World War I also caused some states to pass legislation which barred schools from teaching German and which banned the use of that language on the street, in churches, and even on the telephone. A general hostility toward language-minority groups developed following World War I, and enrollment in foreign language courses declined.

As recently as the 1970's, the use of Spanish by Latino students in South Texas schools was considered a social problem. School districts justified their "No Spanish" rule by stating that English was the language of the United States, that English enhanced students' opportunities for further education and employment, and that it was impolite to speak a language not understood by all.

The CIVIL RIGHTS MOVEMENT of the 1960's helped reduce the practice of linguistic legislation to discriminate against racial and ethnic minorities. Discriminatory literacy tests were outlawed with the VOTING RIGHTS ACT OF 1965, and the BILINGUAL EDUCATION ACT OF 1968 attempted to provide equal educational opportunities for students with limited English proficiency. Although in the 1990's many state and local governments offered voting ballots, driving tests, telephone books, and certain social and information services in a variety of languages, most public discourse and official business in the United States has been conducted in English, leading to continuing charges of language bias.

SUGGESTED READINGS. For a general consideration of the issue of bilingualism, see Kenji Hakuta's *Mirror of Language* (1986). On language and the law, consult Dennis Baron's *The English-Only Question: An Official Language for Americans?* (1990). A publication by the National Education Association, *Official English/English Only: More Than Meets the Eye* (1988), also provides a historical perspective on language restrictionism.

Language schools: Although the many indigenous peoples of America spoke several hundred different languages before the arrival of Europeans and certainly communicated with one another, there is no documentation of formal language schools before European contact. Beginning in the sixteenth century, Spanish missionaries used a variety of methods to learn American Indian languages and to teach the natives Spanish.

Other European settlers who arrived on the Atlantic coast brought with them strong ties to their linguistic and cultural heritage. Many children learned basic academic skills at home, including learning to read in the native language, and many people studied foreign languages with private tutors. Students preparing for careers in the ministry, teaching, or law were provided formal language instruction in Greek, Latin, and Hebrew. Several prominent colonial leaders such as Thomas Jefferson, Benjamin Franklin, and Cotton Mather promoted the study of second languages.

Where large clusters of immigrants settled and established houses of worship, the routine affairs of daily life were conducted in the native language. Churches and religious societies promoted the formal study of the language. Students learned to read from religious materials and were taught both standard vocabulary as well as special religious terms.

German immigrants established German-language schools in Philadelphia as early as 1694. Public and private German-English schools were founded in Baltimore, Cleveland, Cincinnati, Indianapolis, and other midwestern cities during the 1800's. Many of these schools continued until the anti-German backlash associated with World War I forced them to close.

In the mid-1800's when the Cherokee tribe was resettled in Oklahoma, the tribe established schools which taught in the native language. A literacy rate of 90 percent was achieved among members. This went against the general trend of suppressing native languages, as seen through many decades of American Indian education.

The development of public schools in the late 1800's reduced the numbers of students in private school where instruction was provided in languages other than English. The use of English was stressed as part of efforts toward AMERICANIZATION. Language instruction nevertheless often included Latin, German, French, and Spanish.

Large numbers of immigrants arriving at the beginning of the twentieth century created an increased need for ENGLISH AS A SECOND LANGUAGE (ESL) PROGRAMS for adults. Many public schools offered evening classes to promote English literacy and speaking ability, and social service agencies or civic organizations such as the YMCA also took up the cause.

In the late 1900's many ethnic groups organized voluntary language schools in order to help maintain both language and traditional culture. Hebrew schools exist in many communities to teach language and culture as well as religion. "Saturday schools" that teach language, music, and dance are found in Asian, Middle Eastern, and other communities across the country. In many cases, these schools are the only means of maintaining ethnic preservation and are the third and fourth generations' only link to the language of their heritage. Children of temporary Japanese residents in the United States often attend Japanese weekend school where classes in reading, writing, and other subjects are taught in the Japanese language.

SUGGESTED READINGS. Kenneth Chastain has written a detailed history of second language study in the United States in the book *Learning a Second Language*, edited by Frank Grittner (1980). The communities of language groups in the United States are discussed in Nancy Conklin and Margaret Lourie's *A Host of Tongues* (1983). Charles Ferguson and Shirley Heath consider a variety of language-related issues in their edited collection *Language in the USA* (1980). A detailed discussion of the Germans in Pennsylvania can be found in Robert C. Williamson's *Minority Languages and Bilingualism: Case Studies in Maintenance and Shift* (1991).

Laotian Americans: Almost all of the 150,000 Laotians in the United States in 1990 arrived after 1975 as a result of American involvement in Southeast Asia during the VIETNAM WAR. Laos, the least populated and least powerful state—militarily and economically—in Southeast Asia, is a landlocked, mountainous country of about 91,000 square miles inhabited by an estimated 3.5 million people. It is bordered on the southwest by Thailand, on the south by Cambodia, on the west by Burma, on the north by China, and on the east by Vietnam.

Although Laotians have settled in many states, the largest concentrations are found in California and Texas, with Laotian populations of about 58,000 and 10,000, respectively, in 1990. The other states with more than 5,000 Laotians are Illinois, Minnesota, and Washington. In addition to these ethnic Laotians, approximately 90,000 members of the HMONG minority, a tribal people from the mountains of Laos, reside in the United States. More than half of them (47,000) live in California, particularly in and around Fresno. Minnesota, with 17,000 Hmong, has the nation's second largest Hmong community.

History. The ancestors of the Laotians were among the T'ai peoples who migrated south from China between the sixth and the thirteenth centuries. By the end of the era of migration, a number of T'ai principalities had emerged in the areas of modern Thailand and Laos. The strongest of the T'ai leaders were able to become independent of the Cambodian kingdom of Kambuja-desa, then the principal power in the region, and to establish kingdoms of their own. The T'ai prince, Fa Ngum, in 1353 established the realm of Lan Xang ("the Kingdom of a Million Elephants"), the first unified Laotian state. It lasted as a powerful kingdom for 350 years. During the 1700's, however, struggles between rivals for the throne broke the kingdom into three parts. At the same time, Siam (Thailand) and Annam (Vietnam) were becoming the great powers of Southeast Asia, and the three Lao states were caught in the middle.

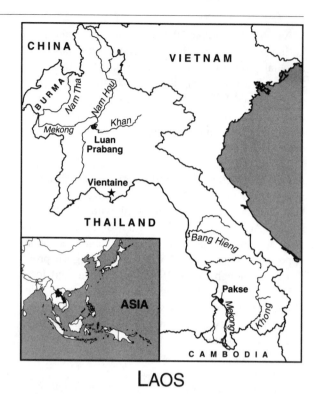

LAOS

In the latter half of the nineteenth century, the French established colonial control over Vietnam and Cambodia. In 1892, the expulsion of two Frenchmen by the Siamese government from the Siamese-controlled Laotian city of Luang Prabang gave the French an excuse to intervene and establish a protectorate over Laos as well.

The divisions in Laotian society that eventually led to civil war, and thereby to Lao migration to the United States, may be traced to the French colonial presence in Southeast Asia. Although there were a number of peasant rebellions against French rule during the late nineteenth and early twentieth centuries, organized resistance to the French did not occur until World War II. During that unsettled period, an anti-French movement, known as the Lao Issara, or "Free Lao," was organized by Laotian exiles in Thailand. This group continued to oppose French control of their country after the war and became allies of the main anti-French movement in neighboring Vietnam, the Viet Minh, led by Ho Chi Minh. In this way, two factions were created in Laos: those, including the king and the royal government, who supported France (and later became American allies), and those who supported the Communist-led Vietnamese.

Laos was granted independence by the French at the 1954 Geneva Conference. The Viet Minh operated in Laos and Cambodia, as well as in Vietnam, and their Laotian allies (now known as the Pathet Lao, or "Lao Nation") favored a Vietnamese-style socialist government in Laos. When the North Vietnamese began the armed struggle to reunify the country under the rule of Hanoi in 1959, Laos was drawn into the war.

The United States entered the fighting in order to preserve a non-Communist regime in South Vietnam. In Laos, this meant that the United States provided advice and military assistance to the royal Lao government to fight an on-again, off-again war with the Pathet Lao. In 1962, the United States organized Hmong tribesmen, paid by the Central Intelligence Agency (CIA), to fight a "secret war" against the Pathet Lao and against Vietnamese troops in Laos.

Since the "Ho Chi Minh Trail," North Vietnam's main supply route to its troops in South Vietnam, ran the length of eastern Laos, the United States began a massive campaign of aerial bombing in 1964 in order to cut the supply line. By 1970, American planes had dropped bombs on two-thirds of Laos. This drove more than 20 percent of the population away from their homes, villages, and fields.

After American troops were withdrawn from Indochina in 1973, the Lao government was forced to negotiate with its enemies and to bring the pro-North Vietnamese leftists into a coalition government. Following the fall of South Vietnam in April of 1975, the leftists in Laos gradually consolidated their political power. By the end of the year, the royal government crumbled, the king abdicated, and the Lao People's Democratic Republic was proclaimed.

Administrators, former soldiers in the royal army, shopkeepers, and technically trained personnel were the first to flee the country. As the new government

Young Laotian Americans born and reared in the United States must often juggle two cultural identities. (Joel Dexter, Unicorn Stock Photos)

In pursuit of the American Dream, some Laotian Americans have found jobs that allow them to enjoy middle-class lifestyles. (Claire Rydell)

attempted to implement Soviet-style economic policies, villagers and farmers also began to take refuge across the border in Thailand. The Hmong tribesmen, seen as the remnants of the CIA's paid army, were fiercely persecuted. Although the socialist government began to pursue more moderate and liberal policies after 1980, about 10 percent of the population fled the country. In the years following the passage by the U.S. Congress of the Indochina Migration and Refugee Assistance Act of 1975, more than a third of these refugees resettled in the United States with the assistance of a variety of government and voluntary agencies.

Language and Religion. The Lao language is closely related to Thai. It is a tonal language; the meanings of words are determined by the pitch or tone at which the words are spoken, as well as by the arrangement of vowels and consonants. There are many regional dialects, but the dialect spoken at Vientiane, the modern capital, is accepted as the standard. Members of the Hmong minority speak their own language, not related to Lao, but almost all Hmong can also speak Lao.

Laos is a Buddhist country and most Laotian Americans remain BUDDHISTS, although some have converted to Christianity. The Buddhists believe that all things in the world are changing and impermanent; attachment to worldly things is thought to lead to suffering. Through meditation and living a moral, disciplined life, a person can overcome his or her own desires and eventually achieve Nirvana, a state in which there is no self and no rebirth. Life and rebirth are governed by the law of karma, in which good deeds, or "merit," help one achieve a better rebirth and earn rewards in the present life while bad deeds do the opposite. Therefore, "making merit" is a central part of religion for Laotians.

Any kind act is a way of making merit, but the most important ways involve becoming a monk; devoting oneself to meditation and discipline; or supporting monks and temples. In Laos, almost all Laotian men are expected to become monks at some time in their lives, usually as young bachelors or elderly retirees. Women may become nuns, but this is not common and nuns do not enjoy the great respect given to monks. During the time that a man is a monk, it is strictly forbidden for him to touch or be touched by a woman, on purpose or by accident.

Laotians in the United States have limited opportunities to become monks, as a result of the work demands of the American economy and because there are fewer Buddhist temples in the United States. In many places, Laotians share temples with Thais, since Thai Buddhist temples are often partly funded by the royal Thai government, and Thais and Laotians have almost identical religious practices. In popular religion, both Laotians and Thais often subscribe to non-Buddhist beliefs in a variety of ghosts, spirits, and demons.

Arts and Culture. The Laotians are known for their love of music and poetry. Their orchestras include a variety of instruments, the most popular of which is the hand-held bamboo pipe organ known as the *khen.* Laotian folktales and legends are frequently set to the music of the khen and sung by balladeers known as *mohlam.* Much of Laotian literature is based on the literature of India, which was a great influence on Laotian culture until modern times. Popular stories and novels, chanted or sung in intricately rhymed poems, deal with events in the lives of the Buddha, with supernatural powers, and with the adventures of ancient kings and heroes. In the United States, where there are few books in the Lao language, the survival of these tales and legends depends on the memories of traditional storytellers.

The most frequent Laotian ceremony is the *baci,* which is held to celebrate almost any important occasion. Participants form a circle around a tree made out of banana leaves and flowers with bits of white cotton string tied to it. The tree is surrounded by foods that symbolize abundance and prosperity. A monk or an older man chants prayers. When the chanting is finished, the participants place the food in the hands of the person or persons being honored and tie the cotton strings around the honoree's wrists while they express wishes for good health and good fortune. It is bad luck to cut these strings and they should not be removed for at least three days. Non-Laotians are welcome at *baci* ceremonies and usually anyone who has contact with a Laotian American community can expect to be invited to this colorful event.

Laotian cuisine is highly seasoned. There are a number of good Laotian restaurants in the United States, particularly in California and Hawaii, and Thai restaurants usually offer several Laotian dishes. Sticky rice is the basic ingredient of Laotian food. The best-known dishes are *lap,* which includes various forms of chopped meat spiced with peppers, and a spicy papaya salad.

Laotians and the U.S. Economy. Despite some initial problems with the English language and the strangeness of American culture, Laotians have adapted well to life in the United States. The majority have found employment, with more than 70 percent of Laotian workers employed in skilled or semiskilled crafts, operation of machinery, and similar blue collar

This Mien woman and child, from a highland tribe in Laos, arrived in California from a Thai refugee camp in 1981. (Eric Crystal)

jobs. As a result of the emphasis placed by Laotian cultural values on strong interpersonal relations, they tend to be cooperative, rather than competitive, in the workplace. Like other Southeast Asian refugee groups, however, Laotians tend to be poorer than most other Americans and are among the poorest Asian Americans.

SUGGESTED READINGS. One of the best general introductions to Laos is *Laos: Keystone of Indochina* (1985) by Arthur J. Dommen. Martin Stuart-Fox's *Laos: Politics, Economics and Society* (1986) offers a detailed description of Laos under its socialist government. For a readable study of the process of resettling Indochinese refugees in the United States, James Tollefson's *Alien Winds: The Reeducation of America's Indochinese Refugees* (1989) is highly recommended. The adaptation of Laotian, Cambodian, and Vietnamese refugees to American society is discussed in *Refugees as Immigrants: Cambodians, Laotians, and Vietnamese in America* (1989), edited by David W. Haines, and in *The Boat People and Achievement in America* (1989) by Nathan Caplan, John Whitmore, and Marcella Choy.—*Carl L. Bankston III*

Latinas: Latino women are a diverse group in terms of their national origins, socioeconomic status, and beliefs about women's roles. Yet all Latinas in the United States share to some extent in the struggle against several simultaneous oppressions. They may be the victims of ethnic discrimination in the American mainstream as well as sexism both inside and outside their ethnic communities. They are often expected to conform to the stereotype of the submissive Latina who is solely dedicated to home and family, rather than to career or community concerns. Historically, they and their female ancestors have been raised in the traditional Latino family, which has been characterized as patriarchal and authoritarian. Having been socialized within a family structure that stresses sex-role differentiation, the Latina faces challenges in asserting herself and achieving both at school and in the workplace. The economic, social, and political leadership of her community has been dominated by men for generations; Latina role models for a more public role are few or little known.

Since the rise of the CHICANO MOVEMENT and FEMINISM in the 1960's, Latinas have increasingly voiced their unique political concerns through organizations and their distinctive social and cultural experience through literature and the arts. By the 1990's, however, their efforts were still most visible at the local rather than the national level.

Historical Background. Latinas can be divided into separate groups based on nationality. The three largest groups are of Mexican, Puerto Rican, and Cuban ancestry. Each Latino nationality group has one or sev-

These four generations of Latinas may have different values and prospects but share a common belief in the importance of family. (James L. Shaffer)

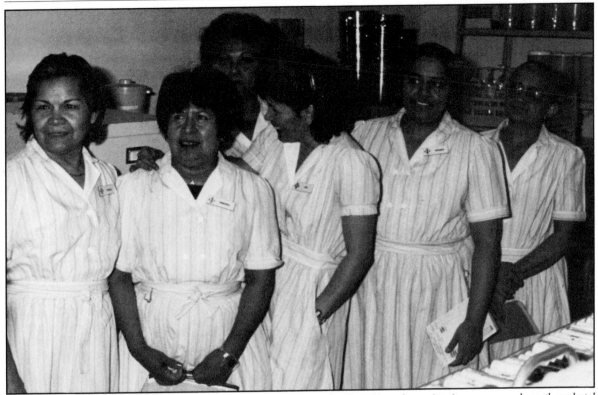

Many Latinas believe that the women's movement ignored the needs of working-class minority women such as these hotel maids. (Robert Fried)

eral periods of migration to the United States, with the exception of those Mexican women residing in what was Mexican territory in 1848. Because of MANIFEST DESTINY and related policies, the present-day American Southwest was seized from Mexico. Mexicans living in this area were given the choice of taking American citizenship or returning to Mexico. Later, Mexicans crossed the border as a result of the Mexican Revolution, during World War II, and at subsequent times of economic hardship.

Both economic pressures and the unique political status of Puerto Rico as a colony prompted the Puerto Rican immigration to the United States. Spain ceded Puerto Rico to the United States at the end of the SPANISH-AMERICAN WAR in 1898. Larger numbers of Puerto Ricans immigrated to the United States at times of economic crisis after the world wars or during the era of technological expansion and American prosperity in the 1950's. In 1952, Puerto Rico was forced to establish itself as an *Estado libre Asociado* (Free Associated State or Commonwealth). Thereafter, because of economic need, there has been a constant flow of peoples between the United States and Puerto Rico. The same holds true of the Dominicans, who share

much social, political, and economic experience with the Puerto Ricans.

Another major Latino group residing in the United States resulted from Cuban emigration in response to the 1959 Cuban Revolution. The most recent groups of Latinos to immigrate to the United States, usually as refugees, are the Salvadorans and Guatemalans who generally arrived in the 1980's. There are smaller numbers of Latinas from other Central and South American countries.

With each Latina national group, there are further distinctions based on political affiliation, class, race, religion, and other factors. Cutting across all these distinctions is the important division between native Latinas and migrant or immigrant Latinas. The latter generally came to the United States in youth or mid-life; the native Latina, on the other hand, is one who was born in the United States or who emigrated early in life and whose language of education is English. Some Latinas are bilingual while others are monolingual, either in English or Spanish. In addition, there are generational distinctions. The third and fourth generations of Latinas are more likely to be Americanized, though many enjoy rediscovering their ethnic roots. These women's degree of commitment to and acceptance of traditional female roles also varies. Thus, it is difficult to generalize about the historical and cultural situation of Latinas.

Liberation Movements' Neglect of Latino Women. The greatest common denominator for Latinas is their experience of belonging to two oppressed groups: women and Latinos. Latinas became more united as a group in the late twentieth century as they realized they faced several oppressions. Furthermore, Latinas soon realized that few of the liberation movements in either the United States or Latin America cared for their specific needs and concerns.

Latina executives such as this one in San Francisco are challenging stereotypes of the passive homemaker. (Robert Fried)

The CIVIL RIGHTS MOVEMENT of the 1950's and the 1960's in the United States concentrated on the subordination and exploitation of African Americans. Because of the movement's lack of focus on women's needs and concerns, a new movement came about.

The WOMEN'S LIBERATION MOVEMENT shifted attention to the inferior status and exploitation of women. This movement stressed the fact that women, regardless of their race, ethnicity, and social class, were subjected to differential and inequitable treatment in all sectors of society. While the women's movement strove to help women attain equal treatment and participation in society, it mainly concentrated on the concerns, goals, and needs of middle-class Anglo women, who were its founders and leaders. Thus, the women's movement did not attract the participation of Latinas and failed to consider minority women's needs and priorities.

Yet another movement gave hope to Latinas, but its results disappointed them as well. The CHICANO MOVEMENT aimed to raise consciousness about Chicano culture and identity while fighting the oppression of Chicanos and other Latinos. Despite this movement's claim to represent all Chicanos, in reality, it only concentrated on male issues and ignored women's particular problems. Once again, Latinas had no voice and were not equally or fairly represented. Because Latinas did not wish to divide the Chicano movement, they subordinated their needs to the good of the larger group.

Thus, Latinas had no voice in the main social protest movements of the 1960's and 1970's. They were neglected not only by the dominant culture of the Anglo man but also by the feminist Anglo woman and the Latina's own oppressed brother, the Latino man.

Latinas have organized in response to neglect by social movements to voice their concerns in various ways. One of the most effective methods has been teaching courses on Latinas in ETHNIC STUDIES programs. Through courses in WOMEN'S STUDIES, Latin American studies, and Chicano studies, Latinas have been able to assert their views on social inequality, sex roles, and cultural diversity and conservation. Art, theater, and literature have provided another way for Latinas to express their experience as a minority group. Organizations are another avenue through which Latinas voice their concerns. For example, the National Network of Hispanic Women (NNHW) is a national organization of Latina professionals, managers, and entrepreneurs that focuses on the needs and concerns of the working Latina. In cities such as Los Angeles, Latinas have been the driving force behind community organizing efforts in the BARRIOS such as United Neighborhood Organization or Para los Niños ("for the children") to improve housing, education, and social services for Latino families.

Family Roles. The traditional stereotype of a Latina is that of a passive homemaker who submits to male authority and devotes herself to raising many children. While some Latinas accept a traditional female role, others support feminist ideals and work on improving conditions for women in society. A Latina may decide to stay at home, work outside the home, or balance both a career and a family. She may be a community activist, a homemaker, and a breadwinner. In other words, many of the traditional stereotypes of Latinas are inaccurate.

Whatever role the Latina pursues, she generally places great emphasis on *la familia*, which includes both the immediate nuclear family and sometimes the

pregnancies among Latinas since the 1980's.

Though the Latina's role is changing as she fulfills a dual role—that of caretaker and provider—she appears to have great influence in the home. She is responsible for the daily chores of the household and affairs of the family, and she shares in the decision-making at home. For example, she tends to be responsible for setting the rules for the children's behavior and the observance of religious and cultural customs.

Work and Education. Latinas' participation in the labor force likewise challenges the "homebody" stereotype. More and more Latinas have joined the labor force in the late twentieth century. Their educational attainment and income, however, are usually lower

Traditionally, Latinas were expected to devote themselves to their domestic roles as wives and mothers. (James L. Shaffer)

extended family of other relatives. As the most important social unit, the family serves as a major source of emotional gratification and support. In addition, Latinas tend to encourage respect for their elders, and aging parents are usually cared for at home rather than in an institution. The Latino family is undergoing change in the late twentieth century, however, as the woman's role is being modified. Among the new stresses on Latino FAMILY LIFE is the sharp rise in teenage

than those of Latino men and Anglo men and women. This low socioeconomic status is typically blamed on the Latina's inadequate education, but discrimination also plays a role. Since in American society, education is the key to social mobility and economic advancement, the Latina, especially if she is a migrant or immigrant, faces several unique problems in school such as language difficulties, inadequate curriculum, and instructional biases.

Cuban American singer Gloria Estefan is a role model for many young Latinas. (AP/Wide World Photos)

Yet another faulty myth sees the Latina as a meek and subordinate person who never ventures beyond the confines of her home. In fact, Latinas have made important contributions to society as their labor force participation increases in both quantity and sophistication. More Latinas are educated, more are registered to vote, and more are taking an interest in community problems and issues. Furthermore, greater numbers of Latinas are enrolling in nontraditional majors in colleges and universities and going on to careers in fields such as engineering, business, construction management, industrial arts, medicine, and law.

Much is still being learned about the contributions of Latinas in the past. By the late twentieth century, Latinas were leaving their mark on various fields. One of the most notable examples is Antonia NOVELLO,

who was appointed U.S. surgeon general by President Bush. Gloria MOLINA served in state and city government in California before becoming one of the five powerful Los Angeles County supervisors in the 1980's, while the more conservative Linda CHÁVEZ served as executive director of the U.S. COMMISSION ON CIVIL RIGHTS in the Reagan Administration. In the arts, prominent Latinas range from pop star Gloria ESTEFAN and salsa legend Celia CRUZ to visual arts innovators such as Patsy Valdez and Amalia Mesa-Bains, as well as a host of gifted Latina writers including Ana Castillo, Mary Helen Ponce, and Sandra Cisneros. Increasing numbers of Latinas are running their own businesses or rising in the corporate world, while others continue community activism in the tradition of Dolores HUERTA, and many make important contributions in such careers as teachers and social workers.

Many contemporary Latinas subscribe to a new philosophy: The Latina can achieve whatever she wants to achieve. Although Latinas often come from poor or working-class families and have had to overcome many barriers, they are drawing on their own experience to encourage the new generations to progress and succeed in life.

SUGGESTED READINGS. For a more detailed account of the historical circumstances of these minority women, consult Alfredo Mirande and Evangelina Enriquez's *La Chicana* (1979). For vivid fictional descriptions of the lifestyle of some Latinas, see Sandra Cisneros' *Woman Hollering Creek and Other Stories* (1991) and *The House on Mango Street* (1989). Gloria Anzaldua's *Borderlands: La Frontera, The New Mestiza* (1987) captures Latinas' struggles in facing numerous oppressions. *Breaking Boundaries: Latina Writing and Critical Reading* (1989), edited by Asuncion Horno-Delgado, Eliana Ortega, Nina M. Scott, and Nancy Saporta Sternback, is a collection of insightful essays.—*Maria Isabel B. Villaseñor*

Latino immigration to Canada. *See* **Canada— Latino immigration**

Latino movement. *See* **Chicano movement**

Latino population—diversity within: The Latino population consists of many diverse subgroups. According to many definitions, this population includes Spanish-speaking people of any country; thus it consists of people with widely divergent histories and customs.

Although often lumped together under the label "Hispanics" or "Latinos," these Americans represent diverse national, racial, and socioeconomic backgrounds. (Robert Fried)

Even with discussion limited to Latinos within the United States, divergences still exist.

The Latino population, sometimes referred to synonymously as Hispanic, is a somewhat artificial construct. Spanish-speaking background constitutes the main linking characteristic among the population; there is little else to define the group. Some definitions of Latinos include people of Portuguese and Brazilian backgrounds with a heritage of the Portuguese, rather than the Spanish, language. Because of differences in background, even the Spanish spoken by Latinos differs, sometimes making it difficult for government agencies such as schools to assemble materials in Spanish that are suitable for all Latinos.

Members of the Latino population have chosen to use the label when it is convenient, but when offered choices for self-identification in polls, very few individuals identify themselves as Hispanic or Latino. (Care must be taken in interpreting poll results, since some Latinos, particularly those in the United States without documentation, are resistant to responding to polls.) Latinos most commonly refer to themselves as

American (if naturalized) or with reference to their country of origin. People with Mexican background thus refer to themselves as MEXICAN AMERICANS or Mexicans rather than as Hispanics or Latinos. In the 1990 U.S. CENSUS, 50.6 percent of Mexican Americans designated themselves as white; 46.7 percent chose the "other" classification, which includes Hispanic; and 1.2 percent described themselves as black.

U.S. Census reports use the label "Hispanic" to define a diverse population rather than using the subdivided populations. Even within that definition, the federal government recognizes that the Hispanic population contains diverse people. A commonly used definition is that a Hispanic is "a person of Mexican, Puerto Rican, Cuban, Central or South American or other Spanish culture or origin, regardless of race." Thus Hispanics can be black, white, or brown in color; a small percentage even have Asian backgrounds.

According to government statistics, in 1990 Hispanics constituted almost 9 percent of the U.S. population. Within the Hispanic population, slightly more than 60 percent had Mexican background, about 12 percent had Puerto Rican background, slightly less than 5 percent had Cuban background, and the remainder had "other" backgrounds, including Central and South American. Clearly, this Hispanic population is not a monolithic group.

Geographic Diversity. Partly as a result of history and partly as a result of choice, the subpopulations of the Latino community have concentrated in different geographical regions. MEXICAN AMERICANS are concentrated most heavily in the Southwest, in regions that formerly were part of Mexico. PUERTO RICANS predominantly live in the Northeast, particularly in New York City, which has the largest immigrant Puerto Rican population in the world. CUBAN AMERICANS predominantly live in the Southeast, particularly Florida. Immigrants from Central America, many of them political refugees of the 1980's and 1990's, have concentrated in the Southwest. In 1988, Hispanics constituted more than half of the population of the area around San Antonio, Texas, and more than one-fourth of the populations of LOS ANGELES, CALIFORNIA, and the MIAMI-Fort Lauderdale region of Florida.

Uses of "Latino" and Other Group Labels. Various connotations are associated with different labels for Latinos. The term "Hispanic" came into common use earlier than did "Latino." It is used commonly to link diverse populations politically, to create a single large constituency for various issues. Politicians use it to define a large population presumed to be in support of various policies, and Hispanics themselves use it when they want to be seen as part of a larger group and thus gain bloc power. For example, the Congressional Hispanic Caucus was created by Latino politicians.

The Latino label itself is popular in Southern California, particularly Los Angeles, as it identifies people with the Latin American countries of Central and South America, many of them recent arrivals. Far less

Floats roll past New York City crowds in the third annual Puerto Rican Parade. (AP/Wide World Photos)

common but still used in the Southwest is the term "Hispano," referring to descendants of Spanish colonists. That identification carried greater status than did other labels in the eighteenth and early nineteenth centuries. "Chicano" came into common use among Mexican Americans in the 1960's, particularly among activists looking for political recognition.

Latinos clearly perceive themselves, as individuals, to be members of different groups, as reflected in concentrations of different subpopulations in different geographic areas. Another indication of this self-perceived diversity comes from the rates of intermarriage between groups. Among couples with at least one Hispanic member (according to the U.S. Bureau of the CENSUS, in 1989), more than 70 percent of Hispanic husbands and wives of Mexican, Puerto Rican, or Cuban origin had a spouse of the same background, with those of Mexican origin being least likely to intermarry. Less than 1 percent of Hispanic men of each subgroup were married to non-Hispanics; about one-sixth of women of each subgroup had non-Hispanic spouses.

History. The histories of the various Latino subpopulations can account for differences in characteristics and beliefs among these groups. Mexicans were absorbed into the United States as a result of the MEXICAN-AMERICAN WAR and the GADSDEN PURCHASE. Cubans began arriving in the United States in large numbers following the 1959 revolution. Puerto Ricans, like Mexicans, became citizens of the United States en masse as a result of the JONES ACT of 1917. Puerto Rico declared itself as a commonwealth of the United States in its constitution of 1952. Many Latinos of Mexican and Puerto Rican descent thus consider themselves to be involuntary Americans, and significant proportions of the home populations desire return of land claimed by the United States. In contrast, a large proportion of the Puerto Rican population favors statehood for Puerto Rico. Mexican immigrants are the least likely to become naturalized citizens, and many make return migrations or trips home. Puerto Ricans travel freely between the island and the United States. Cuban Americans are far less likely to return home because of political conditions in Cuba.

Economic Diversity. Latinos as a group are not as well off economically as the United States population as a whole. Among Latinos, CUBAN AMERICANS are the best off, with the highest levels of education, highest income, lowest rates of poverty, and greatest proportion employed in professional or technical occupa-

tions. In 1985 and 1989 studies, Cuban Americans had far lower unemployment rates than did Mexican Americans and Puerto Ricans living in the United States. Gaps in these areas lessen for children born in the United States to immigrants and for later generations, as all groups tend to assimilate, over time, to become closer to the U.S. averages on various indexes of socioeconomic status. Mexican Americans tended to fall between Puerto Ricans and Cuban Americans on these indexes.

Politics and Ideology. The Latino National Political Survey, conducted in 1989 and 1990 among residents of the United States, revealed several differences in the politics and ideology of Latino subpopulations. Among U.S. citizens, Puerto Ricans strongly agreed with the proposition that there are too many immigrants to the United States, Mexican Americans agreed slightly less strongly, and almost two-thirds of Cuban Americans agreed with the statement. It comes as some surprise that noncitizens of Cuban and Mexican background agreed more strongly with the statement than did citizens with the same backgrounds.

Among all the subgroups, at least 90 percent agreed that citizens and residents of the United States should learn English, indicating a desire to assimilate. About 80 percent of those interviewed, however, favor BILINGUAL EDUCATION. Slightly more than half of Mexican Americans and Puerto Ricans agreed that the government is run by the few in their interest rather than for the benefit of all. Cuban Americans were more optimistic, with only 36 percent agreeing with the statement. Among noncitizens, less than one-sixth of respondents saw the government as being controlled by narrow interest groups.

Generally, Cuban Americans consider themselves to be conservative politically, while Mexican Americans and Puerto Ricans consider themselves to be moderate or slightly liberal. Part of this difference is attributable to the fact that Cuban Americans who could afford to leave Cuba were from the more affluent classes, which tend to be more conservative.

SUGGESTED READINGS. Among the few books to compare various Latino populations are L. H. Gann and Peter J. Duignan's *The Hispanics in the United States: A History* (1986) and Joan Moore and Harry Pachon's *Hispanics in the United States* (1985). More common are books describing various subpopulations, with works on Mexican Americans most prominent. *North from Mexico: The Spanish-Speaking People of the United States* (1968) by Carey McWilliams is a classic look at the experience of Mexican Americans, focusing on social conditions. Issues of self-identification are explored in two works by Peter Skerry: *Mexican Americans: The Ambivalent Minority* (1992) and "E Pluribus Hispanic?," in *Wilson Quarterly* (Summer, 1992), pp. 62-73. *Hispanic Americans: A Statistical Sourcebook* (1991), edited by Alfred N. Garwood, contains valuable statistical tables.—*A. J. Sobczak*

Latino studies programs. *See* **Chicano studies programs**

Latino theater: Two principal Latino theatrical traditions flourish in the United States: Mexican American theater and Puerto Rican theater of the mainland. Contemporary Mexican American theater derives directly from the earliest traditional folk plays that the conquistadores brought to the Spanish Caribbean and Mexico as they migrated northward into New Mexico and California. One cycle, known as *Las Pastorelas*, is still performed primarily at Christmas and Easter in New Mexico and Southern California. It is from this tradition and the unionization struggle of migrant farm workers by César CHÁVEZ that El TEATRO CAMPESINO emerged. The theater's resident playwright and founder, Luis VALDEZ, is best known for his work *Zoot Suit* (1978). This was followed by the founding of the Teatro Chicano, whose performances were also related to the CHICANO MOVEMENT of the 1960's and 1970's and were savagely comic as well as satirical in style. Like the early Mexican American mystery cycle, these groups remain largely amateur in performance and aim at enhancing community solidarity, ethnic identity, and cultural pride, while at the same time effecting social or political change. Their performances tend to mix English and Spanish for bilingual audiences, while other groups such as the Bilingual Foundation for the Arts in Los Angeles perform plays in Spanish and English.

The Puerto Rican theater of the mainland also has its roots in Spanish theatrical tradition. In the 1890's, a new drama emerged reflecting the multiracial and multicultural realities of the island, including consideration of the Indian and African contributions to Puerto Rican culture. The mainland theater of the twentieth century, however, creates and performs works by PUERTO RICANS about the Puerto Rican experience in the contiguous states as well as on the island of Puerto Rico for a fundamentally Puerto Rican audience. The language of performance is Spanish, English, or "Spanglish," a mingled dialect of the two mother tongues. The focus of these plays is upon the community, life in the street, and the problems of survival for Puerto Ricans born on the mainland and residing in American BARRIOS or urban GHETTOS. Performances often take place on the streets as well as in lofts, churches, abandoned film theaters, and parks.

Like Chicano theater, the majority of troupes are amateur, but some professional groups with permanent theaters exist, particularly in New York City. The Puerto Rican Ensemble, for example, formed in the late 1960's and is supported by the New York City Department of Parks, Recreation, and Cultural Activities. It was followed by the formation of Pedro Santaliz's El Nuevo Teatro Pobre de America (New Poor Theater of America), and Teatro de Orilla, directed by Maria Soledad Romero and Rafael Acevedo. The emphasis of each of these groups is upon political action, collective consciousness, and social change.

SUGGESTED READINGS. For background information, see Laurie Kay Sommers' "Inventing Latinismo: The Creation of 'Hispanic' Panethnicity in the United States" in *Journal of American Folklore* 104 (Winter, 1991), p. 32-53, and "Latinismo and Ethnic Nationalism in Cultural Performance," in *Studies in Latin American Popular Culture* 10 (1991), p. 75-86. Book-length studies include Nicolas Karellos' *Hispanic Theatre in the United States* (1984) and Jorge Huerta's *Chicano Theater: Themes and Forms* (1982).

Latino women. *See* **Latinas**

Latinos and higher education: Although many of the earliest explorers of the Americas represented Spain, the English language and culture became dominant in North America as soon as English colonists arrived in significant numbers. Isolated pockets of Spanish speakers remained, particularly in sections of the Southwest that had been parts of Mexico before being annexed by the United States. The number of Latinos was not significant in the American population until the twentieth century, however, when immigration swelled the ranks of Spanish-speaking Americans.

Since the founding of the first colonial schools in the early 1600's, American higher education has been conducted almost exclusively in English, and the assimilation of ethnic subgroups into the dominant culture has traditionally been one of its implicit goals. Therefore, few institutions were established exclusively for Latinos, and there was never a group of Latino colleges existing as a parallel to the historically black colleges for African Americans.

Yet although true Latino colleges have hardly existed in the history of American HIGHER EDUCATION, the diverse cultural backgrounds of the large and growing number of Latino college students have had an impact on American colleges and universities.

a diverse group, and many factors have affected the numbers of Latino students in higher education and helped determine which colleges they attend. Among these factors are the religious preferences, average age, and varied origins of Latinos. Though diverse in their beliefs, Latinos often have Catholic backgrounds,

These Latino high school students have been encouraged to take advanced math and science courses that will prepare them for college. (James L. Shaffer)

Qualified Latino students are much sought by mainstream academic institutions. Since the 1960's, Latino students have increasingly insisted that their cultural identities be respected and maintained. Demands for cultural relevance have led many institutions to initiate changes in college curricula and programs. Beginning in California in the 1968-1969 academic year, CHICANO STUDIES PROGRAMS and departments were created. Important Latino student organizations, such as the MOVIMIENTO ESTUDIANTIL CHICANO DE AZTLÁN (MEChA), were also formed in the late 1960's.

Cultural and Educational Backgrounds. Latinos are

and this leads some to choose Catholic colleges. Statistically, Latinos are also a young group (in 1980, the median age was twenty-two). The number of potential Latino students is therefore very high, and Latino college enrollments increase each year.

Diverse heritages and economic histories exist within the general Latino population. Many Mexican Americans, for example, have rural origins but live in urban areas; though often poor, many have two-parent families and a strong work ethic. More Puerto Rican families, on the other hand, are headed by women. The income of Puerto Ricans is the lowest—and their unemployment rate the highest—of any Latino subgroup. Cuban Americans, most of whom fled Fidel Castro's Communist government after 1959, are largely middle-class; many are professional and politically conservative. These differences have had an impact on the numbers from each group that attend college.

Mexican Americans and mainland Puerto Ricans have low overall levels of education: In 1985, 17 percent of Mexican Americans had fewer than five years of any kind of schooling, and no more than half of those in the twenty-five to thirty-four age category had finished high school. Only 46.3 percent of mainland Puerto Ricans were high school graduates, compared with 73.9 percent of the whole population.

General confusion and controversy over how to approach BILINGUAL EDUCATION has deeply affected

of their unique cultural features. Bilingual education has provoked many-faceted debate, and policies have been inconsistent. One argument holds that since many Spanish-speaking Latino children, especially the youngest, are not yet fully literate in Spanish, speaking only English in school is doubly difficult. Another perspective, however, contends that precollege bilingual education may only intensify the language barrier that Latinos will face in English-based college programs.

College Enrollment Patterns. Statistically, Latinos who graduate from high school are slightly less likely to go to college than white students but are more likely to attend than black students. (The terms "Latino" and "Hispanic," it should be noted, denote an ethnic rather than a racial group.) In 1978 there were 417,000 Latinos enrolled in American colleges; a decade later, the number was 680,000. In 1978, 24,000 Latinos were

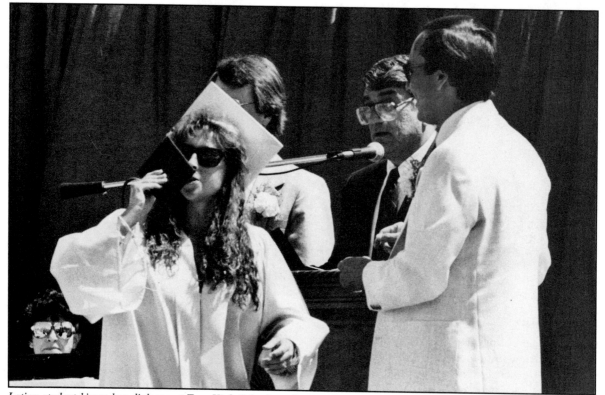

Latina student kisses her diploma at Taos High School graduation. Since the 1970's, increasing numbers of young Latinos have gone on to college. (Elaine S. Querry)

Latino education. As late as 1977, most states required that English be the only language of instruction in public elementary and high schools. From the 1960's onward, however, some support for bilingual education through high school had come from the federal government, spurred by Latinos' push for recognition

in American graduate schools and 5,000 were in professional schools; 1988 figures were 39,000 and 9,000, respectively. In 1988 Latinos made up 0.9 percent of the college undergraduates in Florida and 5.9 percent of those in Texas.

There are wide educational variations among the

main Latino subgroups. A high percentage of Cuban Americans over age twenty-five have college degrees, but the percentages for Mexican Americans and mainland Puerto Ricans are quite small. The relatively low number of non-Cuban Latinos in college has many explanations. Among them are the social and economic conditions that cause high dropout rates in elementary and secondary schools; "tracking" systems that shunt students away from college preparatory subjects; lack of funds; and the migrant lifestyles of some families.

In 1990 the average score of Mexican Americans on the American College Test (ACT), a standard college admissions test, was 18.3, up from the previous year. That of other Latinos was 19.3, compared to a national average of 20.6. Latino students have often entered college with academic deficiencies and with high, sometimes unrealistic job aspirations; nevertheless, they have dropped out of college at only a slightly higher rate than Anglo students.

Predominantly Latino Colleges. The colleges that serve predominantly Latino student populations are mostly located in the West and Southwest, in Florida, and in large cities. Aspects of Latino culture inevitably shape such institutions, but their kinship with Anglo-dominated institutions is also strong.

Institutions of higher education in the United States at which Latinos predominate are a small handful. Saint Augustine College in Illinois, a two-year college with more than 99 percent of its students being Latino (as of 1988), may be the most thoroughly Latino college in the country. Not far behind, in Texas, are Laredo Junior College, Texas Southmost College, Texas State Technical Institute at Harlingen, Laredo State University, and El Paso County Community College. Pan American University, of the University of Texas system, has a roughly 80 percent Latino student population. Some other American colleges with more than 60 percent Latino enrollment (again, based on 1988 figures) include East Los Angeles College, a campus of the Los Angeles Community College system, and Northern New Mexico Community College.

The huge Miami-Dade Community College, with an enrollment topping 43,880 students, has a student population that is about half Latino. Hudson County and Passaic County Community Colleges in New Jersey also have enrollments of Latinos approaching 50 percent. The Colegio Jacinto Trevino, in Mercedes, Texas, has a unique place among predominantly Latino schools. Established in 1977 for Mexican Ameri-

cans, the school trains bilingual teachers in Spanish and English.

Illustrative of the very few bilingual English/Spanish colleges in the United States is Hostos Community College of the City University of New York, a publicly-funded, open admission, coeducational junior college in the South Bronx. Named for a Puerto Rican educator, it was founded in 1968. Hostos was founded on the belief that students reared in Spanish-speaking homes need to develop superior skills in their first language as a means of mastering materials in the mainstream language.

Latino Students and Latino Studies Programs. As early as the 1960's, groups such as the New University Conference (NUC) and the National Council of Teachers of English (NCTE) advocated college courses, textbooks, and programs that would reflect the "cultural and ethnic plurality of American society." Especially in California, Latinos and others advanced initiatives favoring "Third World colleges" devoted to ETHNIC STUDIES. These proposals achieved only limited success in accomplishing their specific goals.

Such radical initiatives, however, did have broad effects on American higher education in that they led to increased attention being given to minority students and to various ethnic studies programs. Many schools, for example, bolstered their counseling programs for Latino students. Moreover, by the 1980's, many mainstream American colleges were trying to attract Latino students with special scholarships and modified admissions standards, hoping to enroll them in proportion to the Latino presence in the population. By the 1987-1988 academic year, the University of California at Berkeley had achieved that goal—a Latino enrollment of 6 percent. In 1986 Latino college students throughout the United States received financial aid at a rate that was very slightly above the national average of 45.5 percent. In 1989 Stanford University made ethnic studies compulsory for all students and established elective "ethnic theme houses" for Latinos and other groups. The gender distribution of the student population of the 1970's, when more Latino men than women were attending college, had been reversed by the late 1980's. One example of the cultural adjustments that have faced Latino students is the occasional conflicts that have been reported between "macho" Latino attitudes and the FEMINISM prominent on college campuses.

Many American colleges offer programs that study Latino culture. Some programs involve academic departments dedicated to the field; others are interdisciplinary programs. CHICANO STUDIES began in California in the late 1960's as a response to student demonstrations and demands for programs that would meet the needs of minority communities. Since then, there has been considerable heated debate over the direction such programs should take and how politicized and activist they should be. There has been friction both within Latino studies programs themselves and between the programs and the universities of which they are a part.

Nevertheless, by 1987 bachelor's degrees in Latino, Hispanic, or Chicano studies were available at twelve schools in nine states and Puerto Rico, and master's degrees were available at SMITH COLLEGE (Massachusetts), VASSAR COLLEGE (New York), and the University of Puerto Rico at Mayagüez. Northwestern University (Illinois) offered a doctorate in Hispanic studies. Bachelor's degrees in Hispanic American studies have also been offered at colleges including Smith College, BRYN MAWR, the University of Miami, and Berkeley.

SUGGESTED READINGS. The history of higher education among Latinos exists in scattered sources. David Riesman's *On Higher Education: The Academic Enterprise in an Era of Rising Student Consumerism* (1980) discusses the role of Latinos in American colleges. Good overall sources include *The College Blue Book* (published every two years) and *The Almanac of Higher Education* (published yearly), which tabulate primary information about Latinos and offer brief profiles of institutions where Latinos predominate. Books that discuss Chicano studies include *Chicano Studies: A Multidisciplinary Approach* (1984), edited by Eugene Garcia et al., and Carlos Muñoz's *Youth, Identity, Power* (1989).—*Roy Neil Graves*

Lattimore, Owen (July 29, 1900, Washington, D.C.—May 31, 1989, Providence, R.I.): Sinologist and journalist. Lattimore spent much of his childhood in the Sino-Russian border region of Asia, and as an adult returned there for both business and journalism. His journey to Inner Mongolia in 1926-1927 led to his 1928 book *The Desert Road to Turkestan*. Through further travel, research work at Harvard and Beijing Universities, seven years as editor of *Pacific Affairs* magazine, and six more books, Lattimore became a leading authority on the history, culture, and politics of central Asia. During the early 1940's, he was the American adviser to Chinese leader Chiang Kai-shek. Lattimore suspended his re-

China expert Owen Lattimore was accused of being both a communist and a spy in the 1950's. (AP/Wide World Photos)

search work in 1950 to respond to allegations made by Senator Joseph McCarthy that he was a spy for the Soviet Union. Although the charges were initially dropped after an investigation failed to yield evidence, Lattimore was once again in the spotlight after a confessed Communist testified that Lattimore had been a Communist Party member. Indicted for perjury in 1952, Lattimore was eventually cleared of all charges. He published an account of his experiences entitled *Ordeal by Slander* (1950). Lattimore established a Department of Chinese studies at the University of Leeds in 1963.

Latvian Americans: The U.S. Census of 1990 listed 100,300 people of Latvian ancestry living in the United States. Though not one of the largest European immigrant populations, Latvian Americans have made significant cultural and scientific contributions to American society.

The Latvian Republic, one of three small states lying on the Baltic Sea, is bordered by Estonia on the north, Lithuania on the south, and Russia and Byelorussia on the east. With an area of about 25,000 square miles, Latvia is approximately the size of West

Virginia. The 1990 population was 2.7 million, with about 52 percent ethnic Latvians and 34 percent ethnic Russians. About 100,000 Latvians live elsewhere in the former Soviet Union, and about 200,000 others live abroad, mostly in the United States, Canada, or western Europe.

Language, Culture, and History. Latvians are a linguistic and ethnic group quite distinct from their Slavic and Baltic neighbors. The Latvian language is somewhat related to Lithuanian but only distantly related to Russian. It is not affiliated with Estonian at all.

Most Latvians are Lutheran, and about 70 percent live in urban areas. Modern Latvian culture combines indigenous forms with German, Russian, Swedish, and Lithuanian elements. There is a rich folk tradition of oral literature, poetry, and music, especially choral works and folk songs.

LATVIA

Several Latvian tribes (or "Letts," as they are often called) established contacts with the neighboring Slavs, Scandinavians, and Finns in ancient times. They gradually fell prey to German and Slavic expansion after the collapse of Rome. Between the thirteenth and sixteenth centuries, the antecedents of modern Latvian language and culture took form under German economic and religious influence.

Until the 1700's, Germans, Poles, Swedes, and Russians fought over various Latvian territories, but by 1795 the whole country was under Russian political control. Latvians were little more than landless peasants until the Napoleonic wars of the first decades of the 1800's emancipated the serfs, and a growing Latvian nationalist movement began. After the Russian Revolution in 1917 and the civil war that followed,

Latvia gained its independence for twenty years (1920-1940), only to become incorporated into the Soviet Union again during World War II. From 1940 to 1990, Latvia was one of the fifteen republics that made up the Soviet Union. On May 4, 1990, Latvia declared Soviet rule illegal, and on August 21, 1991, Latvia declared its independence.

Immigration. The history of Latvian migration to the United States may be divided into four phases: the earliest settlers, the nineteenth century immigrants, the first major influx of immigrants in the early 1900's, and World War II refugees and the Latvian diaspora.

Probably the first Latvians to reach the North American continent were four settlers from Vidzeme who arrived around 1638, along with Swedish, Finnish, and Estonian immigrants. Because the part of Latvia where they lived was ruled by Sweden at this time, it was natural for the Latvians to join the New Sweden colonies at Delaware Bay and Pennsylvania. In 1687 and later in the 1850's, Latvians from the West Indian colony of Tobago (belonging to the Duke of Courland of western Latvia) also migrated to Boston and other parts of New England.

A small but steady stream of Latvians came to the United States during the eighteenth and nineteenth centuries, settling mostly on the East Coast and in the Midwest. In the 1850 U.S. Census, there were more than three thousand people of Latvian-Lithuanian descent living in the United States, with almost two thousand being second generation. By the 1870's there were more than four thousand. These early settlers left their mark with place names such as Mount Riga, New York, and Livonia, Michigan.

Unlike many other immigrant groups, Latvians did not establish many large ethnic enclaves in American cities. A community of several hundred Latvians did, however, develop in the Boston area, the common port of entry for most Latvian newcomers. During the 1880's and 1890's Latvians regarded Boston as the center of Latvian American life.

Like many other immigrants at this time, these early Latvians usually had little English language training, limited capital, and few job opportunities. Upon their arrival they often started out as unskilled laborers, working in factories, packing houses, or textile mills. Some even worked on railroad lines or in lumber camps. Several Latvian American cultural organizations and labor associations assisted these newcomers in finding jobs. The common pattern was for new immigrants to take any manual job temporarily, then gradually find something in their respective trades later on.

In the late 1800's and early 1900's Latvian Americans began to define themselves as a community. Jacob Sieberg (1864-1964), one of the most active of the early Latvian immigrants, published the first Latvian newspaper in the United States—*Amerikas Vestnesis* (American Herald)—from 1896 to 1922 in Boston. Several dozen other Latvian-language newspapers and journals were published in the years before World War II.

Many Latvians immigrated in the early twentieth century for the same reason as most other Europeans: to improve themselves economically. The early part of the century, however, was a period of extreme social upheaval, civil war, and revolution in Russia and its empire. This further encouraged Latvian immigration to the United States. Between 1905 (the end of the Russo-Japanese War, which incited several revolutions in Russia) and 1914 (the start of World War I), more than five thousand Latvians entered the United States. Most of them were experienced artisans, machinists, and factory workers from urban areas. Many others were highly educated socialists and nationalists who left Latvia for political as well as economic reasons. For example, in 1905, a violent uprising in Riga (the present-day capital of Latvia) was put down with much bloodshed. Many of the revolt's leaders left to escape arrest or compulsory military service in the Russian czar's army.

Thus, a fair number of Latvians who arrived in the United States at this time were political radicals. During a demonstration involving the Latvian Workingmen's Association in Boston in 1908, two policemen were killed, eight people injured, and thirty Latvian Americans arrested. Latvian Americans were important participants in the American LABOR MOVEMENT in the first quarter of the twentieth century and helped establish important labor unions such as the Industrial Workers of the World (IWW). Most Latvian political activities, however, tended more toward nationalism than socialism.

By 1920, there were more than thirty thousand Latvians living in the United States. World War I and the Great Depression discouraged most immigration during the interwar years; from 1920 to 1939, less than five thousand new Latvians came to the United States. This period coincided with the two decades of freedom from Russian rule enjoyed by Latvia. It is likely that Latvians probably felt less desire to leave their newly independent nation than when the country was part of either Imperial or Soviet Russia.

In a secret pact between Adolf Hitler and Joseph Stalin, Germany and the Soviet Union divided up much of eastern Europe after the Nazis invaded Poland in 1939. In June, 1940, Latvia was annexed by Stalin, becoming a Soviet republic. German and Soviet armies occupied the country at various times during World War II. By the time the war ended, 240,000 Latvians—about 14 percent of the total population of the country—became refugees fleeing the advancing Red Army. About half of them ended up in Germany and were officially designated displaced persons by the United Nations. Thus began the great scattering, or dispersal, of many Latvian citizens in what is sometimes called "the Latvian diaspora."

Between 1945 and 1950, more than thirty thousand Latvians came to the United States, most of them being refugees. From 1950 to 1959 approximately seventeen thousand more immigrated. The American Latvian Association, the Lutheran Resettlement Service, the American Latvian Relief Fund, and the Latvian Legation helped many of these newcomers by providing transportation, financial aid, credit, and language assistance. While many of these newcomers had to begin their lives in the United States as unskilled laborers, within a decade a majority of them had reclaimed their earlier careers or begun new ones. Probably more than 90 percent of these foreign-born Latvians eventually became U.S. citizens (up from about 60 percent in the 1930's).

The influx of these new Latvian immigrants was beneficial in uniting the Latvian American community. After World War II, many social, cultural, and political organizations formed, and Latvian weekend schools, choirs, and clubs could be found in many American urban centers.

Cultural Contributions. Latvian Americans began making contributions to their new homeland as soon as they arrived on its shores. They worked in American factories and farms and even fought in America's armed conflicts. One of the first casualties of the Civil War was Latvian immigrant Martin Bucin, and several Latvian Americans were highly decorated soldiers and airmen in World War II and the Korean War.

Latvian Americans have been especially productive in scientific and technical fields. The mechanical engineer August Krastins (1859-1942) patented his Krastins gasoline automobile in 1901, seven years before Henry Ford built his first cars. Krastins' company in Cleveland, Ohio, introduced several innovative automotive designs, including electrical ignition systems and circular steering wheels. He also developed refrigerators, phonograph needles, telegraph equipment, and agricultural machinery. John Akermans and Leon Swirbul were both pioneers of early aviation research and airplane construction. Akermans developed one of the earliest twin-engine monoplanes; helped design the B-29, B-47, and B-97 bombers; and was dean of the department of aeronautics at the University of Minnesota until 1960. Swirbul was a brigadier general in the Pacific theater during World War II who, as a former president of Grumman Aircraft, had overseen the manufacture of more than seventeen thousand aircraft for the U.S. Navy. Peteris Krumins (1898-1964) developed the standard method for determining the carbon dioxide content of coal in 1961. Juris Upatnieks was the coinventor of holography (photographs that appear in three dimensions using lasers and polarized light).

Latvian Americans have also been active in government and public service. After studying and teaching agriculture at the University of Nebraska, Karlis Ulmanis (1877-1942) returned to his homeland and in 1918 became the first prime minister of the newly independent nation of Latvia, serving again in 1938 as its last president.

Latvian Americans involved in the fine and applied arts include famed architects such as Gunars Birkerts (b. 1925), Akselis Mangulis (b. 1922), and Visvaldis Palukulis (b. 1923). Painters and sculptors of international renown include Janis Kuga (1878-1969), Nora Drapce (1866-1956), Rikards Maurs (1888-1966), Janis Annus (b. 1935), Svens Lukins (b. 1943), and Ivars Hirss (b. 1931).

A number of modern organizations document the history and culture of Latvians and Latvian Americans. The central organization for all Latvians living abroad is the World Federation of Free Latvians in Washington, D.C. Under the auspices of the American Latvian Association, the Latvian Studies Center was opened in 1983 at Western Michigan University in Kalamazoo. The center's library currently has a collection of more than twenty thousand holdings, one of the largest outside of the former Soviet Union. The Toronto Latvian Studies Center library also has more than eight thousand items.

SUGGESTED READINGS. Being a small minority, Latvian Americans are documented in fewer books and resources than many other ethnic groups. A good start for further research would be two books filled with interesting facts, anecdotes, and pictures: Osvalds Akmentinš' *Latvians in Bicentennial America* (1976) and *The Latvians in America, 1640-1973: A Chronology and Fact Book* (1974), edited by Maruta Kārklis, Līga Streips, and Laimonas Streips. An interesting sociological study of Latvian immigration and cultural adaptation is the two-volume work *Social Change: Major Value Systems of Latvians at Home, as Refugees, and as Immigrants* (1982) by Juris Veidemanis. A later overview of Latvians at home and abroad is *Latvia and Latvians* (1988) by Juris Sinka. Two excellent articles are Inese A. Smith's "The Latvian Diaspora," in *Multicultural Review* 1, no. 4 (1992), pp. 32-38 and Edgar Anderson's "Latvians" in *The Harvard Encyclopedia of American Ethnic Groups* (1980), edited by Stephan Thernstrom.—*James Stanlaw*

Lau v. Nichols (1974): Supreme Court case which ordered that BILINGUAL EDUCATION be offered in American public schools. The case began with a class-action suit (an action brought on behalf of many persons similarly affected) which charged the San Francisco public school system with failure to provide remedial English courses for approximately eighteen hundred Chinese-speaking pupils. Of the 2,856 students of Chinese ancestry then in the San Francisco schools, only about a thousand were receiving supplemental courses in English.

The suit charged that the school system was in violation of two laws: the equal protection clause of the FOURTEENTH AMENDMENT, which says that the state shall not "deny to any person within its jurisdiction the equal protection of the laws," and section 601 of the CIVIL RIGHTS ACT OF 1964, which prohibits recipients of federal funds from discriminating against students on the grounds of race, color, or national origin. Under section 602 of the same act, the Department of Health, Education, and Welfare (HEW) has the authority to issue regulations concerning discrimination to schools receiving federal aid. HEW guidelines state that:

> where inability to speak and understand the English language excludes national-origin minority group children from effective participation in the educational program offered by a school district, the district must take affirmative steps to rectify the language deficiency in order to open its instructional program to these students.

Basing its decision on the Civil Rights Act of 1964, the Supreme Court found that the San Francisco school system, by failing to provide special instruction for non-English-speaking students, had denied them a meaningful opportunity to participate in their schooling, thus violating the act. The Court held that any

fied.) The Court did not rule on whether the San Francisco school district had violated the equal protection clause of the Fourteenth Amendment.

A 1971 study by the U.S. Commission on Civil Rights noted that the problems facing non-English-speaking Chinese children "are dramatically similar"

In Lau v. Nichols, *the Supreme Court ruled that schools must offer bilingual instruction to non-English-speaking children, thus easing the adjustment of immigrant students such as this girl.* (James L. Shaffer)

school district receiving federal monies must provide English instruction for non-English students whose education is hampered by the language barrier. A concurring opinion by Justice Harry Blackmun stressed that if only a few children were involved, he would not regard the decision to apply "conclusively." Therefore, school districts must provide supplemental English language classes only when they have a substantial number of non-English-speaking students. (The minimum number of students necessary was not speci-

to those facing Mexican-American children. Since 1974, the number and diversity of non-English-speaking children enrolled in American public schools has vastly increased, highlighting the importance of *Lau v. Nichols*. *This Supreme Court decision laid the groundwork for the development of controversial bilingual education programs.*

Suggested Readings. For additional information, consult Americo Lapati's *Education and the Federal Government* (1975), *A Digest of Supreme Court De-*

cisions Affecting Education (1978), edited by Perry Zirkel, the Information Plus Series' *Immigration and Illegal Aliens: Burden or Blessing* (rev. ed. 1991), edited by Alison Landis et al., or *United States Reports* (vol. 414, October, 1973, page 563).

Law and discrimination. *See* **Discrimination—laws**

Law enforcement and community relations: Interaction between members of police agencies and the public, whether positive or negative. With the development of formalized community relations programs in police departments since the 1950's, the phrase has often been misunderstood to mean police public relations. Unlike self-serving public relations programs designed for image enhancement, police community relations units were set up to promote mutual understanding between the police and the diverse members of the communities they serve.

Early American Policing. During its infancy, the United States was populated mainly on the Atlantic coast by colonists of English origin, who demanded local control of their government. Initially, cities were patrolled by a volunteer force at night; as volunteers became scarce, however, cities were forced to hire paid police officers.

The first paid daytime police force was established in New York in 1800, based on the London model developed by Sir Robert Peel. Its goals were to reduce crime and increase public safety without undue violation of privacy and property of individuals. American citizens retained control of the police department until 1883, when the Pendleton Civil Service Act created a regulated system of civil service jobs on the federal level. Gradually cities and states adopted the same system, thus putting an end to open political manipulation of police departments.

In the early years, police officers on foot patrols had constant direct contact with the citizenry. Community service was an intrinsic part of the job of the police officer, whose responsibilities included everything affecting the well-being of the citizens. As American society became more urbanized, more populated, more diverse, and more mechanized, positive direct police contacts with the public decreased and the need for public cooperation increased.

Evolution of the Community Relations Problem. Relations between the police and the public began to sour during the Spoils Era and Prohibition (1919-1933), which were characterized by widespread corruption and lawlessness in response to unpopular laws.

After World War II, population shifts caused law enforcement agencies to confront the problem of police and public cooperation. Northern metropolitan areas nearly doubled in population because of an influx of southern blacks. The major industrial cities also suddenly bulged with immigrants of vastly differing ethnic origins and opposing points of view. The police were concerned about real and potential social strife among these groups living in such close proximity.

In 1945, career law enforcement attracted thousands of disciplined young war veterans. With newly available resources, police training programs in human relations were instituted for the first time, focusing on racial, religious, and ethnic conflict.

The first formal Police-Community Relations Division was established in 1957 in St. Louis, Missouri. Similar divisions, commonly known as PCR units, were set up by all large departments in following years to promote communication between the police and public. Ethnic minorities, youth, and the poor criticized the units as being mere public relations ploys, disguising the bigotry and hostility institutionalized in the police force.

Between 1960 and 1963, scandals of police corruption in large cities received nationwide media attention. In the summers of 1964 and 1965, New York and Los Angeles experienced major RACE RIOTS, alleged to have been precipitated by police brutality.

In 1965, President Johnson established the Commission on Law Enforcement and Administration of Justice, which issued a report stressing the need to strengthen police relationships with the communities they serve. A national center for police and community relations was established in 1965 at Michigan State University to provide research and development of training programs and consulting services to interested police and community organizations. That same year, J. W. Wilson of Harvard University led an extensive study comparing the urban police in eight medium-sized communities.

Although scholarly interest in the sociology of police had been stimulated and considerable reform was beginning, the years 1967 through 1969 were tumultuous. Destructive race riots occurred in Detroit, Michigan, and Newark, New Jersey, in 1967. In February of that year, the President's Commission on Law Enforcement and Administration of Justice had actually predicted the riots in these and ten other cities, warning that unless the police frankly and effectively confronted the legitimate grievances of minorities, trouble was inevitable. The violent riots in 1968 following the assassination of Dr. Martin Luther KING, Jr., and during the Democratic National Convention in Chicago reinforced the nation's sudden, acute awareness that racial and social divisions posed serious threats to peace and well-being, and that law enforcement was woefully ill-equipped to cope with the growing public discontent.

The National Advisory Commission on Civil Disorders (popularly called the KERNER COMMISSION)

The commission proclaimed that the nation was moving toward two separate and unequal, black and white societies. Many blacks saw the police as symbols of white power, repression, and racism. This attitude was exacerbated, according to the commission, by a widespread belief among blacks in the pervasiveness of police brutality and double standards of protection for black and white people.

Clearly, law enforcement needed to show a new level of responsiveness to the conflicts breeding in the streets. The Law Enforcement Assistance Administra-

During civil rights protests such as those in Birmingham, Ala., in 1963, white police officers often dealt harshly with black demonstrators. The legacy of police brutality has sparked race riots in many minority communities. (AP/Wide World Photos)

considered both the social problems and the professionalism of the police in its report in February, 1968. It found that the humanity and community relations skills of the old-style patrolman on a regular neighborhood beat had unfortunately been sacrificed in the name of technological advancement.

tion, the Ford Foundation, and other institutions made millions of dollars available to the criminal justice system for the development of increased professionalism and innovative programs to advance police community relations across the country.

Formalized Police Community Relations Programs.

Community relations programs, like any institutional reform, grew from open acknowledgment of a serious problem. Development of effective programs to combat the problem hinged on proper identification of the causes of disintegration of public trust. Scholars from various disciplines analyzed the police function, social processes, and population trends to recommend constructive measures toward building good police-community relations.

Most friction between the police and the public occurred in the urban GHETTOS. African Americans and Latinos made up the greatest percentage of the minority population living in poverty-stricken inner-city slums; however, Asian Americans and Americans Indians living in poor urban areas also complained of discriminatory treatment. Animosity toward the police

was traced to two basic problems: failure to provide adequate protective services and discretionary, over-zealous enforcement of the law in minority communities. Grievances of excessiveness included complaints of police brutality (physical, verbal, and psychological), alleged to be motivated by racial PREJUDICE.

Although racial discrimination could not be eliminated without more basic social reforms, city authorities and police administrators instituted policies and

Police officer gives school children antidrug lecture in an instance of the modern preventive approach to law enforcement. (James L. Shaffer)

programs to provide better protective services and reduce complaints of police abuses in the INNER CITY.

Making the Police More Accessible. Decentralization, team policing, and storefront offices were among the most common approaches to better community relations. Certain metropolitan police departments dispatched specially trained PCR officers into alienated neighborhoods in small storefront offices to make police contact readily accessible to neighborhood residents. These approaches afforded the police higher visibility in the neighborhoods, and returned to the beat patrol approach that put a high priority on community relations. The success of these programs depended on the willingness of the police to assume the

cessful specialized unit for handling domestic disputes was developed in New York City, with specially trained officers assigned to family crisis intervention. Their mission was to reduce tension rather than make arrests.

Most departments also developed speakers bureaus to bring information about police technology, respon-

In community-based policing, law enforcement officers get to know the people in their communities to promote a spirit of cooperation. (James L. Shaffer)

pended on the willingness of the police to assume the role of a community service officer. Ironically, community services had traditionally accounted for the larger percentage of police activity, as opposed to criminal investigation, especially in inner-city neighborhoods. Nevertheless, performing what appeared to be social work, rather than crime solving, was met by considerable resistance in the police forces. One suc-

sibilities, and resources to public bodies such as schools and civic clubs. Although informative, such programs served mainly as public relations vehicles.

Direct community involvement in the maintenance-of-order aspect of police work has been achieved through crime prevention programs, such as neighborhood watch groups, block parents programs, and women's safety programs. Most of these efforts have resulted in a reduction of crime as well as improved communication between police and the community.

New Training and Recruitment Standards. Group encounters, role playing, and other forms of behavior modification became a part of police training in an effort to address police bias toward minorities. The basic idea of sensitivity training was to conduct intensive human relations training under laboratory conditions, supervised by psychologists, sociologists, and other specialists. Members of the groups developed greater insight and sensitivity into themselves, their motivations, and their prejudices toward others. Such training was found to be especially useful for police officers in daily contact with people of diverse socioeconomic backgrounds.

It was recognized that higher educational standards for recruits were vital to the improvement of police and community relations. Better-educated police officers were expected to be less likely to engage in the STEREOTYPING associated with racial bias. Intensive police training programs in human relations have come to include specific training in topics such as police-media relations, police-Spanish speaking relations, and police handling of campus disorders.

In the 1960's, both the President's Commission on Law Enforcement and Administration of Justice and the KERNER COMMISSION urged that law enforcement agencies become more representative of minority communities. Minority recruits became important in the neighborhood police units, particularly where fluency in another language was essential for effective communication.

Civilian Review Boards. Civilian review boards were a forum for citizens with grievances who were seeking redress against the police. They grew in response to complaints that internal investigation of alleged police misconduct was ineffective. Such boards could often be counterproductive, as in New York City, where the police department became more politicized and solidified in its defeat of the civilian review boards referendum in 1966. Other forms of control over police misconduct were instituted, such as peer review panels, field tape recordings of police-public interactions, and citizens' advisory panels regarding policymaking decisions.

Since the early 1960's, dramatic changes have occurred in police composition and procedure in an effort to involve citizens in the peacekeeping aspect of law enforcement. However, tensions between the police and minority groups have continued. In May of 1992, there were violent riots in Los Angeles and other American cities following the acquittal of four police officers accused of violently beating a black suspect. This led to renewed interest in community-based policing, which had been used effectively in cities such as Philadelphia.

Scholars have concluded that real change in police-minority relations depends on change in the larger political, economic, and social spheres of American society. Innovative practices and active citizen involvement, however, have contributed in no small measure to improved relations between the police and the communities they serve.

SUGGESTED READINGS. For a detailed study of one community, see Geoffrey P. Alpert and Roger G. Dunham's *Policing Multi-ethnic Neighborhoods* (1988). For an overview of the topic, see *Police Community Relations: Images, Roles, Realities* (1976), edited by Alvin W. Cohn and Emilio C. Viano. Discretionary law enforcement is discussed in *Arrest: The Decision to Take a Suspect into Custody* (1965), by Wayne LaFave. *The New Blue Line* (1986) by Jerome Skolnick and David Bayley examines in detail how policy is put into practice.—*Kathleen O'Brien*

Leadership Conference on Civil Rights: National conference of civil rights organizations. The Leadership Conference on Civil Rights was begun in 1950 following President Truman's Committee on Civil Rights' report *To Secure These Rights*. Founders were A. Philip RANDOLPH, Roy WILKINS, and Arnold Aronson. At first thirty organizations representing the needs of a variety of minorities were involved. The number has steadily grown. Its goals include providing good jobs with reasonable wages for all who can work, safe and affordable housing, quality education, and medical services. The conference has been instrumental in helping pass all of the major civil rights legislation in the twentieth century.

League of United Latin American Citizens (LULAC): Established in 1929 as a conservative middle- and upper-class organization to promote the social, political, and economic rights and duties of MEXICAN AMERICANS. During World War II it became active in desegregating schools and juries. In 1949 LULAC was influential in the passage of fair employment laws. In the 1990's it remains one of the more influential Mexican American organizations. It sponsors National Education Service Centers, which serve Latino college students, and publishes the monthly *LULAC News*.

League of Women Voters (LWV): Nonpartisan organization founded in 1920 to educate and prepare women for political life. On the eve of passage of the federal woman's suffrage bill, Carrie Chapman CATT, president of the National American Woman Suffrage Association, called on all those who had worked for suffrage to continue to work together in a new organization dedicated to informing the new electorate.

The LWV's focus shifted from women to children in the 1930's. The LWV opposed the addition of sex

Lebanese Americans: Lebanese Americans are prominent members and leaders of the Arab American community. They include adherents of Christian and Muslim sects from both early (nineteenth century) and recent migrations from what is present-day Lebanon.

Historical Background. A large number of Lebanese immigrants came to the United States during the late 1800's and 1900's, when the area then referred to as Mount Lebanon was part of the Ottoman Turkish Empire. Until this empire was dismantled after World

After women won the right to vote, the League of Women Voters was set up to educate the new electorate while advocating women's and children's rights. (Library of Congress)

discrimination to Title VII of the Civil Rights Act of 1964 because of fears that the addition of women as a protected group would create opposition and defeat the entire bill. Most recently the LWV has been known for its publication of voter's guides, supervision of televised presidential debates, and strong stands on a wide array of issues concerning the conduct of public life.

War I, Mount Lebanon proper was essentially a Maronite Christian enclave surrounded by different sectarian groupings (Druze, Sunni, and Shi'a Muslims). All would eventually be "annexed" in 1920 under French mandate to become the entity called Greater Lebanon. It was only after World War II, when Lebanese immigration had already been well established in both South and North America, that the United Nations recognized the independent Republic of Lebanon. For the Lebanese who had settled in the United States before World War I, there may have been less of a dilemma about their identity in the "MELTING POT" of American society than that experienced by the communities of Maronites, Druze, Greek Orthodox, Greek Catholics, and Sunni and Shi'a MUSLIMS who remained in the uneasy crucible of the national identity of Lebanon which was "created" following the collapse of the Ottoman Empire.

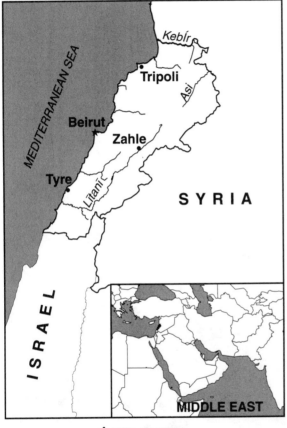

LEBANON

Certainly one of the early causes for Lebanese emigration to North and South America was fear and insecurity brought about by intersectarian strife. In the mid-1800's, when the first cultural and educational ties were being established between Lebanese and American religious schools, Christian Lebanese families began to be attracted to the United States as an alternative to the centuries-old traditional symbol of French "protection" of Maronites. These people hoped for educational and trade advantages, and escape from first the violent intercommunal disturbances of the 1860's and then rising Turkish political repression under the last sultans.

Statistics from the late nineteenth and early twentieth centuries do not distinguish between different segments of the Syrian emigrant population. Lebanese are grouped together with Palestinians and others from areas now located in the independent state of Syria. Most secondary sources agree that about 70 percent of "Syrian" emigrants counted in this period came from Lebanon. In the early 1900's before the IMMIGRATION ACT OF 1917 established national quotas, there was a steady flow of five thousand "Syrian" entries per year on the average. By the time of the Census of 1920, official U.S. records showed some fifty thousand persons of Syro-Lebanese descent in the country. It should be noted, however, that scholars of Arab American emigration believe that actual numbers were considerably higher at the time, given the total of 250,000 Arab immigrants and their descendants in the United States by the 1940's.

Lebanese Identity and Communities. Because Lebanese immigrants represented only a portion of immigration into the United States from geographical Syria, much of what applies to any of the first or subsequent generations that built Arab American communities has a distinctly Lebanese flavor. In fact, however, statistics from the Greater New York area show that the majority of "Syrians" settling in the United States were Christian of either Maronite or Catholic (followed by Greek Orthodox) background. The predominance of these two religious groupings would imply, therefore, that most Syrian communities in the United States, especially in the first half of the twentieth century, were majority Lebanese in composition.

Historically most Lebanese communities were, and still are, to be found in the North Atlantic states, principally in New York, Massachusetts, and Pennsylvania. In the early 1900's, Ohio was the only other state that could compare in numbers of immigrant-founded communities with the three main East Coast states.

Much of the cultural traditions of Lebanese in their adopted American setting would grow in these originally densely settled states, particularly in sections of large cities such as the Atlantic Avenue section of Brooklyn in New York. With the passage of time, however, and particularly during and after the troubled years of the Lebanese civil war (1975 to the late 1980's), new waves of Lebanese immigration into the United States would challenge "old" demographic patterns and the dominant role of East Coast Lebanese communities. By the 1990's, a "new" first generation of Lebanese had spread throughout the United States, with substantial areas of concentration in key cities of California.

It is difficult to compare early Lebanese emigration, with less privileged families coming to the United States to seek a better material existence, with the more complicated patterns visible in the "new wave"

English, made it possible for many to find vocational paths that could lead to faster integration into mainstream American life. Thus, a number of new Lebanese immigrants could be found in the 1980's and 1990's working as teachers, college professors, or other professions. Others opened small businesses, either in the traditional spheres of restaurants and groceries or, notably, in the retail clothing sector.

Members of the Lebanese Socialist Party capture a Lebanese army tank in 1976 at the height of the Lebanese civil war. The conflict prompted a new wave of Lebanese immigration to the United States. (AP/Wide World Photos)

of the last three decades of the 1900's. The religious origins of those leaving Lebanon to escape the effects of civil war have certainly been more varied. In addition to still substantial numbers of Christians, new immigrants include many Muslims, both of Sunni and Shi'a background. Immigrants arriving since the late 1970's had also received a higher level of education in their home country than earlier generations. This, together with a more widespread prior knowledge of

Lebanese American Organizations and Activities. Since the 1890's, Lebanese Americans have had access to newspapers and magazines specializing in news of their communities. The longest operating newspaper, *Al-Hoda* ("Guidance"), was founded and edited in Arabic in New York by Naoum Mokarezel, former president of the Lebanon League of Progress in the United States. A continuing generation of editors has kept the journal alive as the "new" *Al-Hoda.*

Since 1952, two other papers in English, *The Heritage* and *The New Lebanese American Journal*, both published in New York, have thrived by providing both local news of Lebanese American communities and news from the Middle East of interest to these communities.

Beyond general Arab American organizations that attract participation by Lebanese, there are two fraternal bodies, the Lebanese American Association in Boston and the Lebanon American Social Society in Detroit, that provide a network of communication between individual Lebanese Americans and representatives of their communities in all areas of the United States. Unlike other immigrant populations from the Middle East such as Syrian Americans, there is no national religious organization reflecting the communal identity of Lebanese Catholic or Maronite Christians.

Lebanese Cultural Expression in America: Literary Figures. A rich symbol of the vitality of Lebanese culture transplanted in the American environment is to be found in the writings of poets and essayists whose reputations recrossed the Atlantic, not only to gain recognition in Lebanon and other Arab countries, but in Europe and Asia as well. Foremost among these writers, perhaps, is Khalil Gibran. Gibran emigrated to Boston from a Maronite village in Mount Lebanon when he was eleven years old. His writings, which often combined Western style and poetic form with the mystical imagery of Arabic poetry, were translated into many different languages. Significantly, Gibran divided his original writings between his native Arabic and English. His most popular work, *The Prophet*, was originally published in English in New York in 1923 and became a classic work of popular philosophy.

A slightly older literary colleague and biographer of Gibran, Ameen Rihani, came to New York when he was twelve. His first publications were for *Al-Hoda* during his early twenties. Although Rihani would, like Gibran, gain international recognition as a cultural spokesman for his former homeland, his work put more emphasis on historical and political concerns such as studies of the French Revolution and Arabian history. Rihani later became known as an advocate of Syrian independence and Arab nationalism.

In addition to notable activity in the literary sphere, many Lebanese Americans have gained recognition for contributions to their adopted country. These range from scholarship to public service and entertainment. Only a few selected examples may be cited here.

One of the earliest figures to gain international fame in the American university world after the relocation of his family in the United States was Philip Hitti. A Princeton scholar who pioneered the field of Middle East studies in the United States in the 1920's, Hitti wrote *The History of the Arabs* in 1935, which later became a classic.

Individuals of Lebanese origin who have entered public service have been numerous, particularly since the 1960's. Elected representatives have included James Abdnor, who rose to serve in Congress after being elected state senator in Nebraska. Another Lebanese American, James Abourezk of South Dakota, moved from a congressional seat to a Democratic Senate post in 1974, where he served on several committees and became an important spokesperson for Arab Americans. In the same year that Senator Abourezk was elected, Dr. Philip Habib was appointed Assistant Secretary of State of East Asian and Pacific Affairs. His vital services to the State Department expanded greatly in the 1980's, when he became an official U.S. envoy to the Middle East, particularly in Lebanon, the strife-torn country of his family origin.

Public service by well-known Lebanese Americans has not been limited to government careers. Perhaps the most prominent consumer protection advocate in the United States, Ralph Nader began his career in the mid-1960's with the publication of a critique of automobile safety features entitled *Unsafe at Any Speed*. Nader's role as a public figure speaking out for varied consumer interests continued into the 1990's.

In the sphere of popular culture, several Lebanese Americans began careers in the 1950's that would leave indelible marks on the history of American popular music (Paul Anka) and comedy (Danny Thomas).

SUGGESTED READINGS. Two general texts on Lebanese Americans, the first more contemporary and the second more historical, are *The Syrian-Lebanese in America: A Study in Religion and Assimilation* (1975) by Joseph M. Kayal and Philip M. Kayal and *Becoming American: The Early Arab Immigrant Experience* (1985) by Alixa Naff. Gregory Orfalea's *Before the Flames: A Quest for the History of Arab Americans* (1988) discusses the waves of Syrian Lebanese immigration and attempts to assess the impact of the Lebanese civil war on the larger Arab American community.—*Byron D. Cannon*

Bruce Lee popularized Asian martial arts in the United States through his films and kung fu academies. (AP/Wide World Photos)

Lee, Bruce (Nov. 27, 1940, San Francisco, Calif.—July 20, 1973, Hong Kong): Chinese American actor and martial artist. Although born in San Francisco, Lee spent his boyhood in Hong Kong. Lee returned to the United States in 1958 and studied philosophy at the University of Washington. He soon opened a kung fu academy in Seattle, followed by others in Oakland and Los Angeles. His martial arts expertise brought him to acting, and he played Kato in the *Green Hornet* television series from 1966 to 1967. Martial arts films, long an established genre in Asia, appeared in the United States in the early 1970's, and with his performance in *Enter the Dragon* in 1973, Lee became the symbol of the new craze as well as its biggest star. Just ascending to fame, he was killed accidentally during a filming session in Hong Kong. His life became the basis of the 1993 film *Dragon: The Bruce Lee Story.*

Lee, T. D. [Tsung-Dao] (b. Nov. 25, 1926, Shanghai, China): Chinese American physicist. Lee's Chinese mentor and teacher obtained for Lee a government scholarship that enabled him to study in the United States in 1946. He studied at the University of Chicago, earning his doctorate in 1950. Lee worked at the University of California at Berkeley, the Institute for Advanced Study, and Columbia University. In collaboration with his friend and countryman Chen Ning YANG, Lee successfully challenged the generally accepted "parity principle," ushering in a new era in the field of physics. For this work, Yang and Lee shared the 1957 Nobel Prize in Physics (Lee was the second youngest laureate ever) as well as the Albert Einstein Award.

Lesbians: (*See also* **Gay and Lesbian**) Women who choose other women as sexual and significant life partners. The term is derived from "Lesbos," the name of the Greek island that was the home of the female poet Sappho, known as a lover of women. Some lesbians refer to themselves as "born" lesbians, knowing from an early age that they are attracted to other women rather than to men. Others are "political" lesbians—those who consciously reject the patriarchy and its oppression of women. An estimated 10 percent of the adult female population is lesbian.

The term "homosexuality," within which lesbianism is included, came into use in the medical literature of the late nineteenth century. During the Victorian period, it was generally believed that women, especially middle-class and upper-class women, were incapable of homosexual practices. By the 1930's, however, the term "lesbian" had been incorporated into colloquial discourse to identify same-sex female eroticism. Any type of homosexual activity was labeled perverted or unnatural by society at large. Lesbian sexual activity, along with male homosexuality, has been outlawed under various antisodomy laws since colonial times. As of 1992, twenty-two states had sex-crime laws that could be applied to lesbian practices. In modern legal history, lesbians and gays have been barred from equal protection under the law in housing, employment, military service, child custody, and adoption.

The contemporary WOMEN'S LIBERATION MOVE-MENT, CIVIL RIGHTS MOVEMENT, and GAY AND LESBIAN RIGHTS MOVEMENT encouraged women to challenge the belief that lesbians suffer from a mental disease or congenital illness. In 1955, the Daughters of Bilitis was formed to support lesbians and to educate the general public about them. By the 1980's, many large urban areas featured lesbian bars; university and college curricula addressed lesbian issues in GAY AND LESBIAN STUDIES PROGRAMS and diversity courses; women's centers provided social support ser-

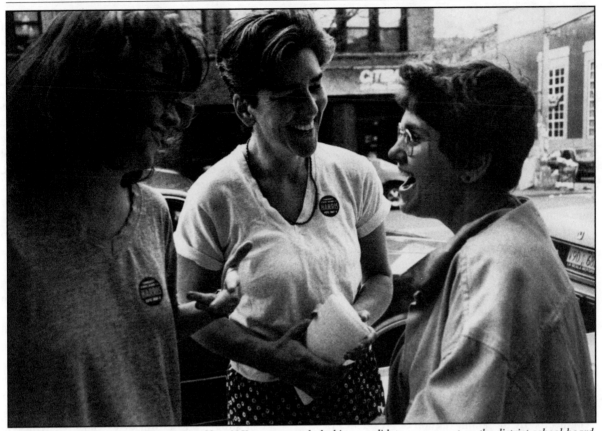

Jill Harris (center), campaigning in Brooklyn, N.Y., as an openly lesbian candidate, won a seat on the district school board.
(Hazel Hankin)

vices for lesbians; and state courts such as California Superior Court had even begun to grant lesbian petitions to adopt a child.

Lesbians have been active in both the gay rights and women's liberation movements, but they have sometimes found themselves in uncomfortable positions in both: They have encountered sexism from gay males and faced uneasiness, even HOMOPHOBIA, in the women's movement. The women's movement (in particular, the NATIONAL ORGANIZATION FOR WOMEN, or NOW) has at times been divided along the lines of sexual orientation, with debate over whether to expend energies and finances to advance lesbian causes. Beginning in the mid-1970's, NOW voted to use a small percentage of its funds to work for lesbian rights.

In the gay community's fight to promote awareness of, and urge funding for, the ACQUIRED IMMUNE DEFICIENCY SYNDROME (AIDS) epidemic, lesbians often felt that they were being excluded, both from research and from the gay community's support networks. Therefore, the Women's Caucus of the Aids Coalition to Unleash Power (ACT-UP) was formed to help women with AIDS gain access to clinical trials and new treatments. (Lesbians had been at first mistakenly viewed by the medical establishment as a low-risk or no-risk population.)

Lesbians are often assumed to be overwhelmingly white and middle class, but this is a misconception. Studies of lesbians frequently ignore issues of race and class, and the lesbian who is African American, Latina, Asian American, or Jewish American suffers from a powerful double bias. Black and Latina lesbians, for example, are more often physically assaulted than white lesbians. Researchers hypothesize that this is because women in these groups are at a greater risk of experiencing violence than are white women. The voice of the lesbian woman of color is more frequently being heard, as in the works of artists such as black poet Audre Lorde.

SUGGESTED READINGS. For a view of cultural diversity among lesbians, see *For Lesbians Only: A Separatist Anthology (1988), edited by Sarah Lucia-Hoagland and Julia Penelope. Other useful reference works are Gay/ Lesbian Almanac: A New Documentary (1983), edited by*

Jonathan Ned Katz; *Lesbian (Out)Law: Survival Under the Rule of Law* (1992) by Ruthann Robson; *The Well of Loneliness* (1928), the seminal and controversial novel of lesbian love by Radclyffe Hall; *Woman Plus Woman* (1989) by Dolores Klaich; and *Odd Girls and Twilight Lovers: A History of Lesbian Life in Twentieth-Century America* (1991) by Lillian Faderman.

Letras de Oro: Spanish-language literary contest for writers living in the United States initiated by the University of Miami in 1986. The contest is open to all SPANISH-LANGUAGE writers in five fields: the novel, poetry, theater, essay, and short story. The contest has attracted work of notable quality from a large number of writers, most of whom live in Florida, New Jersey, Texas, New York, California, Illinois, and Puerto Rico. Many of the writers were born in Cuba, Colombia, Puerto Rico, Argentina, Mexico, Spain, Chile, or Peru.

Liberals: People who believe that government (whether through legislation or court decisions) should take an active role in effecting social change and in improving the well-being of its citizens. This concept of "liberalism" stems from the years of the NEW DEAL programs engineered by the administration of President Franklin D. Roosevelt. Although there are liberal Republicans, in the political arena the term is most often identified with the Democratic Party.

Both Roosevelt and his successor, Harry S. Truman, were Democrats, and the combined twenty years of their administrations (1933-1953) represent the first major thrust of liberalism. When Roosevelt took office, the United States was in the grip of the GREAT DEPRESSION. Roosevelt created myriad work programs, using federal money, to give people jobs and bring a new feeling of hope to a dispirited nation. He also instituted SOCIAL SECURITY and federal bank deposit insurance, both of which have remained in place as widely approved programs.

In the 1960's, the administrations of Democrats John F. Kennedy and Lyndon Johnson carried liberalism into a new era. Liberals in the 1960's were in the forefront of civil rights activism, urging legislation and court action to gain equal rights for African Americans. Johnson, in particular, with his "WAR ON POVERTY" and "Great Society" programs, expanded the New Deal social programs to offer greater government assistance to poor people, older citizens, and African Americans. The strength of the liberals' posi-

tion was dramatically damaged in the second half of the 1960's, however, both by the divisive VIETNAM WAR and by the urban riots and disturbances of those years.

Support for an all-encompassing New Deal liberalism began to erode. Dissatisfaction with paying taxes to support social programs, a perception that crime was escalating to unprecedented levels, and a feeling that the federal government itself was out of control led voters to elect politicians with less liberal agendas. The "Reagan Revolution" of the 1980's was seen as a repudiation of traditional liberalism. Yet millions of Americans maintained, and do maintain, liberal beliefs that government can act powerfully and effectively to create change and redress wrongs done to minorities and underprivileged Americans. The election of President Bill Clinton in 1992 (over moderately conservative Republican George Bush) signified that liberalism was still a present and evolving force.

Liberals, whose numbers include people from all races and ethnic groups, have been among the most prominent and vocal supporters of MULTICULTURALISM. Evidence of their contributions can be drawn from the nation's egalitarian upsurge during the 1960's and 1970's. Liberals and liberal influences were evident in struggles to affirm or extend civil rights; in battles for women's rights and gender equality; in redressing injustices among American Indians and Chicanos; in liberalizing immigration legislation; in unblocking professional and corporate bottlenecks for women and minorities; in reassessing the nation's educational establishments; in reapportioning voting power; in redefining the rights of children and older Americans; in attacking poverty; and in enhancing workers' job security.

SUGGESTED READINGS. The work of liberals from the 1960's to the early 1990's is the subject of many substantive, readable books. Allen J. Matusow's *The Unraveling of America* (1984) critically surveys liberal activism in the 1960's. Archibald Cox's *The Role of the Supreme Court in American Government* (1976) cogently addresses the transformation of civil rights by a liberal Supreme Court. Richard Polenberg's *One Nation Divisible* (1980) treats multicultural issues of race, class, and ethnicity from 1930 to 1980. Other works focused on liberalism include David P. Barish's *The L Word: An Unapologetic, Thoroughly Biased, Long Overdue Explication and Celebration of Liberalism* (1992) and Ronald Beiner's *What's the Matter with Liberalism?* (1992).

Librarians: Professionals working in libraries who communicate knowledge, assist patrons with research, make administrative decisions, set up educational programs, and perform many other varied tasks. Though American libraries were once considered elitist institutions reserved for the upper or educated classes, in the twentieth century they have become increasingly accessible to the diverse American population. Modern librarians have been the prime movers in this change. Far from the stereotyped image of the stern, disapproving guardian of information, they play a positive role in contemporary society, leading people to the knowledge that can empower them. This includes encouraging greater multicultural awareness.

Women and Minorities. Librarianship as a profession dates back to the Sumerian civilization that flourished around 3500 B.C.E. Once a field dominated by priests and scholars, career librarianship has changed in the modern era with the general acceptance of public education. This brought more women into the male-dominated field.

In 1887, the first American library school opened at Columbia University to provide formal training and establish professional standards. The school's founder, Melvil Dewey, made an appeal to college-educated women to become librarians. The reasons for this had little to do with promoting equal opportunity. Rather, in an area where materials were expensive and hard to obtain, budget was a major concern; women were asked to work in this field because they could be hired more cheaply than men. Whereas men were encouraged to apply for librarian jobs for financial reasons, women were called upon to apply for this noble position on the basis of morality and public service.

Some of the areas where women may experience discrimination in the profession are in salary, title, and position. As is the case in many other fields, women are paid less than men for the same position. In a profession dominated by women, the normal salary is much less than for other professions that require the same or less skill. Efforts to attract men to the profession are expected to raise the base salaries of the professionals in this field in general.

Women's superior position in numbers in the field does not imply equal opportunity for advancement. Women are only the majority of librarians in the lower-level positions. They are not equally represented in the higher, executive level positions. In fact, the higher the position and the larger the library, the lower the number of women who are visible in executive

This librarian gives children a friendly welcome to the world of information. Librarians are typically women, including increasing numbers of ethnic minorities. (Jeff Greenberg, Unicorn Stock Photos)

positions. Furthermore, until the 1960's there was no law prohibiting discrimination by gender in job advertisements, and women were mainly encouraged to apply as librarian's assistants rather than for top-level positions.

Minorities share this disproportionate representation in libraries, but for other reasons. Minorities are underrepresented in the profession partly because they are underrepresented both in undergraduate programs and in librarianship graduate programs, and thus lack a basic requirement for the job. With low visibility in the profession, there are few role models for children of color, and hence less motivation for students to seek that career.

Some libraries have pursued AFFIRMATIVE ACTION programs since the 1970's to recruit and hire more minority librarians. A number of librarian organizations share related goals. The Black Caucus of the American Library Association, for example, promotes the profession and better conditions in the profession for African Americans; Reforma (National Association to Promote Library Services to the Spanish Speaking) awards a library science scholarship to a student interested in a SPANISH-LANGUAGE library career. The American Indian Library Association helps tribes set up their own libraries or archives, while the Asian/Pacific American Librarians Association seeks to improve library service to Asian/Pacific communities. Numerous multicultural library organizations, such as the Association of Jewish Libraries, give out annual awards for fine books or distinguished service in their area of interest.

Education. The American Library Association

school. In addition, some academic librarians have Ph.D's or a second M.A. in the field of their academic specialty.

Certain classes such as cataloging and bibliography are mandatory for all library students. Other courses depend on the type of library in which the individual would like to work. There are three main types of libraries: public, academic (from high school to university level), and special (such as those at corporations, hospitals, and nonprofit organizations). Whether one would like to work as a reference librarian, cataloger, archivist, bibliographer, rare books librarian, or systems librarian also determines what course one's education will take.

Public libraries offer vital community services to people of all ages and backgrounds. Here students sign a petition to keep their library open. (Richard B. Levine)

(ALA), a national support organization for librarians, sets standards and accredits schools that offer degrees in library science or library information science. In order to be a professional librarian, a person must generally obtain a B.A. and then an M.A. in library science or information science from an ALA-accredited

Expertise. Librarians play an essential role in the selection of books a library acquires. The selection is based on the needs of the library's users and the specific mission of each individual library. Librarians evaluate the incoming materials for their appropriateness and effectiveness within their particular setting and budget constraints. Knowledge about publishing companies, ordering processes, how to contact less well-known companies for rare sources, and how to obtain gifts or exchanges within the network are crucial to this process. Librarians are also concerned with the materials they do not select; they must be certain that there is no form of censorship or bias in practice. In the 1980's and 1990's, this meant bringing a keen multicultural awareness to book selection to ensure that a diverse range of cultures and viewpoints were represented.

Librarians at public libraries establish many programs to serve the community. These may include providing BRAILLE and talking books; reading to children in story hours and as summer programs; sponsoring child care and hospital programs; teaching adult literacy; and setting up lecture series or discussion groups.

One of the jobs of a specialist librarian is to assist in research. Librarians must not only be familiar with their own area of expertise but also know how to connect that area with other disciplines and assist in research methods outside their specialty. Keeping up-to-date involves both familiarity with new library technology and being aware of major contributions and breakthroughs as well as trends in their area.

A librarian's knowledge is not confined, however, to what lies in the actual physical library. She or he must also be aware of the surrounding cultural, social, and economic environment that affects the library and its patrons. An academic library on a university campus in a small college town requires an emphasis in different areas than a large public library in a major metropolitan area or a medical library with exclusive users.

Library users, especially at large public libraries, come from divergent cultural backgrounds and education levels, requiring assistance in a multitude of subject areas. To communicate clearly and effectively with such a broad clientele requires highly efficient communication skills that can cross cultural, racial, or social boundaries. It also requires awareness of the particular needs of multicultural populations.

Multicultural Awareness. Librarians have responded in various ways to the concerns of the CIVIL RIGHTS MOVEMENT, the drive toward ETHNIC STUDIES and multicultural education, the ETHNIC HERITAGE REVIVAL, and other minority rights and liberation movements since the 1960's. They have aimed for greater inclusiveness in their collections to reflect the history, culture, and political causes of groups that were hith-

erto ignored or poorly represented. They have then tried to use these collections to attract underserved minority populations to the library through, for example, exhibits on Hispanic Heritage Week or a series of readings by African American women authors. Some library systems such as that of Los Angeles County set up entire branches specializing in African American, Latino, Asian American, and American Indian subjects. Public libraries, like other public buildings, have increasingly strived to make their facilities accessible to those with disabilities and to provide more materials in braille or talking book (audio tape) format. In areas with large concentrations of new immigrants, many have boosted their collections of books in the relevant foreign languages. The literacy movement of the late 1900's also inspired some libraries to sponsor adult literacy training and to offer books written in a simplified form of English for patrons with little education. All of this makes for more diverse library patrons as well as materials.

The goal of a library is to make available to all persons—regardless of their origin or background—any information that is accessible to that library. A library concerned with MULTICULTURALISM seeks to incorporate complete cultural diversity. There are certain steps librarians can take to ensure that the proper attention is paid to everyone who would possibly use the library. Collections should represent not only the dominant culture but a pluralistic view. This involves selecting materials in different languages, looking for sources in marginal publishing areas, working together with other libraries, and most especially treating each user as if she or he has a right to be in the library. Making the library more accessible to the community may lessen the alienation some individuals feel in regard to using a library or asking librarians for assistance.

SUGGESTED READINGS. A guide to the profession and related issues is *The Whole Library Handbook* (1991), compiled by George Eberhart. For more information on education and the history of librarianship, see Jesse H. Shera's *The Foundations of Education Librarianship* (1972) and Jean Key Gates's *Introduction to Librarianship* (1976). A good introduction to the literature on librarians and multiculturalism is Roberto G. Trujillo and David C. Weber's "Academic Library Responses to Cultural Diversity: A Position Paper for the 1990's" in *Journal of Academic Librarianship* 17 (July, 1991), p. 157. *Women in Librarianship* (1975), edited by Margaret Myers and Mayra Scarborough, explores the issue of women's role in libraries. Another useful source is *Opportunities for Minorities in Librarianship* (1977), edited by E. J. Josey and Kenneth E. Peeples, Jr.—*Diane L. Hendrix*

Limón, José Arcadio (Jan. 12, 1908, Culiacán, Mexico—Dec. 2, 1972, Flemington, N.J.): Mexican American choreographer and folklorist. Limón came to the United States in 1915 and studied painting at the University of California at Los Angeles before going to New York in 1927 to study dance with Doris Humphrey, Charles Weidman, and Martha Graham. He choreographed his first piece, *Bacchanale*, in 1930. Early notable works include *Danzas Mexicanas* (1939) and the solo *Chaconne* (1942). In 1945, Limón established his own company in New York, generating a long list of works including some based on Mexican legends. His company toured Europe and South America several times in the 1950's and 1960's and worked closely with the Academy of Dance in Mexico City. Since his death in 1972, the Limón Dance Company has continued his work.

Lincoln County War (1876-1878): Struggle in Lincoln County, New Mexico, between rival groups of ranchers and businessmen. Lawrence Murphy, head of the Santa Fe Ring (a group of Anglo ranchers and businessmen) was pitted against John Chisum. Their bitter rivalry escalated into clashes between Anglo cattle ranchers and Mexican sheepherders as well as between professional gunmen hired by both sides. The bloody, lawless struggle therefore involved a complex interweaving of economic factors and racial enmity. Mexican farmers in the area were caught in the middle. Local leader Juan Patrón and most other Mexicans sided with Chisum. The violent "war" finally ended when the new governor of the New Mexico Territory, General Lew Wallace, formed a militia led by Patrón to keep the peace and offered amnesty to those who would stop fighting.

Ling Sing v. Washburn (1862): Important California State Supreme Court decision of 1862 establishing that Chinese immigration into California could not be unduly restricted. The Chinese and other Asians faced a series of restrictive laws passed by California legislators in the wake of the state's GOLD RUSH immigration boom. Many whites complained that the Chinese were too numerous and charged that the immigrants came to California to make their fortunes but had no interest in remaining or in being acculturated. In short, the argument was that the Chinese insulated themselves from the other residents of California. The California Assembly, bowing to public pressure, enacted laws to limit the number of Chinese immigrants and to encourage the Chinese already residing in California to leave.

In May, 1852, the legislature passed a bill requiring the licensing of all nonwhite miners. Chinese reaction to the special three-dollar fee was muted because they did not want a confrontation. The next session of the assembly saw several other laws proposed that would more drastically tax Chinese, or even exclude them from the mines altogether. Faced with these new threats, the Chinese community came together to protest the blatant discrimination.

During the next few years there were further attempts by the assembly to enact heavy taxes on Chinese citizens already in California, along with measures to cut off any other immigration. In addition, there was increasing ANTI-CHINESE VIOLENCE with little attempt by police officers to apprehend the culprits. To make things worse, Chinese were barred by statute from giving testimony in a court of law. Matters came to a head in 1862 as the assembly passed the Chinese Police Tax, which levied a per capita fee of $2.50 a month on all Chinese citizens over the age of eighteen who had not already paid the mining tax or were not engaged in the production of rice, sugar, tea, or coffee. This tax also made additional Chinese immigration into California difficult because it taxed new immigrants prohibitively.

A test case involving a Chinese man named Ling Sing (sometimes written Lin Sing) was brought only two months after the Chinese Police Tax went into effect in April, 1862. Under threat of property seizure, Ling Sing paid the tax, but he also brought suit in a case that reached the California State Supreme Court later that year. The court ruled that the Chinese Police Tax was contrary to the U.S. CONSTITUTION because it attempted to control commerce—new immigrants—from a foreign nation; as the justices pointed out, only the federal government could enact legislation governing foreign commerce and importation. More important, the case represented the first time a Chinese resident of the United States had tried to use the Constitution to overturn a state law. Over the course of the next three decades, the Chinese of California used their new weapon—the courts—to contest and overturn virtually every law or tax that discriminated against them.

SUGGESTED READINGS. More information about the

Chinese fight for equality in California can be found in Corinne Hoexter's *From Canton to California* (1976) and Ronald Takaki's *Strangers from a Different Shore: A History of Asian Americans* (1989).

Literacy testing: Formerly used by both the federal and state governments to determine qualifications for voting. During the nineteenth and early twentieth centuries, it was a popular instrument for denying immigrants the right to vote. Many southern states also adopted literacy testing to obstruct blacks from voting. The VOTING RIGHTS ACT OF 1965 removed literacy testing as a requirement in all states where less than 50 percent of the voting age population had been registered to vote in the 1964 presidential election and authorized inspections by federal authorities. The act was extended in 1970, 1975, and again in 1982.

Lithuanian Americans: Lithuanian Americans are a proud people who have worked hard to preserve their culture in the United States while maintaining strong ties with their homeland. The Baltic state of Lithuania is a country of 34,000 square miles, a little larger than Maine (with a similar climate), that is struggling to maintain its independence.

History. At its height in the medieval period, the Lithuanian Commonwealth flourished under grand dukes and dominated eastern Europe, stretching from

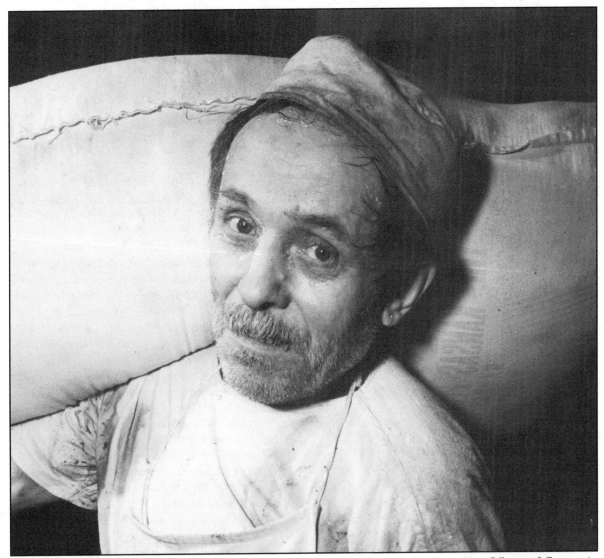

Lithuanian immigrants such as this baker have opened their own small businesses in American cities. (Library of Congress)

Lithuanians celebrate their newly won independence outside the Lithuanian Parliment in 1991. Many Lithuanian Americans actively supported the independence movement in their homeland. (AP/Wide World Photos)

the Baltic Sea to the Black Sea. Lithuania and Poland united as a single nation in 1569, and the Gediminas dynasty ended in 1572. Oppression and wars ravaged the Lithuanian/Polish Commonwealth while the Russian czars conquered and ruled. A declaration of independence was proclaimed on February 16, 1918, after more than a century of czarist rule. Vilnius, the capital, was a political and cultural center not just for Lithuania but also for all northeastern Europe.

In 1939, however, the Ribbentrop-Molotov pact between the Soviet Union and Nazi Germany assigned the three Baltic states of Latvia, Estonia, and Lithuania to the Soviet Union. The Soviet Army occupied the Baltics in June, 1940, and an estimated 600,000 Lithuanians were deported or executed under Stalin. Lithuania then disappeared from European maps for fifty years. Quiet underground resistance continued and eventually erupted on March 11, 1990, with the restoration of Lithuanian independence. Vytautas Landsbergis was elected president. On September 17, 1991, the U.N. General Assembly accepted Lithuania,

Latvia, and Estonia as members of the United Nations. Diplomatic relations within the United States had never actually ceased but were officially reactivated. Lithuanians had experienced the rule of the Gediminas, invasions, captivity, totalitarianism, and democracy.

The Lithuanian language is part of the Baltic family of Indo-European languages. The written form of the language has existed since the sixteenth century translations of the Lord's Prayer and Ave Maria. The most common Lithuanian name is Kazlauskas, which means "billy goat," considered by some as embodying a national trait of stubbornness. There is Slavic influence in many names, since the official language of the Grand Duchy of Lithuania until 1795 was Slavic. Also, under czarist rule, institutions of higher education were only open to Slavs so many Lithuanians changed their names. Prohibition of reading, writing, or publishing anything in the Latin alphabet from 1864 to 1904 created heroes and martyrs in Lithuania. Book carriers, clandestine village schools, and underground newspaper publishers in Prussia all assumed the risk of death, deportation, or imprisonment in Siberia.

Immigration. In 1908, 1,500,000 immigrants from Europe passed through ELLIS ISLAND. The first Lithuanian immigrants were mostly peasants, unlike the educated professionals known as displaced persons (DP's) who came after World War II. The early immigrants were recruited in New York's port of entry to work on the country's railroads; in the coal mines of Pennsylvania, especially in the Shenandoah area; and in the stockyards of Chicago and other major cities where work could be found for people who did not yet know the English language. Happy to escape from Soviet rule, the immigrants sacrificed ordinary luxuries, diligently saved what money they made, and began small businesses of their own such as restaurants, barber shops, saloons, and other services. Social, charitable, religious, and cultural organizations were established as the immigrants became more familiar with the choices, diversity, and opportunities of the United States. For example, Eli Broad, cofounder of Los Angeles-based Kaufman and Broad Home Corporation, was the major donor for the newly named Broad College of Business and Graduate School of Management at Michigan State University.

Today, major centers of the Lithuanian American population are Chicago (with 250,000 Lithuanians); Los Angeles; Philadelphia; Shenandoah, Pennsylvania; Cleveland, Ohio; Paterson, New Jersey; and New York City. The Lake Michigan shorelines in Illinois and Indiana strongly resemble the Baltic Sea and Neringa peninsula of sandy dune beaches and birch tree forests, explaining why many Lithuanian Americans migrated to this region.

Draugas ("The Friend"), a newspaper first published in 1909, continues to serve as a prime communicator for Lithuanian Americans. The Museum of Lithuanian Culture on Chicago's South Side, founded in 1966, has become a model ethnic institution whose aim is to increase ethnic heritage awareness and pride. Its founder, Stanley Balzekas, is an inveterate collector and historian as well as a businessman. Through exhibits, archives, and resources on topics from immigration and genealogy to language and folk art, the museum offers a view of American life from an ethnic perspective.

Several important Lithuanian Americans are educators. Aldona Walker, assistant dean and professor at Loyola University in Chicago, has been a link in helping Lithuania make a transition to post-Soviet educational, social, and health care systems. G. Y. Dryansky,

European editor for *Conde Naste Traveler,* whose great-grandfathers experienced czarist rule, celebrates his ethnic heritage through his writings. A Center for Lithuanian Social Work was established through the efforts of Robert Constable of Loyola and Regina Kulys of the University of Illinois. Algirdas Avizienis, a computer specialist for nuclear missiles at the California Institute of Technology and for National Aeronautics and Space Administration (NASA) interplanetary spacecraft, returned to Lithuania to re-establish Vytautas Magnus University, based on the University of California structure and curriculum.

Leonidas Ragas and Romuladas Povilaitis grew up in Kaunas, Lithuania, immigrated to the United States and became prominent in their field of dentistry. They have established the American Dental Association for

LITHUANIA

Assistance to Lithuania to upgrade dental care in their homeland. Rimgaudas Menickas, chief cardiologist at Illinois Masonic Medical Center, initiated a health care educational exchange between American and Lithuanian universities. George Wiltrakis was chief surgeon of all U.S. military hospitals in Australia and New Guinea during World War II and elected surgeon general of American Veterans of Foreign Wars. Rear Admiral F. E. Bakutis, naval aviator ace, took part in the Apollo missions and was responsible for recovery of the astronauts in the South Pacific for Apollo 10. Alexander Bialaski was first director of the Federal Bureau of Investigation from 1912-1919.

Lithuanian American political activities began in Wilkes-Barre, Pennsylvania, the site of the first American Lithuanian Catholic Congress in 1906. The congress organized Lithuanian Day, a combined political/social event in which participants were entertained by the first Lithuanian Band sponsored by the

St. Joseph Temperance Society. Immigrants held strong loyalties to their friends and family left in Eastern Europe and made every effort to assist them through rallies, fund-raisers, and political activism in attempts to heal the scars of oppression and bring about freedom for their homeland. One of the candidates in the first popular presidential election held in the newly independent Lithuania was Stasys Lozoraitis, who spent fifty years in exile in the United States and in 1991 became ambassador to the United States. Jurist Nadas Rastenis, a member of Maryland's House of Delegates, was nominated for the Nobel Peace Prize and membership in the U.S. Poets Laureate International. Susanne Puisys Shallna was the first Lithuanian American woman attorney and an active representative of the U.S. Federation of Business and Professional Women at the United Nations.

Religion. Lithuania was one of the last European nations to accept Christianity. Lithuanians are mostly Roman Catholic but also include people of the Eastern Orthodox, Protestant, and Jewish faiths. Many young Lithuanians have entered U.S. seminaries to become priests, missionaries, and bishops. Archbishop John Marcinkas, for example, has been special secretary to Pope John Paul II for many years. Often, Lithuanian Americans sustain social, cultural, and community ties through their religious parishes and schools. In Chicago's South Side, several neighborhood elementary schools feed into a highly regarded and thriving high school for young women, St. Casimir-Maria Academy, founded by the Sisters of St. Casimir.

Arts and Sports. Lithuanian culture is rich in folk arts that are passed down informally from generation to generation. Textile weaving, wood and straw holiday ornaments and wax resist-decorated EASTER eggs are typical crafts that Lithuanian Americans preserve at holiday time. One of Lithuania's proudest traditions is the folk song or *liaudies daina*, which often expresses deep love for the homeland. The music was sung by individuals or small groups for many years since organized Lithuanian cultural activities were forbidden. When independence was achieved, many choirs and a national song festival began. Immigrants carried this love of song and dance to the United States with a Lithuanian song festival held in Chicago in 1916. Antanas Pocius helped organize choruses of more than five hundred singers.

Individual Lithuanian Americans made their mark on the American arts. Anna Kaskas joined the Metropolitan Opera as mezzo-soprano. Joanne Akalaitis was director for the prestigious Goodman Theater and New York Shakespeare Festival. David Brenner (Baranauskas), medalist and sculptor, designed the Lincoln penny, seal of the New York City Library, and plaques of Amerigo Vespucci and John Paul Jones. The town of Roslyn, Washington, founded more than a hundred years ago by Lithuanian pioneers, served as the town of Cicely, Alaska, in the television series *Northern Exposure*. Ann Jillian, Ruta Lee-Kalmonyte, Ruth Roman, and Charles Bronson are Lithuanian Americans prominent in Hollywood productions.

Konnie Savickus, Frank Talzunas, Ed (Moose) Krause and other Lithuanian Americans helped their homeland win the 1937 and 1939 European BASKETBALL championships in the Olympics. Frank Lubin of Glendale, California is considered the godfather of Lithuanian basketball, having first taught the sport in 1922. Other sports figures of Lithuanian heritage are Billy Burke, golf pro and winner of the U.S. Open Championship in 1930; Dick Butkus, a Chicago Bears FOOTBALL linebacker inducted in the Pro Football Hall of Fame; Al Kaline, a baseball Hall of Fame member who played for the Detroit Tigers; Jack Sharkey, world heavyweight boxing champion; Johnny Unitas, voted most valuable player and National Football League all-star player; and Johnny Podres of the Brooklyn Dodgers, BASEBALL hero of the 1955 World Series.

Food Customs. The ritual of breaking and sharing wafers of holy bread starts the Christmas Eve (Kucios) meal consisting of twelve nonmeat dishes that represent the twelve apostles of Christ. Marinated herring (*silke*), smelt, rye bread, cheeses, sauerkraut and beet soups, potato pudding (*kugelis*), dumplings (*cepelinai*), mushroom-stuffed buns, and poppyseed milk are all traditional dishes that take extensive preparation. Sweets of fried pastries (*gruzdai*) and coffee cakes are served only after midnight Mass. At weddings, the newly married couple is customarily served *kirupnikas*, a potent honey liqueur of amber color symbolizing fertility and good health, as well as rye bread with a touch of salt for prosperity and for satisfaction flavored with the reality of sorrow.

SUGGESTED READINGS. For additional information on Lithuanian history and culture, see *Timeless Lithuania* by O. J. C. Norem and *The Formation of the Baltic States* (1959) by Stanley W. Page. For background on the experiences and traditions of Lithuanian Americans, see David Fainhauz's *Lithuanians in the USA: Aspects of Ethnic Identity* (1991) and Victor R. Greene's *For God and Country: The Rise of Polish*

General Custer was defeated by Sioux, Cheyenne, and Arapaho Indians at the Battle of the Little Bighorn. (Library of Congress)

and Lithuanian Ethnic Consciousness in America, 1860-1910 (1978). Information specifically on Lithuanian Americans can be found in *Genealogija*, The Lithuanian American Immigration History and Genealogy Newsletter, and *The Observer*, both published in Chicago.—*Marilyn Dargis Ambrose*

Little Bighorn, Battle of the (June 25, 1876): Crucial battle between the attacking United States Seventh Cavalry and a large camp of SIOUX and some ARAPAHO and CHEYENNE Indians protecting their lands. News of the deaths of 270 soldiers under General George Armstrong CUSTER's command stunned the nation, and an outraged

American public demanded government action.

The Sioux, the largest tribe on the Plains, had been guaranteed reservation lands in an 1868 treaty. The reservation covered all of present-day South Dakota west of the Missouri River including the sacred Black Hills, with rights to live and hunt in lands further west until the buffalo were gone. As increasing numbers of white settlers passed through Sioux lands, white soldiers moved in to protect them. The Sioux protested the incursions into their lands, sometimes through armed conflict.

Tension escalated after an illegal government expedition ignored Sioux treaty rights and discovered gold in the Black Hills in 1874. Gold sinkers were not kept out of the Black Hills, in direct violation of the 1868 treaty. When the Sioux protested the flood of miners into their lands, the U.S. government response was to send a commission in 1875 to negotiate relinquishment of the Black Hills. The Black Hills are sacred to the Sioux, who refused to sell or give them the area. As a way to halt escalating violence against the miners, a government ultimatum ordered all Indians to report to the Great Sioux Reservation by early 1876. Many Sioux under SITTING BULL, CRAZY HORSE, and other leaders asserted their rights under the 1868 treaty to hunt outside the bounds of the reservation, but U.S. troops began to round up off-reservation Indians in the spring of 1876.

In June, 1876, large numbers of Sioux along with Cheyennes and Arapahos were gathered in summer camps in western Montana to hunt buffalo and conduct a sun dance, as was customary. Soon after the sun dance the people moved their camp along the Big-horn River and prepared to hunt. Meanwhile the army launched a three-pronged invasion of the Indians' country.

In a series of actions which remain controversial and puzzling, Custer ordered an attack on the Indian village. The Indians responded in defense of their families, and within about thirty minutes Custer and his troops were annihilated. Though the Indians were victorious, their victory set in motion an unyielding government policy that ultimately affected all Plains Indians. Soldiers poured into the Plains, hunted the "hostiles" down, and forced them onto the reservation or killed them. The Black Hills were illegally seized from the Sioux in an 1877 agreement. By the fall of 1877 Crazy Horse was dead, Sitting Bull was in exile in Canada, and the northern Plains tribes were confined to their reservation.

The Battle of the Little Bighorn marked a turning point in Plains Indian history and an end to traditional ways of life. Thereafter Indians' lives would be defined by federal Indian agents and unrelenting government policies that attempted to assimilate Indians into the dominant society.

SUGGESTED READINGS. Dee Brown's *Bury My Heart at Wounded Knee* (1970) provides a good historical background on events leading to the battle. *Black Elk Speaks* (1932) by John Neihardt and *Warpath* (1934) by Stanley Vestal are poignant accounts of Sioux life before and after this battle. W. A. Graham's *The Custer Myth* (1953) is an interesting compendium of military sources.

Little Havana: Cuban section of MIAMI, FLORIDA. Many factors merged to make Little Havana the most important Cuban community in the United States. Cubans had begun to settle the area in the late nineteenth century long before the Castro revolution of 1959. Early immigrants were few in number, but formed a nucleus community within the neighborhood. By the 1950's, property values and retail trade had begun to decline and those who could moved away.

The area offered important opportunities to Cubans who fled the Castro revolution. Low-cost housing was readily available. Displaced Cuban entrepreneurs saw potential in the vacant and dilapidated commercial buildings. Moreover, the neighborhood was centrally located, close to the social services and employment opportunities of downtown Miami as well as Catholic churches and schools. It was also well served by public transportation.

Once Cuban restaurants, markets, nightclubs, and other businesses had been established, the area developed a flavor and attraction of its own, earning the name "Little Havana." During the 1960's, a substantial percentage of Miami's Cuban population lived in the area. By the end of that decade, Little Havana was among the most densely populated parts of Dade County. It was also the center of the Cuban community in the United States with 14 percent of the Cuban population. By the decade of the 1970's, 35 percent of all Latinos residing in the 16 census tracts that made up the area were Cubans.

The profound impact that the Cuban settlement has had on the cultural milieu of Miami and Dade County is made apparent in Cuban festivals like Carnival Miami and the spirited Calle Ocho Open House in the heart of the neighborhood. The environment has been tailored to meet the needs and tastes of its Cuban residents, while also appealing to tourists with its restaurants and nightclubs. It reflects in both obvious and subtle ways the impact of Cuban culture and shows the extent of the ethnic transformation that has taken place. In the early 1990's, there were many Cuban communities in Dade County, but the heart of Cuban Miami in both outlook and culture remained Little Havana.

SUGGESTED READINGS. Probably the most detailed historical, demographic, and cultural survey of Little Havana can be found in *The Cuban-American Experience: Culture, Images and Perspectives* (1984) by Thomas D. Boswell and James R. Curtis. For other good descriptions, see *Miami Now!: Immigration, Ethnicity, and Social Change* (1991), edited by Guillermo Grenier and Alex Stepick III, and Ivan A. Castro's essay on "Little Havana" in *Miami's Neighborhoods* (1982). David B. Longbrake and Woodrow W. Nichols' *Sunshine and Shadows in Metropolitan Miami* (1976) gives a brief view of the enclave.

Background. In May of 1954, the United States Supreme Court delivered a landmark decision in the case of BROWN V. BOARD OF EDUCATION, declaring that racial segregation in public schools is unconstitutional. The decision was unanimous and forcefully articulated, but it was viewed defiantly in much of the South as an intrusion of the federal government into the southern way of life, and an imposition upon alleged "states' rights." The classrooms of the South would become a key battleground in the CIVIL RIGHTS movement.

In the immediate aftermath of the Court's decision, the school board of Little Rock expressed its wish to avoid integration if legally possible. The reputation of Little Rock was a fairly moderate one by southern standards, however, and its public transportation system was integrated without incident in 1956. During the same year, the University of Arkansas in Little Rock was peacefully integrated as well. When the city's school board selected its largest high school, Central High, for a gradual process of desegregation,

Crowds and media gather as the tension mounts over school desegregation in Little Rock, Ark. (Library of Congress)

Little Rock crisis (1957-1959): Massive, violent resistance to school desegregation by white citizens and public officials in Little Rock, Arkansas in a standoff with federal troops. In the autumn of 1957, the city of Little Rock attracted attention from all over the world when U.S. paratroopers were called in to enforce federal injunctions to integrate Central High School.

few local authorities expected serious obstacles.

Nine African American students, who came to be known as "the Nine," were selected on the basis of academic merit to attend Central High School in the fall of 1957. The NATIONAL ASSOCIATION FOR THE ADVANCEMENT OF COLORED PEOPLE (NAACP) challenged the plan in the courts on the grounds that it

Military personnel escort black students to and from Central High during the Little Rock crisis. (AP/Wide World Photos)

was too gradual and that it failed to meet the "deliberate speed" provision of Supreme Court desegregation decisions, but the school board's gradual plan prevailed.

There were few signs of impending trouble during most of the summer of 1957. But as September approached, segregationists began to organize. Orval E. Faubus, the governor of Arkansas, was considered a moderate, and he had often been supported in elections by the African American community. In response to vocal segregationists, he stated in July that the state was powerless before the federal government and that compliance with integration was inevitable. Faubus was coming to realize, however, that he faced stiff competition in the next election and that he would need the segregationist vote to win. Rather suddenly, he began to assist obstructionist groups.

White Resistance. Segregationists engaged in a flurry of litigation in late summer. A newly formed group called the Mother's League for Central High School filed suit to seek an injunction against Central's integration. Governor Faubus was the only witness to testify at the hearing; he warned of potential violence, describing students forming gangs and planning to arm themselves with revolvers while in school. (The police chief of Little Rock later told reporters that the police had no knowledge of such developments.) Faubus declared that it was the worst possible time for integration of the school, citing local white segregationist sentiment. Judge Murray Reed granted the injunction, which was declared invalid the next day by a federal judge, Ronald Davies. The manipulation of the court system on a local level to impede or postpone integration would become routine tactics in Little Rock during the next two years.

On September 2, the day before Central High School opened, the governor declared a state of emergency, and—again invoking the risk of violence—called in the Arkansas National Guard. He instructed the troops to block off several streets in the vicinity of the school on September 3 and to surround the building armed with bayonets. Faubus dissembled concerning the presence of the guard, telling the federal government that the measure was intended only to prevent potential violence while at the same time ordering the troops to admit only white students. The school board instructed the nine black students to stay away from school for their own safety and filed a petition that the board not be held in contempt of court. Judge Davies denied the petition, ordering the board to put into effect its plan of integration.

On September 4, the nine students attempted to enroll at Central High. Eight of the students—Ernest Green, Minnijean Brown, Jefferson Thomas, Carlotta Walls, Gloria Ray, Thelma Mothershed, Terrance Roberts, and Melba Pattillo—were taken to the school as a group. Flanked by local ministers and by Daisy Bates, the director of the local NAACP, the students approached the line of guardsmen. Shoved and taunted by a mob of segregationists as they approached a side entrance of Central High, the students were turned away from the school by Colonel Marion Johnson of the National Guard, who declared that he was acting by order of Governor Faubus. African Americans who were identified by guardsmen as cafeteria workers were escorted into the building to work as usual.

The family of Elizabeth Eckford, the ninth student, had no telephone; she had not been notified of the plan to form a group in order to organize the approach to the school. She took a public bus to the neighborhood of Central, approaching the building alone. The line of guardsmen drew together, blocking her path. Her appearance attracted the attention of a mob of about two hundred rowdy segregationist demonstrators. The mob pressed in close to the fifteen-year-old girl, taunting, catcalling, and shouting abusive epithets. Eckford walked along the line of guardsmen, seeking an opening, then turned and retreated to the bus stop, closely followed by the heckling mob. She bore the abuse with a dignity that was captured in a photograph and in television footage; both received international publicity.

In the face of the violent opposition, the school board called off its plan and sought a suspension of the federal order to integrate. Governor Faubus appeared on television, declaring that the situation was too dangerous to proceed with the integration plan. He further claimed that the language of *Brown v. Board of Education* called for integration at "all deliberate speed," meaning that communities could determine what speed was appropriate.

On Monday, September 9, six of the nine African American students attempted again to enroll in the school but were pushed away from the entrance by a group of white students. For the next eleven days, the Nine remained at home, awaiting a legal resolution. The NAACP took a strong interest in the case, which was emerging as a crucial showdown for integration. Thurgood MARSHALL, the prominent chief counsel of the NAACP, arrived in Little Rock from New York and filed a federal injunction against interference with the integration of the school. Meanwhile, the Eisenhower Administration announced that it would initiate legal proceedings to force Faubus to cease interference. The governor accepted a summons to an injunction hearing in federal court, scheduled for Friday, September 20.

At the hearing, after being overruled several times by the bench, the governor's attorneys gathered up their papers and withdrew from the courtroom. Judge Davies continued the hearing and later ruled in favor of the injunction prohibiting the governor from interfering with integration. Faubus announced that evening that he had withdrawn national guardsmen in compliance with the court order. This move was widely interpreted as a mere change of tactic; the governor was leaving the city police in charge of a potentially explosive situation.

On the night of September 22, the NAACP's Bates was contacted by the superintendent of the school district, who instructed her to gather the Nine by morning. Since the families of the Nine had all been subjected to harassing telephone calls, they had begun to take their telephones off their hooks at night. Bates visited the homes of each of the families throughout the night, rousing them from sleep and instructing the students to gather at her home in the morning.

Rioting and Mob Rule. On the morning of September 23, three African American journalists, James Hicks, Moses Newman, and Alex Wilson, were walking together down a street leading to the school when they were noticed and pursued by an angry crowd. The journalists fled, but they were chased and beaten until word reached the mob that eight of the Nine had entered the school. A day of terrible, widespread race riots ensued. The mob returned to the police blockade at the periphery of the school, screaming hysterically and shouting racial epithets. The mob applauded dozens of white students who emerged from the building in protest. Some of these students told journalists untrue stories of bloody violence within the building—rumors which spread throughout the city, often by radio. At 11:30 A.M. the Little Rock police chief ordered the Nine removed from the school, and they were led under heavy police escort through a rear exit. For the rest of the day, rioting raged in other parts of Little Rock. Forty-five people were arrested. President Dwight Eisenhower, who had been reluctant to take a high profile on the matter, denounced the "disgraceful occurrences" at Little Rock and issued an executive order directing all persons obstructing justice to cease and desist, and to disperse. Eisenhower also returned to the White House from Rhode Island in order to address the nation and to urge compliance with federal desegregation law.

On September 24, the president federalized all ten thousand Arkansas national guardsmen and ordered one thousand federal troops—a unit of paratroopers—into Little Rock to enforce the law. On September 25, the paratroopers surrounded Central High in full battle gear, dispersing the crowds of racists with bayonets. They detained mob leaders and violent resisters in a detention compound on the school's football field. The paratroopers also escorted the Nine's car to Central High and each of the Nine from class to class. The Nine had succeeded in registering only under the protection of an imposing military presence that seemed appalling in its incongruity.

The Uncomfortable Routine. On September 30, the paratroopers pulled out and the Arkansas National Guard took over Central High. Some of them looked the other way when the African American students were harassed or assaulted. Accounts vary concerning the percentage of white students who responded with hostility to the presence of the nine black students. The Nine were spat upon, pushed to the ground, threatened verbally and in writing, lassoed with ropes tied in nooses, and shoved on staircases. Books were knocked from their arms, firecrackers set off in their vicinity to simulate gunfire, ink spilled on their clothes, and hot soup thrown at them in the cafeteria. When members of the Nine complained of the assaults to administrators, school officials were loathe to provoke outrage in the community by accepting the word

of African Americans over white students.

In January, 1958, Minnijean Brown lost her temper in the face of the incessant harassment. In the school cafeteria, she dumped a bowl of chili onto the head of one of her tormentors. She was suspended, then expelled, and soon afterward some white students distributed cards reading, "One down—eight to go." In May, however, the only senior among the Nine, Ernest Green, became the first African American to be graduated from Central High School. The summer of 1958 saw a repetition of the obstructionist litigation of the previous summer. To prevent further integration, the governor eventually closed all four Little Rock high schools for the entire 1958-1959 school year. The atmosphere of hate intensified, with some of the parents of the nine losing their jobs, or being forced from the state by the harassment. All of the nine African American students eventually attended universities.

SUGGESTED READINGS. Several firsthand accounts of the Little Rock crisis were published during the years immediately following the events. Robert Brown's *Bigger Than Little Rock* (1958) discusses reactions and involvement in the crisis by local churches, while Virgil Blossom's *It Has Happened Here* (1959) narrates the crisis from the point of view of the superintendent of Little Rock schools. *The Long Shadow of Little Rock* (1962) by Daisy Bates, the Arkansas NAACP director, details the trials of the Nine from the intimate perspective of their chief sponsor. Elizabeth Huckaby, vice principal of Central High School during the crisis, tells an interesting version of the story in her 1980 book, *Crisis at Central High.—James Knippling*

Little Tokyos. *See* **Japantowns**

Little Turtle [Michikiniqua] (1752, near Fort Wayne, Ind.—1812, Fort Wayne, Ind.): Miami Indian chief in the Northwest Territory of the United States. He was principal commander in the defeat of General Josiah Harmar on the Miami River (1790) and was known for his oratorical powers and military skill. When General Anthony Wayne defeated his people at Fallen Timbers (1794) near present-day Toledo, Ohio, Chief Little Turtle signed the Treaty of Greenville (1795), which ceded a large portion of Ohio to the United States.

Liu, Henry (Liu Yi-liang; Dec. 7, 1932, Liu Jia Tai, Jiangsu Province, China—Oct. 15, 1984, Daly City, Calif.): Chinese American journalist. In 1950, Liu joined the Guomindang party and fled mainland China to Taiwan. In 1967, he came to the United States and eventually settled in the San Francisco Bay Area, where he wrote books on Chinese politics as well as articles for Chinese language newspapers. Although he became an American citizen in 1975, Liu continued to travel to Taiwan and maintained ties with political organizations there, as well as with the Federal Bureau of Investigation (FBI). A revised edition of his biography of Chiang Ching-kuo, the president of the Republic of China, was published in the United States in 1984. His political connections earned Liu suspicion and enemies, and in 1984 he was shot to death in his own California garage. In November, the Taiwanese government arrested two members of a Taiwan criminal gang who confessed their involvement in Liu's murder and alleged that officials of President Chiang's administration had ordered them to kill Liu. Several years later, American authorities arrested and convicted a third gang member for his involvement in the murder.

Navajos off their land. Tired of skirmishes between Navajos and United States troops, such as that at Fort Fauntleroy in 1861 in which twelve Navajo women and children were killed, and eager to force the Navajos to submit to federal government authority, Brigadier General James H. Carleton, commander of the U.S. Army in New Mexico Territory, launched a military campaign in November, 1863, designed to subdue the Navajos completely. Carleton thought his efforts would change the Navajos' traditional way of life and open their former homeland to mining exploration. His plan was implemented by Colonel Christopher "Kit" CARSON, a legendary explorer then serving in the New Mexico militia.

During 1864, Carson ordered 8,354 Navajos gathered at Fort Defiance and Fort Wingate in the central New Mexico Territory to relocate at Fort Sumner along the Pecos River to the southeast. Thus began the "Long Walk," a march of some 300 miles, during which only children and those with disabilities used wagons. Some twelve hundred Navajos escaped the

American Indians camp in front of the White House to protest government misuse of Indian land in 1978 in the Longest Walk, a reference to the Long Walk more than a century earlier. (Library of Congress)

Long Walk of the Navajos (Nov., 1863—Mar., 1864): Tragic episode in the history of conflicts between NAVAJOS and white settlers which temporarily forced the

Long Walk by hiding in remote canyons in their homeland. The Navajo resettlement at Fort Sumner, New Mexico, was a disaster. According to Carleton's plan, the Navajos were to practice farming for food production rather than their traditional hunting and gathering techniques. Crops failed, Navajo deaths increased, and opposition to Carleton's despotism grew.

A congressional U.S. Indian Peace Commission sent two of its members, Colonel Samuel F. Tappan and General William Tecumseh Sherman, to hold treaty negotiations with Fort Sumner Navajos in late spring, 1868. Led by Barboncito, a Navajo chief, the Navajo delegation pleaded to return to their homeland. This policy was agreed to in a June 1, 1868, treaty establishing a 3.5 million acre reservation for the Navajos in their traditional homeland in present-day northeast Arizona and northwest New Mexico. Soon after, the Navajos jubilantly returned home, agreeing not to raid white settlements. The ordeal of the Long Walk was over.

SUGGESTED READINGS. For further historical background, consult Bertha P. Dutton's *American Indians of the Southwest* (1983), a balanced treatment of the sordid affair. Equally helpful is Peter Iverson's *The Navajos* (1990), which includes photographs of the principals involved. Norman J. Bender in *New Hope for the Indians: The Grant Peace Policy and the Navajos in the 1870's* (1989) very helpfully discusses post-Long Walk efforts by the U.S. Bureau of Indian Affairs to acculturate the Navajos.

Longest Walk: Protest march in 1978 from San Francisco to Washington, D.C. Outraged by the BUREAU OF INDIAN AFFAIRS' attempts to exploit American Indian land, more than two hundred American Indians marched across country, led by Clyde Bellecourt of the AMERICAN INDIAN MOVEMENT (AIM). The name of the protest echoes the famous "LONG WALK" endured by the Navajos and Mescalero Apaches in the 1860's.

López, Nancy (b. Jan. 6, 1957, Torrance, Calif.): Latina golfer. Though born in California, López grew up in southern New Mexico. After studying at the University of Tulsa for two years, López burst onto the professional golf scene in 1978, when she was the first winner at the Bent Tree Classic in Sarasota, Florida. She was named Associated Press Athlete of the Year for 1978 and Ladies Professional Golf Association Player and Rookie of the Year in 1979. She has won more than 130 tournaments, and was inducted into the Halls of Fame of the Ladies Professional Golf Association in 1987 and the Professional Golf Association in 1989. Her memoir, *The Education of a Woman Golfer*, appeared in 1979.

Golfer Nancy López has been winning tournaments and honors since 1978. (AP/Wide World Photos)

Lord, Bette Bao (b. Nov. 3, 1938, Shanghai, China): Chinese American writer. Bette Bao Lord came to the United States in 1946 and became a naturalized citizen in 1964. She studied at Tufts University and the Fletcher School of Law and Diplomacy, and served as director of the University of Hawaii East-West Cultural Center. Her first book, *Eighth Moon: The True Story of a Young Girl's Life in Communist China*, appeared in 1964. Lord studied, taught, and performed modern dance with Martha Graham from 1964-1973 and journeyed to China in 1973. Her second book, *Spring Moon* (1981), a novel about social and political life in modern China, earned an American Book Award and remained on *The New York Times* best-seller list for thirty weeks.

Lord Dunmore's War (1774): Attack by the Virginia militia against the Shawnee Indians of Kentucky in 1774. In the 1770's, Kentucky was a rich and valuable hunting ground, and the Shawnees watched as white trappers, traders, and settlers moved onto their land. Early in 1774, the Virginia militia seized what was then called Fort Pitt and renamed it Fort Dunmore, in honor of their colonial governor, John Murray, the earl of Dunmore. The Shawnees tried defending their homeland, but on October 10, at the Battle of Point Pleasant, they were defeated. This battle has sometimes been called the first battle of the AMERICAN REVOLUTION.

Los Angeles, Calif. (founded Sept. 4, 1781): Located 140 miles north of Mexico, Los Angeles is the second largest city in the United States (after New York). The metropolitan Los Angeles area, spread over 464 square miles, has nearly eight million residents and is the largest metropolitan area in the United States. Its multicultural character was set at its founding by forty-four *pobladores* (founders or settlers) in 1781, who included American Indians, African Americans, mestizos, mulattoes of Spanish heritage, and Anglos.

In the U.S. CENSUS OF 1990, 53 percent of the city's population of 3,485,398 was listed as white ("white" here includes some of the Latino or Hispanic population). About 40 percent was of "Hispanic origin (of any race)"; 14 percent was black; 10 percent was Asian or Pacific Islander; half of 1 percent was American Indian. (The figures add up to more than 100 percent because of the overlapping categories used.)

The city's demography changed rapidly in the 1970's and 1980's as increasing numbers of immigrants and refugees from troubled areas such as Southeast Asia, the Middle East, Central America, and Eastern Europe flocked to the city. They were attracted by its sunny Mediterranean-like climate, strong social welfare programs, and—until the recession of the 1990's—excellent work opportunities.

As a relatively young city that saw little growth until the twentieth century, Los Angles lacks the well-defined ethnic neighborhoods of older cities like New York and Chicago. Exceptions include the BARRIO of EAST LOS ANGELES, which has the largest Mexican population of any city except for Mexico City; the Chinese and Vietnamese cluster in New Chinatown close to downtown; and Koreatown, where much of the Korean population lives or works. The South Central part of the city was predominantly black until more Latinos moved in beginning in the 1980's.

Los Angeles has been called "the new Ellis Island" for its absorption of vast numbers of Asian and Latino immigrants since the 1970's. It is also considered one of the nation's most important laboratories for the study and celebration of cultural diversity. The city is home to the largest American communities of Iranians, Salvadorans, and Vietnamese, to name but a few. Recent immigrants have changed the face of the city, from the fashionable mansions of Iranians in Beverly Hills to the Mexican and Central American swap meets and vending carts in the downtown area. Japanese Americans have led the way for other groups with the establishment of Little Tokyo, a thriving commercial and cultural center.

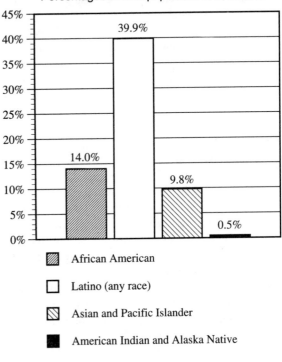

Los Angeles Minority Population: 1990
Percentages of total population of 3,485,000

Legend:
- African American
- Latino (any race)
- Asian and Pacific Islander
- American Indian and Alaska Native

Source: Data are from *Statistical Abstract of the United States, 1992* Table 38. Washington, D.C.: Government Printing Office, 1992.

Tom BRADLEY, the city's first black mayor, took office in 1969 and served until 1993. Despite his influence, and the presence of blacks, Asians, and Latinos on the city council, racial tensions plague Los Angeles and often explode into open conflict. The WATTS RIOTS of 1965 set off a chain reaction of black unrest across the country. The LOS ANGELES RIOTS of 1992, which involved people of all races, were sparked by the acquittal of several Los Angeles police officers tried in the beating of Rodney King, a documented act of police brutality that galvanized the nation. The events of 1992 also seriously strained Korean American-African American relations in the city.

SUGGESTED READINGS. John Anson Ford's *Thirty Explosive Years in Los Angeles County* (1961) foresaw the city's social dislocation, as did Rodney Steiner's

Los Angeles: The Centrifugal City (1981). Robert M. Fogelson's *The Fragmented Metropolis: Los Angeles, 1850-1930* (1967) and Bruce Henstell's *Sunshine and Wealth: Los Angeles in the Twenties and Thirties* (1984) provide interesting studies of how the city grew. Ricardo Romo's *East Los Angeles: History of a Barrio* (1983) is a brilliant scholarly study of Latino Los Angeles. *The City Observed: Los Angeles* (1984) by Charles Moore and others is also an insightful study, while the controversial *City of Quartz: Excavating the Future in Los Angeles* (1990) by Mike Davis covers many multicultural issues.

Los Angeles riots (1992): Nominally caused by the acquittals of four white police officers accused of beating an African American motorist, the riots left more than forty people dead and caused at least $1 billion worth of damage to the city. Although the acquittals certainly triggered the violence, the root cause of the civil unrest was the result of the overwhelming poverty and sense of despair among the underclass of Los Angeles.

On March 3, 1991, Rodney King's car was stopped by police following a high speed chase. He allegedly resisted arrest and was subsequently beaten into submission by officers on the scene. Unlike most disputes between the police and those under arrest, the beating was videotaped by a private citizen. The tape seemed to show that the officers used excessive force in subduing King. Consequently, four members of the Los Angeles Police Department—Sergeant Stacey Koon, Officer Lawrence Powell, Officer Theodore Briseno, and Officer Timothy Wind—were ordered to stand trial for brutality. After more than a year of delays, and after a change of venue to Simi Valley, a predominately white suburb, of Los Angeles, the four were acquitted of all charges in May, 1992. Almost immediately, rioting broke out in predominantly black and Latino South Central Los Angeles, and then spread north into the San Fernando Valley and south to Long Beach. It proved to be the deadliest and costliest civil disturbance in the United States since the WATTS RIOTS of 1965.

Many Angelenos were outraged by the verdicts and referred to the riots as a "rebellion," much as they called the 1965 events the "Watts rebellion." Unlike the earlier disturbances, however, many of the rioters in 1992 (a mix of African Americans, Caucasians, and Latinos) seemed more interested in looting for profit than they did in making a political statement. In some areas, they attacked African American and Latino businesses as quickly as those owned by Asian Americans and European Americans. Particularly hard-hit were Korean American-owned stores in black neighborhoods, traumatizing the immigrant community and bringing AFRICAN AMERICAN–KOREAN AMERICAN RELATIONS to a new low.

Some residents of the region interpreted the disturbances to mean that life on the margins of American society—regardless of one's color—is unacceptable, while others saw the riots as simple lawlessness. In either case, no one had anticipated the rage that erupted, which meant that the city was caught completely off-guard. Despite pleas from Mayor Tom BRADLEY and President George Bush, who promised a federal investigation into the brutality charges, the rioting continued for two days after the verdicts had been announced. Even a statement from Rodney King asking for peace went unheeded. Hundreds of buildings were burned.

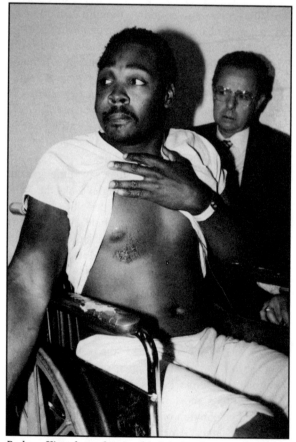

Rodney King, here showing his injuries from a police beating, became the touchstone of the civil disturbances in 1992. (AP/Wide World Photos)

Authorities in Southern California were slow to react to the growing violence; in many sections of Los Angeles there was no LAW ENFORCEMENT at all as people took to the streets to loot and destroy. By the time the police department had mobilized, the situation was out of control. It was not until the police were reinforced by the California Highway Patrol, the National Guard, and federal troops that relative peace returned to Los Angeles.

This mural reflects the national suffering associated with the violent beating of both African American Rodney King and European American Reginald Denny before and during the Los Angeles riots. (Aneal Vohra, Unicorn Stock Photos)

In the weeks following the riots, the city of Los Angeles and the U.S. government announced plans to rebuild the riot-torn areas, as well as programs to help those needing assistance. A year later, however, few businesses in the areas hardest hit had been rebuilt. On April 24, 1993, a federal jury convicted Koon and Powell of depriving King of his civil rights; Briseno and Wind were again acquitted. Although Los Angeles had braced itself for another round of rioting, the streets remained calm.

SUGGESTED READINGS. Two books on the Los Angeles riots are John Salak's *The Los Angeles Riots: America's Cities in Crisis* (1993) and Sue L. Hamilton's *Los Angeles Riots* (1992). Considerable coverage and analysis of the riots can be found in periodicals as in "L.A.'s Broken Dreams," in *Time* (April 19, 1993), p. 26, and Edwin Diamond's "It's Deja Vu All Over Again," in *New York* (June 1, 1992), p. 40.

Los Lobos: Musical group. Los Lobos is a rock and roll, Tex-Mex band consisting of David Hidalgo on guitar and accordion, Conrad Lozano on bass, Luis Perez on drums, and Cesar Rosas providing guitar and vocals. The group developed a strong Los Angeles following in the mid-1970's with their style bridging the gap between traditional Mexican songs and contemporary American music. Their albums include *Just Another Band from L.A.* (1978), *How Will the Wolf Survive?* (1984), and *By the Light of the Moon* (1987). Their 1987 sound track for the film *La Bamba*, and its title track were both number-one hits. In 1988, the group released a collection of traditional Mexican songs in Spanish on the album *La Pistola y El Corazón*. The album *Kiko and the Lavender Moon* appeared in 1992.

Louisiana Purchase: Acquisition of a large tract of territory by the United States from France in 1803. The tract consisted of the western half of the watershed of the Mississippi River and its tributaries. Although the boundaries were not defined in the treaty itself, they ultimately included all or part of thirteen present-day American states from Louisiana north to the Canadian border and from the Mississippi west to the Rocky Mountains. This effectively doubled the size of the young American republic.

Louisiana had belonged to Spain from 1763 to 1800; Napoleon Bonaparte's France acquired it in 1800 in return for Spanish dynastic considerations in Europe. Napoleon envisioned this territory on the continent of North America as part of a French empire in the Caribbean Sea and the Gulf of Mexico. The colony of Santo Domingo (Haiti) on the island of Hispaniola was a key to such an empire; however, it was in the hands of Toussaint L'Ouverture, a former slave who had led a revolt against white rule in 1794. Unable to muster sufficient forces to retake the colony and beset by other power struggles in Europe, Napoleon gave up his West Indian ambitions and offered Louisiana to the United States for about $15 million.

President Thomas Jefferson was taken by surprise by the offer but perceived the possibilities that Louisiana offered for future American expansion.

This 1819 map of the United States shows the new territory west of the Mississippi acquired in the Louisiana Purchase. (Library of Congress)

He recommended the treaty to the Senate, which approved it on October 20, 1803. The next year, Meriwether Lewis and William Clark were sent on an expedition to explore the region. The vague boundaries were further defined in treaties with Great Britain in 1818 and with Spain in 1819.

This addition to the national domain had significant implications for the future of American society, economy, and politics. The southern portion of the purchase, which became the state of Louisiana in 1812, brought elements of Spanish and French culture into the American republic. Some areas of French culture remained into the twentieth century, especially in the "Cajun" region of southern Louisiana. SLAVERY existed in Louisiana at the time of the purchase, and the future of the institution in this region became a recurring issue as its population grew, causing major political controversy in 1820, 1850, and 1854. During much of the period from 1820 to 1846, U.S. public policy regarded the Great Plains area as a permanent home for Indian tribes from both east and west of the Mississippi; after that time, the increased incursion of white Americans into those regions began a policy of restricting American Indians to ever-smaller reservations. Railroad development brought many European immigrants to the northern Plains.

SUGGESTED READINGS. A classic account of the diplomacy of the purchase may be found in Samuel Flagg Bemis' *John Quincy Adams and the Foundations of American Foreign Policy* (1949); a more up-to-date account may be found in Alexander DeConde's *This Affair of Louisiana* (1976). Population development in the region is recounted in Ray Allen Billington and Martin Ridge's *Westward Expansion* (5th ed., 1982). The fate of American Indians can be studied in Francis P. Prucha's *American Indian Policy in the Formative Years* (1962) and in Bernard W. Sheehan's *Seeds of Extinction: Jeffersonian Philanthropy and the American Indian* (1973).

Low riders: Customized cars that have had their springs shortened so that the chassis rides close to the ground. The cars are often equipped with hydraulic lifts that can be controlled by the driver while cruising. A person who drives or rides in such a car is also referred to as a low rider. The term is chiefly used in the southwestern United States and is often identified with young Mexican Americans, who have their own distinctive low rider culture complete with slang, fashions, car designs, and magazines.

Lowell mill girls: New England farm girls who became an important labor source for the early textile mills in Lowell, Massachusetts. The dormitory-style housing of the mill town created a community of workers. In addition to their relatively high wages, the women had other cultural opportunities unavailable in their home towns. Competition forced management to lower wages in the mid-1830's, and the female operatives responded with strikes—an unprecedented collective move by women workers. In 1845, the Lowell Female Labor Reform Association succeeded in stopping a work speedup and lobbied for the ten-hour day. Owners eventually replaced the mill girls with families of Irish immigrants.

Loyalty oaths: Solemn promises to act in the interests of a person or organization. JAPANESE AMERICANS who were confined in internment camps during WORLD WAR II were required to sign loyalty oaths to demonstrate their fitness to be drafted into the U.S. military. Although many Japanese Americans were citizens of the United States, many whites doubted the strength of their loyalty to the United States. GERMAN AMERICANS and ITALIAN AMERICANS, however, were not asked to swear to their loyalty. As a result of anticommunist fervor during the Cold War, federal employees and teachers, among others, were required to sign loyalty oaths affirming that they were not Communists.

Luce, Clare Boothe (Apr. 10, 1903, New York, N.Y.—Oct. 9, 1987, Washington, D.C.): Writer and politician. In 1919 Luce became active in the women's SUFFRAGE MOVEMENT. She was assistant editor for *Vogue* magazine in 1930, then managing editor for *Vanity Fair* in 1931; that same year, she published her first novel, *Stuffed Shirts*. She published her most notable play, *The Women*, in 1937.

Luce re-entered politics in 1940. Luce was the first women elected to Congress from Connecticut, and she served from 1943 to 1947. From 1953 to 1957 she was ambassador to Italy, considered one of the more important governmental appointments for a woman at the time.

Members of a Chicano low riders club near Phoenix, Ariz., in 1980. (AP/Wide World Photos)

Manuel Luján served as a member of Congress for twenty years before becoming secretary of the interior. (U.S. Department of the Interior)

Luján, Manuel, Jr. (b. May 12, 1928, San Ildefonso, N.Mex.): Latino politician. Luján studied at the College of Santa Fe and St. Mary's College in California before going into the insurance business in Santa Fe and Albuquerque. He was elected to the U.S. House of Representatives from New Mexico in 1969, serving twenty years as a member of the Interior and Insular Affairs Committee and Energy and Environmental Subcommittee. From 1989 to 1992, Luján served as U.S. secretary of the interior under President George Bush. Attempting to balance environmental and economic interests, he often encountered controversy on such issues as offshore drilling and endangered species.

Luke, Keye (June 18, 1904, Guangzhou, China— Jan. 12, 1991, Whittier, Calif.): Chinese American actor. Luke was reared in Seattle, Washington, where he was graduated from high school. He began his acting career with Fox West Coast Theaters and RKO Studios. His debut film was *Painted Veil* in 1934. Over the next four decades, Luke appeared in hundreds of films. Luke was best known as the brash Number One Son in the Charlie Chan films of the 1930's, and then as the blind philosophic Master Po on the television series *Kung Fu* from 1972 to 1975. Other notable films include *The Good Earth* (1937), *Love Is a Many-Splendored Thing* (1955), and *The Hawaiians* (1970). Luke was also featured in the Broadway and touring productions of *Flower Drum Song* from 1958 to 1960. He made his final film appearance as an acupuncturist in Woody Allen's *Alice* (1990).

Lutherans: Followers of the theology of Martin Luther (1483-1546), German leader of the Protestant Reformation. Luther was ordained in 1507 and became vicar of the Roman Catholic church in 1515, overseeing more than a dozen monasteries. He then underwent a spiritual crisis, prompted by his own sense of unworthiness and sin. Despite his prominence, he believed that he, like all human beings, was depraved and that a righteous God could only send him to everlasting damnation if He judged Luther by his efforts to promote good in the world.

This spiritual crisis led Luther to formulate the key theological position of Lutheranism: the death of the sinful self and the rebirth of self in Christ. Thus, human beings are justified before God through faith and faith alone. Because of Original Sin, salvation can never be earned through good works; instead, meritorious action by human beings is an effect of "justification"—standing before God as if one had never sinned. Christ's sacrifice makes justification possible. Because a person feels the joy of salvation through faith, he or she performs good deeds spontaneously, a consequence of regeneration through Christ. The Christian is a forgiven sinner acting from the joy of God's forgiveness.

Luther thus attacked the authority of Catholicism, though his open revolt was precipitated by the sale of indulgences in 1517. Appalled by the vulgarity of the sale, Luther posted his Ninety-five Theses on the church's door at the University of Wittenberg, an act that sparked the Protestant Reformation.

For Luther, faith—not indulgences—brought God's forgiveness and salvation. The Church, then, should not dispense indulgence as a disguised effort to win funds, but should instead act as a community of the faithful, who rejoice together in God's grace. Christ has already paid the supreme penalty for human sin in His Crucifixion, Luther argued, and the Church is organized for the purpose of praising Him. The Christian life is thus a life of radical freedom: the free response of the human being to Christ's love. The world is where the Christian enacts this freedom; the world is the means by which people serve one another through Christ.

Luther's view of the Church changed the Christian conception of vocation. For Luther, one vocation is as good as any other. To become a monk and enter a monastery is not necessarily better than any other kind of work, for all work should be a "priesthood" to believers. Even the most lowly laborer carries out God's calling to His creation.

The United States, through the late nineteenth and early twentieth centuries, saw a great immigration of Lutherans. As Sydney E. Ahlstrom writes in *A Religious History of the American People* (1972), "No Protestant communion was so thoroughly transformed by the later nineteenth century immigration as was the Lutheran." Lutheranism spread throughout the eastern seaboard, and in the twentieth century, Scandinavian and German immigrations flooded the Midwest and the Northern Plains.

SUGGESTED READINGS. Sydney E. Ahlstrom's study *A Religious History of the American People* (1972) discusses Lutheranism from the Reformation through its development in America in the twentieth century. For specialized studies of Luther, see B. A. Gerrish's *Grace and Reason: A Study in the Theology of Luther* (1962) and R. H. Fife's *The Revolt of Martin Luther* (1957). For discussions of the Reformation, see R. H. Bainton's *Studies on the Reformation* (1963) and F. H. Harbison's *The Age of the Reformation* (1955).

Lynching: Murder, typically hanging, done at the hands of an angry mob. Lynching of African Americans reached epidemic proportions during the late nineteenth and early twentieth centuries. According to statistics compiled by such civil rights leaders as W. E. B. DU BOIS, at least twenty-five hundred African Americans were lynched from 1884 to 1900 and another eleven hundred from 1900 to 1918. Recent research suggests that actual numbers were significantly higher, because many lynchings were never officially reported; thus, the exact number will never be known. Generally, the problem seemed worse in Mississippi, Alabama, Louisiana, and Georgia, but none of the former slaveholding states escaped the scourge of lynching. On many occasions reformers lobbied for a federal antilynching law, but southern politicians managed to defeat their efforts until language in the CIVIL RIGHTS ACT OF 1964 cited lynching as a violation of a victim's civil rights.

Most lynching victims were African American males, some of whom were rumored to have committed high crimes. Rape of a white woman seemed to be the most serious allegation, other than that of murder of a white person. Many of the victims were in jail (in supposed protective custody) awaiting a trial that never came because a white mob got there first.

Examples of lynching demonstrate the extent to which racism and miscarriages of justice flourished in the South. In 1918 at Shubuta, Mississippi, a white dentist, E. L. Johnston, impregnated two African American women, Maggie Howze, age twenty, and Alma Howze, age sixteen. When a twenty-year-old African American named Major Clark told Johnston that he wanted to marry one of the women, Johnston told Clark to leave "his" women alone. Later Johnston was murdered—apparently either by Clark or by a white man who had earlier accused Johnston of seducing his wife. A white mob gathered and hanged the Howze women, Major Clark, and his fifteen-year-old brother from a bridge spanning the Chickasawha

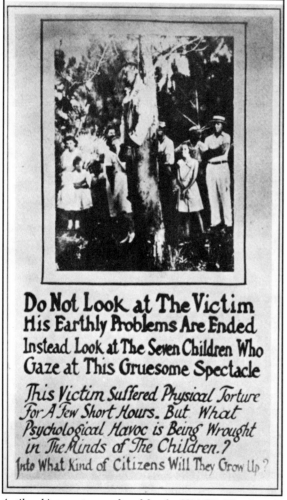

Antilynching poster produced by the NAACP. (The Associated Publishers, Inc.)

	U.S. LYNCHINGS: 1882-1968	
State	African American	Non-black
Alabama	299	48
Arizona	0	31
Arkansas	226	58
California	2	41
Colorado	3	65
Delaware	1	0
Florida	257	25
Georgia	492	39
Idaho	0	20
Illinois	19	15
Indiana	14	33
Iowa	2	17
Kansas	19	35
Kentucky	142	63
Louisiana	335	56
Maine	0	1
Maryland	27	2
Michigan	1	7
Minnesota	4	5
Mississippi	539	42
Missouri	69	53
Montana	2	82
Nebraska	5	52
Nevada	0	6
New Jersey	1	1
New Mexico	3	33
New York	1	1
North Carolina	86	15
North Dakota	3	13
Ohio	16	10
Oklahoma	40	82
Oregon	1	20
Pennsylvania	6	2
South Carolina	156	4
South Dakota	0	27
Tennessee	204	47
Texas	352	141
Utah	2	6
Vermont	0	1
Virginia	83	7
Washington	1	25
West Virginia	28	20
Wisconsin	0	6
Wyoming	5	30
Totals	3,446	1,297

Source: Data are from W. Augustus Low, ed., *Encyclopedia of Black America*, p. 542. New York: McGraw Hill, 1981.

River. Of the four, only Major Clark was suspected of a crime.

Lynching did not end in the early 1900's. For example, in 1947 a young South Carolina African American was lynched after being held in jail on suspicion of the murder of a taxicab driver. After twenty-eight white men publicly admitted that they participated in the lynching, they were tried but found not guilty by an all-white jury. Continuing to occur even into the 1950's, lynching eventually earned the United States condemnation by many international organizations. By the late 1960's, the number of lynchings declined; however, even as the United States approached the twenty-first century, murders and other hate crimes committed by people with racist motives continued to occur.

SUGGESTED READINGS. David Chalmers' *Hooded Americanism: The First Century of the Ku Klux Klan* (1965) gives good coverage of the topic, as do C. Vann Woodward in *Origins of the New South, 1877-1913* (1951), Arthur Raper in *The Tragedy of Lynching* (1933), and Walter White in *Rope and Faggot: A Biography of Judge Lynch* (1929). Also see the National Association for the Advancement of Colored People's (NAACP's) *Thirty Years of Lynching in the United States, 1889-1918* (1919) and Robert L. Zangrando, *The NAACP Crusade Against Lynching, 1909-1950* (1980).

Lyon, Mary (Feb. 28, 1797, Buckland, Mass.—Mar. 5, 1849, South Hadley, Mass.): Educator. Known as an

Mary Lyon, founder of Mount Holyoke Female Seminary, was honored with a postage stamp in 1987. (AP/Wide World Photos)

innovative teacher, Lyon used contemporary news articles as a basis for discussion and brought geography alive with maps that could be colored. She is best known as the founder of Mount Holyoke Female Seminary, now Mount Holyoke College, in 1837. Among Lyon's published work is *A Missionary Offering* (1843).

M

Ma, Yo-Yo (b. Oct. 7, 1955, Paris, France): Chinese American cellist. Born into a musical family, Ma began on the violin but soon moved to the cello. He had his Carnegie Hall debut at the age of nine and attended a professional children's school before studying at Harvard University. Upon graduation from Harvard in 1976, Ma began touring widely and recording. He has performed with such figures as Pablo Casals, Isaac Stern, and Leonard Bernstein and has been guest artist with the New York and Los Angeles Philharmonic Orchestras, among dozens of others in the United States and Europe. Ma received Grammy Awards in 1984, 1985, and 1986 and was the first solo winner of the Avery Fisher Prize in 1978.

Chinese American cellist, Yo-Yo Ma graduated from Harvard University before pursuing an international career as a guest soloist and recording artist. (AP/Wide World Photos)

McCarran-Walter Act. *See* **Immigration and Nationalization Act of 1952**

McCarthyism: Practice of condemning and punishing Americans, especially alleged Communist Party members, as security risks without sufficient evidence or proper legal procedure. The term is named for Senator Joseph McCarthy of Wisconsin, who came to national attention after he made a speech in 1950 in which he claimed to have a list of more than two hundred communists in the U.S. government. His beliefs took hold at the height of the Cold War when Americans feared the developing nuclear capabilities of the Soviet Union and the People's Republic of China. McCarthy's particular target was the State Department, which he believed was assisting the international movement of communism by harboring a network of communist spies.

McCarthy's charges set off a wave of investigations and interrogations by his Senate committee and other agencies that cost many government employees their jobs. McCarthy's influence and power reached its zenith in 1954 when he claimed that the U.S. Army was riddled with communists subverting the goals of the United States. The result of these charges was the televising of the Army-McCarthy hearings before a Senate committee, during which McCarthy grew increasingly vicious and reckless in naming alleged communists and sympathizers. The American people rejected McCarthy after viewing him at some length, the Senate formally censured him at the end of 1954, and he died of alcoholism in 1957.

McCarthyism provided a voice for those who thought that the United States was slipping from its position of world dominance as a result of its betrayal by the well-educated WHITE ANGLO-SAXON PROTESTANTS (WASPs) who had devised the NEW DEAL and led the country during the GREAT DEPRESSION and WORLD WAR II. Frightened people reacted against the liberalism that had guided the country for a generation and anyone who bore its stamp. A jingoistic pride in all things "American" (as defined by McCarthy and his supporters) complicated U.S. relations with other countries. Coupled with the earlier hearings of the House Committee on Un-American Activities in the 1940's, which had generated a blacklist of presumed communist sympathizers in the entertainment field, and the emotionally chilling fallout from the Alger Hiss case, in which a prominent New Dealer was convicted in 1949 of lying about spying for the Soviet Union, McCarthyism made Americans from all walks of life and all income levels suspicious of one another.

Ordinary Americans feared a communist conspiracy of which their next door neighbors might be a part; leftist and liberal citizens and politicians were afraid to assert themselves. The sense of mutual distrust lasted long after the senator's own impact had faded.

SUGGESTED READINGS. Joseph McCarthy makes his case in *McCarthyism: The Fight for America* (1952). The most objective and well-researched biography of the senator is Thomas C. Reeves's *The Life and Times of Joe McCarthy* (1982). Michael Paul Rogin analyzes some of the negative effects of the senator's work in *The Intellectuals and McCarthy: The Radical Specter* (1967). William F. Buckley and L. Brent Bozell defend McCarthy in *McCarthy and His Enemies* (1954). Various viewpoints are presented in the anthology *The Meaning of McCarthyism* (1965), edited by Earl Latham.

McCoy, Elijah (May 2, 1844, Colchester, Ontario, Canada—Oct. 10, 1929, Eloise, Mich.): African American inventor. Born of American parents who had left Kentucky to escape slavery, McCoy contributed to modern industrial operations by inventing and refining automatic lubricators used to oil engines and machinery. These employed a drip cup, and regulated oil flow by means of a stopcock; previously such lubrication had been done manually. After Emancipation, McCoy moved to Ypsilanti, Michigan. Eventually he held more than fifty patents. The phrase "the real McCoy" may have come into use as a reference to the quality of McCoy's devices.

Machismo: Condition or posture of exaggerated masculinity, from the Spanish word for maleness or masculinity. Machismo is multicultural and global in its manifestation, but it is most strongly associated with Spanish and Latino culture. Encompassed within the concept of machismo is the belief that men should be strongly dominant over women and should protect them from others; women are expected to remain in a subservient role. Other primary aspects of machismo are loyalty to one's group of male friends and relatives and intimidation of men outside one's group.

In the United States, behaviors associated with machismo are exhibited by men of all ethnic backgrounds. Social and cultural traditions have led to the prevalence of machismo and related "macho" attitudes and behavior among MEXICAN AMERICAN males as well as Latinos from the Caribbean, Central America, and South America, but similar attitudes are also no-

tably prevalent among African American males. Males in these groups have often been frustrated in their attempts to obtain jobs providing sufficient income to support their families and have been angered by the discrimination they have faced at the hands of whites. Some have therefore sought to prove their worth, strength, and virility by asserting their dominance in an arena where their control is nearly unchallenged: their families. Some of these men seek to prove their virility by marrying at an early age and fathering large families. Despite the challenges of poverty and discrimination, many Latinos choose not to allow their wives to work outside the home, encouraging them to perform traditional domestic chores such as cooking, cleaning, and caring for children.

Among the social problems that have been linked to machismo are violence toward women and membership in GANGS. Strong male dominance over women can foster courteousness and gentleness toward the "weaker" sex, but it can also lead to abuse if a woman is seen as a convenient, docile target on which to vent one's anger and frustration. Many of the outward signs of gang loyalty in the 1980's and 1990's—wearing special colors or similar clothing, intimidating outsiders by verbal or physical harassment, and expressing dismissive or proprietary attitudes toward women—were derived from the loyalty to one's brotherhood that developed as expressions of machismo among Latinos and African Americans.

Magazines—women's: Among the first and most successful of the mass magazines in both the United States and Great Britain. Despite their success, women's magazines have generally been considered, both by readers and by advertisers, to be addressed to a specialized audience as reflected in the content of the articles as well as the advertisements. In the early 1990's, there were some fifty titles on the newsstands which might be considered women's magazines. While there are many periodicals directed primarily at a male audience—*Sports Illustrated*, *GQ*, *Esquire*, and *Playboy* among them—these magazines have no unifying ideology and do not focus on the totality of "masculinity" or the position of males in society. It has been suggested that women's interests have been more homogeneous than men's interests because women were culturally socialized to accept responsibility for home life irrespective of their employment status or social class. Many women's magazines have reinforced these cultural patterns in conveying what some scholars call the "cult of femininity."

Editor Helen Gurley Brown, shown here in front of a cover shot of model Christie Brinkley, has shaped the content of Cosmopolitan *magazine to appeal to young, upscale women interested in contemporary fashion as well as advice on health and personal relationship issues.* (AP/Wide World Photos)

There is evidence that there are shared ideological messages in all women's magazines regardless of their classification or editorial intent. Traditional women's magazines aimed at working-class and middle-class readers tend to define women primarily in terms of their relationship to men. Magazine covers for fashion as well as more traditional home magazines often feature beautiful young female models or celebrities whose flawless complexions, impeccable hair, and designer-label clothes present a highly idealized image of women. The content of these magazines has been influenced to some extent by changes in women's roles within American society. During World War II, women's magazines featured patriotic articles encouraging women to make sacrifices on the home front in support of the war effort. Postwar magazines of the 1950's contained advertising and articles that focused on modern conveniences that assisted women in their proper roles as homemakers. As the proportion of women who worked outside of the home increased during the 1960's, 1970's, and 1980's, new magazines began to focus on the special interests and concerns of working women.

Traditional Women's Magazines. Seven women's magazines that had the highest circulation in the United States during the early to mid-twentieth century were collectively referred to as the "seven sisters." This label had remained even though most of these magazines have attempted to develop their own identities in a fierce competition for advertising dollars. *Redbook*, known for adopting the image of their ideal reader as "the Juggler," targets young mothers between the ages of twenty-five and forty-four, many of whom work outside the home. *McCall's* and *Ladies' Home Journal* have traditionally appealed to a more mature audience able to indulge themselves in personal activities outside the scope of childrearing. *Woman's Day* and *Family Circle* began life as free periodicals, generally loaded with recipes and food buying tips that appealed to female customers in retail grocery stores. In their modern incarnations as inexpensively priced magazines, both have continued to rely upon store sales rather than subscriptions. *Good Housekeeping* includes tips and features that appeal to the same homemaker audience, while *Better Homes and Gardens* has emphasized more home improvement and interior decorating projects than the other "sisters."

Competitors for the low-end retail buyer's money include magazines such as *First for Women*, which sold its earliest editions in 1989 for only 25 cents. New entries that have been targeted at affluent subscribers include magazines such as *Victoria*, which contains lavish fashions, collectibles, and interior designs reminiscent of the Victorian period.

Feminist and Career-Oriented Magazines. During the 1970's and 1980's, several new women's magazines were founded to address the concerns of newly liberated American women who benefitted from the civil rights gains achieved by the WOMEN'S MOVEMENT. The forerunner of these new periodicals was *Ms.*, which was first published in 1972 under the leadership of one of its founding editors, feminist Gloria STEINEM. Noteworthy for its refusal to accept advertising deemed inconsistent with its principles, *Ms.* struggled for years to balance its operating budget and still be responsive to the criticisms levied by its readers. In 1990, the magazine ceased publication in its old format and returned with an advertising-free format that required a higher cover price and a stronger dependence on subscriber loyalty. From the beginning,

Ms. has carried fiction, poetry, international news, and analysis of current events that reflect its feminist concerns. The success of *Ms.* in appealing to a niche audience inspired the founding of *Essence*, a magazine devoted to the accomplishments and concerns of African American women. Subtitled "For the Woman Who Wasn't Born Yesterday," *Lear's* has dedicated itself to the fashions, health concerns, and cultural interests of mature American women. Career-oriented magazines include *Working Woman, Executive Female*, and *Working Mother*, while periodicals such as *Savvy, New Woman*, and *Self* have focused on health and self-image concerns facing women. These magazines have focused on career issues such as AFFIRMATIVE ACTION programs, SEXUAL HARASSMENT, and job performance while also addressing complications such as finding adequate childcare, preparing quick and healthy meals, and maintaining a fitness regimen.

Fashion and Bridal Magazines. Numerous magazines have been published to keep American women informed on the latest developments in fashion. Maga-

Fashion magazines appeal to many women who want to escape from the less than glamorous routine of their own lives. (Mary Langenfeld)

zines such as *Vogue, Elle, Glamour, Mademoiselle*, and COSMOPOLITAN feature seasonal photographic layouts of clothing, makeup, and hairstyle fashions as well as personal advice columns, health information, short fiction, and other essays designed to appeal to contemporary women. More than a century old, Cosmopolitan has been transformed under the influence of editor Helen Gurley BROWN. Designed to appeal primarily to women between the ages of eighteen and thirty-four, the magazine has discarded a stodgy, traditional image in favor of frank discussion of a wide range of sexual matters, including orgasm, infertility, birth control, sexually transmitted diseases, and date rape. The 1989 advent of *Mirabella* magazine heralded the beginning of a new trend toward including lesser-known models with realistically proportioned figures and showcasing practical, somewhat more affordable clothes.

While some of the women's magazines of the 1930's and 1940's carried features aimed at teen readers, more specialized fashion magazines developed as teens began to earn and spend more money. *Seventeen, Teen*, and *Sassy* are among the magazines catering to young females by featuring clothing, hair, and beauty trends for teens as well as profiles of young celebrities, short fiction, and articles on relationships, high school and college life, and teen employment.

Bridal magazines constitute another subdivision within the category of fashion magazines. Periodicals such as *Bride's* and *Modern Bride* feature the latest trends in bridal fashion supplemented by planning lists for the first-time bride and groom, trends in household goods and interior decorating, honeymoon travel tips, and advice on bridal etiquette as well as issues confronting newlyweds. As in other fashion magazines, the advertising featured in bridal magazines reinforces the themes of its editorial contents.

As business enterprises aimed at attracting advertising revenues, women's magazines have chosen different methods for developing a healthy subscriber base. Some magazines have revamped their image and content in an attempt to reflect the interests of their audience or to attract a new readership; while others have retained features that have been successful over the course of many years to ensure the loyalty of a core readership. As more and more women have become involved in shaping the editorial and advertising content of these magazines, women's magazines have become more effective mirrors of contemporary women's issues rather than mouthpieces for dominant cultural images of women.

SUGGESTED READINGS. For a comparative analysis of American and British contemporary women's magazines, see Marjorie Ferguson's *Forever Feminine: Women's Magazines and the Cult of Femininity* (1983). A somewhat dated but extensive historical analysis of American women's magazines can be found in Cynthia White's *Women's Magazines 1693-1968* (1970). For an analysis of how women are portrayed in women's magazines as well as other forms of mass culture, see Kathryn Weibel's *Mirror Mirror: Images of Women Reflected in Popular Culture* (1977) and *Hearth and Home: Images of Women in the Mass Media* (1978), edited by Gaye Tuchman, Arlene Kaplan Daniels, and James Benet.—*Gretta Stanger*

Magyar Americans. *See* **Hungarian Americans**

Mah-jongg: Chinese game popular since the nineteenth century. The game is played with more than one hundred tiles engraved with Chinese characters and divided into suits. The object is to obtain a certain combination of tiles to complete a winning hand. Before World War I, each province in China had its own version of the game and a different name for the game in the local dialect. Playing mah-jongg, often throughout the entire night, was a common form of recreation for early Chinese immigrants, and teaching the game to children was an important way to maintain traditional culture. After World War I, the name "mah-jongg" was copyrighted and a standard form of the game was introduced. This form of the game was very popular throughout the English-speaking world in the 1920's and continues to be played.

Mainstreaming: Practice of integrating people with disabilities into regular schools and classrooms rather than separating them because of their disabilities. Mainstreaming is thought to give people with disabilities a greater chance of achieving educational independence. It has been generally championed by the disability rights movement and mandated, wherever practical, by legislation such as the AMERICANS WITH DISABILITIES ACT (ADA) OF 1990. The practice remains controversial, however, because of the logistical difficulties and high costs it may entail.

Malcolm X (Malcolm Little; May 19, 1925, Omaha, Neb.—Feb. 21, 1965, New York, N.Y.): African American Black Muslim leader and civil rights activist. A street hustler in New York City in his teens, Malcolm X took to drugs, gambling, and robbery. Caught with stolen goods, he was sentenced in 1946 to ten years in prison.

While serving a total of seven years in prison, Malcolm X took correspondence courses and read much in the prison's library. It was here that his brother, Reginald, visited him and introduced him to the teachings of the NATION OF ISLAM. In Detroit, Reginald had converted to Islam and followed the Honorable Elijah MUHAMMAD. Won over, Malcolm began writing to Muhammad from prison, receiving occasional replies.

Studying Muhammad's teachings, Malcolm learned that black history had been left out of the history books and that blacks had a glorious history of their own. He became a zealous recruit for Muhammad's teachings. After his release in 1952, he delved more deeply into Islam, met Elijah Muhammad, and changed his name to Malcolm X in rejection of names imposed by whites during SLAVERY. Malcolm actively recruited new members for Temple Number One in Detroit, helping to triple its membership. In the summer of 1953 he became the temple's assistant minister.

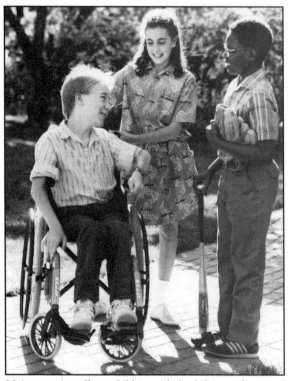

Mainstreaming allows children with disabilities to learn and interact with able-bodied children in classrooms and on playgrounds. (Jim and Mary Whitmer)

At the height of his popularity in the early 1960's, Malcolm X addressed huge crowds of African Americans eager to hear his message of black nationalism. (AP/Wide World Photos)

In the 1960's, the Nation of Islam was flourishing and Malcolm was its rising star, representing it frequently in the media. By 1963 he had angered both whites and blacks by criticizing civil rights leaders and their campaigns. Himself "a creation of the Northern white man and of his hypocritical attitude toward the Negro," as Malcolm later said, he scorned northern liberals and denounced the concept of INTEGRATION, urging complete separation of the races. In spite of this Malcolm was a popular lecturer with white audiences. He particularly favored speaking at colleges, where he appreciated the open, searching minds of students and professors.

Jealousy of Malcolm's notoriety grew within the Nation of Islam, particularly at the Chicago headquarters. The Nation's official paper, *Muhammad Speaks,* wrote less and less about the minister whose fame threatened to eclipse that of Elijah Muhammad. Malcolm's ties with his mentor were broken when he lost faith in Muhammad after the latter was charged with adultery. In return, Malcolm was silenced by Muhammad's orders. Malcolm left the Nation of Islam in 1964, founding the ORGANIZATION OF AFRO-AMERICAN UNITY.

The new organization embraced black people of all faiths, attracting many members repelled by the rigidity of Nation of Islam. Malcolm X wanted an active program to eliminate political, economic, and social exploitation of African Americans. Accused at times of inciting violence, Malcolm insisted that he was for justice and if that meant violence, so be it. His views mellowed after a visit to the Muslim Shrine of Mecca in Saudi Arabia, where he was impressed by the possibilities of multiracial brotherhood. By 1965 Malcolm's public speeches emphasized an inclusive approach: All peoples were welcome in the fight against RACISM. He continued to insist, however, that black and white people must work for justice separately among their own people.

Death threats and government surveillance increased against Malcolm X, yet he continued a busy lecture schedule. On February 13, 1965, his New York City home was firebombed. On February 21, 1965, while lecturing in New York's Audubon Ballroom, Malcolm was shot dead by assassins. While many African Americans have long venerated this articulate, passionate leader, other Americans only came to a belated appreciation of him with the film *Malcolm X* by Spike Lee (1992).

SUGGESTED READINGS. For a compelling look at Malcolm X's life and teachings, see *The Autobiography of Malcolm X* (1965). An analysis of his influence is given in "Voices from the Veil" in Gordon Taylor's *Chapters of Experience* (1983). An interpretation of Malcolm X's political significance is featured in *Garvey, Lumumba, and Malcolm: Black National-Separatists* (1972) by Shawna Maglangbayan.

Manifest Destiny: Popular nineteenth century belief that God had ordained that the United States should cover the entire North American continent, from coast to coast. This destiny brought responsibilities as well as rights. It was the Anglo-Saxon Americans' duty to spread liberty and opportunity across the continent. This belief was used as a justification for the removal and relocation of American Indians from their traditional lands and for the Spanish-American War in 1898. The term was first used by John L. O'Sullivan in 1845, referring to the annexation of Texas.

Mankato, Minn.—mass executions (Dec. 26, 1862): Hanging of thirty-eight American Indians following the Sioux Uprising at Mankato. The historical context of this event, framed within the INDIAN WARS of the Great Plains, must be fully understood in order to see the inevitability of the uprising and the injustice of the execution.

The treaties of 1851 and 1858 had, in effect, exchanged 28 million acres of INDIAN TERRITORY for annual annuities, to be distributed on the reservations. The monetary portions of these annuities, however, were consistently withheld; in fact, plundering and graft by local and territory officials occurred regularly. By inflating their claims, traders and merchants also cheated the Indians out of their rightful share. Throughout the 1850's and early 1860's, the Indian situation was desperate, and Little Crow, the leading chief of the Sioux, argued for giving up the annuities. His unsuccessful efforts in diplomacy were distrusted by more militant chiefs, who believed that Little Crow

had been compromised by his association with the whites.

Sioux frustration finally found a release when, on August 17, 1862, four Indian youths murdered five white settlers over a senseless argument about chicken eggs. Militant tribal leaders, after much debate, decided to defend the youths and, along with Little Crow, led war parties against the white settlers the next day. The white farmers, most of whom were of German and Scandinavian descent, were unprepared for the attack and untrained in Plains warfare; more than four hundred whites were killed, with hundreds more fleeing to Fort Ridgely. Minnesota Governor Ramsey called upon General Henry H. Sibley to put down the uprising. Sibley responded grimly: "I will sweep them," he said, "with the besom [broom] of death."

The Sioux were unable to withstand Sibley's onslaught. Strategically, they made a serious mistake by dividing their forces: Little Crow led an attack against Fort Ridgely, and other chiefs attacked New Ulm, but both moves were repulsed. On September 23, the Sioux regrouped to ambush Sibley's forces at Woodlake, Minnesota, but were soundly defeated. Sibley captured more than two thousand Indians and established a military commission to try the captives.

The commission found 303 Sioux guilty of murder, and they were sentenced to hang. Almost all of the Indians, however, were convicted on little or no evidence. President Abraham Lincoln called for the court records, and he pardoned all but thirty-eight Sioux—over the vehement objections of Minnesota officials. On December 26, the thirty-eight were hanged simultaneously.

There were to be more consequences of the uprising. Little Crow, who had worked so hard to win Indian approval of the treaties, was murdered the next year, and his assassin was voted a $500 reward by the Minnesota legislature. Sibley continued his pursuit into Dakota Territory, where he killed more than five hundred Sioux in one battle. The Sioux lost their reservation and were forced onto a reservation in Nebraska, where their descendants live today; others escaped to Canada. The Winnebago tribe, who had nothing to do with the uprising, also lost their reservation.

SUGGESTED READINGS. For further information consult Robert M. Utley, whose *The Indian Frontier of the American West, 1846-1890* (1984) contextualizes the event. Specialized studies on the Minnesota Up-

This engraving depicts the mass hanging of thirty-eight Indians involved in a Sioux uprising against white settlers in Minnesota in 1862. (Library of Congress)

rising and its aftermath include Kenneth Carley's *The Sioux Uprising of 1862* (1961), Robert H. Jones's *The Civil War in the Northwest* (1960), and Chester M. Oehler's *The Great Sioux Uprising* (1959).

Mankiller, Wilma (b. Nov. 18, 1945, Stillwell, Okla.): Cherokee Indian chief. Mankiller's last name is inherited from an eighteenth century warrior ancestor. She was the first woman to serve as Principal Chief of the CHEROKEES (1985), whose sixty-seven thousand members live mainly in Oklahoma. Mankiller was inducted into the Oklahoma Women's Hall of Fame in 1986.

Manlapit, Pablo (Jan. 17, 1891, Lipa, Batanga, Luzon, Philippines—1969, Philippines): Filipino American labor organizer. Manlapit came to Hawaii in 1910 to work for the Hawaiian Sugar Planters' Association. Fired for involvement in a strike, he moved to Hilo, started two newspapers, and studied law at night. After completing his law studies, Manlapit became the first Filipino law-

yer to practice in Hawaii. In 1918, he organized workers to form the Filipino Federation of Labor and in 1920 began the Higher Wages movement. When labor demands were denied, Manlapit called a strike that lasted 165 days but resolved nothing. Another strike four years later led to a confrontation in Hanapepe, Kaua'i in which sixteen strikers and four police officers were killed; Manlapit went to prison for conspiracy in the strike. In 1932 he established a new union, but in 1934 was convicted on federal charges. He requested that his sentence be suspended and chose to be exiled to the Philippines. Manlapit was active in Filipino labor activities and served in various Filipino administrations before his death.

Manpower programs: Government job training and job finding programs of the 1960's and 1970's directed at easing unemployment, especially in urban areas. The Manpower Development and Training Act of 1962 set aside funds for vocational training, basic education, and

The Manpower Development and Training Act of 1962 provided federal funds for vocational training including educational programs at trade schools such as this one in New Mexico. (AP/Wide World Photos)

other types of support for unemployed and underemployed Americans. Its centers reached 2.3 million people, many of them poor African Americans, between 1966 and 1973. Another well-known program that created new jobs and staffed innovative community programs was the COMPREHENSIVE EMPLOYMENT AND TRAINING ACT (CETA) OF 1973. Both programs were phased out in the 1980's.

Mansfield, Arabella (Bella Aurelia Babb; May 23, 1846, Sperry Station, near Burlington, Iowa—Aug. 2, 1911, Aurora, Ill.): Arts professor, suffragist, and, in 1869, the first woman to be admitted to the bar in the United States. She and her husband, John Mansfield, were both teaching at Iowa Wesleyan University when they applied for law school, but on earning their degrees, neither practiced. In 1870 Mansfield earned a Masters of Fine Arts. In 1886 she took a job teaching music history and aesthetics at DePauw University. She became dean of the art school in 1893, and dean of the music school in 1894. She was active in establishing the Iowa Woman Suffrage Society.

Manuelito (c. 1818, near Bear Ears Peak, Utah—1894): Principal chief of the NAVAJOS. Manuelito led his people in the war in New Mexico, which resulted in the Long Walk (1863-1866) to Bosque Redondo. He went to Washington, D.C., in 1874 to plead the case of his people regarding the poor land and living conditions at Bosque Redondo. A new treaty was signed which gave the Navajos a reservation in the Chuska Mountains, and the Navajos never again made war on the Caucasians.

March on Washington (Aug. 28, 1963): Culminating event of the early CIVIL RIGHTS MOVEMENT. This massive gathering brought more than 200,000 black and white Americans to the federal Mall in support of solving the nation's racial problems.

In 1941, A. Philip RANDOLPH, president of the BROTHERHOOD OF SLEEPING CAR PORTERS, called for a march on Washington protesting President Franklin D. Roosevelt's failure to address discrimination against African Americans in NEW DEAL programs and in the defense industry. The march was cancelled when Roosevelt responded to Randolph's threat by issuing an executive order forbidding discrimination by defense contractors and establishing the Fair Employment Practices Committee to address charges of racial discrimination.

Returning to the same strategy in 1963, Randolph, his associate, Bayard Rustin, and other African American leaders such as Martin Luther KING, Jr., planned a second march that would urge Congress to pass a stalled civil rights bill. The march's primary objective was to demonstrate how strongly public opinion favored voting rights and desegregation.

Rustin coordinated the staging of the march. He publicized it through local organizations nationwide and arranged for old school buses to transport thousands of people to Washington, D.C. Since the groups backing the event—the NATIONAL ASSOCIATION FOR THE ADVANCEMENT OF COLORED PEOPLE (NAACP), the NATIONAL URBAN LEAGUE, King's SOUTHERN CHRISTIAN LEADERSHIP CONFERENCE (SCLC), and the more radical STUDENT NONVIOLENT COORDINATING COMMITTEE (SNCC)—represented different constituencies, the program for the day had to be ironed out in a series of meetings. In the interest of promoting unity, everyone was asked to temporarily put aside their rivalries. The most heated battle was resolved when SNCC's John Lewis, who planned harsh criticisms of the Kennedy Administration, changed his speech at the last minute to preserve the atmosphere of goodwill.

The long day of activities was a huge success. Clergy, well-known entertainers, politicians, and civil rights leaders, both black and white, performed, delivered speeches, and led songs and prayers. King concluded the program with his now-famous "I Have a Dream" oration. Using powerful biblical phraseology, he inspired the world with the statement of his belief

The 1963 March on Washington was cosponsored by several leading civil rights groups—the NAACP, the Urban League, the SCLC, and the SNCC. (AP/Wide World Photos)

and faith that people of all races and backgrounds would someday be united.

Less than three months later, President Kennedy was assassinated and the fate of the civil rights legislation was put in the hands of President Lyndon Johnson. Invoking the memory of Kennedy and applying his usual political savvy, Johnson pushed through the landmark CIVIL RIGHTS ACT OF 1964. It authorized the federal government to enforce desegregation of public accommodations and outlawed discrimination in employment and on public facilities.

SUGGESTED READINGS. For further discussions of the march, as well as Civil Rights movement histories such as Taylor Branch's *Parting the Waters* and Rhoda Lois Blumberg's *Civil Rights: The 1960s Freedom Struggle* (1984). Biographies of Martin Luther King, Jr., such as David Garrow's *Bearing the Cross* (1986) and Stephen Oates's *Let the Trumpet Sound* (1982), also contain information about the march.

Mardi Gras: Elaborate pre-Lenten holiday and festival first introduced in Paris in 1827 and held annually in New Orleans, Louisiana, and in some other cities in the southern United States. Mardi Gras season begins on Twelfth Night, and ends at midnight on Shrove Tuesday, immediately before the First Day of Lent (Ash Wednesday). The festival derives from the ROMAN CATHOLIC custom of purification through the confession of sins. Since about 1857 in New Orleans, a highlight of Mardi Gras has been a procession of floats and torchlights organized by local organizations called krewes. Mardi Gras is also celebrated as Carnival in other parts of the world, especially in Latin America and the Caribbean.

Mariachi: Traditional Mexican music ensemble that originated in Jalisco, Mexico, and spread throughout Mexico and the American Southwest. Mariachi groups played in marriage ceremonies and used stringed instruments. The original instruments utilized were a *guitar-*

Mariachi bands in the U.S. perform at restaurants, festivals, weddings, masses and—as pictured here—at Las Posadas celebrations before Christmas. (Robert Fried)

rón (a large bass guitar), a *vihuela* (a smaller guitarlike instrument), two violins, and a guitar. Later trumpets were added. Mariachis wear a distinctive costume, usually black, which includes boots, tight decorated pants, a short jacket, and a wide brimmed sombrero. They may be found playing a variety of *ranchera* songs and dances at MEXICAN AMERICAN parties, weddings, restaurants, festivals, and Catholic masses. Mariachis are known for their sentimental serenades and the performance of "Las Mananitas" on birthdays. Their music became popularized to non-Mexican Americans in the 1980's through the performances of pop singer Linda RONSTADT.

Mariel boat lift (1980): Migration to the United States of about 125,000 Cuban refugees. The boat lift occurred after President Jimmy Carter announced that anyone from Cuba would be welcomed in the United States. Over a period of five months, thousands of Cubans fled the fishing port of Mariel, in boats large and small (the "freedom flotilla"), heading for Florida. The United States was quickly faced with two unanticipated problems: the sheer number of the penniless immigrants and the fact that some of them were Cuban criminals and mental patients whom Fidel Castro had taken the opportunity to deport. The U.S. Coast Guard attempted blockades, but they were mostly unsuccessful. Upon the immigrants' arrival, thousands were detained in refugee or resettlement camps or in prison. Early worries about the "Marielitos" proved unfounded, however, and by 1990 an impressive 85 percent of them were employed. About 2,600 were in American prisons, hospitals, or other institutions, and about 400 more had been returned to Cuba.

Marine Corps, Women's Reserve. *See* **Women's Reserve in the Marine Corps**

Maroons: Fugitive slaves living in the New World, especially in Jamaica and Haiti. After escaping from plantations, they lived in small groups in isolated areas and used guerrilla tactics to harass their former owners and to help other slaves escape. Although their life was not easy, the maroons preferred this hardship to being enslaved. They often made short-lived alliances with British, French, or Spanish arrivals against the existing nationality in power in order to make gains. In Jamaica, the maroons were granted land and some self-governance in 1738. In Haiti, they were instrumental in bringing about an end to slavery in the revolution of 1791.

Marriage: Since the social upheavals of the 1960's, the institution of marriage has been in transition. It is no longer seen as the only socially acceptable way for men and women to meet economic, sexual, and procreative needs in American society. The sexual revolution relaxed prohibitions on sex outside of marriage, prompting increasing numbers of couples to live together without legal sanction. The WOMEN'S MOVEMENT as well as the MEN'S MOVEMENT questioned traditional gender roles and challenged the value of marriage per se, leading some to abandon marriage and others to try to make it a more equitable partnership. Women entered the work force in large numbers, becoming less economically dependent on men. The GAY AND LESBIAN RIGHTS MOVEMENT encouraged more homosexuals to "come out" rather than conform to social expectations through heterosexual marriage. With greater emphasis on personal fulfillment during the 1960's and 1970's and greater impatience with the limitations of marriage, divorce rates began to rise. Perhaps partly as a consequence of these various social forces, Americans began to delay or forgo both getting married and having children. In the 1950's, the married couple with male breadwinner, female housewife, and at least two children was the norm for American households; by the 1990's, it was the exception.

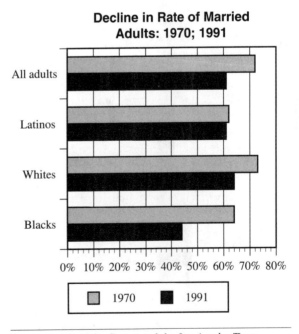

Decline in Rate of Married Adults: 1970; 1991

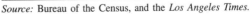

Source: Bureau of the Census, and the *Los Angeles Times*.

Views about marriage and marital patterns are as diverse as the composition of households in the United States. Aspects of arranged marriages can still be found among some groups such as Gypsies or Southeast Asian refugees, but most Americans freely choose their mates. Weddings remain a primary focus of family and community celebration as well as an occasion for the expression of ethnic, religious, or gender identity. What happens after the wedding varies tremendously, from married couples who consciously share the tasks of earning a living, making decisions, running a household, and rearing children to those who prefer a more conventional division of labor along gender lines. There is a broad range of approaches to marriage and gender roles even within social classes and ethnic groups. The conventional pattern was probably more common in the late 1900's, yet compared to mid-century, it had already been altered by the many challenges to the institution of marriage.

"His" and "Hers" Marriages. For both men and women, marriage is a social relationship that, in a monogamous society, changes one's primary social unit from "individual" to "couple." This change in status may be where the similarities of marriage for men and women end. Most societies are patriarchal, giving higher status and greater power to males. Through marriage women become wives, and this basic element of kinship systems places men in control of women. Some writers describe the differential effects of marriage on men and women by saying that within every marriage there are two marriages—"his" and "hers." Such a fact has far-reaching implications for women who enter the institution of marriage.

Theorists of a "his" and "hers" marriage point out that marriage involves the exchange of women by men and not vice versa. Women become instruments or objects that bind kinship groups and communities together. In American society this property exchange by men can be seen in the custom of the father giving the bride away in marriage ceremonies. This exchange signifies the transferral of the father's property (his daughter) to the new owner (her husband). Women's subordinate position vis-a-vis her husband and the denotation of ownership by the husband is further exemplified by men entering and exiting the marriage ceremony as "Mister." Women traditionally enter as "Miss" and exit as "Mrs.," although the modern option of "Ms." is also available for both states. Additional evidence that women are to be submissive and men dominant is found in the traditional exchange of vows where women promise to obey their husbands, but no such promises are expected of husbands.

Contemporary feminism and the women's liberation movement of the 1970's and 1980's in the United States revealed many of the meanings behind these rituals. This reexamination led to the rewriting of marital vows to exclude women's promises of obedience and to women retaining their maiden names in various forms. Nevertheless, in traditional Western weddings and cultures, male-dominant and woman-submissive attitudes are still reflected in marriage ceremonies and customs. In MEXICAN AMERICAN marriages, for example, these attitudes reflect the "MACHISMO" or "cult of virility" notion associated with males and the "cult of spiritual superiority of women" (associated with notion of virginity)—concepts introduced by the Spanish conquistadors and the CATHOLIC church.

Housework and Marital Roles. Marriage roles are sharply defined by gender. While some changes have occurred in American society, norms still specify, implicitly or explicitly, that the responsibility for HOUSEWORK falls on the wife. That this social status carries with it low prestige and low economic value is found in the frequently heard phrase "I don't work; I'm only a housewife." This conception of the housewife role is curious, given that the work housewives do is socially and economically valuable. Nevertheless, housework is unpaid, repetitive work with no scheduled hours and no time off, not even for holidays. The fact that housework has a private rather than public nature, and is intermingled with love and caring, is blamed for its devalued status. For some women it is the absence of rigid schedules, the private nature of housework, and working for loved ones that make them appreciate the role of housewife. Whether women like or dislike the role of housewife, they are the ones who usually end up doing most chores at home. And, the qualifications for becoming a housewife appear to be only two—marriage and gender.

In 1988, married women made up close to 60 percent of the total civilian workforce in the United States. Most wives shared the provider role because the family needed the added income. Yet when wives enter the labor market and assume a share of the traditional male provider role, husbands do not necessarily share the housewife role. While some husbands and wives say housework should be equally shared, this is not usually the case in reality. Wives do spend fewer hours on housework when they are employed,

Many couples continue to exchange vows in traditional religious marriage ceremonies. (Photo Agora)

cial CLASS, race, and ETHNICITY that influence the amount of time spouses spend on housework, although research findings in this area are inconsistent.

The presence of children in a household increases housework time, and it is again women's time that is most significantly affected. Wives with an infant typically spend about seventy hours a week on housework. If a wife is also employed, her housework time will decrease to fifty hours a week including twenty on child care, but her husband's contribution typically increases by only four hours.

Both the academic and popular literature have examined the phenomenon of "househusbands" in the United States, and the greater egalitarianism in the division of the household labor between spouses in contemporary marriages. A review of available evidence indicates that "househusbandry" is neither common nor growing in popularity. Many "househusbands" are either temporarily out of work or are actually wage earners who have offices in their homes.

Many studies of marital power use a resource theory in studying decision making by married couples to determine which spouse has more power. Overall, findings suggest that husbands are more powerful than wives in that they directly or indirectly make more family decisions. There were conditions, however, under which this tends to vary. Specifically, the spouse who brings more "resources" to the marriage—for example, income, social status, or education—was likely to be more powerful. Typically, this was the husband, but it was found that as wives' resources increased, they gained leverage relative to their husbands. Full-time homemakers tended to be relatively powerless. For couples who believed that men should be the primary family breadwinner, men tended to be more powerful regardless of the earnings of either partner.

The Motherhood Mandate. Phyllis Schlafly wrote, "Why should a man marry a woman who refuses to be a mother to his children? He can get everything else he wants from women at a price much cheaper than marriage." As her quote illustrates, for women, having children is often viewed as a requirement for marriage and, in many cultures, is a primary justification of female existence. In cultures and groups where strict Catholicism is practiced, women who cannot bear children tend to be pitied, and women who are voluntarily child-free are viewed by others as misguided, maladjusted, or selfish. Because of these views, many women who have difficulty conceiving feel like failures and go to extraordinary lengths to

but their husbands' contributions do not increase significantly; more often, they can afford to hire someone else to do the home-related work. It has been found that even if a husband is unemployed, a wife with a forty-hour work week does most of the housework. This arrangement is sometimes referred to as employed wives carrying a "double work load" or "second shift."

When husbands and wives do equally share housework, one of the most important factors influencing their behavior is their shared belief that housework is not "women's work," but rather something family members should do for one another. Additionally, there are several demographic factors such as age, so-

In many marriages, husbands choose to devote more time to yard work and other outdoor chores rather than contribute to indoor housework. (Mary M. Langenfeld)

bear children. While the motherhood mandate is being challenged in the United States and childless marriages are increasing, couples who decide not to have children usually encounter disapproval and curiosity. This may explain why in the United States nine out of ten married women do become mothers.

Having children changes the lives of parents, but especially the lives of wives. New mothers find themselves not only more involved in child care activities than they had expected, but also doing more of the housework, regardless of the previous division of labor between couples and regardless of their employment status. One major result of a traditional division of labor when a young child is present in the home is that marital satisfaction tends to decline, especially for the wife. Mothers of young children are under great stress, much greater than that of their husbands regardless of their labor force participation. The emotional and physical work involved in caring for and being responsible for a young, dependent child is tremendous, yet the myths of motherhood imply that such work should be assumed easily and eagerly by "good mothers." For single mothers without a supportive family network or sufficient income, the strains are even greater. In some cases women experience stress because their lives and identities are completely defined in terms of marital and family roles. Through marriage they lose their individual identity or a sense of "self" that is separate from wife and mother.

Spouse Abuse. Murray Straus, one of the leading pioneers in the study of family violence, has frequently been cited as saying that "for wives the marriage license is a hitting license"—it gives men the right to abuse their wives. Like child abuse, wife abuse historically has been condoned in western societies. English common law permitted husbands to "correct" their wives and children. The law even prescribed the method: with a stick no thicker than the husband's thumb, hence the phrase "rule of thumb." In the United States until the late 1800's, husbands could legally beat their wives. Although the laws have changed, attitudes remain remarkably similar.

Wife beating appears to be the most common form of family violence across cultures, and beatings severe enough to kill or permanently injure wives have been found in 58 percent of societies where wife beating was present. It was also found that there were three reasons that wife beating occurred: for suspected infidelity, for failure to perform her wifely duties, and for no reason or any reason. The latter was found to be the most common reason across societies. These ideas are particularly problematic for women where men's "honor" and "shame" are culturally tied to the behavior of female family members, as in some Arab or Mediterranean societies, including immigrant communities.

Women often accept blame if they are battered. They try to change themselves or the circumstances that they think led to the abuse, and most hope that their husbands will change. They usually find that the abuse is unpredictable and that virtually anything may trigger it. Living under such conditions lowers self-esteem and generates feelings of hopelessness. Intimidation and the threat of violence are often sufficient to keep women paralyzed with fear in an abusive relationship. Spousal violence may also include marital rape, a controversial topic. Numerous shelters and hotlines for battered women sprang up across the United States in the 1970's and 1980's, increasing public sympathy for wives in this predicament.

Divorce. According to some statistics, the United States has one of the highest DIVORCE rates in the world, although these rates vary according to social class, religion, and ethnicity. Surprisingly, when divorces occurred prior to the INDUSTRIAL REVOLUTION, fathers were far more likely than mothers to be given legal custody of children. Later, childrearing experts began to emphasize the superiority of the mother in child care, and by the beginning of the twentieth century it was commonly accepted that children needed to be with their mothers. The courts adopted this principle.

Parenthood changes the lives of married couples and often places extra demands on wives. (Hazel Hankin)

Today mothers continue to receive custody of their children in most divorce cases. Even in joint custody agreements women usually receive physical custody of children. The parenting experiences of single fathers and mothers are quite different. Since single fathers are typically middle- or upper-class and well-educated, financial difficulties in rearing children alone is not one of their common complaints. Rather, their most common concerns are being treated as incompetent parents and feeling constrained in their social lives and careers because of the demands of parenting. Single mothers, however, are less likely than men to hold high-status, high-income occupations. Their employment constraints are more often inflexible work schedules and inadequate salaries. Even finding a job may be difficult, particularly if a woman has been out of the labor market for many years, has little work experience, and has developed few salable skills. Not surprisingly, the biggest problem of single mothers is money.

Families with a female head of the household represent almost 60 percent of poor families with children under eighteen. Of the almost 6.3 million female-headed households with children under eighteen in 1987, more than half (54.7 percent) were living below the POVERTY line. When race is taken into account, the figures are even more startling: 45.2 percent of white female-headed families, 66.9 percent of black female-headed families, and 72.4 percent of Latino female-headed families were living in poverty.

Some observers blame no-fault divorce laws for the poverty of many female-headed households. Under no-fault statutes, either the husband or wife may file for divorce on the grounds of "irreconcilable differences" and neither is blamed for the failure of the marriage. Although elimination of the question of fault has made divorce somewhat easier, it has also changed the economic outcome. Built into this is the notion that men and women are equally capable of providing an income. Yet many women's roles as mothers and housewives during marriage leave them at a disadvantage in the job market at the time of divorce, according to sociologist Lenore Weitzman: "When the legal system treats men and women 'equally' at divorce, it ignores the very real economic inequalities that marriage creates."

Weitzman's research on the impact of no-fault statutes in the United States, combined with other studies, indicates that within the first year after a divorce women and their dependent children suffer a 73 percent drop in their standard of living, while men enjoy a 42 percent rise. Some observers believe that no-fault divorce and a long history of nonenforcement of child support laws have been the major contributing factors in the feminization of poverty.

SUGGESTED READINGS. The ideas presented in this article are more fully discussed in Susan Basow's *Gender: Stereotypes and Roles* (1992); Claire Renzetti's and Daniel Curran's *Women, Men, and Society* (1992); and Jean Stockard's and Miriam Johnson's *Sex and Gender in Society* (2d ed., 1992). Richard Gelles and Claire Cornell present an overview of domestic violence in a very short and readable book entitled *Intimate Violence in Families* (1990). Accounts of the effects of divorce on women as a result of the stress on gender equality is vividly expressed in Lenore Weitzman's *The Divorce Revolution: The Unexpected Social and Economic Consequences for Women and Children in America* (1985).—*Sharon K. Araji*

Marshall, Thurgood (July 2, 1908, Baltimore, Md.—Jan. 23, 1993, Washington, D.C.): African American Supreme Court justice. A liberal who has been called the "lawyer of civil rights," Marshall was a judge on the

Circuit Court of Appeals (1962-1965), the first black U.S. solicitor general (1965-1967), and the first black associate justice of the Supreme Court (1967-1991). After graduation from law school (1933), Marshall worked with the NATIONAL ASSOCIATION FOR THE ADVANCEMENT OF COLORED PEOPLE (NAACP) as first director of its Legal Defense and Education Fund (1939-1961). He traveled the South and argued cases before the U.S. Supreme Court—notably BROWN V. BOARD OF EDUCATION (1954), which overturned the "separate but equal" doctrine and opened the way to school desegregation.

Martinez, Bob (b. Dec. 25, 1934, Tampa, Fla.): Cuban American educator and politician. Martinez began teaching in Hillsborough County, Florida, schools in 1958, and was executive director of its Classroom Teachers Association from 1966 to 1975. He opened a restaurant in Tampa in 1975, served as Tampa's mayor from 1979 to 1986, and was governor of Florida from 1987 to 1991. As Governor, Martinez led the National Governors Association in its efforts to stem drug trafficking and substance abuse. He was also cochair of the U.S. delegation to El Salvador to monitor the 1989 elections. Martinez spoke at the Republican National Convention in 1988. In 1991, he was appointed to serve as director of Drug Control Policy under President Bush.

Maryland Act of Religious Toleration (1649): Provided the death penalty and loss of property to anyone who blasphemed God, denied that Jesus Christ was the son of God, or denied the existence of the Trinity (although these were not enforced). It further provided freedom to practice any religion that included belief in Jesus Christ and did not conspire against the established civil government. Those who prevented others from worshipping as they chose were given fines, public whippings, or imprisonment. The law was initiated by Lord Baltimore to keep Maryland from being considered intolerant of Protestants.

Matsunaga, Masayuki "Spark" (Oct. 8, 1916, Kukuilula, Kauai, Hawaii—Apr. 15, 1990, Toronto, Ontario, Canada): Japanese American politician. After receiving a Bronze Star and a Purple Heart for his Army service

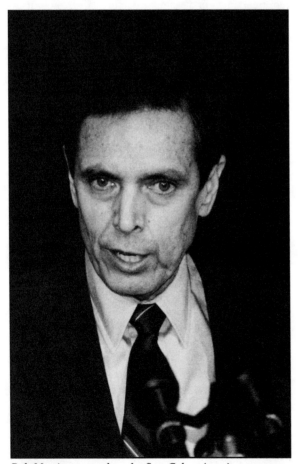

Bob Martinez served as the first Cuban American governor of Florida from 1987 to 1991. (AP/Wide World Photos)

Japanese American Spark Matsunaga fought in World War II and went on to serve Hawaii in the U.S. House of Representatives and the Senate. (AP/Wide World Photos)

in World War II, Matsunaga worked for the War Assets Administration. He earned his J.D. from Harvard University in 1952, and returned to Honolulu to work first in the public prosecutor's office and then in private practice. As a member of the Democratic Party, he served as a member of the Hawaiian Statehood Delegations of 1950 and 1954 and of the Hawaiian Territorial Legislature from 1954 to 1959. He was elected to the U.S. House of Representatives from 1962 to 1976 and served as a senator from 1976 on. Matsunaga distinguished himself as a champion of veterans' interests and of space exploration. He was a member of the Japan-American Society and author of a 1976 book, Rulemakers of the House.

Anthropologist Margaret Mead is known for her pioneering cross-cultural studies of women's roles, sexuality, and family life. (AP/Wide World Photos)

Mead, Margaret (Dec. 16, 1901, Philadelphia, Pa.—Nov. 15, 1978, New York, N.Y.): Anthropologist. Mead studied cultural anthropology at Columbia University with Franz Boas and Ruth Benedict, earning her Ph.D. in 1929. The first of her many field studies of Oceanic and other cultures resulted in the book *Coming of Age in Samoa: A Psychological Study of Primitive Youth for Western Civilisation* (1928). In 1948 she became the Director of Columbia University's Research in Contemporary Cultures in the midst of her long career as a curator at the American Museum of Natural History (1926-1978). Mead is known for her pioneering cross-cultural research on women's roles, sexuality, and family life, and for her lively interest in contemporary social issues such as racism and the arms race. She is the author of more than forty books, among them *Sex and Temperament in Three Primitive Societies* (1935), *Male and Female: A Study of the Sexes in a Changing World* (1949), in which she links child rearing to broader social patterns, and *Culture and Commitment* (1970).

MEChA. *See* **Movimiento Estudiantil Chicano de Aztlán**

Media portrayals of women and minorities: The roles of women and minorities in the American mass media illustrate both the potential and the problems of American MULTICULTURALISM. Social and cultural variety is preserved, strengthened, and disseminated in a broad variety of ways in the media. Among them one might include black performances, from mid-nineteenth century theater to the work of Bill COSBY, Bernard Shaw, and Oprah WINFREY in 1990's television; the presence of women as stars from the earliest days of motion pictures to the present; and the exuberance of local cultural diversity as expressed in music, video, radio, and the press.

Nevertheless, in many cases, members of America's diverse ethnic and social groups have been depicted in the media as objects rather than agents—as figures in the background, targets of humor, victims, or threats rather than complex individuals who shape the world around them. Moreover, heroic minority roles were for decades seen not as opportunities for nonwhite actors but as "challenges" for showcasing the flexibility of European American film stars wearing makeup. An ongoing transformation of more recent decades has seen younger men and women taking charge of the creation, production, and distribution of films. Many of them have created images which suggest the pluralistic changes occurring in American culture.

As American filmmaking developed after its earliest years, its cultural diversity was actually reduced as powerful producers limited its representations to those of their own narrowing vision.

Early Motion Pictures and the Studio Era. Early silent films incorporated women both as aesthetic figures and as characters within dramas. In the new and

Since her screen debut in Children of a Lesser God *(1986), Marlee Matlin has broken stereotypes by portraying a positive image of people with disabilities.* (Merrick Morton)

relatively unspecialized production of silent cinema, women also were involved in all aspects of writing, production, design, and direction. Silent films also became a golden opportunity for Asian and Latino actors, from Sessue Hayakawa to Ramon Navarro, as well as for ethnically based production companies. African Americans, however, were generally barred from starring roles except in films with all-black casts. American Indians, although sympathetically portrayed at times, were also rare as lead actors apart from a few productions such as Edward S. Curtis' *In the Land of the Headhunters* (1914).

With the advent of sound films, the rise of the star system, and the consolidation of major studios in the 1920's and 1930's, the presence of women and minorities declined, despite the individual value and interests of the most famous white female stars. More and more, the model couple depicted in films became Anglo-Saxon, while ethnic minorities as well as older actors or performers with disabilities were relegated to supporting or villain roles. In mainstream motion

pictures, women of color were cast in stereotypical secondary roles. African Americans played domestics, while Asians and Latinos were depicted as seductive, dangerous or mysterious. American Indians were generally scripted as perpetual enemies—always in groups—of white cowboys. In cases where scripts called for more active and positive nonwhite figures, the "ethnic" role might well be taken by a European or Euro-American actor—whether Luise Rainer (*The Good Earth*, 1937) or Katharine Hepburn and Walter Huston (*Dragon Seed*, 1944) as Chinese peasants, Jeanne Crain and Ava Gardner as mulattoes (*Pinky*, 1949 and *Show Boat*, 1951), or the multitude of Euro-Americans cast as Latinos or American Indians. Actors whose names denoted even a non-English European heritage often found themselves repackaged and renamed. Among them were Edward G. Robinson (born Emanuel Goldenberg), Linda Christian (Blanca Rosa Welter), Jeff Chandler (Ira Grossel), and Doris Day (Doris Von Kappelhoff).

It is also important to note how the work of minority actors has been recognized by their peers in the Academy of Motion Picture Arts and Sciences. The first Academy Award (Oscar) won by any black appearing onscreen went to Hattie McDaniel in 1939,

Despite being relegated to stereotyped character roles in his later career, Sessue Hayakawa played numerous leading roles during his early silent career and was nominated for an Oscar as best supporting actor in The Bridge on the River Kwai *(1957).* (AP/Wide World Photos)

followed by Sidney POITIER (1963), Louis Gossett, Jr. (1982), Denzel Washington (1989), and Whoopi Goldberg (1990). Except for Poitier's award, all these awards were for supporting roles, a category which reflects the status of minority actors in most films. Rita MORENO won the first Academy Award given to a Latina in this category for *West Side Story* in 1961. Haing S. NGOR, a Cambodian immigrant in his first role, received the award for best supporting actor in 1985 for his role in *The Killing Fields,* and American Indian Graham Greene was nominated in the same category in 1991. Marlee Matlin won the Academy Award for best actress for her portrayal of a deaf woman in *Children of a Lesser God* (1986), a role which broke from the long Hollywood tradition of having characters with disabilities portrayed by actors who do not have them. The total number of Academy Awards won by members of minorities does not equal those won by actors of Euro-American heritage playing minority or "disabled" roles. Despite the severe limitations and restrictions placed on them by the Hollywood establishment, performers of color could find roles in certain areas. Among them were the films of African American filmmaker Oscar Micheaux, the occasional all-black Hollywood production such as *Cabin in the Sky* (1943), and unusual cases such as the all-Asian musical *Flower Drum Song* (1961)—in which Japanese actors played some of the primary Chinese roles. The roles of African American women in early black cinema illustrate other problems. They were often light-skinned, middle-class heroines, vulnerable and demanding male protection; thus they portrayed only a fragment of African American life and were caught in general American gender stereotypes.

Changes in the 1970's and 1980's. Women and minorities began to take charge of mainstream productions in greater numbers in the 1970's, a process which has slowly increased in subsequent decades with directors such as Melvin Van Peebles, Robert Townsend, Penny Marshall, Barbra Streisand, and Spike Lee. The first feature-length American film in general distribution directed by a black woman was Euzhan Palcy's 1989 *A Dry White Season.* African American filmmaker Julie Dash followed in 1992 with her independently produced *Daughters of the Dust.*

Asian, Latino, and American Indian women and men have been more active in documentary and independent productions, where the nature of their struggles to gain expression has often provided their subject matter. Independent filmmaking has also provided a home for many lesbian and gay films. Lesbian sexuality had been exploited as pornography for a male audience for many years, but once gays and LESBIANS themselves were able to become creators and controllers (rather than objects) of films, they were better able to depict the realities of their lives.

The experiences of women and minorities in film and television differ according to class, race, and national heritage. African American actors and directors, for example, became more visible during the civil rights period of the 1960's, paving the way for more recent generations of well-known actors and directors. Certain figures—Bill Cosby, Eddie Murphy, Oprah Winfrey, and Arsenio Hall among them—stand out as well for the control they exercise as multimedia stars and producers.

Asian Americans, on the other hand, have had less presence since the days of silent films. The careers of Asian actors have been complicated by exclusion acts, the enemy status of Japan in World War II, and later political differences between the United States and China. Moreover, Asians are often depicted according to Euro-American perceptions of exoticism, often being stereotyped as geishas or martial arts experts. Their roles on television have been sporadic, relegated to villains, servants (as in *Bonanza* or *Bachelor Father*), or members of an ethnic ensemble cast (Jack Soo in *Barney Miller*).

Latinos often have found themselves, by contrast, playing any "foreigner" except a Latin American or providing "local color" within an exotic plot. As among Asian and black actors, a more activist generation has begun to take center stage since the 1970's, although Latino characterizations on television often have been limited to stereotypical portrayals in urban shows such as *Miami Vice* in which diversity contributes to "atmosphere" (*L.A. Law* and *Hill Street Blues,* with their strong Latino characters, were notable exceptions).

American Indians have perhaps been least recognized as heroes in their own right despite their prominence in Westerns or as objects of study in academic documentaries. Even "sympathetic" films, from *Broken Arrow* (1950) to *Dances with Wolves* (1990), have essentially provided opportunities or background for white heroes rather than recognizing American Indian actors. Stereotypes have been challenged, however, in films such as *Thunderheart* (1992) and the documentary *Incident at Oglala* (1992). American Indians on television continue to find limited roles.

Actress Candice Bergen's portrayal of an unwed mother on the television situation comedy Murphy Brown *unleashed a storm of controversy in 1992 surrounding the issue of "family values."* (AP/Wide World Photos)

Despite a few isolated exceptions, severe limits remain for actors with disabilities. For example, sighted actors are frequently called upon to play blind characters. It is true that audiences can immediately sympathize with a blind character played by an actor they already know well. On the other hand, such casting excludes those actors who might effectively represent their own voices and experiences.

Bill Cosby's television situation comedy The Cosby Show *appealed to a broad audience and counteracted stereotypes of black urban life by portraying the experiences of an upscale African American family.* (AP/Wide World Photos)

Radio and Television. Radio, partly because of the relatively low costs of production and the relative ease of public access, has provided a voice for many minority communities, especially in areas where ethnic concentrations have sustained broadcasts in Spanish, Chinese, and many other languages. Federal broadcast regulations have encouraged minority and female ownership (although it remains limited) as well as programming that is community oriented. Women and minority radio broadcasters have made dramatic advances both in their presence on the air and in their work in key decision-making areas such as sales.

The situation in television broadcasting is more complex; for one thing, the production and distribution of television programming is more complicated and much more expensive than the relatively straightforward radio programming. Television programming encompasses drama, situation comedies, sports events, game shows, and national and local news. In television's early days, programs often reproduced racist stereotypes. A prime example was the black minstrelsy of *Amos 'n' Andy,* which moved to television from radio in the early 1950's. Today, women and members of minorities routinely host major national talk shows, and comedy programs and some daytime dramas assemble surprisingly diverse casts. Nevertheless, only African Americans seem to have made real strides in prime-time drama series. Diversity also has characterized newscasts and public service broadcasts, particularly since the mid-1980's, although there are clearly limits on positions of power for women and minorities behind the camera and in the boardroom in many segments of American television.

Despite the real advances in media portrayals of women and minorities that have gradually occurred since the 1960's, there are pitfalls that remain. For example, there is a general failure to recognize that people often belong to multiple communities whose culture and status do not coincide with the neat, simplistic categories into which the mass media prefer to place people. Examples of the types of complex characterizations that remain unacknowledged might include an elderly Latina who uses a wheelchair or a gay man of mixed Asian and African racial background. Such combinations suggest how complex these multiple communities can be.

Moreover, both the use of token representations of minority supporting characters and the presentation of "all-minority" programming risk producing new versions of typecasting. The image of the United States presented on screens, over the airwaves, in print, and in live performance should make audiences wonder not only who constitutes American society but also how that society will change and can be changed in the future.

SUGGESTED READINGS. Overviews are presented in *Ethnic and Racial Images in American Film and Television: Historical Essays and Bibliography* (1987) by

Allen L. Woll and Randall M. Miller and in *Ethnic Images in American Film and Television* (1979), edited by Randall M. Miller. Studies of minority representation in the media were pioneered in work on the African American experience, including Donald Bogle's *Toms, Coons, Mulattoes, Mammies, and Bucks* (1973) and Thomas Cripp's *Slow Fade to Black: The Negro in American Film, 1900-1942* (1977). Asian roles were discussed by many collaborators in Russell Leong's *Moving the Image: Independent Asian Pacific American Media Arts* (1991). Darrell Hamamoto examined "The Contemporary Asian-American Family on Television" in *Amerasia Journal* 18, no. 2 (1992), pp. 35-55. George Hadley-Garcia has chronicled the complex roles of Latinos in the mass media in *Hispanic Hollywood* (1990). Ally Acker's *Reel Women* (1991) considers the roles of women in direction and production as well as the diversity among women of color in film production.—*Gary W. McDonogh with Cindy Hing-Yuk Wong*

Medicine. *See* **Health and medicine**

Medicine men—traditional American Indian: Popular term derived from the label applied by French explorers to American Indian healers and supernatural specialists. The common element shared by these specialists was an apparent ability to enter into contact with and consciously utilize the power of supernatural forces. Medicine men treated disease, found game, sought out hidden knowledge, and officiated at communal rituals. The domains in which these supernatural specialists held sway varied from culture to culture, as did the attributes associated with them. Contemporary social scientists prefer more specialized labels, such as shaman and shamanism for these practitioners and their spiritual system.

Among smaller hunting and gathering cultures, specialists drew on the power of personal guardian spirits. Since most adults in the group also had guardian spirits, the power of the specialist differed from that of the ordinary person primarily in degree, not in type. Within such cultures, the medicine man was commonly a shaman: He or she was a part-time specialist with the ability to enter ecstatic trance to tap into supernatural power. In some groups, cults developed around "medicine bundles" which were jointly owned by clans or other kin-based groups. The power of these sacred objects could be utilized by a clan member on the occasion of ceremonies or by individuals engaged

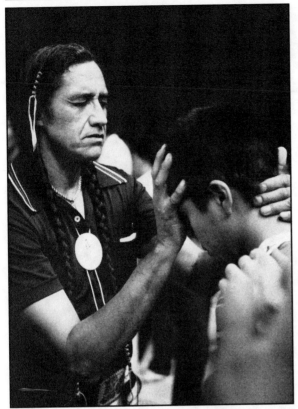

This Flathead medicine man inherited his position as spiritual leader of the tribe. (Odette Lupis)

in specific enterprises such as warfare. Among agriculturally based societies, the role of medicine man became institutionalized in the secret societies that sponsored the major religious ceremonies of the villages. In such cultures, the supernatural practitioner who did not operate within the confines of a recognized ceremonial organization was likely to be accused of witchcraft.

As the role and nature of medicine men varied from culture to culture, so too did their training. In some cases, particularly in the case of the shaman, the individual might be called to the profession by a supernatural signal—a special vision, a psychological trait such as susceptibility to trance, or a physical condition such as epilepsy. In other cases the calling might be inherited from a family member. One could be obligated to the calling in return for having been cured by a member of a medicine society. Whether power was acquired through a supernatural omen, as a birthright, or via apprenticeship, those entering the profession found it necessary go through an often lengthy and arduous process of learning to control their power through songs and rituals, and to convince others of

its efficacy by mastering "stage skills" such as ventriloquism and sleight of hand.

SUGGESTED READINGS. Ake Hultkrantz provides a comprehensive overview of the medicine man and related issues in *The Religions of the American Indians* (1979). *Teachings from the American Earth: Indian Religion and Philosophy* (1975) by Dennis and Barbara Tedlock presents a range of perspectives on the role of the Native American medicine man. Valuable studies of particular cultures are found in Vera Laski's *Seeking Life* (1958) and Gladys Reichard's *Navajo Medicine Man* (1977).

Melting pot theory: One of several theories that attempted to characterize the process of immigrant ASSIMILATION in the United States, sometimes referred to as fusion. The theory emerged as a reaction on the part of "old immigrants" to the massive waves of immigrants from southern and eastern Europe from 1880 to 1914. The idea of the melting pot was first advanced by J. Hector St. John de Crèvecoeur. In his *Letters from an American Farmer* (1782), he noted that the United States was made up of individuals of many nations, although he spoke only of Europeans melting into a new American race. He believed that the process of combining the different groups would produce a new and superior group. Presumably, the differences between ethnic groups would simply melt away.

The term "melting pot" was popularized by the English Jewish playwright Israel Zangwill. His play *The Melting Pot*, first performed on Broadway in 1908, was a romantic, optimistic outlook for the future. The play spoke of a dissolving of hatreds and rivalries between groups, from which the new identity of the "real American" would emerge.

The melting pot theory was challenged in the debate on immigration and assimilation that raged during the interwar years. Supporters of NATIVISM considered the presence of southern and eastern European, as well as Asian, immigrants threatening. They pressed Congress to enact national QUOTAS in restrictive IMMIGRATION LEGISLATION. The new immigrants were viewed as inferior; they were no more accepted than American Indians, African Americans, and Latinos had been by most white Americans. Doubts surfaced that the diverse American peoples would ever "melt."

One view held that the English colonists and their descendants had established a culture that all future immigrants had to adopt. This was referred to as Anglo-conformity. Others saw the "old" immigrants (including

The distinctive cultural backgrounds of these teenage campers enrich their perspectives on life, challenging the melting pot theory's notion that ethnic differences will simply melt away. (Dale D. Gehman)

those from northern and central Europe) as having established the "American" culture which, once established, would compel the adaptation of all future immigrants. The latter process is more dynamic in that it suggests a continuously evolving culture.

Social scientists now generally agree that the idea of a "melting pot" was a myth, an idealistic concept that was attractive but unrealistic. INTERMARRIAGE has occurred among various Europeans, but far less frequently among Europeans and people of color. There is a mainstream American or DOMINANT CULTURE, but many ethnic groups continue to maintain aspects of their unique cultures as well. The melting pot theory has been succeeded by CULTURAL PLURALISM in which culturally distinct groups live together in the same society in relative harmony and by MULTICULTURALISM, which recognizes the distinct experiences and perspectives of diverse groups.

SUGGESTED READINGS. For a comprehensive theoretical analysis of assimilation, see Milton M. Gordon's *Assimilation in American Life* (1964). A more critical view of assimilation is presented by Andrew M. Greeley in *Why Can't They Be Like Us?* (1971) and by Nathan Glazer and Daniel Patrick Moynihan in *Beyond the Melting Pot* (1963). Ronald Takaki's *A Different Mirror: The Making of Multicultural America* (1993) presents the paradigm of cultural pluralism that has replaced the concept of the melting pot.

Mennonites: Religious subculture originating in the Protestant Reformation of sixteenth century Europe, especially in Switzerland, Germany, and the Netherlands. The name Mennonite comes from Menno Simons, who unified the persecuted and dispirited Anabaptists in the Netherlands and North Germany; eventually the label Mennonite came to be applied to Anabaptists elsewhere. Early Mennonites were persecuted by civil authorities as well as by ROMAN CATHOLIC, LUTHERAN, and Reformed state church authorities for their pacifism, their insistence that church membership be voluntary and church matters free of state control, and their practice of rebaptizing adult believers previously baptized as infants in a state church (Anabaptist means "rebaptizer"). Early Mennonites were tortured and killed for their beliefs. In a broad sense, Mennonites deserve credit for establishing the principles of religious freedom and separation of church and state now accepted by most Americans but considered heretical and subversive in sixteenth century Europe.

The AMISH split from the Mennonites in 1693 over the issue of the severity of internal church discipline, with the Amish taking a more extreme position and remaining more sectarian ever since. The HUTTERITES differed slightly in practicing communal living and communal ownership of property.

Both Mennonites and Amish arrived in Pennsylvania at the invitation of fellow pacifist William Penn in the early 1700's. Together with like-minded QUAK-ERS, they issued the first public protest against SLAVERY in North America at Germantown. Significant numbers of Mennonites eventually settled in Indiana, Ohio, Kansas, and California, as well as Ontario and the western provinces of Canada. Many of the Canadian Mennonites came from Russia in the late 1800's and early 1900's, some narrowly escaping a second Mennonite "Holocaust" as Russian Communist leaders forcibly broke up thriving Mennonite colonies and sent many Mennonites to labor camps in Siberia. Most contemporary North American Mennonites retain the pacifism of their ancestors, and a strong desire to help others victimized by persecution or natural disasters. Mennonite Disaster Service and Mennonite Central Committee are respected relief and development organizations.

Mennonites number about one million worldwide, with the largest concentrations in the United States

These Mennonite church members take pride in upholding their religious and social traditions, including a commitment to pacifism and a desire to help others who have become victims of persecution or natural disasters. (Photo Agora)

and Canada, but with growing numbers in Africa, Asia, and Latin America, mostly as a result of mission activity. In North America several thousand African American, Latino, Asian American, and American Indian Mennonites, along with many white "non-ethnic" Mennonites belong to the church as a result of both mission work and marriage to "ethnic" Mennonites of German origin.

Mennonites are divided by degree of sectarianism and self-imposed separation from the non-Mennonite world. More progressive than the Amish and Hutterites, Mennonites are increasingly behaviorally assimilated to the mainstream culture but often retain strong commitments to pacifism, simplicity of life, mutual aid, and service to others.

SUGGESTED READINGS. J. Howard Kauffman and Leo Driedger's *The Mennonite Mosaic: Identity and Modernization* (1991) details characteristics of the progressive Mennonite groups. A comprehensive reference work is Cornelius J. Dyck and Dennis Martin's *Mennonite Encyclopedia* (1990). See also Calvin Redekop's *Mennonite Society* (1989) and Dyck's *An Introduction to Mennonite History (1981)*.

Men's movement: Efforts to reassess traditional men's roles and reconnect men with their emotions and basic nature. This movement, which emerged in the 1970's and 1980's, would seem to be a reaction to FEMINISM and the women's movement, but its roots and inspiration actually date back much further. Since the INDUSTRIAL REVOLUTION in the early 1800's, there has been a diminishing of American men's relating well to their fathers. Previously, in traditional agricultural societies, men worked with their fathers and identified with the older men in their communities. As the Industrial Revolution progressed, however, men went off to work in locations separated from their homes. Their sons could no longer work beside them and learn from them, and men gradually became alienated from one another because they never learned to trust other men.

Today, many men spend less than ten minutes a day in conversation with their sons. Most men have no idea what passions, hopes, and dreams inspired their fathers, and most fathers are not aware of the yearning of their sons to become close to them. The men's movement calls for men to gather together to explore the inner feelings that they have buried since childhood. They must become aware of what strangers they are to their fathers and to their sons.

Another dimension of the need for the men's move-

ment involves the role expectations that men adopt and that ultimately fail them. Men are not supposed to exhibit pain, fear, love, nurturing, grief, or a host of other emotions. This emotional denial and suppression dooms men to frustration, alienation, and impoverished relationships with other males and often with females. The poet Robert Bly suggests that men should grieve together over the loss of human relatedness, which they have abandoned in their attempts to be proper men.

Poet Robert Bly, a leading figure in the men's movement of the early 1990's. (Jerry Bauer)

The men's movement encourages male bonding by sharing feelings, not just sharing sports or adventure. To state openly exhilaration and fear, hope and dread, anger and love is the goal of this bonding. Before the challenge of the men's movement, male bonding was characteristically one-dimensional, with most emotion going unspoken; men had to assume or guess their friends' emotions if they cared to examine them at all. The men's movement has influenced American men's interaction to the extent that more activities now center on conversation and sharing emotions, rather than only sharing space and time in activity. This is done through ongoing men's groups (patterned after encounter groups and the consciousness-raising groups of the WOMEN'S LIBERATION MOVEMENT), special retreats, and new rituals such as initiations for teenage boys.

SUGGESTED READINGS. An excellent book on the men's movement is *Iron John: A Book About Men* (1990) by Robert Bly. Other helpful sources are *Fire in the Belly: On Being a Man* (1991) by Sam Keen; *Men's Friendship* (1992) by Peter M. Nardi; *Troubled Men: The Psychology, Emotions, Conflicts, and Therapy of Men* (1988) by Reuben Fine; and *The Making of Masculinities: The New Men's Studies* (1987) by Harry Brod.

Meredith, James Howard (b. June 25, 1933, Kosciusko, Miss.): African American integration pioneer. Meredith was the first black to integrate the previously all-white University of Mississippi. In the face of heavy resistance and backed by federal troops, the twenty-nine-year-old veteran gained admission to Ole Miss in 1962, later earning his B.A. there. He studied law at Columbia University (1968) and gradually embraced conservative

James Meredith was the first African American granted admission to the previously all-white University of Mississippi. (AP/Wide World Photos)

positions. He ran for Congress as a Republican (1972); worked as a stockbroker and investor; advocated black entrepreneurship; and was the first black on the staff of conservative North Carolina Senator Jesse Helms (1989). His book *Three Years in Mississippi* (1966) is autobiographical.

Methodists: Members of a Protestant denomination that traces its beginnings to the eighteenth century English reformer, John Wesley. In an age of religious formalism and philosophical rationalism, Wesley sought to revitalize Christian life through the cultivation of religious experience and personal holiness within the context of religious fellowship. To this end, Wesley formed small religious societies—fellowships of committed Christians within the Church of England devoted to regular Bible study and lively worship which included extemporaneous prayer, testimonies and witnessing, and mutual encouragement. Methodist also believed that the Christian life ought to express itself in moral transformation.

Though Methodism began in England, British immigrants, especially from Ireland, brought this new form of Protestantism to North America. Before the American Revolution, Methodism was a religious society related nominally to the Church of England. That situation changed in 1784, when at the "Christmas" Conference in Baltimore Methodists became an independent denomination, the Methodist Episcopal church. During the next half century, Methodists proved remarkably successful. By 1820, they surpassed the BAPTISTS as the largest Protestant church in America; at mid-century, there were more than one million Methodists, with Baptists at about half their number.

A consequence of future significance for the Methodists was the success of their itinerant preachers in the conversion of blacks to Christianity. These new black members were often given formal responsibilities within the Methodist churches, and those with special talents became exhorters and preachers. By 1794, former slave Richard Allen laid the foundation for a black denomination when he created the first black Methodist church. After a struggle with white Methodists for control, Allen's congregation united with several other black Methodist churches in 1816 to form the AFRICAN METHODIST EPISCOPAL CHURCH. A similar separation occurred in New York with the creation of the African Methodist Episcopal Zion church (1820). In 1866 the black members of the

Although the vast majority of Latinos are Catholic, some have formed Methodist congregations, such as those who attend this church in Los Angeles' Historic Olvera Street district. (Martin A. Hutner)

Methodist Episcopal church, South formed a third black Methodist denomination, the Colored (now Christian) Methodist Episcopal church. Together, these institutions proved significant forums for black leadership.

The history of Methodism in America has been one of separation and union, and, even though the question of SLAVERY accounts for important splits within the church, other matters have shaped its institutional character. The desire to return to Methodism's evangelical roots or to Wesley's teaching of Christian perfection accounts in part for the formation of the Wesleyan Methodist Connection (1843) and the Free Methodists (1860). Issues relative to Hispanic and American Indian Methodist churches have also challenged Methodism to reassess its missions and governing structure. The overwhelming tendency in twentieth century Methodism has been centripetal and ecumenical, a fact particularly evident in the union of 1939 that led to the creation of the Methodist church

and then in 1969 the United Methodist church.

SUGGESTED READINGS. William Warren Sweet's *Methodism in American History* (1954) offers a standard history. Carol V. R. George's *Segregated Sabbaths: Richard Allen and the Emergence of Independent Black Churches, 1760-1840* (1973) and Harry V. Richardson's *Dark Salvation: The Story of Methodism as It Developed Among Blacks in America* (1976) place the African American Methodists in perspective. Though targeted for a Methodist audience, Justo L. Gonzalez' *Out of Every Tribe and Nation: Christian Theology at the Ethnic Round Table* (1992) and Homer Noley's *First White Frost: Native Americans and United Methodism* (1991) are also useful.

Métis: Offspring of Indian mothers and European fathers who joined together as a distinct people among the full-blooded indigenous inhabitants of Canada during the nineteenth century within the large area that lies west of Lake Superior. They were receptive to the missionaries' influence, and, as a result, were very religious. The Métis whose fathers were French followed the Catholic missionaries and were excellent hunters. The Métis whose fathers were Scottish and English, however, followed the Protestant missionaries and tended toward the sedentary lifestyle of planting and gathering. Contemporary Métis have been active in movements to bring greater rights and cultural recognition to native Canadians.

Mexican American Legal Defense and Education Fund (MALDEF): Founded in 1968 to protect the legal rights of MEXICAN AMERICANS and to assist them with an educational grants program. MALDEF played a prominent role in civil rights cases affecting Mexican Americans in the early 1970's. Later it was involved in cases dealing with BILINGUAL EDUCATION, voter disenfranchisement, the undercount of Latinos in the 1970 census, and political redistricting plans to give Latinos a stronger voice in government. With headquarters in San Francisco and offices throughout the Southwest and in Washington, D.C., the group publishes a quarterly newsletter called *MALDEF*.

Mexican American Political Association (MAPA): Group founded in 1959 in Fresno, California, by a group led by Eduardo Quevedo, who became the first president, and Bert Corona, who succeeded him. MAPA has helped Mexican American political candidates with endorsements, financial backing, and campaigning. Its success in electing Mexican Americans to the U.S. Senate and state legislature as well as state and municipal judgeships led to the formation of a Texas MAPA. Membership declined in the 1970's, however, and an attempt to grow nationally failed. Consequently it remains essentially a California organization.

Mexican-American War (1846-1848): The United States' victory over Mexico in the Mexican-American War resulted in a significant U.S. territorial expansion. The war was costly to the United States in terms of lives lost, yet it was a generally popular war among Americans. The causes of the war were complex; relations had not been smooth between the United States and Mexico beginning in the 1820's.

Causes of the War. From its inception, many Americans believed that the United States represented a new system of government based upon liberal democratic principles and would, in turn, serve as a beacon for the future of humankind. As such, many felt that the United States should serve as an example for other nations to follow. Others, however, went further and argued that the United States had a special responsibility actively to spread its values throughout the Western Hemisphere and protect the new republics of Latin America from European domination. Finally, many Americans believed that it was the destiny of the United States to unify much of North America from ocean to ocean under its direct political control.

Initially, many Mexican intellectuals admired the American political system and hoped to emulate the United States' example. Mexico's unsuccessful attempt to suppress the Texas Revolution of 1836, however, produced a significant alteration of Mexican perceptions of the United States. Despite Washington's official policy of neutrality, the sympathy and encouragement extended by many Americans to the Texans was apparent. Hence, the Mexicans increasingly came to view the United States as a hegemonic power that threatened Mexico's territorial integrity and possibly its independence. Consequently, Mexico's political elite became increasingly resistant to suggestions that Mexico make any concessions to Washington.

Following the establishment of its de facto independence, Texas claimed the Rio Grande as its boundary with Mexico. Notwithstanding the weakness of the

The American victory over the troops of General Antonio Lopez de Santa Anna at the Battle of Buena Vista in 1847 marked the closing phase of the Mexican-American War. (Library of Congress)

Rio Grande claim, when the United States annexed Texas in 1845, President James Polk accepted Texas' claim to the Rio Grande. Since it rejected Texas' legitimacy as an independent entity within any boundaries, an inexcusable affront to Mexico's national dignity. Indeed, as the Mexican tide of nationalism rose, most Mexican leaders expressed a preference for war with the United States rather than submit to a national hu-

Zachary Taylor's leadership during the Mexican-American War led to his nomination to succeed Polk as president in 1848. (White House Historical Society)

Mexico believed the issue of the Rio Grande line was largely moot. Similarly, the Mexicans rejected the United States annexation of Texas and considered it miliation. In addition to the Texas question, tension between the United States and Mexico was further exacerbated by a financial dispute centering upon Mexico's default in April, 1843, on the payment of more than $2 million in claims to the United States. Finally, by the mid-1840's, many Americans hoped to add Mexico's semiautonomous province of California to the United States. The Polk Administration also hoped to acquire New Mexico. Indeed, on a series of occasions from 1835 onward, Polk's predecessors had attempted to purchase these areas, especially northern California and San Francisco Bay, but these efforts had ended in failure. Undaunted, Polk retained hope that these areas could be acquired peacefully, but, for the moment, the Texas issue complicated all other aspects of Mexican-American relations.

Prelude to War. Soon after taking office, President Polk moved to resolve the various outstanding issues by adopting a grand strategy designed to apply military pressure on the Mexican government while simultaneously offering it the option of a negotiated settlement. Polk ordered a show of naval force along Mexico's Gulf Coast, while at the same time directing Brigadier General Zachary Taylor to lead an army of observation into southern Texas. Thus, by the end of July, 1845, a large body of U.S. troops were in position at Corpus Christi. Meanwhile, the administration launched a diplomatic initiative. U.S. emissary John Slidell was authorized to negotiate a border treaty recognizing the Rio Grande line, resolve the claims issue, and purchase California and New Mexico. By early 1846, however, Slidell's mission had foundered on the related factors of Mexican nationalism, Mexico's political instability, and diplomatic protocol complications.

Polk responded to Slidell's failed diplomacy by increasing the military pressure on the Mexican government in an effort to prod it to negotiate. Hence, Taylor was directed to move his forces to the Rio Grande, but not to engage in hostile actions unless war was declared or Mexican forces initiated hostilities. Taylor's movement began on March 8, 1846, and by the end of the month he had about four thousand troops deployed near the mouth of the Rio Grande. In response, the Mexicans increased their military presence south of the river to more than five thousand men. Meanwhile, in Mexico City there were demands for war against the United States to defend Mexico's national honor and territorial integrity.

On April 25, Mexican cavalry clashed with an American patrol on the north side of the Rio Grande, resulting in sixteen Americans killed or wounded. News of this skirmish, however, did not reach Wash-ington until May 9. By that time, Polk had already decided to increase pressure on Mexico again and call upon Congress to declare war on Mexico. Thus, the news of the armed clash merely reinforced Polk's decision by providing the administration with a hostile act by Mexican forces. The president sent his war message to Congress on May 11 and the following day the House of Representatives and the Senate opted for war by votes of 174 to 14 and 40 to 2, respectively. Despite the vote, many Americans, particularly those in New England, did not support "Mr. Polk's War," viewing it as an obvious southern conspiracy to expand SLAVERY.

Conduct of the War. Even after the declaration of war, President Polk remained committed to his grand strategy of gradual pressure designed to induce the Mexicans to submit to the administration's limited objectives. Hence, the administration formulated a four-fold military strategy. Mexican forces had moved en masse north of the Rio Grande, but they were defeated and driven southward. Taylor then moved his reinforced army across the Rio Grande and embarked upon the first component of Polk's military strategy: the seizure of northern Mexico. On September 24, Taylor captured Monterrey, after which he strengthened his hold on northern Mexico. By mid-November, the U.S. Navy occupied the important coastal town of Tampico.

Colonel (later Brigadier General) Stephen W. Kearny was responsible for the second element of Polk's military strategy: the seizure of New Mexico. Leading his force from Ft. Leavenworth, Kansas, Kearny occupied Santa Fe. After dispatching reinforcements to join Taylor's army, Kearny led his remaining force across New Mexico to California where it assisted in the third component of the administration's strategy: the seizure of California.

In California, U.S. naval forces had already occupied Monterey (July 7), San Francisco (July 9), Santa Barbara (August 4), and San Diego (July 29). The seizure of these California coastal towns was reinforced by the "Bear Flag Revolt" and the brief establishment of the "California Republic" in June by American settlers in the Sacramento Valley, a movement which came to be led by Captain John C. Frémont. Thus, when Kearny's force arrived in California in December, the region had already been placed under American control, although a revolt against U.S. authority in southern California was in progress which Kearny assisted in suppressing. By mid-January, 1847, California was securely in American hands. Finally, the fourth element of Polk's military strategy, the blockade of Mexico's ports, was ably executed by the U.S. Navy.

Despite these gains, however, the president's grand strategy initially failed since the Mexican government continued to refuse to negotiate a settlement. Impatient to end the war, Polk again escalated the military pressure by authorizing a campaign designed to capture Mexico City. In January, 1847, U.S. military forces began repositioning in preparation for the assault on Veracruz, reducing Taylor's force in northern Mexico to approximately five thousand men. Attempting to capitalize upon the weakening of Taylor's army, the new Mexican President, General Antonio Lopez de Santa Anna, took personal command of the Mexican army. Although superior in numbers, Santa Anna's force was defeated by Taylor's army at the Battle of Buena Vista on February 23, 1847. Following their defeat, the Mexicans retired southward and, except for guerrilla warfare, large-scale fighting in northern Mexico ceased.

After landing south of Veracruz and successfully laying siege to the city in March, Major General Winfield Scott's army quickly moved inland. Although Santa Anna attempted to block Scott's advance at Cerro Gordo, his force was outmaneuvered by the Americans, who spent months reorganizing before beginning their attack on Mexico City. Finally, on September 14, following the withdrawal of the defeated Mexican army and the surrender of the city by its civil authorities, General Scott's victorious army converged in the Grand Plaza of Mexico's capital. The U.S. flag was raised over Mexico's National Palace, thus beginning the United States's nine-month occupation of Mexico City.

The Treaty of Guadalupe Hidalgo. Meanwhile, Polk had appointed Nicholas Trist to conclude a peace treaty with Mexico. Trist had been instructed, at minimum, to secure recognition of the Rio Grande boundary and to acquire New Mexico and California. In addition, if possible, Trist was to acquire lower California and transit rights across the Isthmus of Tehuantepec. In return, he was authorized to pay up to $30 million, plus assume the claims which Mexico owed the United States. Armed with these instructions, Trist arrived in Mexico in early May of 1847 and immediately attached himself to Scott's army. Following the September capture of Mexico City, a new Mexican government finally opened negotiations, ultimately

leading to the TREATY OF GUADALUPE HIDALGO signed by Trist and Mexican negotiators on February 2, 1848. Under the terms of the treaty, Mexico recognized the Rio Grande boundary, as well as U.S. acquisition of New Mexico north of the Gila River and of California. The treaty did not secure the Polk Administration's extended objectives of acquisition of lower California or isthmus transit rights. For its part, the United States agreed to pay $15 million to Mexico, as well as abandon its prewar financial claims. On March 10, 1848, the U.S. Senate ratified the treaty by a 38-14 vote and in May, the Mexican Congress also approved the treaty. On June 12, 1848, amid Mexican and American artillery salutes, the U.S. flag was replaced by the flag of Mexico in the Grand Plaza of Mexico City.

For the United States, the victorious war yielded clear title to Texas, control over the vast Southwest, and possession of immensely rich California. With the signing of the Treaty of Guadalupe Hidalgo, some 80,000 Mexicans became residents of the United States. The majority of these residents remained on their lands rather then return to Mexico. These new American citizens constituted a majority in the Southwest until the continuing influx of Anglo Americans deprived most of them of their lands and their status by the end of the nineteenth century. Despite their unjust treatment, these Mexican Americans persisted and continued to carry on their rich cultural traditions.

SUGGESTED READINGS. The classic study of the Mexican-American War is Justin Smith's *The War with Mexico* (2 vols., 1919), while more recent studies include K. Jack Bauer's excellent *The Mexican War, 1846-1848* (1974), Robert W. Johannsen's *To the Halls of Montezuma: The Mexican War in the American Imagination* (1985), and Otis Singletary's *The Mexican War* (1960). Alexander De Conde's *History of American Foreign Policy* (1963) and Samuel F. Bemis' *A Diplomatic History of the United States* (1955) are standard works which place the war into its wider context. Finally, *The West Point Atlas of the Civil War* (1962), edited by Vincent J. Esposito, provides superb maps useful for following the military operations.— *Howard M. Hensel*

Mexican Americans: Mexican Americans occupy a unique place among the many groups that are said to have immigrated to the United States in that, historically, not all Mexican Americans actually came to the United States; rather, the United States came to them. In 1848, after the MEXICAN-AMERICAN WAR, the United States took over the northern part of what had been Mexico. Thus, thousands of Mexican citizens—and their future children—suddenly became Americans living in the southwestern United States. Other terms, including "Chicano" and broader terms such as "Latino," "Latin American," "Spanish American," and "Hispanic," which also refer to immigrants from many other countries, have also been used to refer to Mexican Americans. Mexican and other Spanish-speaking people often call themselves *la raza* meaning "the race." This refers to their shared language, culture, and heritage, not specifically to physical racial characteristics.

The Alamo, a famous Texas landmark, is one of several missions founded during the Spanish colonization of Mexico and the Southwest. (Robert Fried)

Both Mexicans and Mexican Americans have played unique and important roles in the historical, cultural, and linguistic evolution of the United States. They have historically been highly concentrated in the southwestern states, especially California, Texas, New Mexico, Arizona, and Colorado. There are, however, many large communities of Mexican Americans in other parts of the country. Latinos, including Mexican Americans and other Spanish-speaking peoples, constitute the second largest and fastest growing minority in the United States. By the year 2000, the United States may have the world's third largest Spanish-speaking population.

Early Mexican History. By the time the English colony of Jamestown was established in 1607, Spanish explorers and conquerors had already been on the North American continent for nearly a hundred years. Hernán Cortés, Álvar Cabeza de Vaca, and Francisco Coronado, to name a few, had explored large areas of the South and Southwest while establishing control over much of the indigenous Indian population. In 1521, New Spain, as the Spanish colony was called, encompassed all of the present-day Southwest, Mexico, and Central America down to the Isthmus of Panama. Spanish influence in this area was destined to leave an indelible mark.

The area known as present-day Mexico was once home to a succession of highly developed Indian civilizations. Evidence shows that as long ago as 2000 B.C.E., there were thriving, complex societies of Indians, called Mesoamericans, inhabiting the area, including the Olmec, Maya, Toltec, Zapotec, Mixtec, and Aztec civilizations. The Indian cultures were highly organized social and political systems with complex writing systems and advanced achievements in architecture, mathematics, and science.

In 1519, Cortés arrived in the Aztec capital city of Tenochtitlán. The Aztec, who called themselves the "Mexica," had originally been a nomadic tribe of hunters and gatherers from the north. Their legends claim they came from an area called Aztlán, which is believed to be located in the southwestern area of the United States.

After the fall of Tenochtitlán, there followed three centuries of Spanish domination. During this time, the cultures of the Europeans and the indigenous Indian populations blended. *Mestizos* of mixed Indian and Spanish ancestry represented a mingling not only of blood lines and history, but also of diverse patterns of life. Roman Catholicism was introduced, along with the Spanish language and political structures, but much of daily life remained shaped by Indian traditions, making Mexican culture unique among the Spanish colonies.

Mexican Independence and Loss of the Northern Territory. By the time Mexico fought for independence from Spain in the early 1800's, the Spanish-Mexican

UNITED STATES

Tijuana

Juarez

Rio Bravo del Norte

NORTH AMERICA

Sonora

Yaqui

BAJA CALIFORNIA

Gulf of California

Fuerte

Rio Grande

Monterrey

Gulf of Mexico

Guadalajara

Mexico City

Usumacinta

YUCATAN

Balsas

PACIFIC OCEAN

Acapulco

GUATEMALA

BELIZE

MEXICO

influence was already entrenched in the northern region. Santa Fe was established as the territorial capital and missions were active from San Antonio to San Diego. Agriculture, mining, and the spreading of Christianity among the Indians were motivation for the Spanish colonization efforts in the Southwest.

During the move for Mexican independence (1810-1821), there was much strife within the new government, and the northern territory was left to its own devices. Contact with Anglo American explorers and traders from the United States was expanded. At first

encouraged by the Mexican government, the growth of the Anglo population was later viewed with suspicion, especially in Texas. The Mexican government made efforts to curb the influx by passing laws to inhibit foreign settlement and to hinder foreign trade. These efforts, however, were largely ineffective.

By the 1830's, the Anglos in Texas greatly outnumbered the Mexicans. Both Mexican and Anglo Texans wanted self-determination with more local power, and they staged the Texas Revolt in 1835. The Texans were victorious and from 1836 to 1845, Texas was

Mexican Immigration to the United States: 1820-1989

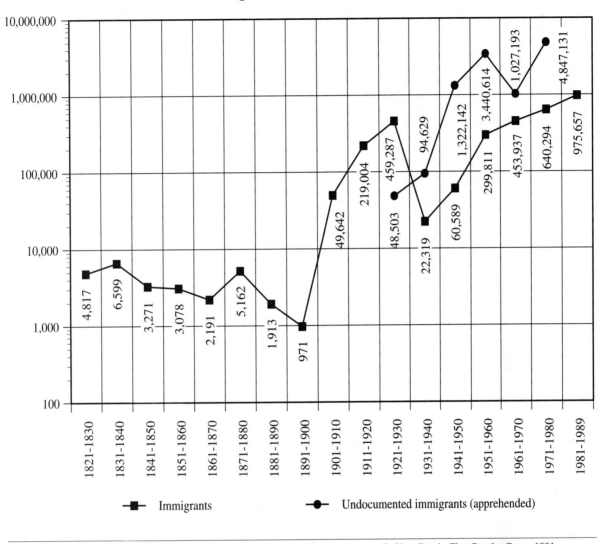

Source: Data are from Paula Lannert, *Mexican Americans*. American Voices series, p. 43. Vero Beach, Fla.: Rourke Corp., 1991.
Note: An additional 4,674,000 Mexicans also arrived under the *Bracero* program between 1941 and 1967.

essentially an independent country. Mexico, however, never officially accepted this status. In 1845, when the U.S. government offered Texas statehood and annexed it into the Union, the Mexican government was drawn into military conflict.

The Mexican-American War (1846-1848) was ended by the TREATY OF GUADALUPE HIDALGO and resulted in Mexico losing almost half of its territory to the United States, including what is now California, Nevada, Utah, New Mexico, Colorado, Wyoming, and part of Arizona. The U.S. government gave the Mexi-

can residents a choice of becoming U.S. citizens or moving to Mexico. Almost 80 percent remained, becoming the first large group of American citizens of Mexican descent living in the United States.

American Citizenship and Minority Status. With the acquisition of the Southwest, the nationalistic doctrine of MANIFEST DESTINY seemingly justified the political, economic, and sociocultural domination of the conquered people. In the years following the war, the process of dispossessing the Mexicans of their property and DISFRANCHISING them of their rights began.

Folklórico dance troupes are a hallmark of Mexican American cultural celebrations. (Martin A. Hutner)

The Mexicans did not understand the language, culture, or political and legal structures of Anglo American society, and they were quickly outnumbered and overwhelmed. Agricultural and other menial jobs, high unemployment, POVERTY, and segregated living conditions came to characterize the life of most Mexican Americans in the Southwest by the end of the nineteenth century.

In the twentieth century, waves of immigration ebbed and flowed from Mexico into the United States, with an ever-increasing number of Mexicans deciding to live north of the border. Relations with dominant Anglo society have been strained and violent at times as the Mexicans struggled to claim their right to participation in the life of the nation. Mexican Americans are unique among American minority groups in having maintained strong cultural and linguistic ties through unique circumstances of geographical proximity to their homeland. Other immigrant groups have traditionally experienced a fading out of such ties after two or three generations. Mexican Americans, however, have remained a distinct, identifiable group bound by experiences of language and culture.

In the latter part of the twentieth century, especially after the CIVIL RIGHTS MOVEMENT of the 1960's, Mexican Americans made some legal progress toward rectifying past injustices. Organizations such as the MEXICAN AMERICAN LEGAL DEFENSE AND EDUCATION FUND, the UNITED FARM WORKERS, and the SOUTHWEST VOTER REGISTRATION EDUCATION PROJECT brought attention to some of the special needs of Mexican Americans, while the CHICANO RIGHTS MOVEMENT of the 1960's and 1970's radicalized the younger generation of American-born Mexicans. There were some economic and political gains as more Mexicans moved into the upper and middle classes, registered to vote, and took advantage of AFFIRMATIVE ACTION programs. Other efforts focused on protecting language rights and viewing BILINGUALISM as a resource rather than a liability. There remains, however, much to be done to make the American dream fully accessible to all Mexican Americans.

Contemporary Immigration. When the United States acquired the Southwest in 1848, there were approximately eighty thousand residents of Mexican descent in the region. By the 1880's, Mexicans had become a poor, landless minority who generally lived apart from Anglo American society. As the U.S. economy began to expand and industrialization moved into the Southwest, there was a greater need for cheap labor to work in the growing agri-business. Economic and political instability in Mexico at the turn of the century also sent thousands of Mexicans north. This movement included many poor peasants as well as wealthy Mexicans seeking the safety and stability of the United States. Between 1900 and 1930, about a million Mexicans immigrated, bringing the total Mexican American population to nearly three million. At first the Mexicans were welcomed into the economy. Menial jobs that had previously been filled by Chinese, Japanese, and Filipino immigrants were now open to Mexicans because Anglo RACISM had led to the exclusion of Asians from immigration and the work force.

When the GREAT DEPRESSION shattered the U.S. economy in the 1930's, hard times beset the Mexicans, especially the new immigrants. White immigrants left the Dust Bowl for the Southwest to compete for the few available jobs. As competition and XENOPHOBIA grew, there was a move to repatriate the Mexican workers. By 1940, nearly 500,000 people of Mexican descent had been sent back to Mexico. Some went willingly, while others were deported without benefit of legal proceedings.

World War II again brought a new demand for unskilled labor in agriculture. The *bracero* program, begun in 1942, was an agreement between the U.S. and Mexican governments to allow seasonal farm workers to migrate to the United States during farm seasons and return to Mexico at the end of the season. The arrangement worked well for business interests in both countries and was not discontinued until 1964 under President John F. Kennedy. During the twenty-two years of the *bracero* program, some 4.8 million Mexican workers entered the United States. These workers were, in theory, supposed to return to Mexico, but one of the effects of the program was a dramatic increase in the migration of undocumented workers.

Smuggling immigrants across the border illegally became a highly profitable business in the 1950's. To curb the flow, the U.S. government set up "OPERATION WETBACK" in which illegal workers were rounded up and deported back to Mexico. By 1955 almost two million Mexicans had been sent back to Mexico, and illegal border crossings seemed to be under control.

Mexican Americans such as this Colorado rancher and priest are concerned about environmental issues such as water use and grazing rights. (James L. Shaffer)

"Operation Wetback" had mixed results for Mexican Americans. There were more jobs available once the cheap, imported labor was gone, but many of those deported were family members of those who remained behind. Many U.S. citizens of Mexican descent also suffered serious infractions of their civil rights when they were threatened and forced to prove their citizenship in order to avoid deportation themselves.

Whatever effect the operation had on illegal immigration was temporary at best. When the *bracero* program ended in 1964, undocumented workers began pouring across the border again. There have been many attempts to control the borders, such as the IMMIGRATION REFORM AND CONTROL ACT OF 1986, which set financial penalties for employers who hire undocumented workers. The 2,000-mile-long border is difficult to patrol, however, and the flow of undocumented aliens continues. This influx, combined with legal immigration and high birth rates, has contributed to the Mexican Americans being the fastest-growing minority in the United States.

Cultural Contributions. The Mexican legacy in the Southwest is profound and far-reaching. It encompasses diverse facets of life including economic structures, the arts, language, and even the legal system. With the wild horses, longhorn cattle, and sheep that were introduced by the early Spaniards, the Mexican influence on American agriculture and ranching cannot be denied. The system of organizing the livestock industry—even the way cowboys dress and entertain themselves in rodeos—can be traced back to the Mexicans. Mexican irrigation systems, and farming and mining techniques also contributed to the economic development of the area.

Another Mexican mark on life in the Southwest concerned legal codes that had been established by the Spanish. Many of these codes were adapted and made into American laws. For example, the idea of community property rights in a marriage is of Spanish origin, whereas English common law gives all control of property to the husband. Another example of Mexican law being incorporated into the U.S. legal system concerned water utilization rights—a critical issue in the arid Southwest.

Aesthetically it is impossible to travel through the Southwest and not see Spanish and Mexican influence in the architecture, including design and construction materials. Colorful Mexican clothing, music, and dance pervade the cultural milieu, both in their pure Mexican forms and in hybrids such as Tex-Mex.

The impoverished conditions faced by this woman and her son demonstrate that much remains to be done to make the American Dream fully accessible to all Mexican Americans. (AP/Wide World Photos)

Throughout the Southwest, Mexican food and Spanish words are ever-present reminders of Mexican heritage. Entire neighborhoods, such as EAST LOS ANGELES, maintain the language, customs, and values of their residents' native regions of Mexico. Holidays such as Mexican Independence Day and Day of the Dead are widely celebrated, and the Catholic religion remains dominant.

The contributions of Mexican culture and Mexican American people touch the mainstream of American life even beyond the borders of the Southwest.

SUGGESTED READINGS. For more information regarding Mexican Americans see Matt S. Meier and Feliciano Rivera's *Dictionary of Mexican American History* (1981). A more analytical treatment of the Mexican American experience is offered by Rudy Acuña in *A Mexican American Chronicle* (1971) and in Julie Catalano's *The Mexican Americans* (1988). L. H. Gann and Peter J. Duigman's *The Hispanics in the United States: A History* (1986) presents an overview of Mexican Americans as well as of other Latino groups.—*April L. Haulman*

Miami, Fla.: Like Los Angeles, New York, Houston, and Seattle, Miami is one of several metropolitan centers that would probably have experienced continuing decline after the 1960's—as did Philadelphia and Detroit—without an influx of immigrants. The city is known for its historic resorts and mild weather—an environment that has attracted many retirees to the area and has contributed to the growth of the city's Jewish population. The Consolidated Metropolitan Statistical Area around Miami grew to include a population of 3,001,000 by 1988, making Greater Miami (Miami and Dade County) the nation's eleventh largest metropolis and one of its densest centers of Latino, African American, and Caribbean (largely Haitian and Dominican) cultures.

Thirty-five percent of Greater Miami's population are Latinos, mostly Cuban immigrants and their descendants. Within the thirty-four square miles constituting the city of Miami, CUBAN AMERICANS are an absolute majority with 56 percent of all inhabitants. From the Cuban revolution in 1959 until 1990, more than one million Cubans fled their home island, nearly 800,000 of them settling in Miami, a city that has subsequently been dubbed "Little Havana." In an unprecedented American demographic revolution, Latinos in company with 535,000 African American inhabitants, have transformed the non-Latino white community into a distinct minority.

Partly because a large segment of Cuban immigrants came from Cuba's middle and professional classes, their collective efforts revitalized what experts had depicted as a declining American city. This resurgence is confirmed by the city's twenty-five thousand Cuban American business establishments as well as by the successful launching of Latino political leaders. BOB MARTINEZ moved from local prominence to governor and then to positions in Washington, D.C., while Jorge Mas Canosa, a millionaire Cuban exile, led the powerful anti-Castro Cuban American National Foundation to international recognition.

In 1993, after years of controversy, Miami elected to become the nation's first officially bilingual city, equalizing the uses of Spanish and English. Miami's predominantly Latino cultures have successfully transplanted not only their native language but also their religions, carnivals, holidays, and foods.

Various conflicts have challenged Miami residents, both between and within ethnic groups. Cuban Americans have parted politically over relations with Cuba. Divisive issues have also erupted between Latinos and Anglos, exemplified by public quarrels between the Anglo-owned *Miami Herald/El Nueva Herald* and Latino leaders. The MIAMI RIOTS in the 1980's underscored differences between blacks and Latinos, and non-Latino whites.

SUGGESTED READINGS. Thomas D. Boswell and James R. Curtis' *The Cuban-American Experience* (1984) is a readable study that covers several American cities as well as Miami. For more detail on Miami's multiethnic population, see *Miami, Now!: Immigration, Ethnicity, and Social Change* (1992), edited by Guillermo Grenier and Alex Stepick III. Eleanor M.

Rogg's *The Assimilation of Cuban Exiles* (1974) examines the "melting pot" hypothesis, while Richard R. Fagen, Richard A. Brody, and Thomas J. O'Leary's *Cubans in Exile* (1968) provides an early analysis of Cuban interactions in Miami and elsewhere. Bruce Porter and Marvin Dunn assess community divisions in *The Miami Riot of 1980: Crossing the Bounds (1984).*

Miami riots (1980's): Series of civil disturbances sparked by altercations between police officers and minority residents. There were four such riots in the 1980's.

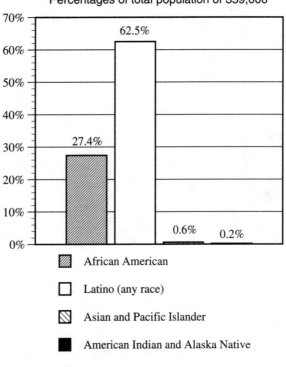

Miami Minority Population: 1990

Percentages of total population of 359,000

- African American
- Latino (any race)
- Asian and Pacific Islander
- American Indian and Alaska Native

Source: Data are from *Statistical Abstract of the United States, 1992* Table 38. Washington, D.C.: Government Printing Office, 1992.

The first, as well as the worst of these, occurred between May 18 and May 20, 1980, in Liberty City, a section of northwest Miami, Florida.

The origins of the 1980 riots can be traced to an incident involving the police and Arthur Lee McDuffie, an African American insurance manager and former Marine. When on December 17, 1979, he was seen speeding on his motorcycle, a police officer gave chase. Twelve additional officers from the Dade County and Miami police departments joined the

In 1989, Miami police officers arrested this looting suspect involved in the violence of the fourth round of rioting in the city. (AP/Wide World Photos)

twelve-minute chase, with McDuffie reportedly running red lights and traveling at speeds of up to one hundred miles per hour.

Upon arriving at the scene a short time later, one police officer noted that McDuffie's face "looked like it had been sprayed with a can of red paint." Although conscious at the time, McDuffie lapsed into a coma and died four days later at a local hospital from head injuries. Inconsistencies in official police reports prompted suspicions of a police cover-up. The original police statement reported that McDuffie had been injured when his motorcycle crashed. The officers also claimed that McDuffie had attempted to resist arrest and had to be subdued.

A department investigation into the incident resulted in the dismissal of eight Dade County police officers, five of whom were indicted on thirteen counts, including second-degree murder in the beating death of McDuffie

and tampering with evidence in the case.

The case was heard by an all-white jury. Two officers testified for the prosecution in exchange for immunity, and a third officer testified for the prosecution after charges against him were dropped. Testimony revealed that McDuffie was beaten to the ground with nightsticks and flashlights, after surrendering, and that his motorcycle was run over to make it appear that he had wrecked it.

The seven-week trial ended with the jury's acquittal of all five officers on all counts after only two hours and forty-five minutes of deliberations. The verdict was seen as an outrage by the African American community, which did not believe that justice had been pursued in the trial. The impact of inflation, high unemployment rates, and increasing resentment over public assistance being given to newly arrived Cuban refugees of the MARIEL BOAT LIFT had combined to create a volatile climate.

An angry mob, which quickly grew to more than five thousand people, stormed the Dade County Public Safety facility on May 18, 1980, in protest of the verdict. The violence quickly spewed out into the streets as arsonists torched buildings, looters ransacked businesses, and snipers fired randomly in the dark. Police cars, fire trucks, and ambulances were pelted with rocks and gunshots as they responded to calls to quell the violence and the fires, and to treat the injured. Motorists, mostly white, were dragged from their cars and savagely beaten.

Governor Bob Graham ordered the mobilization of the National Guard, and one thousand heavily armed troops were sent in to assist local law enforcement agencies in regaining control. An 8:00 P.M. curfew was imposed until the violence was contained. The U.S. Department of Justice sought to indict the former police officers for violating McDuffie's civil rights. The three days of random looting and violence left eighteen people dead and more than four hundred injured. The riots resulted in $1 million worth of property damage to the area and about eleven hundred arrests.

The second and third Miami riots of the 1980's were related. In December of 1982, Officer Luis Alvarez shot and killed twenty-year-old Nevell Johnson, an African American male who was confronted in a video arcade in the Overtown community. Alvarez claimed that Johnson was carrying a gun under his shirt. Civil unrest in the wake of the shooting left two dead and several people injured.

Alvarez was tried and acquitted of any wrongdoing in Johnson's death. The jury returned the not-guilty verdict within two hours of beginning deliberations. The Overtown community again exploded in two nights of violence, resulting in a number of injuries and arrests.

The fourth riot occurred in January, 1989, after the acquittal of Colombian-born police officer William Lozano, who had been tried in the shooting death of motorcyclist Clement Lloyd, a twenty-three-year-old African American male, in Overtown. Tension and outrage erupted into three nights of looting and violence, which caused about $1 million worth of property damage. One person was killed, twenty-two were wounded, and 385 were arrested.

In the wake of the riots, mayor Xavier Suarez established an investigative committee, made up of five African American residents of Overtown and five police officers, to examine the riots. He also suggested that potential police officers be given extensive psychological testing to screen out those who are racially biased or prone to violence. The riots indicated that the problems and frustrations—particularly the feelings of racist persecution—faced by urban African Americans had not improved since the 1960's.

SUGGESTED READINGS. *The Miami Race Riots of 1980: Crossing the Bounds* (1984) by Bruce Porter and Marvin Dunn includes detailed information about the riots and about the history of race relations in Miami. Sources that examine the broader context of urban disturbances include *Race and Inequality: A Study in American Values* (1985) by Paul M. Sniderman and Michael Gray Hagen, *The Truly Disadvantaged: The Inner City, the Underclass, and Public Policy* (1987) by William Julius Williams, and *Voices of Freedom: An Oral History of the Civil Rights Movement from the 1950's Through the 1980's* (1990) by Henry Hampton and Steve Fayer (with Sarah Flynn).

A commercial building in Miami burns during the 1980 riots, which erupted shortly after several police officers were acquitted on charges that they had beaten an African American motorcyclist to death following his arrest for speeding. (AP/Wide World Photos)

Middle Passage: Transatlantic portion of the journey that slaves made from their homes in Africa to their owners in the New World. It is called the "Middle" Passage because it was the second of three journeys made by enslaved Africans. The first was the journey from their homeland to the coast of Africa (often as a prisoner of war). The second or middle passage was the journey from a coastal port of Africa to a coastal port in the New World. The third or last passage was the journey from the New World port to the farm, mine, or plantation for slave labor. Other names for the Middle Passage are the Atlantic Passage and the One-Way Passage.

Slavery and the Triangle Trade. The Middle Passage was the second leg of the triangle trade. The triangle trade was the voyage of a slave ship from its home port to the slave-selling regions of coastal Africa, from Africa to the New World slave-selling port, and then from the New World slave port to a New World or European trading port and back home. Profits were made at each corner of the triangle not only by buying and selling slaves but also by carrying cargoes other than slaves from the New World to Europe (or from the Caribbean to New England).

The slave ships would begin their voyages in Europe or in New England. There the ships' holds were filled with trade goods such as liquor, firearms, ammunition, cloth, cooking utensils, and jewelry. These were used to acquire human cargoes in Africa in a process known as the assortment trade. Since there was no set standard of money in the different societies which traded slaves, the value of the slaves was set as equal to a certain amount of trade goods. The value was adjusted based on the condition of the slaves traded. Factors which affected the value of the slaves included their health, age, gender, and ethnicity. In general, young men brought the highest prices, but women and children were also valued.

In Africa (mostly in the coastal regions of western and central Africa, but extending to the east coast and the island of Madagascar) slaves were often obtained from professional middlemen whose jobs were to

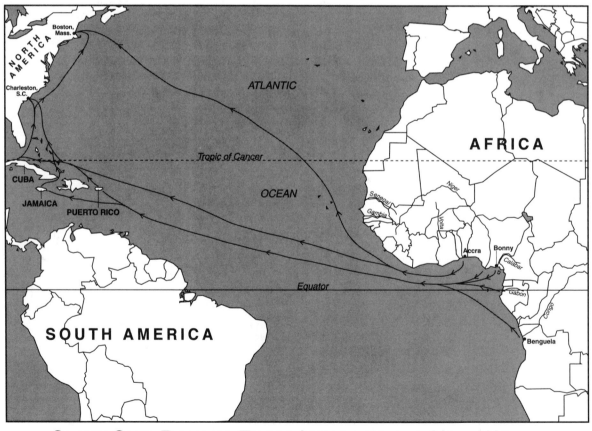

SLAVE SHIP ROUTES FROM AFRICA TO THE NEW WORLD

Source: Adapted from Thomas Howard, ed., *Black Voyage: Eyewitness Accounts of the Atlantic Slave Trade*. Boston: Little, Brown and Co., 1971.

Africans who ultimately endured the Middle Passage were forced to march to the coast under heavy restraint by middlemen who traded prisoners of war and criminals into slavery in exchange for European merchandise. (The Associated Publishers, Inc.)

trade prisoners of war and criminals for the European goods. (It is critical to note that Africans were not selling "their own people" into slavery, as is often asserted. Most of those who became enslaved were of different ethnic groups/nationalities than those who were trading them.) These enslaved people were held at the coast of Africa in dungeonlike forts until enough had been collected to fill the slave ship. After being inspected for disease and fitness, the collected slaves were then transferred to the slave ship and, in some cases, were branded and/or baptized. The slaves were then transported to the New World in a journey which averaged five weeks but could exceed three months under unfavorable conditions. The total number of people taken as cargo in the Middle Passage is estimated to be approximately twelve million.

The third leg of the triangle trade was the transportation of raw materials from the New World to Europe or other New World ports. Among the goods commonly carried were sugar, tobacco, cotton, coffee, gold, dried fish, and furs. Many of the goods transported from the New World (particularly from the Caribbean and Brazil) were produced by the labor of slaves. Thus, in addition to being

significant to the captains and ship owners as an economic commodity to be bought and sold, slaves were also the source of labor to produce other cargo. After arrival in Europe or New England and the sale of the New World goods, the slave ships would return to Africa and the cycle would continue.

Treatment of Slaves During the Middle Passage. Conditions for the slaves aboard the slave ships varied greatly. The treatment of the human cargo was at the discretion of the captain or the ship's owner. The slaves were a valuable commodity which could bring a large profit when sold. Despite the value of this cargo, the slaves were often subjected to conditions which actually reduced their economic worth. For the Middle Passage as a whole, mortality rates are estimated at approximately 20 percent, though in some cases this percentage was much higher. There are examples of captains who treated the slaves on their ships with less brutality in order to ensure higher rates of survival and thus higher profits. This was not the norm, however; many owners and captains packed more slaves aboard in order to offset the loss of life caused by the poor treatment given to the slaves. The

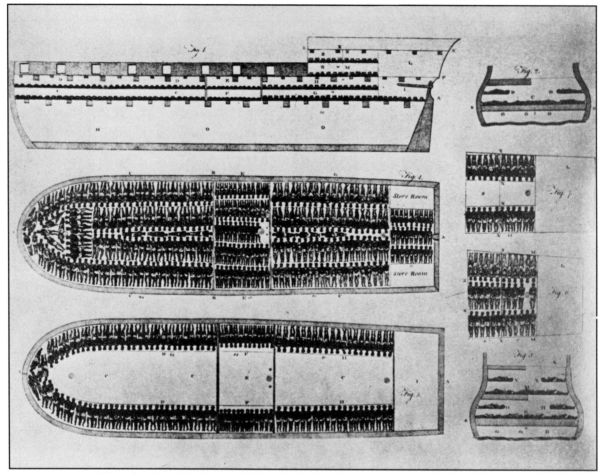

Plan of a slave ship shows tightly packed quarters. (The Associated Publishers, Inc.)

logical contradiction involved in valuing slaves as cargo but ignoring their needs as human beings is difficult to understand; however, it was part of the larger pattern of dehumanization which underlay the New World slave systems.

Overcrowding brought its own problems. The slaves were often packed into lower decks with no room to stand and as little as 12 inches between them. Men and women were put into separate areas; men were usually chained together in twos, while women and children were often left unchained. In some cases, slaves would remain in the holds for as long as twenty-three hours a day, coming above deck only to exercise, pray (in a European language which few of the enslaved could speak), and allow the crew to clean out the slave decks. Toilet facilities were minimal or nonexistent, and diarrheal diseases such as amoebic dysentery were extremely common. Many contemporary reports discuss the stench and general uncleanliness of the slave decks of the ships. The spread of disease among the slaves was rapid and often fatal because of the cramped conditions, the minimal opportunities for personal hygiene, and sometimes the lack of adequate food. Slaves who were ill (particularly with infectious diseases such as smallpox, cholera, or dysentery) were thrown overboard to protect the rest of the cargo and crew.

During the Middle Passage, slaves ate whatever food had been brought on board by the crew. Often, this would include foods familiar to the enslaved. Keeping the slaves well-fed and healthy was a goal of the ship owners in order to ensure that the slaves brought the highest price possible when sold in the New World. As a result, the slaves sometimes ate better than the crew.

Often the slaves were from a number of different ethnic groups and thus could not communicate in a common language. Women suffered a particularly cruel fate aboard the slave ships—one which anticipated their treatment in the New World—as victims of rape. The rape of slaves was a tolerated practice that added to the general process of dehumanization that slavery engenders.

The imposition of the category of property onto the slave during the Middle Passage is clearly illustrated in the case of the slave ship *Zong*. In 1781 the *Zong* had a cargo of 440 slaves. As a result of poor weather and poor navigation, the voyage took much longer than expected; a number of the slaves and crew sickened, and some died. To save the rest of the slaves, the captain ordered 132 sickly slaves thrown overboard. Later, the insurance company was sued to pay for the loss of cargo (slaves) which resulted from this act. Loss of human life was never the issue raised in court, only the loss of property. The ship owners won and were paid for the lost cargo.

Resistance of Slaves During the Middle Passage. The brutal and unfamiliar situations in which the enslaved Africans found themselves created misery and confusion. Acts of resistance against this condition naturally arose. Captains and crews feared rebellion and directed much thought to heading off any possible revolt. It was fear of violent rebellion that caused slavers to chain male slaves (female slaves were seen as less dangerous). Also, to deal with potentially rebellious slaves, slave ships' storerooms contained torture devices.

Slave uprisings did occur occasionally. Attempted rebellions were put down harshly, as there was fear that the idea of rebellion would spread if not punished in a severe and dramatic fashion. One of the most famous examples of an attempted rebellion on a slave ship is that of Tomba, a man of Sierra Leone, who was taken as a slave in 1721. With the assistance of several other captives, he revolted against the crew, but the rebellion was soon discovered and put down. One of the "conspirators," a woman, was stabbed to death, and the other participants were made to eat her flesh and organs. Thus, an extreme, dehumanizing punishment was enforced for a highly feared offense against the system of slavery. A number of other slave revolts have been recorded, few of them successful.

While active rebellion was the most dramatic form of resistance, the most common form was not directed at the crew but at the captives themselves—suicide. It was known that while the slaves could still see the coast of Africa, they were very likely to try to jump overboard. Once out at sea, attempted suicide was also common. The method of suicide that was most feared by the crew was one known as fixed melancholy, a condition in which the slave gave up the will to live, specifically the will to eat. Inducements such as jewelry and alcohol were brought aboard the ships to keep the slaves content. If the more benign inducements were not effective, more direct action was taken. There was a device known as a "speculum oris" (mouth opener), which was used to force-feed recalcitrant slaves. Heated pokers, hot lead, and thumb screws were also used to try to induce slaves to eat (and thus survive to be sold in the New World markets).

Effects of the Middle Passage on African Americans. The lasting effects of the Middle Passage are difficult to assess. Certainly the health of the first generations of Africans to arrive in the New World was severely affected by the traumatic voyage. Mortality rates for these immigrants were extremely high, and fertility rates were extremely low. Some scientists argue that the Middle Passage acted as an agent of biological selection on the population of Africans who came to the New World, keeping only the fittest alive. The high rates of hypertension and cardiovascular disease in contemporary African Americans have been suggested to be results of selection for those aboard the slave ships who could best retain salt in their bodies. Slaves who could not retain salt experienced higher rates of dehydration (from diarrhea or exposure) and thus higher rates of mortality. Much of the social, psychological, and biological legacy of slavery has yet to be explored.

SUGGESTED READINGS. A popular approach to this subject is the novel *Middle Passage* by Charles Johnson (1990), which is well researched and thought provoking. For a detailed analysis of the slave trade and the Middle Passage in particular, *The Making of the African Diaspora in the Americas, 1441-1900*, by Vincent Thompson (1987), is excellent. *The Interesting Narrative of the Life of Olaudah Eauiano or Gustavus Vassa, the African,* in *The Classic Slave Narratives* (1987), edited by Henry Louis Gates contains a rare firsthand account of the Middle Passage from a slave's point of view that was first published in 1814.—*Timothy J. McMillan*

Midwives: Usually women who care for mothers during pregnancy and childbirth. The word midwife, derived from Middle and Old English, means literally "with woman." Mentioned in the Bible and discussed in an-

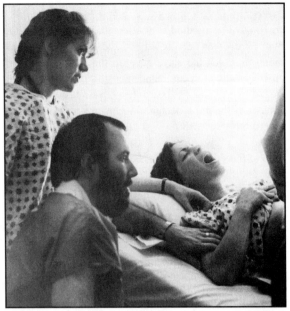

Midwives have encouraged the practice of natural childbirth and the supportive presence of family members during labor in hospital settings. (Photo Agora)

cient medical texts from Egypt, Greece, China, India, and Japan, midwives were the first obstetricians. They continued to dominate the field well into the 1600's and 1700's.

Because midwives were responsible for bringing life into the world and were therefore responsible for matters of inheritance, citizenship, and maintenance of public health, they were, during Roman and medieval times, accorded an important status by civic, royal, and priestly officials. Male physical examinations of women were prohibited by both the Islamic and Christian religions, so midwives treated many medical problems, often administering herbal cures. Because of their knowledge, and also because the birthing process was considered miraculous and mysterious, midwives were thought to possess special powers. During the witchcraft hysteria in early modern Europe, midwives became the natural objects of fear, accusation, and persecution. This, along with scientific advancements and the expansion of formal training in medicine caused midwifery—a vocation based primarily on experience and folk tradition—to be scornfully criticized.

As a result, in the sixteenth and seventeenth centuries, stricter midwifery regulations and licensing rules were enforced, giving "legitimacy" to the often poor and illiterate midwives. The increasing scientific sophistication of the medical field—largely closed to

women—lowered the midwife's status, however. After the publication of various obstetrical treatises and the invention of the forceps (a tool that eased birth, which midwives were not permitted to use), aristocratic women began to have physician-attended births and midwives came to be mainly employed by the rural population and the underprivileged.

In the United States, midwives played an active part from the colonial period through the nineteenth century. Female slaves often became midwives, serving as birth attendants, wet nurses, and housekeepers. Among poorer families, the midwife was usually a relative or friend. The midwifery tradition lasted longer in the South were there were large rural and African American populations. In 1910, half of all reported births in the United States were attended by midwives; by 1930, that number had been vastly reduced.

With the expansion of American medical schools, physicians successfully argued that midwives—most of whom were immigrant or black women—were ignorant, uneducable, and a threat to American health. As midwives became a scapegoat for high infant mortality rates, most American women chose physician-attended or hospitalized childbirth.

During the 1960's and 1970's, natural methods of childbirth became encouraged and respected. With the rise of contemporary FEMINISM and disenchantment with the male-dominated medical profession, midwives once again became an alternative to the often unnecessary and considerably more expensive services of physicians. More women sought the woman-centered approach of midwives, who treated the birth process as a normal, natural event rather than a crisis requiring medical intervention. In addition to traditional lay midwives, who relied on practical experience attending births, the United States saw a surge in the number of certified nurse-midwives (CNMs), who received specialized training as an extension of nursing programs. In the 1980's, a number of American hospitals hired CNMs to facilitate low-risk births and train residents in low-intervention techniques. According to the National Center for Health Statistics, nearly 140,000 hospital births in 1990 were attended by midwives—seven times as many as in 1975—while the number of nonhospital midwife-attended births doubled to 21,000 over the same period. Yet by the early 1990's, some states still had laws restricting midwifery practice and eligibility for health insurance reimbursement.

SUGGESTED READINGS. For an overview of American midwifery, read Judy Barrett Litoff's *The American Midwife Debate* (1986) and Dorothy C. and Richard W. Wertz's *Lying-In: A History of Childbirth in America* (exp, ed. 1989). For more specific studies on the tradition of African American midwifery, see Sharon E. Robinson's article "A Historical Development of Midwifery in the Black Community:1600-1940," in the *Journal of Nurse-Midwifery* 29, no. 4 (1984), pp. 247-250, and Debra Ann Susie's *In the Way of Our Grandmothers: A Cultural View of Twentieth-Century Midwifery in Florida* (1988). For a general and feminist-oriented account of midwifery, see Barbara Ehrenreich's *Witches, Midwives, and Nurses: A History of Women Healers* (1973).

Migrant Children Education Assistance Act of 1960: Law that provides special programs and funding to meet the educational needs of the children of migrant labor parents who cannot attend school continuously during the regular term. The programs were enacted to help these children achieve their potential and become beneficial members of society. Money for personnel, as well as transportation and meals for the students and summer schools for children who cannot attend the required number of days during the regular school year, is included. All school districts that have migrant children can apply to participate in this program.

Migrant workers: Farm workers who travel from place to place harvesting crops. In 1992, there were an estimated 1.5 to 2.5 million migrant workers in the United States. Despite their role as the backbone of AGRICULTURE—the country's largest single business—migrant workers are arguably the poorest paid, most readily exploited group of American workers. Since few of them vote and many are undocumented immigrants who live on the fringes of society, migrant workers have been called "the forgotten people."

Migrant workers began to appear on the scene more than a century ago when large landholdings, specialization, and mechanization changed the face of American agriculture. Farmers found it cheaper and more efficient to hire many workers temporarily at harvest time rather than to keep a small number of workers year-round.

In August, 1942, the United States signed an agreement with Mexico for the importation of Mexican nationals to be used as farm laborers in the United States. The following year, the United States govern-ment made similar arrangement for workers from Newfoundland, Canada, Jamaica, British Honduras, Barbados, and the Bahamas. Of all the alien farm workers brought to the United States during World War II, more than two-thirds came from Mexico under the *bracero* program. In the early 1990's, the majority of migrant workers continued to be foreign-born, with many documented seasonal workers from Mexico and the Caribbean as well as undocumented workers from these regions and from Central and South America.

Each year, thousands of migrant workers arrive in every state to pick fruit, chop cotton, scrap beans, top onions, bunch carrots, and pull corn. In the East, migrant workers travel from south to north, beginning in South Carolina in May, and moving to North Carolina and Virginia in June. By late summer, they have passed through Pennsylvania into New Jersey, New York, Delaware, Maryland, and Maine. By October, the upstate crops are in and the workers then travel

These Mexican migrant workers are harvesting bell peppers in southern Florida. (Michael L. Kimble)

back to the southern tip of Florida.

Migrant workers can be divided into two major groups: migrant families and unattached migrants. Migrant families are generally small, complete units under the direction of an employable head. They tend to be isolated from the activities of local communities because they are always in transit. There are a number of problems that plague migrant families. For example, they suffer from inadequate medical care and educational opportunities. Since the MIGRANT CHILDREN EDUCATION ASSISTANCE ACT OF 1960, there have been efforts to provide seasonal schools and social service programs to help these families.

Unattached migrants are men of various nationalities who often live together in housing provided by the growers. Some, such as Yemeni migrant workers from the Middle East, send their wages to their families back home; others are single men who cannot find work elsewhere.

The television documentary *Harvest of Shame* (1960) first exposed other Americans to the shocking abuses and poor working and living conditions endured by migrant workers. As a result, some protective legislation was passed. In 1962, Chicano leader César CHÁVEZ started the United Farm Workers Organizing Committee to unionize migrant workers in California, who were mainly Mexican and Filipino. The UNITED FARM WORKERS, the first union of its kind, negotiated a number of more favorable contracts with growers after some bitter strikes and nationwide grape and lettuce boycotts. Yet even in 1992, a congressional report noted a pattern of continuing abuse by employers as well as high rates of tuberculosis, pesticide poisoning, disabling work injuries, and other health problems among migrant workers, who rarely made more than five thousand dollars per year.

SUGGESTED READINGS. For profiles of earlier migrant families or unattached migrants, see Nels Anderson's *Men on the Move* (1940). Truman Moore's *The Slaves We Rent* (1965) has a good discussion of the moving patterns of the migrants. See also Oded Stark's *Migration of Labor* (1991) and Jan Young's *The Migrant Workers and Cesar Chavez* (1972).

Migration and Refugee Assistance Act (1962): Authorized the president of the United States to continue membership in and funding for the Intergovernmental Committee for European Migration. The president may also give money to the United Nations High Commissioner for Refugees (UNHCR); to specific REFUGEES if such help is in the United States' interest or benefits its defense or security; and to agencies providing educational, health, and resettlement assistance to refugees.

Migration legends, American Indian. *See* **American Indian migration legends**

Military: Even before the AMERICAN REVOLUTION established the British colonies in North America as a new nation, the military forces responsible for colonial defense reflected a plurality of cultural backgrounds. In time, protests against British rule led to the violence of the 1770 Boston Massacre; the massacre's first casualty was Crispus Attucks, an African American who had escaped from SLAVERY to pursue a career as a seaman. Individuals known for their patriotism during the colonial period represented a strikingly pluralistic spectrum. Paul Revere, the Boston-born son of French immigrant parents originally named Rivoire, was immortalized for his ride to Lexington on April 18, 1775, to warn the

A West Point graduate of Scots descent, Ulysses S. Grant served as commanding general of the Union Army during the Civil War and led the Union forces to victory in a series of decisive battles. (National Portrait Gallery, Smithsonian Institution)

town's minutemen that the British were coming. Peter Salem, Prince Estabrook, and Lemuel Hayes were among the black Americans who fought alongside white militiamen during the first skirmishes of the American Revolution.

The United States Army was formally established on June 14, 1775, when the Second Continental Congress created George Washington's Continental Army. From the originally planned infantry force of 20,000, it was gradually approved to consist of 80,000 troops. In actuality, it never numbered more than 30,000, and seldom could more than 15,000 be mustered for battle. Men and officers of several ethnic and cultural backgrounds played an indispensable role in the American Revolution (1775-1783). After the American Revolution, many of the foreign-born volunteers returned to Europe. Others remained in America, and their descendants became more or less ASSIMILATED.

One of the most highly regarded revolutionary military strategists, Baron Friedrich Wilhelm von Steuben, was an

Ely S. Parker, a Seneca Indian, served as Grant's military secretary during the Civil War and transcribed the documents at Appomattox that ended the war. (Library of Congress)

immigrant volunteer from Prussia (part of present-day Germany) appointed to serve as Inspector General of the Army by General Washington. Using Prussian training methods and issuing his commands in German that was translated by interpreters to the American troops, von Steuben transformed the poorly trained, tattered, and weary soldiers wintering at Valley Forge into a well-disciplined, skilled army; these men subsequently returned to their own units and spread von Steuben's teachings throughout the Army. Von Steuben also published a training manual and helped restructure the Army's battle tactics and troop formations.

Two remarkable military leaders were from Poland. Thaddeus Kosciuszko put his superb academic and practical background to good use as chief of engineers and as an authority on artillery, the field in which he authored the first American instruction manual. He planned numerous fortifications including West Point, which he later suggested as the location of the training academy. Kosciuszko contributed substantially to the British surrender at Saratoga—a turning point in the war. Casimir Pulaski was an equally famous Polish volunteer in command, first, of four highly trained regiments of cavalry and then of the Pulaski Legion, a multiethnic combination of cavalry and light infantry, uniting such diverse fighters as "Light Horse" Henry Lee, one of the Scots-descended Lees of Virginia, and Colonel Michael Kovats, a Hungarian hussar. The legion is credited with saving Washington's army from destruction at the Battle of Brandywine and contributed to the victories in South Carolina at Warren Tavern and Charleston. In 1779, Pulaski was mortally wounded in battle in Savannah, Georgia.

In 1777, the Marquis de Lafayette crossed the Atlantic to fight under Washington. Wounded at Brandywine, Lafayette recovered to fight again at Saratoga and finally at Yorktown, where some 6,000 French troops fought with Washington. Admiral de Grasse, commander of the French fleet sent to support Washington, positioned his twenty-eight ships to cut off any escape of Cornwallis' forces at the decisive battle of Yorktown.

American Indians. The American Indians had long been involved on both sides of various colonial conflicts in North America, either as tribal units or as individual participants. Although many American Indians were subjected to physical and cultural GENOCIDE, some of their descendants have shined as heroes in what was often a hopeless struggle for sovereignty.

Pima Ira Hayes was one of the four Marines who participated in the historic flag raising on Iwo Jima. (National Archives)

Notable leaders include PONTIAC, a brilliant Ottawa war leader against the British in 1763; TECUMSEH, a remarkable Shawnee chief who fought with the British during the War of 1812 and was killed in battle in 1813; Ely S. PARKER, a Seneca who achieved the rank of lieutenant colonel during the Civil War and served as military secretary to General Ulysses Grant; and such Sioux military leaders as RED CLOUD, CRAZY HORSE, and SITTING BULL who, in the 1870's, fought the last valiant, but ultimately futile battles for their ancestral lands and heritage. During the post-Civil War frontier conflicts with many Indian tribes, the U.S. Army recruited Indians from various tribes to serve as military scouts; fifty black Indians of the Seminole tribe served with distinction during the Plains Indian wars in a unit known as the Seminole Negro Indian Scouts.

It was not until 1924 that American Indians were granted U.S. citizenship and with it a chance for fuller, more regular participation in the military. Some 25,000 American Indians served in the armed forces during WORLD WAR II. Groups of NAVAJO soldiers serving in the Marine Signal Corps, known as NAVAJO CODE TALKERS, formed invaluable communication

teams during the war; Oneida, Chippewa, and CO-MANCHE soldiers performed similar duties. Enemy forces were unable to decode intercepted messages because of the unfamiliarity of American Indian words and phrases. Other American Indians made significant contributions. Major General Clarence Tinker, an Osage, was given command of air force operations in Hawaii in 1941, while Joseph James "Jocko," a Cherokee, was conspicuous for brilliance and heroism in the battles of Iwo Jima and, promoted to vice admiral, commanded the Seventh Fleet through the last year of the Korean War. Ira HAYES, a Pima, has been immortalized as a heroic participant in the American flag raising on top of Mount Suribachi on Iwo Jima, (pictured with him was Sergeant Michael Strank, a Slovak immigrant; the photographer who captured this famous historic and symbolic event was Joe Rosenthal, of Jewish parentage).

African Americans. Although free blacks had served in colonial militias and slaves probably served as laborers and support staff in various local conflicts against the Indians, African Americans began to be officially recruited as soldiers during the American Revolution. In November, 1775, the British assured freedom to rebel slaves and invited them to join His Majesty's troops; within a month, the Black Ethiopian Regiment was formed. While at that time George Washington allowed only "free Negroes desirous of enlisting" to join his forces, by 1778 slaves were included and each of his brigades had an average of 42 black soldiers. By 1783, some 5,000 African Americans served under his command.

According to a 1798 rule by the Secretary of War, "no Negro, mulatto, or Indian was to be enlisted," but by 1812, "Free Men of Color" were allowed to form a battalion. Again, during the CIVIL WAR, blacks were initially excluded, but later were used in "limited" capacities. On January 1, 1863, President Lincoln's EMANCIPATION PROCLAMATION declared all slaves in the Confederate states free; the Union's first black volunteer unit, the 54th Massachusetts Colored Infantry, was formed shortly after the proclamation was issued. Subsequently, the numbers of African American participants in the Union forces grew rapidly. In addition to some 186,000 African American combat troops, there were more than 200,000 members in the so-called "service" units; some 37,000 blacks died and 23 black soldiers were awarded Medals of Honor.

After the Civil War, new military opportunities were available to African Americans. In 1866, Congress created six black regiments. Some of these black troops were assigned to keep order in the South during RECONSTRUCTION, but most were assigned to protect frontier settlers in the West. Nicknamed "buffalo soldiers" by the Indians because of the texture of their hair, these African American soldiers fought with distinction during the Indian wars; seventeen received medals of honor for their heroism. In 1877, Henry O. Flipper became the first African American to graduate from West Point. During the 1898 SPANISH-AMERICAN WAR, experienced African American units helped save Theodore Roosevelt and his less experienced Rough Riders when they were under severe fire from Spanish troops.

were systematically scattered to fight in different locations, and were often placed under French command. No fewer than 170 black soldiers of the legendary 367th Regiment alone were awarded the French Croix de Guerre. Two African Americans achieved the rank of first lieutenant: Benjamin O. DAVIS, SR., and John E. Green. Colonel Charles YOUNG, a West Point graduate, was forced into temporary retirement in order to avoid his well-deserved promotion to the rank of general.

World War II marked the beginning of greater opportunities for African Americans in all branches of the armed services. Only shortly before the war in October of 1940, Colonel Benjamin O. Davis, Sr., was

Members of the all-black 367th Regiment served under French command during World War I; some 170 members received the French Croix de Guerre. (National Archives)

During WORLD WAR I, about 367,000 African Americans were called for duty. The famous all-black Ninety-second and Ninety-third Divisions were formed, but their units were still led by white officers,

appointed the first black brigadier general of the Army. In July, 1941, President Franklin D. Roosevelt had signed the Executive Order 8802 providing for equal opportunity in the war effort. Progress toward equality

Colin Powell became the first African American to serve as Chairman of the Joint Chiefs of Staff, the highest military position in the United States. Here Powell signs autographs for soldiers who fought in the Persian Gulf War. (AP/Wide World Photos)

was slow, but steady. The number of black participants in World War II rose to more than 700,000 in the Army; about 165,000 in the Navy; 17,000 in the Marine Corps; and 5,000 in the Coast Guard. The first African American heroes in the Navy all worked in the messman's branch, among them Dorie Miller. During the Pearl Harbor attack on December 7, 1941, Miller hauled the wounded captain of the U.S.S. *Arizona* to safety, then took his post behind an anti-aircraft gun he had never been trained to operate and successfully brought down four Japanese fighter planes. Miller was decorated with a Silver Star and cited for bravery by Fleet Admiral Chester Nimitz. In 1944, a group of African Americans known as the "Golden Thirteen" were commissioned as the first black naval officers. Despite these achievements, the status of blacks in the Navy was nearly unchanged as late as 1945, when 19 out of every 20 black seamen were assigned menial kitchen duties in the mess hall.

Black marines, too, served in racially segregated units throughout World War II. With some exceptions, segregation prevailed also in the Army. Despite their limited opportunities and training, many black units distinguished themselves in the European theater of operations, including the 320th Barrage Balloon Battalion; the 333rd Field Artillery Battalion, which received a presidential citation for bravery in Normandy; and the 761st Tank Battalion, which fought in six European countries. The Tuskegee Airmen, also known as the "Lonely Eagles," constituted what was possibly the nation's most famous black combat unit; some hundred members of the unit received the Distinguished Flying Cross.

As integration and equality were not yet achieved, President Harry S. Truman issued Executive Order 9981 in 1948, ordering "equality of treatment and opportunity" for all who served in the country's defense. During the KOREAN WAR, the American Army units fighting in Korea eventually were fully integrated, units at home had begun the process of integrating, and American forces in Europe were still segregated. By the end of the war in 1953, the Army had nearly 1,000 black officers and more than 50,000 enlisted personnel; the Marine corps had 19 black officers and almost 25,000 enlisted personnel. In 1952, Frank E. Petersen was the first African American to be commissioned as a Marine Corps pilot (he retired in 1988 with the rank of lieutenant general). The Air Force had taken the lead in integrating its forces; after the war, Benjamin O. DAVIS, JR., became the second black of general rank and the first brigadier general in the Air Force in 1954 (he retired in 1970 with the rank of lieutenant general).

During the VIETNAM WAR, the percentage of African Americans in the services grew. Because many of them were not full-time college students eligible for deferment of military service, a disproportionate number of blacks were sent into combat. During the mid-1960's, Martin Luther KING, Jr., took a strong antiwar

Japanese Americans in the 442nd Regimental Combat Team were awarded some 18,000 individual decorations in addition to many unit awards for their services during World War II—making them the most decorated military unit in American history. (Library of Congress)

stance. In a speech, King protested that young black men were being sent "to guarantee liberties in Southeast Asia which they have not found in Southwest Georgia and in East Harlem." Despite opposition to the war at home and racial discrimination on the battlefield, some African Americans rose within the military to become senior officers. By 1971, Samuel L. Gravely became the first African American to reach the rank of rear admiral in the U.S. Navy. Daniel "Chappie" James, one of the nation's most prominent Air Force pilots during the Vietnam War, became the first African American to reach the rank of four-star general in 1975.

President Richard Nixon's decision in 1973 to replace the Selective Service System with an all-volunteer military force resulted in an even greater shift within the military. The black presence in the Army increased from 12 percent in 1968 to 28 percent in 1989. African Americans took special pride in President George Bush's 1989 appointment of General Colin L. POWELL, the Harlem-born son of black Jamaican immigrants, as chairman of the Joint Chiefs of Staff, the highest position in the military. By mid-1992, the official statistics on minorities in the military (including African Americans, Latinos, Asians, and other ethnic minorities) reported that 17 percent of officers and 42 percent of enlisted members of the Army were of minority status. The corresponding percentages were 9.8 and 30.4 for the Navy; 9.4 and 30.3 for the Marines; 10.8 and 21.5 for the Air Force; and 12.5 and 29.7 respectively for all branches of the military. While minorities are very strongly represented in the military, their presence constitutes but one category of pluralism.

Asian Americans. While more than 100,000 Japanese Americans languished in World War II relocation camps, thousands of others volunteered to fight for the United States. Two JAPANESE AMERICAN combat units, the 100th Infantry Battalion and the 442nd Regimental Combat Team, received close to six thousand awards and medals from the United States, in addition to many others that were awarded by governments of Italy and France. Several thousand Japanese Americans served as members of the Military Intelligence Service, using their Japanese language skills to serve as interpreters and translators in the Pacific theater. Immediately following the attack on Pearl Harbor, China declared war on Japan and became an ally of the United States; patriotic response in the CHINESE AMERICAN community soon followed. More than 13,000 Chinese Americans volunteered or were drafted to serve in the armed forces during World War II. Although many Asian Americans had served with distinction in battle and went on to pursue highly successful careers in peacetime, they did not begin to rise to the highest echelons of military command until the 1980's. Vernon Chong, of Chinese parentage, was promoted to major general in the Air Force in 1987, while Rear Admiral Ming E. Chang was listed as Naval Inspector General in 1988.

Latinos. Members of Spanish-speaking ethnic groups and their descendants have usually been listed under such collective names as Hispanic, Spanish, or Latin Americans. They include not only immigrants who arrived directly from Spain but also immigrants from South and Central America and their descendants. Latinos include many individuals of racially mixed backgrounds, such as Mexicans, Cubans, Puerto Ricans, and Filipinos.

As in the American Revolution, so also in the Civil War, Latinos fought on both sides of the conflict. The most prominent Union officer of Spanish descent was David G. Farragut. Son of an immigrant of Spanish ancestry from the island of Minorca, Farragut took command of the naval blockade of the Gulf Coast that was instrumental in achieving Union victories at New Orleans and Mobile. In 1866, he was commissioned admiral of the U.S. Navy.

During World War I, many Latinos distinguished themselves in combat, including Marcelino Serna, a MEXICAN AMERICAN hero on the French front, but they received little study and recognition. David Barkley, a hero in France, was the first Latino to receive the Army's Medal of Honor; the award was bestowed in 1989, some 71 years after his death. Similarly, no systematic data were maintained on Latinos during World War II, although it is estimated that some 500,000 served in the armed forces. Mexican Americans from two New Mexico National Guard artillery units were stationed at American outposts in the Philippines before the attack on Pearl Harbor; many of them were killed at the battle of Bataan and most of the survivors became prisoners of war. Pedro del Valle, a marine from Puerto Rico, fought in several campaigns of World War I, led in commanding positions during World War II at Guadalcanal, Guam, and Japan, and eventually rose to the rank of lieutenant general. During the Korean War, Colonel Manuel J. Fernandez, Jr., became a flying ace who ranked third in that war and 60th among the top U.S. Air Force

aces of the two world wars and the Korean conflict combined.

After World War II, other Latinos were named to high positions of command, including Horacio Rivero, the first Latino four-star admiral in the Navy, and Richard E. Cavazos, the first four-star general in the Army. In 1971, Latinos constituted 1.3 percent of officers and 3.4 percent of enlisted members in the Armed Forces; the respective percentages rose to 1.9 and 4.6 in 1989.

European Americans. The Welsh, Irish, Scots, and Scots-Irish, reflecting their historical experience as opponents of English control of their homelands, were among the first and most enthusiastic advocates of the American colonies' complete independence from England and were superb fighters in the American Revolution.

The armed services have always reflected the great diversity of European ethnic groups resident in the United States. The Department of Defense has, so far, kept no systematic data on individual European ethnic groups and their contributions to, and high-ranking officers in, the military. Only a few illustrative highlights can here be offered.

Scots and Scots-Irish, along with their descendants, made significant contributions to American military efforts. John Paul Jones, an immigrant from Scotland who had landed in Philadelphia in 1775, became a legendary hero of the revolutionary navy. Other outstanding individuals include Henry Knox during the American Revolution, Sam Houston in the War for Texan Independence (1835-1836), Union General Ulysses Grant and Confederate General Robert E. Lee as supreme commanders of their respective forces during the Civil War, and General Douglas MacArthur as commander of American armies in the Pacific during World War II, supervisor of the reconstruction of Japan after the war, and commander of the U.N. Forces in Korea until 1951.

The Irish also made significant contributions. During the American Revolution, General John Sullivan, of Irish parentage, commanded the American Army in Canada and later replaced Virginian Charles Lee as commanding general of the right wing of Washington's army. John Barry, an Irish-born and -trained seaman who commanded a number of George Washington's ships during the war, was appointed commodore of the peacetime navy in 1794. The Irish played a crucial role in the Civil War, having contributed leaders such as Brigadier General Thomas Meagher, who led the heroic Irish Brigade; General Philip Kearney, who lost his arm in the Mexican War and his life in the Civil War; General Phillip Sheridan, the son of Irish immigrants, who was viewed as the Union's finest cavalry leader; and General George Meade, who was in command of the Union Army at the decisive battle of Gettysburg. During World War II, Irish accomplishments were epitomized by William Daniel Leahy, who was promoted to fleet admiral in 1944 and became the only officer who served as both chairman of the Joint Chiefs of Staff and of Naval Operations. In the early 1990's, the Boston-born four-star General Gordon R. Sullivan served as Chief of Staff of the U.S. Army.

Some of the most prominent soldiers of German descent include immigrant Civil War generals Carl Schurz, Peter S. Osterhaus, and Franz Sigel, in addition to more than 500 German-born Union officers; General John J. Pershing, who received the nickname "Black Jack" for his command of black troops during the Spanish-American War, served in command of the American Expeditionary Force against Germany in World War I, and rose to the rank of General of the Armies; Air Force General Carl Spaatz, who led bombing raids against Germany and Japan during World War II; German-born General Walter Krueger, who served as commander of the war in the Pacific; Admiral Chester W. Nimitz, commander-in-chief of

One of the most distinguished American military leaders of German descent, Dwight D. Eisenhouer here addresses paratroopers on the eve of the Normandy Invasion during World War II. (Library of Congress)

the U.S. Pacific Fleet; and General Dwight D. Eisenhower, supreme commander of the Allied Forces in Europe. General H. Norman Schwarzkopf, the son of a distinguished lieutenant general and great grandson of a German immigrant who came to America in 1852, served with distinction as commander of operations during the Persian Gulf War in 1991.

American military leaders of French descent include Admiral George Dewey, the hero of the Spanish-American War; Lieutenant General Leonard Gerow, commander of the U.S. Fifth Corps in Europe during World War II; Brigadier General James P.S. Devereux of the Marine Corps; and John C. Garand, inventor of the U.S. Army's semiautomatic rifle.

The Dutch contributions include General Alexander A. Vandegrift, Marine Corps commander from 1944 to 1947; General James A. Van Fleet, who served in World War II and the Korean War; and General Hoyt S. Vandenberg, Air Force commander and chief of staff during World War II.

The Norwegians gained recognition with their Norwegian Battalion, trained for winter fighting to help liberate Norway during World War II, while their Marine battalion, known as Carlson's Raiders, distinguished itself in the Pacific. Major General Leif J. Sverdup served in the Army Engineers Corps under General MacArthur, while Air Force four-star General Lauris Norstad proceeded from the North African campaign to the position of Director of Operations of the Mediterranean Allied Air Forces in World War II and was commander of North Atlantic Treaty Organization (NATO) at the time of his retirement in 1963.

Slovenian Americans in the military include Marine Captain Louis Cukela, the only hero to win two Congressional Medals of Honor in World War I; Major General John S. Lekson, Chief of Staff of the Second Field Force in Vietnam; four-star General Ferdinand Chesarek, U.S. military representative to the United Nations and commanding general of the Army Materiel Command; Lieutenant General Anthony Burshnick, vice commander-in-chief of the Military Airlift Command during the Persian Gulf War; and Vice Admiral Ronald J. Zlatoper, who was appointed chief of Naval Personnel and deputy chief of Naval Operations for Manpower, Personnel and Training, in 1991.

Many other ethnic officers served in the defense of the United States, among them Rear Admiral George P. Colvocaresses, of Greek descent, who fought in the Spanish-American War; Major General Eduardo Ferrero, of Italian descent, and Brigadier

General Henry Cist, of Russian descent, who fought as Union officers in the Civil War; Rear Admiral Fred Edward Bakutis, a World War II naval aviator and flying ace of Lithuanian descent; Brigadier General David Sarnoff, of Russian descent, whose work with Navajo Code Talkers played such an important role in the U.S. Signal Corps during World War II; Air Force Major General Walter Tkach, Medical Corps (Slovak), who was also President Richard Nixon's personal physician; and four-star General John Shalikashvili, a refugee from Soviet Georgia, who took supreme command of NATO in 1992.

Women officers and enlisted personnel served in a great variety of military assignments during the Persian Gulf War and were honored as veterans in many postwar parades such as this one. (Frances M. Roberts)

Here Oveta Culp Hobby takes the oath of office after being appointed to serve as commanding officer and director of the Women's Army Corps (WAC) during World War II. (AP/Wide World Photos)

Women. Although women constitute the single largest minority group that has experienced discrimination in the military, they have made important contributions to military defense since the American Revolution. In all wars, women played a significant role as nurses; some women were involved in military intelligence work; a few, disguised as men, took part in actual combat. Legendary heroine Molly Pitcher, who took her husband's artillery position at the battle of Monmouth in 1778, is believed to have been a second-generation German American named Mary Ludwig Hays. Some women combined multiple roles: African American heroine Harriet TUBMAN served the Union cause as nurse, soldier, scout, and spy. Clara BARTON's service as superintendent of nurses for the Union's Army of the James led to her organization of the American Red Cross association and her participation in military relief efforts as late as the Spanish-American War. The advent of World War I brought opportunities for women to serve as nurses and ambulance drivers in Europe. By the end of World War I, about 20,000 women served in the Army Nurse Corps and 1,400 in the Navy Nurse Corps.

In addition to the nursing corps, new organizations were formed to encourage women to assist as military volunteers during World War II. In May, 1942, the Women's Army Auxiliary Corps (WAAC) was established by Congress; in July, 1943, the WOMEN'S ARMY CORPS (WAC) replaced the volunteer auxiliary and provided servicewomen with the same rank and pay as their male peers. The Women's Reserves in the Marine Corps, the Navy's Women Accepted for Voluntary Emergency Service (WAVES), and the Women's Airforce Service Pilots (WASP) branch of the Army Air Force were all formed to provide opportunities for women to meet the wartime crisis.

In the 1970's, the U.S. military abolished the separate women's branches and integrated women into general military units, providing women with greater opportunities for advancement. In 1970, Anna Mae Hayes, chief of the Army Nurse Corps, became the first woman brigadier general in America. In 1971, the Air Force promoted Jeanne M. Holm to Brigadier General. Alene B. Duerk, chief of the Navy Nurse Corps, became the first female rear admiral in 1972. Hazel Winifred Johnson, who had earned a master's degree in nursing and a doctorate in educational administration in addition to having had a distinguished career in the Army Nurse Corps, became the first African American woman to attain the rank of brigadier general. On October 1, 1991, the Air Force issued a list of its female general officers, showing two major generals (Jeanne M. Holm and Norma Brown) and fourteen brigadier generals.

In mid-1992, 12.6 percent of officers and 11.2 percent of enlisted members of all branches of the military were women. The corresponding percentages were: 13.4 and 11.7 for the Army; 12.1 and 10.0 for the Navy; 13.9 and 14.6 for the Air Force, and 3.1 and 4.7 for the Marines. In all branches of the military, twenty percent of all female officers and 39.3 percent of all enlisted women were classified as being of minority status (African American, Latino, and other ethnic backgrounds). In the wake of the Navy's Tailhook scandal, in which sexual harassment charges were leveled against male participants attending a convention of naval aviators, the Secretary of Defense announced in 1993 that women would be allowed to compete for combat positions. This news was especially welcomed by women who wished to complete their training as fighter pilots in all aviation divisions of the armed forces.

Gays. Gay men have always served in the U.S. military, although they were officially banned from service between 1943 and 1993. It was no accident that the ban coincided with the start of the COLD WAR, when people's private beliefs and propensities came under intense government suspicion. Servicemen could be investigated and discharged on the mere suspicion of being homosexual. By the 1980's, more women were active in the military and the GAY AND LESBIAN RIGHTS MOVEMENT had become well-established. Increasing numbers of military people began to declare their homosexuality openly and to fight for reinstatement through the courts and the media when they were discharged. They claimed that their sexual orientation

had no impact on their ability to serve their country and that, indeed, gay men and lesbians were among the most capable, dedicated people in the armed services.

The issue came to public prominence during the presidential campaign of Bill Clinton in 1992. He promised to lift the ban on gays in the military as a civil rights measure but met strong opposition in Congress and the Pentagon. Critics charged that the admission of homosexuals would lower morale, prevent combat effectiveness, and fundamentally change the character of the military. Those in favor of lifting the ban, including some African American civil rights leaders, countered that the same predictions had been made by those opposed to the racial and sexual integration of the military in previous decades.

In July, 1993, after six months of debate, the Clinton Administration put forth a compromise that would allow gays to join the military as long as they did not declare their homosexuality or openly engage in homosexual conduct; military investigations of alleged homosexuals would be discouraged unless there was sufficient evidence that they were violating these conditions. The compromise measure—dubbed "don't ask, don't tell, don't pursue"—was hailed as a step forward by some, but it disappointed others on both sides of the issue. It was expected that by the end of the twentieth century, the issue would be decided in the courts, although the U.S. Supreme Court had thus far refused to consider cases of discrimination against gays in the military or to apply FOURTEENTH AMENDMENT protection to other gay rights cases.

The U.S. military has to a great degree exemplified the nation's motto, "Ex pluribus unum"—From many, one. It remains an impressive example of MULTICULTURALISM at work in the defense of America as a land of liberty and opportunity.

SUGGESTED READINGS. For a general history of the armed services, see Allan R. Millett and Peter Maslowski's *For the Common Defense: A Military History of the United States, 1607-1983* (1984). James M. Morris' *History of the U.S. Army* (1992) presents a scholarly overview of the Army, while Clark G. Reynolds' *Famous American Admirals* (1978) is a valuable collection of short biographies of top Navy commanders. Two invaluable overviews of the role of minorities in the U.S. military are *Black Americans in Defense of Our Nation* (1991) and *Hispanics in America's Defense* (1990), both produced by the Department of Defense. *Women in the Military: An Unfin-*

ished Revolution (1982) draws upon author Jeanne Holm's firsthand knowledge of the military as one of a handful of top-ranking female officers.—*Edward Gobetz*

Military academies: Private secondary boarding schools devoted to military discipline and training. The emergence of these academies in the United States began with the founding of the U.S. Military Academy at West Point in New York in 1802. A common goal of military academies is to instill in the cadets a belief of their moral and intellectual superiority over those who would serve under their command. The academies differ from other schools in that the curriculum is college preparatory, but there is a strong emphasis on mental and physical discipline, self-control, orderliness, and most especially, training for leadership. The students must dress in military uniforms. The staff is usually comprised of former military personnel. The idea behind creating the acad-

emy is to empower citizens with the ability and knowledge necessary to defend the country while still working with society and providing a service of higher education. Another service similar to military academies is the Reserve Officers' Training Corp (ROTC), which exists both at colleges and high schools. This has become a popular alternative to a full-fledged academy, but works toward the same goal of offering citizens a general education while training them to become officers in the military.

Beginning in 1976, the nation's military academies at West Point (Army), Annapolis (Navy), and Colorado Springs (Air Force) became coeducational, admitting both men and women. While women cadets have received training on par with that of men, it was not until 1993 that women graduates were allowed to compete for assignments to train as combat fighter pilots. Nevertheless, the military academies remain virtually untouched by other societal trends, especially

Cadets practice precision drill routines on the campus of the Citadel, a military academy in South Carolina. (Jeff Greenberg, Unicorn Stock Photos)

those in educational reform. Thus, while enrollment policies reflect an opening of doors to women and other minorities, the mission of the school and the manner in which the curriculum is carried out have not changed since the school's beginnings. The military academy does not allow educational reforms that affect the public schools to affect them because they believe their mission is different. Reforms for public schools are considered irrelevant to the military academy's mission, which is to create military leaders, not simply graduates.

SUGGESTED READINGS. In *West Point: America's Power Fraternity* (1973) K. Bruce Galloway and Robert Bowie Johnson take a close look at the premiere American military academy. This work includes both the militaristic view of the academy as well as interviews with some of its cadets. George V. Fagan's *The Air Force Academy: An Illustrated History* (1988) provides an account of another military academy. For more insight into life at a military academy and the ROTC program, see Gene Lyons and John Masland's *Education and Military Leadership* (1959) and Joseph Ellis and Robert Moore's *School for Soldiers* (1974). Carol Barkalow's *In the Men's House: An Inside Account of Life in the Army by One of West Point's First Female Graduates* (1990) and Donna Peterson's *Dress Gray: A Woman at West Point* (1990) provide perspectives on coeducational life at the academies.

Miner, Myrtilla (Mar. 4, 1815, near Brookfield, N.Y.—Dec. 17, 1864, Washington, D.C.): Educator. Appalled at the slave conditions she had observed while teaching at a girls' school in Mississippi, Miner became a determined abolitionist. In 1851 she opened the Colored Girls School in Washington, D.C. She received support from Harriet Beecher STOWE and Henry Ward Stowe, and the QUAKERS (Society of Friends). By 1858 six of her former students had begun their own schools. The school was closed in 1860 but reopened after Miner's death, a testament to the dire need for the abolition of SLAVERY and the education of African Americans.

Minimum wage laws for women and children: Laws passed at the state level in the United States, soon after other labor laws had begun to be legally accepted, to help those workers considered least able to gain wage improvements on their own: women. For the lowest-paid workers, a minimum wage provides a floor below which wages cannot sink. Although limits on working hours per day or week and laws restricting night work for

women were becoming common in the early 1900's, the regulation of wages was much slower to gain legal acceptance. Hours limitations were justified because they were consistent with the goal of "protecting" women, whose primary function was viewed as wives and mothers within the home (the 1908 Supreme Court case *MULLER V. OREGON* involved hours limitations). Gaining better pay for their work might have enabled women to be more self-sufficient in their own right—clearly not a goal of legislation designed to limit women's participation in the workforce in general.

Advocates of minimum wage laws pointed out that "supply and demand" would not raise wages for women because the wage structure itself was far lower for women than men, and employers took advantage of this to pay women less than survival wages. Doctrines of "freedom of contract" and noninterference in the market were used by employers to oppose all labor laws. Employers argued that they were not responsible for supporting their workers, and that paying workers above their "workworth" would only drive wages down for all workers so that the minimum would become the maximum. This did not happen. Instead, employers were pushed to use labor more productively.

In 1912, Massachusetts became the first state to set up a wage rate commission. Compliance was voluntary, however. Minimum wage legislation for women and male minors aged fourteen to seventeen was enacted in California in 1913, and several other states as well. When the U.S. Supreme Court struck down a Washington, D.C., minimum wage law for women workers in Adkins v. Children's Hospital (1923), calling it "price-fixing," it surprised supporters and opponents alike, because by then other types of work limitations (such as hours per week) had become accepted by the courts.

Minimum wage legislation was decisively declared constitutional in *West Coast Hotel Co. v. Parrish* (1937). No men workers were covered by minimum wage laws until after the FAIR LABOR STANDARDS ACT (FLSA) was passed in 1938 as part of Depression era NEW DEAL legislation. The FLSA established a federal minimum wage for both men and women, and a standard work week of forty hours with time-and-a-half for overtime. This act covered only one in four workers, however; the lowest-paid workers, many of whom were minority women, were in occupations excluded from the minimum wage.

Employers have consistently opposed extending, and favored excluding youth from, minimum wage re-

Minimum wage legislation for women workers helped improve the earning power and, in some cases, the working conditions of women laborers such as these oyster shuckers. (Library of Congress)

quirements. When a lower "youth" or "training" wage is permitted, teens are used to displace adult workers, weakening the bargaining power of other workers. Until the mid-1960's the minimum wage rose in real purchasing power; it remained relatively stable in the 1970's and then eroded sharply throughout the 1980's. This made it a less meaningful standard, or floor.

SUGGESTED READINGS. For a history of wage legislation, see Ronnie Steinberg's *Wages and Hours* (1982). For a broader discussion of labor legislation see *Protecting American Workers* (1986) by Sar Levitan, Peter Carlson, and Isaac Shapiro.

Mink, Patsy Takemoto (b. Dec. 6, 1927, Paia, Maui, Hawaii): Japanese American politician. After studying zoology and chemistry at the University of Hawaii and earning her law degree at the University of Chicago, Mink spent more than a decade in private practice in Honolulu. She cofounded Oahu Young Democrats in 1954 and served in the Territorial and State Legislatures from 1956 to 1964. As a member of the U.S. House of Representatives from 1965 to 1977, Mink sponsored the National Overseas Education Act of 1967 and chaired the U.S.-China Committee. She opposed the Vietnam War and strove to be responsive to her multiethnic Hawaiian constituency. She also took special interests in education, people with disabilities, and issues con-

cerning the U.S. Pacific Territories. Mink served as assistant secretary of state under President Jimmy Carter and returned to Congress in 1990.

Patsy Mink became the first Japanese American woman to serve in Congress when she was elected as a U.S. Representative from Hawaii in 1964. (AP/Wide World Photos)

Minorities, media portrayals of. *See* **Media portrayals of women and minorities**

Minority business enterprise. *See* **Office of Minority Business Enterprise**

Minority group: Group of people in a subordinate position in society whose differential treatment is based on their shared characteristics. Minorities may be racial, ethnic, or religious groups. Members of minorities often face prejudice and discrimination against them from society's dominant group. A minority group may actually be quite large numerically; what distinguishes a minority is not small size but lack of power and equal access to resources such as education and jobs. In the United States, for example, women are sometimes considered a minority group although they make up the majority of the population; in South Africa, blacks are a minority even though they compose about 70 percent of the population.

Minority status, Supreme Court rulings on. *See* **Supreme Court rulings—discrimination and minority status**

Missionaries and American Indians: From the earliest contacts until the present, efforts to convert American Indians to Christianity had not only direct effects such as the decimation of the mission Indians, but also important secondary effects, such as the shaping of modern Indian religious movements.

In the sixteenth century, ROMAN CATHOLIC mission-aries accompanied by military contingents served as the advance guard of the Spanish Empire in New Mexico and Arizona. Building missions near PUEBLO settlements, Franciscan missionaries attempted for more than two hundred years to bring these sedentary farmers into the Christian fold and under Spanish control. The Franciscans, who generally did not attempt to understand or accommodate Pueblo culture, failed to replace native religion with Roman Catholicism. Many converts displayed a superficial acceptance of Christianity, but secretly adhered to traditional beliefs. Policies based on the Pueblo model were imposed on the nomadic California Indian cultures in the eighteenth century. Again, failure to recognize cultural differences resulted in superficial conversions and thousands of native deaths.

In the northeastern and midwestern United States into Canada, as well as in the contemporary southeastern states of Mississippi and Louisiana, French missionary practice presented a marked contrast to Spanish policies. Beginning in the mid-1600's, French Jesuits made a concerted effort to share the Indian lifestyle, subordinating their interests to those of the native population. These idealists, rather than suppressing all indigenous religious practices, emphasized consistencies between Christianity and American Indian beliefs, encouraging rather than forcing the conversion process.

After minor PURITAN and QUAKER proselytizing efforts in the English colonies in the seventeenth century, the eighteenth and nineteenth centuries saw the task of Christianizing American Indians taken up by

Religious revitalization efforts, such as the Ghost Dance ceremony pictured here, represented attempts by American Indian tribes to throw off the influence of white Christian missionaries. (Smithsonian Institution)

individual Protestant denominations (such as the PRES-BYTERIANS, CONGREGATIONALISTS, and Moravians) and religious coalitions (such as the Society in Scotland for Propagating Christian Knowledge and American Board of Commissioners for Foreign Missions). Soon, Christian evangelism became intertwined with a zeal to educate and acculturate the Indians. Perceiving official corruption as an impediment to acculturation, President Ulysses S. Grant created the Board of Indian Commissioners (composed of Christian laymen) and invited church involvement in reservation affairs. Ensuing reforms led to the General Allotment Act (or DAWES ACT, 1887), which permitted the apportionment of reservation lands among individual American Indians. Educational and political programs of the Christian reform groups, who perceived the adopting of white culture as the only salvation for the natives, forced the weakening of tribal identities. These assimilationist policies prevailed until the passage of the INDIAN REORGANIZATION ACT (1934).

The breakdown of tribal identity permitted the development of the PAN-INDIAN movement of the late 1800's. Ironically some of this movement's developments, such as the GHOST DANCE of 1890 and the NATIVE AMERICAN CHURCH, blend Indian and Christian elements, thus revealing a legacy of the missionary experience.

SUGGESTED READINGS. For a concise and readable introduction to missionary activities among American Indians, see Henry Warner Bowden's *American Indians and Christian Missions* (1981). Insights into the relationships between church and state in American Indian affairs are provided by R. Pierce Beaver's *Church, State, and the American Indians* (1966). Relationships between Christianity and Pan-Indian movements are considered in Alice Marriott and Carol K. Rachlin's *Peyote* (1971) and Weston LaBarre's *The Ghost Dance* (1970).

Missions, Spanish. *See* **Spanish missions**

Missouri Compromise (1820): Measures passed by the U.S. Congress to end the country's first serious tensions over the issue of SLAVERY. As the United States expanded westward in the early part of the nineteenth century, both slaveholders and abolitionists moved into the new territories, and the federal government did nothing to encourage or restrict slavery there. In 1812, Louisiana became the eighteenth state—a slave state. In 1819, the Territory of Upper Louisiana sought admission to the Union as the State of Missouri. Its proposed state constitution permitted slavery. When a bill to admit Missouri came before the House of Representatives, an amendment was proposed to prohibit bringing more slaves into Missouri and to grant freedom eventually to the children of the slaves then living there. The two houses of Congress could not agree on the amended bill, and the issue was unresolved when Congress adjourned in March, 1819.

Suddenly the issue of slavery in Missouri became a topic of intense national interest. In newspaper letters and editorials, in public meetings and church services, in state legislatures and local taverns, the debate raged. In the South, this marked the beginning of proslavery literature, such as pamphlets offering biblical justifications for the institution. For most white Americans, the question of slavery was not so much a moral issue as it was political. The real issue was whether addition of another slave state to the Union would make the southern states more powerful.

Missouri lay north of the line which divided slave states from free. For Northerners, admitting Missouri as a slave state would be an insufferable encroachment into their territory, and an intentional act of aggression on the part of southern slaveholders. The slaveholders, however, claimed they were merely seeking to transport their private property—human slaves—into the new territories and live peacefully there. Did the North intend to lay claim to all the unsettled territory west of the Mississippi? The North and South argued bitterly, until both sides were threatening to secede from the Union.

Congress addressed the issue again in 1820 and offered a compromise. Missouri would be admitted as a slave state, and Maine (which had recently broken off from Massachusetts) would be admitted as a free state. This brought the total to twelve slave states and twelve free states. Although Missouri itself had slaves, its southern boundary at 36°30' latitude marked an important new line: No territories north of that line would be permitted to accept slavery in the future.

The compromise worked for a time. Both sides accepted it as fair, and for the next twenty to thirty years, there was no serious political strife in the nation over the issue of slavery until the period just before the CIVIL WAR.

SUGGESTED READINGS. For a fuller look at the issues involved, see Glover Moore's *The Missouri Controversy 1819-1821* (1953). A fascinating but somewhat dated look at Missouri's view can be found in *Missouri's Struggle for Statehood* (1916) by Floyd C.

Shoemaker. See also *The Awakening of American Nationalism, 1815-1828* (1865) by George Dangerfield for a shorter but very lucid account.

Model minority: Term often applied to Asian Americans referring to their overcoming obstacles peacefully to achieve success. Although Chinese, Japanese, Koreans, Filipinos, Vietnamese, and other Asian American peoples historically have been the targets of racial PREJUDICE and DISCRIMINATION, the model minority concept emphasizes the relative economic and educational success that they have achieved. Users of the term also highlight the fact that such success has been achieved, by and large, without the violent confrontations that have often characterized white-African American and white-Latino interaction. In short, the term "model minority" underscores the high degree of ASSIMILATION that Asian Americans have attained, especially in the twentieth century.

Proponents of the concept point to two pieces of evidence to support their contention of Asian American success. First, Census Bureau data reveal that Asian Americans have a higher median income compared not only to other minority groups but also to white Americans. Second, on the educational front, Asian Americans have the highest percentage of adults (among persons aged twenty-five to twenty-nine and forty-five to fifty-four) who are high school graduates. Moreover, Asian Americans are overrepresented, relative to their actual numbers in the total population, at the most prestigious colleges and universities in the United States. Such educational achievement is held to reflect the emphasis on education in most Asian cultures, and family and cultural pressures to succeed.

Critics of the model minority concept argue that such a term is really a veiled critique of African Americans, Latinos, and other minorities, for failing to achieve the same success as the model minority. Implicit in this view is the notion that hard work and educational attainment provide the same dividend to all minorities. The model minority concept also ignores the importance of salient characteristics such as skin color that have prevented the easy assimilation of certain minority groups into the dominant society.

In addition, critics point out that the indicators of Asian American success are problematic. First, Asian American median income is inflated because most of them live in urban areas and in three states—California, Hawaii, and New York—where incomes in general are higher. Almost two-thirds of Asian American families have two or more wage earners, compared to slightly more than one-half of white families. Asian Americans also work more hours and have had to acquire more education (in the face of dominant group discrimination) to attain their income success. Lastly, while Asian American educational statistics are impressive, among some subgroups there has been an increase in the high school dropout rate.

Among other indicators of success used to define them as a "Model minority," Asian Americans have excelled in education, as reflected by their unprecedented rate of graduation during the 1980's and 1990's. (Jim and Mary Whitmer)

The model minority concept also ignores the great diversity within the Asian American population. Many recent rural REFUGEES, especially from Laos and Vietnam, have unemployment rates of 80 percent. A higher percentage of people are poor in New York's CHINATOWN than in the city as a whole. College-educated Asian Americans may actually experience downward mobility (as in the case of many Korean shopkeepers) in response to linguistic, cultural, and racial barriers that impede their economic mobility.

SUGGESTED READINGS. Charles Mindel, Robert W. Haberstein, and Roosevelt Wright, Jr.'s, *Ethnic Families in America* (3d ed., 1988) provides an overview of cultural characteristics of Asian Americans. Also instructive in this regard is Harry Kitano and Roger Daniels' *Asian Americans* (1988). The best short account of the model minority is Ronald Takaki's "The Harmful Myth of Asian Superiority," in *The New York Times Magazine* (June 16, 1990, p. 15).

A leading Chicano political figure in California, Gloria Molina served in the California State Assembly before becoming the first Latina elected to the Los Angeles County Board of Supervisors in 1992. (AP/Wide World Photos)

Molina, Gloria (b. May 31, 1948, Los Angeles, Calif.): Mexican American politician. Molina founded the Comision Femenil de Los Angeles, a Chicana political group, in 1973. She worked in various legislative positions in Congress, the Department of Health and Human Services, and the California State Assembly before becoming a California State Assembly member from 1984 to 1988. In 1988, Molina was elected to the Los Angeles City Council, where she has championed issues affecting women, children, minorities, and the poor. She cofounded the Hispanic American Democrats and the Centro de Nios, and was named Hispanic of the Year by *Caminos* magazine (1982) and Woman of the Year by both the Mexican American Federation (1983) and *Ms.* MAGAZINE (1984).

Molly Maguires: Nineteenth century secret society principally composed of Irish American coal miners in the anthracite region of eastern Pennsylvania. The group borrowed its name and its tactics from an Irish tenant association organized to protest the domination of oppressive landlords. The Molly Maguires, who formed a miners' union in 1875, used secrecy and their collective power to intimidate mine bosses and supervisors with the intention of achieving better living and working conditions. Ultimately, their tactics included murder and arson. Information obtained by James McParlan, a Pinkerton detective who infiltrated the group, was used to convict twenty suspects who were sentenced to public execution. McParlan was hired by Franklin B. Gowen, president of the Philadelphia and Reading Railroad, a company that owned extensive coal lands. The first executions took place on "Black Thursday," June 21, 1877.

Momaday, N. Scott (b. Feb. 27, 1934, Lawton, Okla.): Kiowa/Cherokee Indian author. Momaday spent his childhood on Indian RESERVATIONS in the Southwest. His best-known work is *House Made of Dawn* (1968), a novel about a young man unable to be at home either in white society or in his ancestral culture. The novel won the Pulitzer Prize. Other works include *The Way to Rainy Mountain* (1969), about Kiowa legends told in relation to history and Momaday's own youth; *The Gourd Dancer* (1976), a book of poems; and *The Names: A Memoir* (1976).

Montalbán, Ricardo (b. Nov. 25, 1920, Mexico City, Mexico): Mexican American actor. Montalbán made films in Mexico from 1942 to 1946, before coming to the United States. He has appeared in more than twenty American films including *Fiesta* (1947), *Sayonara* (1957), *Sweet Charity* (1969), *Star Trek II: The Wrath of Khan* (1982), and *The Naked Gun: From the Files of Police Squad!* (1988). He founded the Latino group Nosotros in 1969. Montalbán became a regular on television as the suave host Mr. Roarke on *Fantasy Island* (1978-1984), for which he won an Emmy Award in 1978. He starred on *The Colbys* from 1986 to 1987 and was featured in numerous commercials, especially for Chrysler automobiles. In 1988, Montalbán received the Golden Aztec Award from the Mexican-American Foundation.

Mexican American actor Ricardo Montalbán has had a distinguished career in film and television. (AP/Wide World Photos)

Montgomery bus boycott (Dec. 1, 1955—Dec. 20, 1956): First large-scale protest against racial SEGREGATION in the Deep South. The boycott was an important step in removing the legal barriers which had been used to separate blacks and whites in many states since the nineteenth century. The boycott also made household names of its leaders, such as African Americans Rosa PARKS, Ralph David Abernathy, and Martin Luther KING, Jr.

Historical Background. On May 17, 1954, the Supreme Court of the United States ruled in BROWN, ET AL. V. THE BOARD OF EDUCATION of Topeka, Kansas, that racial segregation in public schools was a violation of the U.S. CONSTITUTION. Public schools were ordered to begin desegregating "with all deliberate speed" a few months later; however, the ruling did not challenge segregation in any other area of public life. Most states in the Deep South chose to adopt a policy of "massive resistance" to delay as long as possible the implementation of the Court's decision and perhaps to defeat it completely.

In Montgomery, Alabama, the African American community had a long-standing concern with improving the treatment of black riders of the city bus system. Almost 80 percent of the regular users of city buses were African Americans, but a city ordinance as well as state laws required white patrons to sit in the front of the bus while black riders sat at the back. An African American who sat toward the front of the bus because all rear seats were full could be forced to stand if white passengers boarded and found no seat. Bus drivers were expected to enforce this law and could call on city police if they met resistance.

E. D. Nixon, an employee of the Southern Railroad, and head of the state office of the NATIONAL ASSOCIATION FOR THE ADVANCEMENT OF COLORED PEOPLE (NAACP) was a recognized leader in the African American community. He had often raised the issue of treatment of blacks and had frequently held meetings and negotiated with white leaders to improve racial conditions. He and other concerned black citizens had been discussing a bus boycott throughout 1955 but had not found a suitable case over which to make an issue. At least three people had been arrested for violating the segregation laws, but each time Nixon chose not to press ahead for various reasons.

Rosa Parks was a friend and former part-time employee of Nixon. She was a seamstress in the alterations department of a Montgomery department store, but she also worked from time to time for Nixon at the NAACP. By her own description Parks had a long history of actively resenting mistreatment based on her race. In 1955, she attended a training session at the Highlander Folk School at Monteagle, Tennessee, on

Rosa Parks, whose refusal to comply with segregation laws touched off the Montgomery bus boycott, is shown here being fingerprinted after being indicted by a grand jury on antiboycott charges. (AP/Wide World Photos)

how to use nonviolent actions to challenge injustice and achieve racial harmony. On December 1, 1955, these factors combined to cause Parks to decide on her way home from work to disobey an order from a bus driver that she give up her seat to a white person.

Parks was arrested for violating the segregation law but was quickly released on bail when Clifford Durr, a prominent white attorney of Montgomery, intervened on her behalf. Almost as soon as she arrived home following her release, Nixon came to Parks's house to suggest that hers would provide the test case needed to break the bus segregation law. After discussing the issue with her husband and her mother, Parks agreed.

Conduct of the Boycott. Parks had been arrested on a Thursday. On Friday, as word of the planned challenge to bus segregation spread throughout the black community, several members of the Women's Political Council got together to talk. This group of middle- and upper-class professional black women issued a statement calling for a one-day boycott of the city buses on Monday, December 5. Nixon saw one of their flyers and liked the idea. He quickly began calling black ministers to enlist their aid in organizing a long-term boycott. It was almost a case of leaders run-

ning to catch up with followers before the leaders were left behind.

Nixon also acted in a shrewd fashion to make sure the entire African American community knew of the boycott. On Saturday, December 3, Nixon called a friend, Joe Azbell, a white reporter for the Montgomery *Advertiser*. Azbell wrote a story for the Sunday edition of the *Advertiser* which treated the proposed boycott as an exposé of the local NAACP but which also guaranteed every African American in Montgomery knew of the plan.

There was to be a mass meeting to support the boycott at the Dexter Avenue Baptist Church on Monday night, December 5. Prior to that meeting several black ministers met with Nixon to plan strategy. Fearing reprisals, the ministers talked about how to have a boycott with no one person as leader. Nixon accused the group of cowardice, and the young pastor of the Dexter Avenue Church responded that he was not afraid. The meeting then elected twenty-six-year-old Martin Luther KING, Jr., to lead the Montgomery Improvement Association (MIA), the organization which would coordinate the boycott. At the mass meeting that night, King gave a masterful speech which energized and unified the entire African American community.

The commitment to a long-term boycott would place the African American community under considerable stress, because most of its members depended on public transportation to reach their jobs. Although the geographical size of Montgomery would allow people to walk wherever they needed to go, the time involved would make that less than practical. The sponsors of the boycott attempted to alleviate this problem by providing up to twenty thousand rides daily by carpooling using private cars.

These carpools were organized by setting up phone banks to coordinate the effort, using African American churches as gathering places for drivers and riders, and, eventually, purchasing a fleet of nineteen station wagons. When no company in the state of Alabama would insure the vehicles, a policy was taken out with Lloyds of London. To help the black community handle the stress of the boycott, regular mass meetings were held to encourage the people. The crowds at these meetings were so large that as many as seven simultaneous meetings had to be held in separate churches. At one meeting an elderly woman, known locally as Mother Pollard, provided the movement with lasting inspiration when she said, "My feet are tired, but my soul is rested."

While the boycott was underway, leaders of the MIA and city officials were meeting in an attempt to end it. Many proposals were put forward by both sides, but the negotiations went nowhere because neither side was willing to accept compromises. The MIA insisted on ending segregation, while the City of Montgomery insisted on retaining it.

The intractable attitude of the city officials was seen in their ordering the police to follow carpool drivers and arrest them on even minor offenses. King was arrested more than once on such charges. At one point 115 boycott leaders were charged with criminal indictments for conspiracy. Some elements in the white community turned to violence, bombing the houses of King and Nixon.

called "the unforgettable image of old black women walking in the sun."

The question of bus segregation came before the Supreme Court in the fall of 1956. On November 13, 1956, the Supreme Court ruled that state and local laws requiring bus segregation were unconstitutional. This order was transmitted to Montgomery city officials on December 20. A final mass meeting that night declared that the boycott was over.

Impact of the Boycott. On the final night of the boycott King addressed a mass rally. His words on that occasion summed up one important impact of the protest. The African American citizens of Montgomery had learned they could work together to achieve community goals. The leaders of this community had re-

This empty downtown bus confirms the success of African American residents in Montgomery in using alternative forms of transportation to support the bus boycott. (AP/Wide World Photos)

Not all opposition to segregation was expressed by staying off the buses. The NAACP, taking its usual legalistic approach, brought a suit in the federal court charging that segregation on public buses was a violation of rights guaranteed by the Constitution of the United States. The U.S. District Court agreed with the contention of the NAACP, but the Attorney General of the State of Alabama appealed to the Supreme Court.

During the summer of 1956 the boycott continued, and it became national and international news. Well over a hundred reporters visited Montgomery to write about the boycott, to do profiles of various leaders, and to make the world aware of what one reporter

mained true to their trust and not given in to either inducements or threats. The individual citizens had learned that in the face of force, nonviolence was a powerful counterbalance. The black churches had become centers of militant movement for change as well as being places of worship. Every person who had a part in the boycott now had a renewed sense of dignity and purpose.

The Montgomery Improvement Association was disbanded as soon as the boycott was over; however, King, Abernathy, and other African American leaders traveled to Atlanta a few days later to form another group with a broader purpose. This group, the SOUTHERN CHRISTIAN LEADERSHIP CONFERENCE (SCLC), would go on to lead protests and demonstrations against segregation across the United States. It was as leader of this organization that King would become internationally recognized as the spokesman for the CIVIL RIGHTS MOVEMENT. This role would carry him to Washington, D.C., for his "I Have a Dream" speech and to Memphis, where he met his death. The Montgomery bus boycott started King down the road which would eventually lead a young, unknown pastor of a black Baptist church to be chosen winner of the Nobel Peace Prize.

The events in Montgomery also showed African Americans new and effective ways of combating racial segregation. Until the MIA was formed, the NAACP was the only active civil rights organization focusing exclusively on racial matters. The NAACP had traditionally dealt in court litigation only. Now, the new weapon of mass action was added to the arsenal of those fighting injustice. This approach was later used by racial and ethnic groups around the world. While court suits could have old, negative laws overturned, the mass action approach proved able to rouse the conscience of a nation to take new, positive action. The Montgomery bus boycott was a first step toward removing artificial barriers that kept Americans apart on the basis of race.

SUGGESTED READINGS. The Civil Rights movement is dramatically depicted in the Pulitzer Prize-winning *Parting the Waters* (1988) by Branch Taylor. *Let the Trumpet Sound: The Life of Martin Luther King* (1982) by Stephen B. Oates is a readable and thorough biography which analyzes the causes of key events in King's career. A very readable, honest, and rewarding collection of first-person memoirs is Howell Raines's *My Soul Is Rested: Movement Days in the Deep South Remembered* (1977). The standard history of racial segregation is *The Strange Career of Jim Crow* (1974) by C. Vann Woodward.—*Michael R. Bradley*

Montoya, Joseph Manuel (Sept. 24, 1915, Pena Blanca, N.Mex.—June 5, 1978, Washington, D.C.): Mexican American politician. Montoya received his law degree from Georgetown University in 1938 and was admitted to the New Mexico bar in 1939. While still at Georgetown, he was elected to the New Mexico state legislature, where he served from 1936 to 1946. He became the state's lieutenant governor in 1946, entered the U.S. House of Representatives in 1958, and moved on to the Senate in 1965. Montoya was known for his opposition to the Vietnam War and came into the spot-

light as a member of the Senate Watergate Committee. Throughout his career, he worked for the interests of farmers, labor, consumers, American Indians, and Spanish-speaking citizens, and he tried to link militant Chicano organizations with mainstream political institutions.

Mexican American politician Joseph Montoya served in Congress for many years and came to prominence as a result of his role on the Senate Watergate Committee. (AP/Wide World Photos)

Moon, Sun Myung (Yong Myung Moon; b. Jan 6, 1920, Kwangju Sangsa Ri, Korea): Korean American religious leader. On Easter Sunday, 1936, Moon had a personal vision of Jesus Christ that initiated a nine-year course of religious study. After working in Japan during World War II, he returned to Korea, took a new name, and set up his own church. In 1952 he wrote his opus, *Divine Principle*, and two years later established the UNIFICATION CHURCH. The church appeared in the United States in 1959, but it was Moon's tours of major American cities in the early 1970's that drew thousands of followers and enormous publicity and controversy. Moon ended his personal ministry in 1976 but was soon rocked with financial scandal. In 1982, he was convicted of tax evasion in New York City and given an eighteen-month prison sentence.

Moreno, Rita (Rosa Dolores Alverio; b. Dec. 11, 1931, Humacao, Puerto Rico): Puerto Rican actor and dancer. Moreno started Spanish dancing as a child, and soon developed her dancing, singing, and acting to Broadway and professional levels. Her Broadway credits include *The Sign in Sidney Brustein's Window* (1964-1965), *Gantry* (1969-1970), *The Ritz* (1975), and the female version of *The Odd Couple* (1985). Moreno is also known for her roles in such films as *West Side Story* (1961), *Carnal Knowledge* (1971), *The King and I* (1956), and *Singin' in the Rain* (1952). Moreno is listed in the *Guinness Book of World Records* as the only performer to win all four major performing awards: a 1962 Academy Award as Best Supporting Actress, a 1973 Grammy for Best Recording, a 1975 Tony for Best Supporting Actress, and Emmy Awards in 1977 and 1978.

Puerto Rican entertainer Rita Moreno is credited as the only person to win all four major performing awards—an Oscar, a Grammy, a Tony, and an Emmy. (APA)

Morita, Noriyuki "Pat" (b. June 28, 1930, Isleton, Calif.): Japanese American actor. Morita's difficult childhood included an early case of spinal tuberculosis and four years of internment in Arizona with his family during World War II. During the 1960's Morita began as a stand-up comic in San Francisco and Los Angeles nightclubs. After moving to Hawaii in 1972 seeking greater acceptance of Asian American performers, Morita landed the role of Arnold on the television show *Happy Days*. He became best known for his portrayal of the Japanese handyman and strong karate master Miyagi in the 1984 film *The Karate Kid*, for which he received an Academy Award nomination for Best Supporting Actor.

Japanese American actor Pat Morita, shown here in the mid-1970's after his success on the television situation comedy Happy Days, *paid tribute to his ethnic heritage in his portrayal of Japanese handyman Mr. Miyagi in the* Karate Kid *film series. (AP/Wide World Photos)*

Mormons: Members of the Church of Jesus Christ of Latter-day Saints, founded in 1830 by Joseph Smith (1805-1844). Smith grew up in western New York during an era of intense religious searching. Disturbed by the conflicting doctrines proclaimed by revivalist preachers who "burned over" this district, Smith retired to the woods for prayer. There he was visited by heavenly personages who told him that all the existing creeds were corrupt. Shortly thereafter, another celestial visitor, the angel Moroni, directed Smith to Hill Cumorah, where he allegedly discovered gold plates containing an addition to the Bible that had been buried there many centuries before. Smith translated the hieroglyphics on the plates using two divining stones (Urim and Thumim) and published the work as *The Book of Mormon* (1830). The book contained a fascinating historical account that not only linked the young American nation with the biblical past but also gave its inhabitants the possibility of playing the leading role in the "latter" days of God's great historical drama. Smith's revelation called for the gathering of "the Saints" and the building of Zion—God's kingdom on Earth. According to Smith's teachings, Mormons, as the group came to be called, would restore the true Christian church on the North American continent.

The Book of Mormon relates a sacred history of the pre-Columbian inhabitants of North America. Among other claims, the book explains that the American Indian tribes are descendants of the lost tribes of Israel, who migrated to the American continent many years before the birth of Jesus. After Jesus' resurrection, He came to America to correct various doctrines and ritual practices. Eventually, an evil "dark-skinned" tribe wiped out the noble "light-skinned" peoples, but the sacred plates were preserved in the hills of upstate New York until Smith discovered them. Unfortunately, the racial overtones in this account spawned discrimination in the Mormon church. Not until the 1970's were African Americans allowed leadership roles in the church hierarchy.

Smith's religious revelation immediately attracted fervent believers and determined enemies. Settlers were attracted to Mormonism because it injected the arduous pioneering process with divine purpose: A young nation, seemingly relegated to the backyard of civilization, was suddenly at the heart of the divine plan. On the other hand, the Mormons' exclusivity, intensity, and practices such as polygamy resulted in persecution. Until 1847, when Brigham Young led "the Saints" to refuge in what would become the state of Utah, Mormons were driven from every settlement they established. Smith died at the hands of an anti-Mormon mob in Carthage, Illinois. Today Mormons direct a successful worldwide religious organization from their headquarters in Salt Lake City, Utah. They are known for their large families, conservative values, and extensive missionary work.

SUGGESTED READINGS. For a comprehensive account of Mormon history and beliefs see Leonard Arrington and Davis Bitton's *The Mormon Experience: A History of the Latter-Day Saints* (1979) and Thomas O'Dea's *The Mormons* (1957). Jan Shipps's *Mormonism: The Story of a New Religious Tradition* (1985) and Wallace Stegner's *The Gathering of Zion* (1981) are useful in chronicling the impact Mormonism has had and continues to have on American culture.

Morrison, Toni (Chloe Anthony Wofford; b. Feb. 18, 1931, Lorain, Ohio): African American author, editor, and educator. In 1981 *Newsweek* called Morrison the best practicing black writer in the United States. She was educated at Howard University (B.A., 1953) and Cornell (M.A., 1955) and has taught English at various universities including Yale and Princeton. In 1965 she became a senior editor/writer at Random House in New York City. Since 1970 she has written six novels, as well as other books. *Beloved* (1987), chronicling the recollections of a former slave, received a Pulitzer Prize; the novel *Jazz* (1992) was a best-seller. In 1993 Morrison became the first African American woman to receive the Nobel Prize in literature.

As a book editor, Toni Morrison was extremely influential in assisting the careers of many African American women authors. (AP/Wide World Photos)

Motherhood: Until the social changes of the 1960's, motherhood was generally held to be an all-consuming role that women assumed upon the birth of a child. The devoted mother sacrificed her personal needs and ambitions to ensure the well-being of her children, whether in the American colonies of the 1750's or the suburbs of the 1950's. This ideal of motherhood was venerated as a "sacred calling" to which all women should aspire. Notions about motherhood were linked to prevailing social views on the role of women generally, consigning them to the private or domestic sphere.

The WOMEN'S LIBERATION MOVEMENT and relaxation of sexual mores that began in the 1960's challenged ideals of women as wives and mothers as part of an overall critique of women's place in society. More effective means of birth control allowed women greater choice in when or whether they bore children. Some women began to reject the imperative to become mothers, just as some rejected social conventions about marriage or sexuality. Large numbers of women entered the work force, delaying motherhood until they had established their careers or combining motherhood in a delicate balancing act with their working lives. Women began to marry later, divorce more readily, or remain single. Options for motherhood expanded radically to include lesbian mothers and rising numbers of single mothers (through choice, lack of marriage, or divorce).

By the 1980's the diversity in styles of motherhood was comparable to the diversity in American family life. Fast disappearing was the stereotype of the suburban housewife doting over her two children as she waited for her breadwinning husband to return from work. Greater variety in types of families has meant new routes to motherhood. While giving birth to a child remains the most common route to the status of motherhood, it may also be gained socially upon the ADOPTION of a child, the acquisition of stepchildren with a subsequent marriage, or the taking in of foster children.

Giving birth to a child does not inevitably result in the assumption of motherhood. Infant mortality rates in the United States are among the highest in the Western industrialized world. Some mothers may give up their infants to be adopted, while some adoptive mothers may lose their children to the biological mother. A surrogate mother who bears a child for others under a contract arrangement may not even define the baby she is carrying *in utero* as hers. The Baby M case in the 1980's increased public awareness of the complexities of surrogacy and demonstrated the stark differences between the biological process and the social process of becoming a mother.

Mothers are typically expected to assume responsibility for their children's education, including spending time helping their children learn to read. (James L. Shaffer)

Cultural Values. There is more to motherhood, of course, than the acquiring of children. Motherhood is associated with styles of childrearing that are consistent with deep-seated cultural values. Within each ethnic and religious group, there are long-standing customs regarding the propriety of a variety of mothering behaviors. These may include but are not limited to the following issues: breast versus bottle feeding; diapering and toilet training; discipline and safety; sleep habits; comforting styles; timetables for physical and mental development; and views about a mother's place (at home, at work, or both). For example, some fundamentalist Christians subscribe to strict rules of parental control based on what they feel is biblical sanction. Many cultures, both within and outside the United States, find it normal to have babies and young children sleep with the mother or both parents rather than in their own beds. These very personal decisions about parenting are influenced not only by one's culture but also by one's social class, education, and individual personality.

A strong cultural prescription in American society is the expectation that couples will produce children.

Pressures toward childbearing are rooted in much earlier times when the high death rate necessitated a pronatalist stance. This cultural ideal has promoted a division of labor within the family by placing childrearing responsibilities on the mother, while placing the responsibility for the economic well-being of the family upon the father or oldest male within the household.

American cultures vary widely in their expectations about when women should have children, how many children they should have, and how much emphasis they place on shaping young girls for their future role as mothers. Yet virtually all groups in the United States seem to share the belief that the primary responsibility for childrearing falls on the mother. Indeed, this is considered "natural" as an outgrowth of the process of giving birth and women's supposed maternal instinct—the propensity not only to produce life but to nurture it. Some feminists have rebelled against this notion, which implies that motherhood and mothering are both biological imperatives for women and that those women who do not feel such instincts or cannot bear children are abnormal. Others have celebrated the importance of nurturing but called for greater sharing of the nurturing role to accommodate changes in women's lives in the late twentieth century.

Females of active working age constitute close to half of the total work force in the United States and Canada. Increasing numbers of unmarried and divorced women are solely, or mostly, responsible for the economic well-being of both themselves and their children. Yet the reality of females assuming financial responsibility for families they head, or sharing that role with their partners, has had little effect on social expectations for mothers. Mothers are generally still expected to assume major responsibility for childrearing, as well as the majority of other household tasks. Typically, mothers are also expected to take charge of their children's formal and informal education, and religious training or observance. Thus, they may find themselves with two jobs: one paid in the workplace and the other unpaid at home.

By the late 1900's, there was considerable debate about the role of fathers in bringing up children. Popular books and articles on fatherhood in the 1980's and 1990's implied that American males were participating more fully in parenting activities. This may be an accurate observation for some households where there are unusually involved fathers. Empirical studies of the respective contributions of mothers and fathers to various types of HOUSEWORK and childtending activities, however, indicate that the average contribution of fathers has changed little since the advent of contemporary FEMINISM: It has increased by only a few minutes per week. Women are still given child custody in a majority of DIVORCE cases. The 1980's, however, saw the advent of the male househusband raising the children while his wife went to work, as well as a rise in the number of men heading single parent households. These and other experiences have led some men to question traditional models of fatherhood individually or through the MEN'S MOVEMENT, providing yet another influence on the changing institution of motherhood.

Historical Perspective. The important role of the mother in both the family and in society has long been

Modern American women are rearing their daughters with new expectations about and models of motherhood. Here, an African American mother carefully guides her daughter across playground equipment at a local park. (James L. Shaffer)

assumed. Yet history reveals that the father was central in domestic activities and the education of his children until the mid-nineteenth century in the United States. The shift for both fathers and mothers, casting them in far more separate roles, came with the INDUSTRIAL REVOLUTION.

Until the 1830's, the home was the center of American economic life. Entire families worked side by side in heavy domestic and farm labor, or produced goods in cottage industries and workshops. In agrarian society, each child had value as a potential worker to help support the family as a subsistence unit. Couples had many children to ensure their productivity and secure old age, and as a hedge against high child mortality rates. In colonial America, it was typical for women to have as many as twelve children, spending many years bearing, nursing, and rearing them in addition to carrying out their other economic obligations to the household.

With industrialization came many changes in family life. The center of production shifted from the home to the factory and from the countryside to the cities. Men went out to work while women were left home in charge of children and domestic tasks. The home became a refuge from the pressures of modern URBAN LIFE. Although women and children sometimes took part in factory work, this was increasingly frowned upon as inappropriate. According to feminist theorist Adrienne RICH, it was at this time that the home became idealized as a sacred precinct and the institution of motherhood came to be seen as what leaders of the day termed a "sacred calling." Mothers were expected to devote themselves to the welfare of their husbands and children in the home, exerting a redeeming moral influence.

Thus, the ideal of motherhood as solely devoted to mothering is a relatively recent phenomenon in American history. Many nonindustrial societies and subcultures, as well as Americans living outside the DOMINANT CULTURE, have never lived by this ideal, however, either by choice or by circumstance. Instead, women have combined economic activity and child care relying on the help of female relatives. Such a system prevailed, for example, among African Americans under the institution of SLAVERY; among early twentieth century immigrants who worked in the GARMENT INDUSTRY; and among Americans from RESERVATIONS to the INNER CITY who could depend on the support of the extended family. Although most contemporary American women, including mothers, work

outside the home, society has been slow to offer crucial support such as child care, perhaps because Americans are reluctant to part with traditional ideals about motherhood. Modern psychology has also tended to uphold the status quo, stating that devoted mothering is the key to children's mental health, and that there is no substitute for such mothering.

Family Planning. The letters and journals of American women from prior eras often point to the hardships of pregnancy and childbirth at a time when birth control was rare and maternal death in childbirth was common. Improved health care and BIRTH CONTROL options have had a great impact on the nature of American motherhood, certainly easing its physical challenges.

Usually the pressure to have large numbers of children is decreased as the death rate of a country falls, thus increasing the chances for each child to reach adulthood. Other changes brought on by industrialization tend to move children from being considered assets to being considered liabilities. Increasingly, the options to postpone, limit, or perhaps forgo having children are more likely to be selected. In the 1990's 1.8 children per couple became the average in the United States.

In a society in which there are numerous highly effective techniques of birth control, one might assume that all births are planned. There is evidence that some couples do make careful decisions about having children similar to the decisions they make in other major situations such as buying a house or car. Many pregnancies are unplanned, however, and circumstances of motherhood vary widely between and within different age groups and subcultures.

Teenage Mothers. Unmarried young females who became pregnant had limited social options before the 1960's. They suffered strong social censure and could not generally continue in school or, sometimes, work. Many married in accordance with standard social expectations. Those who remained single were pressured to offer their babies for adoption. The WOMEN'S MOVEMENT and sexual revolution of the 1960's expanded options for many women, as did the legalization of ABORTION in *ROE V. WADE* (1973). On the one hand, some women were able to avoid teenage motherhood through the use of BIRTH CONTROL and abortion; on the other hand, there was less social stigma attached to unmarried teenagers bearing, keeping, and raising their own children. Teenage mothers became increasingly common in the late twentieth century United

States in all ethnic groups. The mothers were sometimes isolated but often had contact with and assistance from other family members in childrearing.

Teenage motherhood presents numerous challenges to the young women themselves, as well as to the family members and social agencies that support them. The rise in teenage mothers among Latinas during the 1980's, for example, has been a source of concern to that largely CATHOLIC community, while some African American community leaders warn against teenage motherhood as a leading cause of high rates of POVERTY, crime, and other social problems in the GHETTO. Because teenage mothers are likely not to finish high school, they tend to have a harder time finding good jobs; those who must support themselves often find it difficult to rise out of poverty. Many teenage mothers have limited role models for the daunting task of motherhood. They are often the product of a single female-headed household and live in neighborhoods where such circumstances are relatively routine. Media investigations of teenage motherhood suggest that teenagers are motivated to have children because they have little confidence in their ability to contribute to

society or little love in their lives. Thus, while the phenomenon of "children having children" dismays many adults and strains the nation's health, social service, and educational agencies, becoming mothers appears to give hope and a sense of identity to some teenagers.

Some schools have recognized the importance of incorporating specialized programs for teenage mothers to allow them to complete their education. These may include daycare for the children and special classes for the teenagers on the care of infants and parenting older children. Only a few programs like one in Newark, New Jersey, are targeted to reach teenage fathers and their needs; the young mothers are largely the ones seen as responsible. The feminist ideals of shared parenting roles, therefore, may be far from the reality of most teenage mothers.

Clearly, the ideals and realities of contemporary American motherhood are very much in flux. Many women still want children and cherish their opportunity to be nurturers, but they also want the options of working outside the home and sharing housework and child care with their partners. American social policy

With the increase in the number of American mothers working outside the home, many families have greater financial resources to provide for their children's needs. (Jim and Mary Whitmer)

on family issues such as maternity leave and child care has not kept pace with the changes in women's lives in the late twentieth century. Nevertheless, a new generation of American women is rearing their daughters with a new set of expectations about motherhood and a new set of models for mothering styles.

SUGGESTED READINGS. For a discussion of numerous cultural practices, see Parenting in a Multicultural Society (1980), edited by Mario D. Fantini and Rene Cardenas. Arlene S. Skolnick and Jerome H. Skolnick capture the diversity within the family in their edited volume *Family in Transition: Rethinking Marriage, Sexuality, Child Rearing, and Family Organization* (7th ed., 1992). Diversity, conflict, and change in contemporary American families is detailed in *Breaking with Tradition* (1992), by Marci E. Bedard. An exploration of the issues that new technologies create concerning birth, adoption, infertility, abortion, medicalizing motherhood, and more can be found in Barbara Katz Rothman's *Recreating Motherhood* (1989). A comprehensive analysis of perspectives on women as mothers in several cultures and a discussion of their satisfaction with their lives as mothers can be found in *On Being a Mother* (1983) by Mary B. Boulton. See also Adrienne Rich's *Of Woman Born: Motherhood as Experience and Institution* (rev. ed., 1986.—*Gretta Stanger*

Motown Industries: Company best known for its recording and publishing divisions specializing in African American popular music.

Berry GORDY, Jr., founded the Motown Record Corporation in his native city of Detroit in 1958. The company enjoyed moderate success until, in 1960, Motown produced its first million-seller record, "Shop Around," by the Miracles (featuring Smokey Robinson). In the 1960's, Motown became one of the leading record producers in the industry and the most successful black-owned business in the United States. Its records not only attracted black music enthusiasts, but whites in the United States and abroad.

Besides the Miracles, the company's stable of performers boasted such African American artists as the Temptations, Four Tops, Supremes, Martha Reeves and the Vandellas, Marvin Gaye, Stevie WONDER, and Gladys Knight and the Pips. The success of the company can be attributed not only to the talents of its singers and its pool of studio musicians but also to producer-song writers Smokey Robinson, Norman Whitfield, Eddie Holland, and Lamont Dozier, who created the unique

Motown sound. The music drew from elements of BLUES and GOSPEL music and amplified the beat of its usually up-tempo songs with hand claps, finger snaps, bongos, and other percussive devices.

Motown moved its headquarters to Los Angeles in 1971. Throughout the 1970's, the company continued to reign as the most successful producer of African American popular music by signing such acts as the Jackson 5 and the Commodores (featuring Lionel Richie). The company also created a film division producing vehicles for its stars, most notably Diana Ross in *Lady Sings the Blues* (1972) and *Mahogany* (1975).

The success of African American producers, songwriters, and recording artists at Motown Industries earned millions of dollars for label owner Berry Gordy, Jr., shown here in 1988 on the night of his induction into the Rock 'n' Roll Hall of Fame. (AP/Wide World Photos)

The profitability of the black music entertainment business led other major recording companies aggressively to pursue and sign African American artists with their labels. Some of Motown's most prominent stars—the Jacksons, Diana Ross, and Marvin Gaye—signed multimillion dollar contracts with other record labels. Despite the financial incentive to remain, these artists cited the need to gain greater artistic freedom by breaking away from Gordy's paternalistic managerial style as the primary reason for leaving Motown.

By the early 1980's, Motown appeared less willing to be an innovator and adapt to new trends in popular music such as HIP-HOP CULTURE and RAP MUSIC. In 1988, Gordy sold the recording division of Motown for $61 million to MCA, Inc., and an investment group called Boston Ventures. Initially, Motown made attempts to regain its prominence in the music industry. It retained mainstays such as Stevie Wonder and Lionel Richie, nurtured new groups such as the Boys, re-signed Diana Ross, and lured veteran musicians such as Ray CHARLES and the Pointer Sisters to sign with the company. In the 1990's, however, Motown became embroiled in lawsuits against its owners over the handling of record distribution and the commitment to investing in the company's future growth.

The influence of Motown on American popular culture cannot be overstated. Songs such as "I Heard It Through the Grapevine," "My Girl," "What's Going On," and "Heatwave" are still as popular as they were when first recorded years ago. Its music is often heard in films such as *The Big Chill* (1983), on television shows such as *The Wonder Years* and *Murphy Brown,* and on countless commercials. As a tribute to its inestimable achievements, a 1983 television special—*Motown 25: Yesterday, Today, Forever*—featured memorable appearances by nearly all of the company's most prominent alumni.

SUGGESTED READINGS. For a history of Motown and its unique style of music, see Don Waller's *The Motown Story* (1985). Informative articles on Motown can also be found in Ian Hoare's *The Soul Book* (1975), Jim Miller's *The Rolling Stone Illustrated History of Rock & Roll* (1980), and Jon Futrell's *The Illustrated Encyclopedia of Black Music* (1982).

Mott, Lucretia Coffin (Jan. 3, 1793, Nantucket, Mass.—Nov. 11, 1880, near Philadelphia, Pa.): Abolitionist and suffragist. In 1821 Mott became a Quaker minister, and in 1833 she founded the Philadelphia Female Anti-Slavery Society. She met Elizabeth Cady STANTON, suffrage leader, when the two women arrived at the Anti-Slavery Convention in London in 1840 only to be told that women delegates were not allowed. In 1848 she joined Stanton in organizing the First Women's Rights Convention in Seneca Falls, New York. She founded and ran the Philadelphia Association for Relief and Employment of Poor Women. She is the author of *Discourse on Women* (1850), in which she attributes women's inferior status to repression.

Mound builders: Ancient peoples, primarily of the Mississippi basin, who constructed various structures of earth or stone. The mounds range in shape (cones, pyramids, human and animal forms, walls and various geometric shapes) and in function (tombs, monuments, and fortifications). While little is known about the tribes who created these structures, it is assumed that they did not predate the beginning of the Common Era. The inclusion of some European objects in some mounds near the Great Lakes indicates that the practice of mound building survived to early Columbian times, but by the sixteenth century, Spanish explorers found tribes merely using the structures, not creating them. The ancient mound builders may have belonged to the same race as the Aztecs, Mayas, and Incas and may have been the ancestors of several American Indian tribes in the United States. They attained an impressive level of technological advancement—creating pottery, weaving fabric, and hammering copper into implements and decorative ornaments.

Movimiento Estudiantil Chicano de Aztlán

(MEChA): Activist Chicano student group formed in 1969 from a merging of similar Mexican American organizations at the historic Chicano Coordinating Council on Higher Education in Santa Barbara, California. The name translates as "Chicano Student Movement

A Quaker minister and abolitionist, Lucretia Mott became a leading figure in the fight for women's suffrage. (Library of Congress)

of Aztlán," with its acronym meaning "wick" in Spanish and "match" in Caló. Many leaders of the CHICANO MOVEMENT and CHICANO STUDIES PROGRAMS were associated with MEChA. Through its branches on college campuses, the group continues efforts to bring about social, economic, and political change in both the university and the broader community.

Moynihan Report: Analysis of underlying causes of racial inequality, written for the Johnson Administration by assistant secretary of labor Daniel Patrick Moynihan. The report, officially titled *The Negro Family: The Case for National Action*, was issued in July, 1965, at the request of President Lyndon Johnson to document barriers to achieving full racial equality in spite of the passage of landmark CIVIL RIGHTS LEGISLATION. It blamed problems in the African American community on "the deterioration of the Negro family," tracing the growth of a matriarchal family system that demeaned black men from the SLAVERY era through JIM CROW LAWS and the GREAT MIGRATION to urban areas to modern welfare laws that favored families with a female head of household. The report was strongly criticized by civil rights leaders for placing the blame on African Americans themselves rather than on a RACIST society. Nevertheless, it raised important issues that were still being debated by social workers, policymakers, and black community leaders in the 1990's.

Daniel Patrick Moynihan was President Lyndon Johnson's assistant Secretary of Labor when he undertook his controversial investigation of the social problems affecting black family life. (Library of Congress)

Ms. magazine: Most prestigious feminist magazine published in the United States. It was founded largely through the efforts of Patricia Carbine and Gloria STEINEM, its editor for sixteen years who is still closely associated with the journal. *Ms.* was originally included in the December 15, 1971, issue of *New York* magazine, which sold out in eight days and brought in thirty-six thousand subscriptions. An independent volume 1, number 1 came out in July, 1972; by the end of the year, *Ms.* had 175,000 subscribers. It swiftly became the voice of contemporary FEMINISM and the WOMEN'S LIBERATION MOVEMENT.

Ms. has had two lives. The first (1972-1989) was characterized by its attempt to find a niche within the commercial WOMEN'S MAGAZINE market that would not compromise its integrity as a feminist publication—a goal it was never able to completely meet. *Ms.* began a second life in 1990 when it changed owners and went to a no-advertisements format in order to gain greater editorial control. Robin Morgan became editor-in-chief of the new *Ms.*; Steinem kept her close ties.

Ms. was a pioneer in proving that women are interested in—and will pay for—a woman's magazine focusing on substantial issues rather than merely on food, home decorating, beauty, and relationships. From the start, *Ms.* emphasized social and political issues of special concern to women. A groundbreaker in other ways as well, *Ms.* challenged long-standing conventions with covers featuring a woman in glasses (Billie Jean KING), a girl in braces, and older women.

Steinem and her staff struggled from the start to change the exploitive look and role of ads in women's magazines. Refusing sexist ads, they asked corporations to design advertisements that appealed to women's intellects, wide range of interests, and expanding roles. They were not very successful in this cause.

Ms. also hoped to break free of closely linking ads and content in women's magazines, a practice that has an especially strong hold on this genre of journalism. Yet the magazine depended too much on advertising revenue to demand the editorial and layout freedom the management wanted. When the magazine changed ownership in 1990, it took the risky step of changing to a no-ads format. Since then, it has proudly flaunted its "editorially free with no advertising" status. Unshackled from demands of advertisers, it has ventured far from the look and tone of other women's magazines. The risky experiment has paid off; *Ms.* now supports itself through its readership, despite hefty subscription rates.

Striving to be as inclusive as possible in its feminist coverage and audience, the new *Ms.* regularly features articles on international issues (reported by women native to the country where the story is set) and on LESBIAN and race-related issues along with its more conventional gender topics. It often highlights women in sports and in the arts, and regularly publishes fiction, poetry, and photography by women artists.

SUGGESTED READINGS. The best way to understand the history and aspirations of *Ms.* is to go to the magazine itself, which has featured a number of editorials on its goals and policies. A good, but brief, summary of its early history can be found in *American Mass-Market Magazines* (1990), edited by Alan Nourie and Barbara Nourie; for an appraisal of its more recent merits, see *Magazines for Libraries* (1992), edited by Bill Katz and Linda Sternberg Katz.

Gloria Steinem, shown here in 1969, served as editor-in-chief of Ms. *magazine between 1971 and 1990. (AP/Wide World Photos)*

Muhammad, Elijah (Elijah Poole; Oct. 10, 1897, Sandersville, Ga.—Feb. 25, 1975, Chicago, Ill.): Militant African American religious and political leader. A controversial force in the fight for black self-direction, Elijah Muhammad was born Elijah Poole, the son of sharecroppers and former slaves. By the 1960's he was head of the Chicago-based NATION OF ISLAM, or Black Muslims, holding considerable religious and political power. Anti-white, he advocated BLACK NATIONALISM, racial pride, SEGREGATION, self-defense, and "BLACK POWER." He has often been revered by black militants but scorned as suspect by black moderates and whites. He quarreled with Muslim leader MALCOLM X before the latter's assassination in 1965.

Elijah Muhammad, charismatic leader of the Nation of Islam, was a strong advocate of racial pride and black nationalism. (AP/Wide World Photos)

Muller v. Oregon (1908): Landmark Supreme Court decision that set the trend toward protective legislation for women workers during the "sweatshop era" in the early 1900's. The effects of industrialization and long hours on workers' lives and health had aroused the concern of social reformers and labor advocates. Yet attempts by state legislatures to pass laws limiting employers' power over workers' lives were often struck down by the courts.

From the 1890's through the early 1920's, all regulation of working conditions was challenged by employers. They contended that such laws were a violation of both the employer's and the worker's right to contract "freely" the conditions of labor and violated the "due process" clause of the U.S. CONSTITUTION. Those favoring restriction laws argued that some might be acceptable for women if not for men, because of women's greater physical frailty, especially concerning childbearing. Woman's primary function focused around her domestic duties in the home, they claimed, and when she worked outside the home for wages, the state could legitimately intervene in the interests of the "future generation," to "protect" a woman's health.

Curt Muller, a laundry owner in Portland, Oregon, challenged a 1903 state law limiting the hours women could work in industrial work to ten per day and sixty per week. He had the support of an employers' organization dedicated to opposing labor unions and promoting employers' interests, and the American Bar Association. Louis Brandeis, who later became a U.S. Supreme Court justice, defended the law for the state of Oregon, using an innovative type of argument based on factual evidence rather than law and precedent. He cited evidence collected by social reformers Josephine and Pauline Goldmark, which pointed to the dangers of overwork and the effect of fatigue on the human body. Even small motions, if repeated over and over, are a source of fatigue that is especially detrimental for women, the evidence suggested.

The Court agreed with the Goldmarks' evidence that standing for hours on her feet is injurious to a woman, and, "as healthy mothers are essential to vigorous offspring," it decided that it was a matter of public interest to preserve women's health. Justice Brewer's opinion upholding the Oregon law stated: "That women's physical structure and the performance of maternal functions place her at a disadvantage in the struggle for subsistence is obvious. This is especially true when the burdens of motherhood are upon her." The Court not only held that women were physically in need of protection but also said that even if all social, educational, and legal barriers were removed, women would still need the "protection" of law. This case set the precedent for numerous state laws limiting women workers' participation in the workforce as equals with men. Such laws are now considered sex discrimination and counter to the CIVIL RIGHTS ACT OF 1964.

SUGGESTED READINGS. For a discussion of *Muller v. Oregon* in its historical context, see Susan Lehrer's *Origins of Protective Labor Legislation for Women 1905-1925* (1980). For specific reference to legal cases see J. Ralph Lindgren and Nadine Taub's *The Law of Sex Discrimination* (1988).

Multicultural education: Effort to bring multicultural perspectives and experiences to general studies in American schools with the goal of increasing Americans' appreciation of cultural diversity. The United States has always been a multicultural society, but one in which ethnic and cultural differences have often been ignored by the majority. MULTICULTURALISM began as a reaction and alternative to the MELTING POT THEORY of ASSIMILATION. Under the concept of the United States as a melting pot, immigrants were expected to give up their identity, language, and cultural values and to fuse into one ideal American culture. While Anglo-conformity was somewhat attainable for western European immigrants who resembled the majority culture, it was unrealistic for non-European groups. AFRICAN AMERICANS and other racial minorities became the "unmeltable ethnics" whose educational and career aspirations often went unfulfilled. School curricula continued to center on the cultural aspects of Western civilization, while the study of other cultures and languages was not taken seriously.

In its early years, multicultural education focused primarily on improving intergroup relations within American society. Technological advances, changes in world democracies, and increased interdependence among nations broadened the concept of multicultural education to include a global perspective: It became imperative that individuals learn to communicate effectively across cultures. During the 1980's, marginalized groups such as people with disabilities, OLDER AMERICANS, and homeless people were brought under the umbrella of multicultural education along with women and ethnic minorities. An ongoing debate within the field has been the degree to which multicultural education should stress the differences between people as opposed to focusing on human similarities.

Historical Development. The push for what was officially termed "multicultural education" began in the 1970's under the influence of the CIVIL RIGHTS MOVEMENT and the ethnic heritage revival. Related efforts, however, date back to international studies programs begun in the 1920's and 1930's and early projects on intercultural relations in urban schools. Previously the public schools had been seen as agents of Americanization, especially when confronted with the huge immigrant influx of the late 1800's and early 1900's. It was the challenge of meeting the educational needs of African Americans that ultimately led some educators to perceive a need for multicultural education.

Until the mid-twentieth century, those African American children who received an education did so in segregated schools with inferior resources. The historic 1954 U.S. Supreme Court decision in BROWN V. BOARD OF EDUCATION outlawed school segregation, but educational inequality persisted, along with pervasive RACISM, PREJUDICE, and DISCRIMINATION against blacks in American society. The Coleman Report, issued in 1966 after a series of race riots, suggested that a lack of educational opportunity was a major cause of economic inequality and racial unrest. The CIVIL RIGHTS ACT OF 1964 and the BILINGUAL EDUCATION ACT OF 1968 were efforts to provide greater economic and educational equity for racial and ethnic minorities. The Civil Rights movement, CHICANO MOVEMENT,

and other forces that pressed for such legislation helped bring about greater awareness of cultural diversity and the contributions made by members of minority groups.

The ideas behind these social change movements eventually coalesced in early efforts for multicultural education. Colleges and universities took the lead by establishing ethnic studies and women's studies programs in the 1960's and 1970's, inspiring the public school system to follow suit. Early programs were limited in scope: An individual teacher might make a point of having students learn about the life of Martin Luther KING, Jr., for example, or plan festivities to celebrate Mexican Independence Day. In the mid-1970's, multicultural education became more systematized as a pedagogical strategy for replacing the melting pot ideal with the concept of CULTURAL PLURALISM. Proponents rewrote curricula and developed new teachers' guides to integrate multicultural perspectives into various subject

At the height of the Black Power movement, some African American educators began to argue for the adoption of Afrocentric curricula and all-black classrooms, such as were instituted at the Liberation School in Nashville, Tenn. (AP/Wide World Photos)

The main goal of multicultural education, as demonstrated by this geography lesson in which students locate their ancestral homelands, is to develop instructional approaches that encourage respect for and awareness of cultural diversity. (James L. Shaffer)

areas, especially social studies, language arts, and the fine arts. Educators with this view got a boost from the popularity of Alex HALEY's novel Roots: The Saga of an American Family (1976) and the surge of public interest in genealogy, oral history, and other aspects of ethnic heritage that followed the *Roots* miniseries on television.

As more marginalized groups began to make their voices heard in the 1970's and 1980's, multicultural education programs tried to be ever more inclusive. They embraced the concerns not only of ethnic minorities but also of women, homosexuals, people with disabilities, and others, often prompting controversy. By the last part of the 1980's, few new multicultural education programs or theories were being promoted. There are several possible causes. Claims of REVERSE

DISCRIMINATION in AFFIRMATIVE ACTION programs and admissions QUOTAS increased hostility between the DOMINANT CULTURE and MINORITY GROUPS, as well as among minorities themselves. Cuts in funding for schools and social services during the Reagan and Bush administrations made it difficult to start or sustain new programs. Many school districts felt they had already done their part to encourage multicultural awareness by celebrating such events as Asian American Heritage Month.

Yet in the late 1980's and early 1990's, RACISM resurfaced, with white supremacist groups reclaiming their place in the spotlight. HATE CRIMES were on the rise. The LOS ANGELES RIOTS of 1992, the worst in the nation's history, reawakened Americans to continuing socioeconomic inequities between whites and people of color. Projections indicate that in the twenty-first century, most urban Americans will be of non-European background; that was already true of many urban American public school districts in the 1980's. More and more Americans began to realize that their country is a global democracy whose citizens must acquire the necessary skills to function effectively across cultures. There seemed to be a continuing need for multicultural education which would help to shape well-informed, responsible citizens who view cultural diversity as a sign of unity and strength.

Definition, Goals, and Objectives. Multicultural education is a reform movement as well as a teaching and learning process that values cultural pluralism and fosters understanding among people of different backgrounds in an interdependent world. Advocates believe that schools must restructure their priorities, commitments, and processes to reflect the cultural diversity of a global society. Multicultural education is a multidisciplinary field. For example, the concepts of culture and proxemics (spatial separation between people) come from anthropology, while insights into prejudice, discrimination, racism, CLASS, and gender derive from sociology. Psychology aids in examining cultural variations and differences in teaching and learning styles, while social philosophy provides a perspective on cultural pluralism, equality, and democracy. Ethnic studies, drawing from the social sciences, literature, and history, provide a balanced perspective on minority cultural groups based on historical antecedents and social realities.

The main goal of multicultural education is to develop instructional approaches that help eliminate racist attitudes and behaviors and help promote respect for cultural diversity. Through multicultural education, individuals learn to function effectively in more than one culture without rejecting their own cultural identity. Students learn to perceive and understand multiple cultural interpretations of values, beliefs, attitudes, and behaviors while eliminating ETHNOCENTRIC views, STEREOTYPES, and racist attitudes. They become critical thinkers capable of viewing the world and others more objectively as they study cultural differences within their historical and international contexts.

Curricula and Materials. Ideally, multicultural education is broadly inclusive and permeates the total school curriculum, providing knowledge and understanding of cultural differences in historical context. It should integrate multiethnic and global (Eastern and

The range of cultural diversity represented by these three schoolchildren is beginning to be reflected in the ethnic mix of American teachers—a change crucial to the success of multicultural education. (Cleo Freelance Photo)

Western) perspectives within the traditional curriculum and be directed toward all students, regardless of ethnic background.

Traditional American school curricula have reflected the values of the white Anglo-Saxon middle-class majority and presented information from a western European point of view. This Eurocentric perspective has neglected the achievements and contributions of cultural minorities. Effective multicultural programs have launched curricular reforms that enable students to view concepts, issues, and events from a multicultural perspective and to make decisions on important social issues. In this way, students assume responsibility for their own education.

Many schools take a less integrated approach by simply adding a multiethnic perspective or unit to an existing traditional curriculum or by focusing on the contributions of minority groups to American culture through the celebration of heroes and holidays. This approach, especially common in the 1970's, was seen by many as too limited, however, by the mid- to late-1980's, multiculturalists favored the social action approach and redesigned curricula to integrate multiculturalism fully into every aspect of school life. Through this type of educational reform, schools can correct stereotypical perceptions about culturally different groups.

In the course of multicultural studies, students are exposed to key concepts and definitions, such as ACCULTURATION, assimilation, cultural pluralism, cultural relativism, discrimination, and racial prejudice. In addition to the study of theory and concepts, students engage in activities such as role-playing and simulation in order to benefit fully from multicultural education. Interdisciplinary and comparative approaches are commonly used in designing multicultural curriculum. Ethnic and multiethnic studies, minority studies, women's and gender studies, BILINGUAL EDUCATION, special education, cultural awareness programs, human relations and conflict resolution, and values clarification are examples of various curricular approaches. Examples of ways to incorporate multiculturalism into the curriculum could include studying African masks in art history, ancient Mayan concepts of numbers and time in mathematics, the foreign-language press in journalism, and the American Indian origins of lacrosse in physical education.

Proponents of multicultural education find that textbooks and other instrumental materials must be examined carefully for bias. Textbooks may ignore the contributions of women and other minorities, stereotyping them in traditional, subordinate roles and neglecting to devote equal space to their accomplishments. Other biases may contribute to unrealistic historic portrayals of cultural groups. Using antebellum SLAVERY as a starting point for the study of African American history rather than beginning by tracing its roots in African civilizations may give students the false impression that African Americans had no cultural traditions of their own before contact with white Europeans. Career stereotyping in textbooks, such as the portrayal of MEXICAN AMERICANS solely as migrant workers, is especially damaging, so educational materials from stories in elementary-school readers to illustrations in high school textbooks should include profiles of minority individuals in positions of power, such as physicians, attorneys, and school administrators.

Staffing. Multicultural education is best implemented when school personnel represent the full range of American cultural diversity. Educators must be aware of differences in teaching and learning styles, must be aware of cultural bias in standardized testing, and must make an effort to interact with culturally different individuals inside and outside the community. Students and community members have proved to be excellent resources in multicultural classrooms, whether in sharing PUERTO RICAN recipes or in leading a discussion about the INTERNMENT OF JAPANESE AMERICANS.

Meaningful multicultural education requires staff who are multiculturally sensitive, competent, and aware. School districts can foster this awareness through preservice and inservice training for teachers and other personnel, including intercultural field experiences. Educators who effectively present a multicultural curriculum respect and affirm cultural diversity, develop methods appropriate for dealing with diverse learning styles, and foster critical thinking and problem solving. Such teachers encourage students to analyze events from different perspectives and to search for bias or historical inconsistencies.

Model Programs. School districts and schools have designed many prototype programs to encourage students to share cultural knowledge and general understanding of other lifestyles since the 1970's. In Hartford, Connecticut, the Annie Fisher School, predominantly made up of minority students, and the all-white Morley School developed a cooperative program called "Across the Lines" to lessen racial isolation. Students wrote to each other using electronic mail and planned joint ventures such as a visit to a science museum. After various opportunities for intercultural interaction, post-testing of the students revealed that stereotypes they had previously held about one another were now seen as wrong and unfair.

Elsewhere, in an "Immigrant Assistance Program," elementary students wrote letters to older Russian and other European immigrants to learn about the immigrants' background while helping them prepare for citizenship exams. In California, numerous model programs for immigrant students have covered not only cultural orientation and bilingual education but also the mediation of intercultural conflict and improved relationships between schools and immigrant parents. Navajo Culture: A Bridge to the Rest of the World, a program of the Greasewood Toyei Consolidated

School in Arizona, encourages integration of NAVAJO culture into the curriculum, thus emphasizing bicultural education. In many Boston schools, teachers are encouraged to draw from the rich cultural backgrounds of students and parents through having students conduct family interviews and participate in multicultural panel discussions.

Colleges and universities are also actively involved in incorporating multicultural awareness classes and field experiences in teacher education programs. For example, the Teachers for Alaska (TFA) program at the University of Alaska, Fairbanks, prepares educators to teach in small, remote INUIT villages. Students majoring in education at Indiana University are encouraged to spend six to eight weeks applying the theories of multicultural education while teaching in an American Indian community. Ball State University requires education students to have field experiences in inner-city schools as well as suburban areas to encourage multicultural interaction.

SUGGESTED READINGS. Additional information on multicultural education can be obtained from the following sources: *Multicultural Education: Issues and Perspectives* edited by James A. Banks and Cherry A. McGee Banks (1989); *Comprehensive Multicultural Education: Theory and Practice* by Christinne Bennett (1986); *Research and Multicultural Education: From the Margins to the Mainstream,* edited by Carl A. Grant (1992); *Multicultural Education. A Teacher's Guide to Content and Process* by Hilda Hernandez, (1989); *Affirming Diversity: The Sociopolitical Context of Multicultural Education* by Sonia Nieto (1992); *Multicultural Education; A Cross Cultural Training Approach* edited by Margaret D. Pusch (1979); *Empowerment Through Multicultural Education,* edited by Christine Sleeter (1991); and *Multicultural Teaching: A Handbook of Activities, Information, and Resources* by Pamela L. Tiedt and Iris M. Tiedt, (1990).—*Maria A. Pacino*

Multiculturalism: Term coined in the late 1980's to refer to a new kind of CULTURAL PLURALISM, which stresses the inclusion of multicultural perspectives and empowerment of members of minority groups in all aspects of public life. Unlike the idea of cultural pluralism promoted in the early 1900's, which was conceived by white sociologists as a response to massive immigration, multiculturalism in the 1980's and 1990's has been developed by activist members of cultural minorities to redress what is seen as a continuing pattern of unjust

exclusion. Proponents take a broad approach to inclusiveness that embraces members of various marginalized groups, such as women and people with disabilities. Still too new a concept to be precisely defined, multiculturalism has been the topic of intense debate in higher education and public policy. Used loosely in ordinary conversation, however, it may simply refer to an awareness of diversity in American culture.

"Multicultural" means composed of many cultures, as when citizens of the same nation reflect a plurality of ethnic and social identities. By this definition, most modern nation states are multicultural. The United States, which heralds itself a nation of immigrants, is clearly so. In celebrating diversity, Americans acknowledge multiple streams of creative wisdom and endeavor. *E pluribus unum* ("in many, one"), the motto of the United States, suggests hybrid vitality and the distinctive tolerance of democracy.

Despite its appeal as an idea, cultural pluralism has also presented complex problems since it was first advocated in the United States in the early 1900's. Unrest based on ethnic conflict has emerged as one of the most contentious issues of the post-COLD WAR era. Domestically and abroad, old hatreds have rekindled in violence while new animosities erupt over REFUGEES and recent immigrants. The challenge facing multicultural societies in general, and the United States in particular, is how to negotiate the dilemmas inherent in a culturally diverse citizenry.

Opinions about how to solve the problems of cultural diversity are themselves divided. These disagreements frame the contemporary policy debate over what has come to be known as "multiculturalism." On one side of the controversy, proponents argue for changes in public institutions to recognize and accommodate the many different cultural traditions reflected in the population. Opponents argue that such changes, especially in schools and the workplace, will weaken the unity of society and the competitiveness of the American economy.

Pluralism versus Assimilation. The argument broadly divides those who favor cultural pluralism from those who advocate ASSIMILATION. Pluralists contend that liberty and democracy entail the right to retain one's own heritage and to be secure against cultural domination by the majority. They emphasize the benefits of diversity and the need to encourage tolerance and mutual respect among different groups in society. In contrast, assimilationists favor the rapid transition of minorities and immigrants into the "main-

This 1887 engraving of immigrants arriving in New York Harbor reflects the ethnic diversity of some of the peoples who came to the United States. (Library of Congress)

stream," including acquisition of English and adoption of the DOMINANT CULTURE's values and behaviors. According to this view, peace and prosperity depend on a strong common culture. Those who are different are obliged to change if they wish to succeed.

The forces of assimilation versus pluralism have long been in conflict in the United States, born in the dispossession of American Indians and the enslavement of Africans by European settlers. For most of American history, however, official policy has favored assimilation. Laws and procedures have discouraged retention of cultural differences while sanctioning discrimination that prevented the assimilation of non-European ethnic groups. This contradiction lies at the heart of the contemporary debate on multiculturalism. Assimilationists failed to deliver on promises of equal opportunity, resulting in wide socioeconomic gaps between Caucasians and people of color over many generations. Cultural differences have persisted in spite of predictions to the contrary and against active efforts to make those predictions come true. By the 1990's, thirty years after the height of the CIVIL RIGHTS MOVE-

MENT, most observers agreed that racial, ethnic, and class divisions in American society were growing wider. Controversies over multiculturalism are about new ways to solve this problem.

Origins of the "Culture Wars." Throughout the 1980's, cuts in social services and worsening poverty in inner-city neighborhoods deepened the alienation of AFRICAN AMERICAN and Latino youth. The flow of immigrants from Asia and Latin America accelerated greatly, taxing public services and heightening ethnic tensions. The WOMEN'S MOVEMENT gathered strength, especially in response to curbs on legal ABORTIONS. Homosexuals mobilized against growing threats from the religious right and the government's handling of the ACQUIRED IMMUNE DEFICIENCY SYNDROME (AIDS) EPIDEMIC.

Multiculturalism became a slogan in the 1980's for the common goals of activist women, gays, and ethnic minorities, who demanded greater inclusion in positions of power and a major reinterpretation of American history and culture. Reactions coalesced against these demands, drawing support from the highest levels of the government, most notably the Secretary of Education (William Bennett) and the Director of the National Endowment for the Humanities (Lynn Cheney). By the end of the decade, struggles over academic curricula, preferential hiring, and the essential definitions of truth, knowledge, and art had erupted into what some have labeled the "culture wars."

Concerns about curriculum reform in New York State public schools influenced the National Park Service's presentation of multiculturalism in exhibits at its immigration museum on Ellis Island. (James L. Shaffer)

University campuses became a primary field of engagement. Perceived as bastions of liberalism, the site of student activism in the 1960's, and incubators of knowledge and culture, universities were perhaps a logical context. One popular theory about what is behind multiculturalism suggests a conspiracy of former radical student activists who are now middle-aged professors. Although some multiculturalists fit this age profile, many do not. For example, Stanley Fish, of Duke University, and Catherine Stimpson, of Rutgers, are two well-known proponents of multiculturalism who were educated in the 1950's, when campuses were very quiet, while David Horowitz, an ardent

critic of multiculturalism, was formerly editor of *Ramparts*, the leading leftist magazine in the 1960's.

Inclusiveness and the Academic Debate. The debate on multiculturalism tends to split along a political axis between right and left, old ideas versus new ones. Another line bisects men from women and people of European descent from people of color. Sexual orientation and disabilities offer further distinctions. Diversity and difference, per se, compose the central philosophical issue. Demands for inclusiveness are made not only to remove the existing barriers to assimilation but also to redefine the body politic as a multicentric, "multivocalic" (many-voiced) quasi-federation composed of equally regarded, coexistent, culturally self-determining communities.

Multiculturalism in this sense is aimed at leveling hierarchies, at assigning equal value to the lives and traditions of all Americans, regardless of color, ethnicity, gender, sexual orientation, or any other condition that differentiates. The source of social differences and the nature of intergroup relations among groups are explained historically by the political domination of one group (often referred to as "hegemony"). Advocates believe that college curricula should reflect various cultural traditions, purging the implication that European heritage is somehow superior.

Among academics, literary criticism emerged at the forefront of the debate with arguments about the "canon"—that is, the official list of great works that students study. In restricting greatness to a limited number, the canon sanctions a hierarchy; and, because the authors of the existing canon are overwhelmingly white and male, it explicitly devalues works by women and all people of color. In contrast, Henry Louis Gates, of Harvard University, argues that a truly adequate liberal education requires reckoning the "comparable eloquence of the African, the Asian and the Middle Eastern traditions." Students need a global perspective and a critical understanding of their total culture. Failure to achieve this will handicap them in their future lives. Defenders of the canon, such as Irving Howe and John Searles, argue that reduced emphasis on the great ideas of Western civilization is partly responsible for the crisis that already exists in the American educational system. According to this view, declining test scores and rising drop-out rates are the result of too much curricular experimentation in the 1960's and 1970's. Education based on a disciplined, acknowledged "common core" of knowledge is needed to reverse these trends. These same ideas

Ethnic student organizations on college campuses are vocal supporters of multicultural "rainbow" curricula, as seen in this rally on behalf of a Chicana/Chicano studies department at UCLA sponsored by Asian Pacific American students. (Bob Myers)

are echoed in popular books by E. D. Hirsch (*Cultural Literacy*, 1987) and Allan Bloom (*The Closing of the American Mind*, 1987).

Defining American Culture. Debates over the relative value of literary accomplishments extend to the question of cultural values generally. Should public education teach that all cultural systems are equally valid? Should variant lifestyles, such as those of lesbians, be represented and legitimized in lessons taught to students? Whose version of history should be presented, that of the European Americans who "won" the West or American Indians who lost it?

The much-publicized struggle over the New York state public school curriculum reform touched on all these issues. Proposals to introduce an AFROCENTRIC

perspective, for example, brought forth accusations of reverse ethnocentrism, along with a scornful appraisal of the scholarship underlying that perspective. Diane Ravitch, formerly the assistant U.S. secretary for education, bitterly complained about the "war on so-called Eurocentrism" in the New York curriculum. Arthur Schlesinger, Jr., noted LIBERAL historian, added his voice to this complaint in *Disuniting America* (1991), arguing that it is folly to maintain that Western traditions are no more influential or important than others in American life.

Supporters of the "rainbow" curriculum include Molefi Asante of Temple University, who notes that Ravitch and other detractors do not seem to know very much about the non-Western traditions they dismiss

African American scholar and critic Henry Louis Gates has been an influential figure in the debate about multiculturalism and political correctness. (Harvard Afro-American Studies)

as less significant. He points to Ravitch's disparaging reference to the IROQUOIS LEAGUE, a precolonial federation of American Indians in New York. In discussing the League's inclusion in the new curriculum, Ravitch muses that readers "might wonder what it is," as if obscurity proved its unworthiness. Ravitch's apparent lack of knowledge about Indians indigenous to her own state points to the root of the problem multiculturalism is intended to solve. The American curriculum has traditionally excluded vast sectors of human endeavor by women and ethnic minorities, thus omitting important knowledge and wisdom. These omissions also lead to an exaggerated assessment of the ideas and accomplishments of western Europe.

Two issues are at stake here. The first concerns ETHNOCENTRISM, or the belief that one's own culture is the best. Some question whether European-derived cultural achievements are intrinsically more important (as Schlesinger maintains), or whether people of European ancestry are simply enamored with thinking that they are. The second issue involves the extent to which most Americans meaningfully share a broad set of values and experiences that are the makings of a common culture. Some doubt that all Americans can be gathered onto a foundation of beliefs and institutions created by white men whose central ideas were forged in the European Enlightenment.

Ethnocentrism is bias, by definition. If other traditions have gone unexamined, it is hard to give an unbiased judgment about their value. The debate on multiculturalism has shaken the confidence of some scholars in assessing Western or white male traditions and cultural assumptions. For example, although perhaps little known, the Iroquois League, or the *Haudenosaunee*, was indeed an important political achievement. Long before Europeans arrived, the five nations of the Iroquois established a formal system of representative governance that can only be labeled "democracy." Assertions that European colonists planted democracy on North American shores, or that the Greeks were the original inventors of this idea, show ignorance as well as arrogance. Multiculturalists argue that their opponents, especially those with liberal credentials such as Schlesinger and Howe, are unwittingly limited by their own educational experiences. To break this cycle, it is necessary to restructure the educational process.

Community versus Tribalization. Even many of those who see the dangers of ethnocentrism in the present system are dubious about finding viable alternatives. They fear that cramming so many different perspectives into education not only is inefficient but also may produce a "tribalized" community and may deepen existing societal divisions. Dinesh D'Souza, author of *Illiberal Education* (1992), weaves together anecdotes from several major universities that, he claims, demonstrate the ill effects of the new emphasis on race and gender. In promoting what he terms the politics of "victimization," multicultural courses and sensitivity workshops justify and encourage hatred of Caucasian students and professors based on historical wrongs done to people of color. The rise in ethnic conflicts on campuses are an unfortunate response to these provocations, D'Souza asserts.

Troy Duster, a University of California, Berkeley, sociologist who has studied his own campus, disagrees with D'Souza's analysis and conclusions. He argues that ethnic tensions reflect the simple fact that Berkeley has changed from an overwhelmingly white campus to one where white students will soon be in the minority. "There is tension and sometimes even open conflict over resources, turf, and 'ownership' of the place," he explained in 1991. These new realities demand a measured response from university leaders, a constructive means of achieving mutual respect through shared understanding. Students who know little about the history of ethnic minorities in the United States are prone to dismiss complaints of discrimination as exaggerated or unfounded. The ethnic, WOMEN'S, and GAY AND LESBIAN STUDIES PROGRAMS that D'Souza considers "victimization studies," Duster and others regard as a needed corrective to the sanitized Eurocentric history taught in most high schools.

The importance of community, and the value to the individual in having a supportive group, are other dimensions of the argument. Students from the same ethnic group often draw together on campus, partly out of defense and partly because they can help one another to succeed and they enjoy one anothers' company. White students who express dismay at the evident self-segregation of minority students apparently are unaware of the highly segregated patterns in their own socializing. ETHNICITY persists, many argue, because the communities in which individuals are raised have value in forging a sense of identity and in offering needed support. Attachment to ethnic cultural traditions thus reflects the defining experiences of youth and the needs of young adulthood.

On campus, and in the larger social context, other groups have formed communities voluntarily, based on sexual orientation, disabilities, age, and other nonethnic criteria. These communities have developed many of their own cultural traditions based on shared values and experiences. Multiculturalism is regarded as a positive affirmation of these varied subcultures and a basis for eliminating prejudice against their members. Inclusion entails mutual respect and a more relativist perspective on cultural accomplishments.

Values and Standards. Cultural relativism—a belief in the essential worthiness of all cultures—is linked to the larger debate about standards. Opponents of multiculturalism express concern that standards of excellence are being dismantled in a fruitless quest for egalitarianism. The question of standards involves admissions, hiring, and tenure issues, as well as the content of course curricula in HIGHER EDUCATION, and hiring and advancement in public sector jobs. In this respect, the debate is an extension of the controversy over AFFIRMATIVE ACTION.

Central to curricular reform are demands to increase the numbers of women and minority faculty and administrators, and for active efforts to recruit a student body more representative of the society at large. Opponents maintain that a shortage of qualified ethnic minorities makes such goals unattainable and that lowering standards to include more minorities will diminish the quality of university education or the effectiveness of the work force. Multiculturalists, however, see traditional standards as another example of the "hegemonic" character of the prevailing system, pointing to cultural bias in testing and institutional bias in

To overcome the ignorance caused by ethnocentric perspectives, monuments such as the Civil Rights Memorial in Montgomery, Ala., help publicize the struggle to guarantee equality for all Americans. (AP/Wide World Photos)

the evaluation of minority and women candidates for hiring and promotion.

Added to complaints about lowered standards is the argument that preferential admissions and financial aid have directed the anger of white students toward the beneficiaries of these policies, thus adding fuel to ethnic conflict. Within faculties, similar policies have produced "protected" classes of colleagues who are both envied and stigmatized.

In addition, the establishment of so-called "hate-speech codes"—which prohibit insensitive language and verbal harassment toward minority groups—has provoked a stormy backlash. Opponents of these codes argue that they only intensify the problems they were designed to solve. Free speech and academic freedom are jeopardized by these well-intended, but misguided, policies, critics say. Opponents of hate-speech codes have formed an organization, the National Association of Scholars, with a large membership drawn from many campuses. They and other CONSERVATIVE organizations have waged a vigorous campaign to influence academic policy, legislators, and the public at large. In the early 1990's, there was a spate of articles in all the major news magazines that warned of "thought police" and a "big chill" on campus.

"Political Correctness." The capstone phrase in this aspect of the debate is "POLITICAL CORRECTNESS" (often shortened to "PC"). The meaning connotes orthodoxy, in this case an inflexible demand that RACISM, SEXISM, HOMOPHOBIA, and condescension toward people with disabilities be eliminated from campus life. On a perhaps trivial level, it refers to awkward language practices in which sexist pronouns are replaced—with, for example, "she/he"—and the terms used to describe groups are re-negotiated to reflect the desires of the groups themselves. More substantively, PC also refers to efforts by some students to disrupt the classrooms of professors with un-fashionable views. For example, Vincent Sarich is a physical anthropologist at Berkeley who teaches undergraduates that race and gender do correlate with biological differences in human abilities. His views, which are shared by few of his colleagues in anthropology, have been contested bitterly, with some students demanding that he be fired or at least not allowed to teach the offending course.

Controversies over Sarich and other professors, demonstrations to prevent the appearance of certain conservative speakers such as Jeane KIRKPATRICK or William Bennett, and sanctions against ethnic slurs uttered by students have been collectively characterized as the "new MCCARTHYISM." The reference is to the virulent campaign waged against communists and progressives by Senator Joseph McCarthy during the 1950's. Supporters of multiculturalism decry the comparison as exaggerated and ironic. Catherine Stimpson argues that the term "politically correct" was originally coined by leftists to mock the theoretical excesses of certain Marxists who were prone to abandon reason in pursuit of the correct line. This gesture of self-criticism has transformed into a clarion for conservatives, some of whom were directly involved in the suppression of thought and speech (not to mention dismissals and blacklisting) that occurred under the banner of the original McCarthyism. Stimpson points to the lack of comparable circumstances in the present controversy; no one has been fired, books are not being removed from libraries, and measures taken against the politically "incorrect" have been timid and frequently ambivalent.

Conclusion. The greatest significance of the ongoing debate about multiculturalism and political correctness has been to raise public awareness about the complex issues of diversity. As Henry Louis Gates observes, "whatever the outcome of the culture wars in the academy, the world we live in is multicultural already." D'Souza and Duster may disagree about why ethnic conflicts occur but not about whether they occur, nor about the urgency of finding solutions to these problems. In his book entitled *Beyond the Culture Wars* (1992), Gerald Graff argues that it is time for both sides in the academic debate to stop trying to stifle each other's point of view and instead "teach the conflicts." Within the best tradition of the liberal arts, competing perspectives on multiculturalism should be fully aired and subjected to critical analysis. Gates offers a similar recommendation: "Beyond the hype and the high flown rhetoric is a pretty homely truth: There is no tolerance without respect—and no respect without knowledge." This also applies to how multiculturalism is seen in the media, the halls of government, the corporate world, and the community centers and homes of Americans of all backgrounds.

SUGGESTED READINGS. An excellent summary of the debate on multiculturalism, including excerpts from hard-to-find sources, is contained in the anthology entitled *Debating PC* (1992), edited by Paul Berman. Books by opponents of multiculturalism are more abundant and accessible than books by proponents. Roger Kimball's controversial critique of the modern university, *Tenured Radicals* (1990), drew considerable attention and reaction in the early 1990's. Arthur Schlesinger's slim volume, *Disuniting America* (1991), is mainly a defense of liberal individualism but is also highly critical of contemporary trends in education. Perhaps the best-known assault on these trends is Dinesh D'Souza's *Illiberal Education* (1992). This book, which excoriates some of the most prestigious universities in the United States, was the subject of numerous editorials and talk shows and has sold out several editions.

One of the more influential figures on the other side of the debate is Henry Louis Gates, chair of Afro-American Studies at Harvard. In his book, *Loose Canons* (1992), he offers a collection of essays on race and culture that articulate the rationale for a multicultural perspective on art and society. See also Gerald Graff's *Beyond the Culture Wars: How Teaching the Conflicts Can Revitalize American Education* (1992) on contemporary multicultural scholarship and a dispassionate, thorough exploration of the debate.— *Susan D. Greenbaum*

Multiculturalism—Canadian policy: Promotes the enhancement of cultural diversity while working to eliminate RACISM in Canadian society. Multiculturalism has a somewhat different history and meaning in Canada than it does in the United States. Though both countries have indigenous populations, a legacy of immigration, and great cultural diversity, Canada has opted to support this diversity directly through government policy and funding. Its view of intergroup relations is based on a model of INTEGRATION rather than ASSIMILATION to a DOMINANT CULTURE or the isolation of separate groups. This policy was an outgrowth of Canadian efforts to support BILINGUALISM and biculturalism of the French- and English-speaking populations, as in the Official Languages Act of 1969.

Canada's first multiculturalism policy, announced in 1971, aimed to help minority groups preserve and share their culture while removing cultural barriers. It supported research on Canadian ethnic groups, the learning of heritage languages, and the activities of groups serving immigrants and minorities. In 1972, the government appointed the first Minister of State for Multiculturalism. Ten years later, race relations was added to the program's mandate. This was reinforced in 1988 with the passage of the Canadian Multiculturalism Act, which stressed efforts to eradicate racism and DISCRIMINATION, particularly in federal institutions. The act states, in part, "The Government of Canada recognizes the diversity of Canadians . . . as a fundamental characteristic of Canadian society and is committed to a policy of multiculturalism designed to preserve and enhance the multicultural heritage of Canadians while working to achieve the equality of all Canadians in the economic, social, cultural and political life of Canada."

In 1991, the government established the Department of Multiculturalism and Citizenship to achieve these goals while bringing all Canadians into full participation in the society. The department spends $27 million (Canadian) per year on multicultural programs such as support for festivals and the arts; academic research; language study; immigrant organizations; and antidiscrimination projects that promote cross-cultural understanding in business, education, and the judicial system. The policy remains controversial with some Canadians.

Multiracial movement: Advocates greater recognition and awareness of the distinctive identity of people of mixed racial ancestry. The population of Americans with parents of different races has grown since the 1960's with the rise in INTERMARRIAGE. In addition, movement activists say many Americans, particularly people of color, have been multiracial for generations—a fact reinforced by genealogical research as part of the ethnic heritage revival of the 1970's. These people often feel they do not "fit in" with one particular ethnic group and have trouble finding a label that suits them. Several organizations (such as Project Race in Atlanta, Georgia) and publications (such as *Interrace* in Beverly Hills, California) have emerged to provide support to people of multiracial background and make their needs known to the public. A major goal of the movement is the addition of a multiracial category to the U.S. Census—a proposal that was under study by a congressional subcommittee in 1993. The movement is controversial with some people of color, who believe that seeking a multiracial label is an effort to deny one's blackness (or Asian or Indian ancestry) and lessens the strength of minority groups.

Mura, David Alan (b. June 17, 1952, Great Lakes, Ill.): Japanese American poet. After studying at Grinnell College and the University of Minnesota, Mura taught writing through the COMPAS' Writers-and-Artists-in-the-Schools program and the Loft in Minneapolis. His first volume of poetry, *A Male Grief: Notes on Pornography and Addiction*, appeared in 1987, followed by

After We Lost Our Way (1989), the nonfiction *Turning Japanese: Memoirs of a Sansei* (1991). A National Endowment for the Arts Literary Fellow in 1985 and Pushcart Prize Winner in 1990, Mura writes about the Asian American experience, male sexuality, and racism. He has been published in *New Republic*, the *American Poetry Review*, and numerous Asian American anthologies.

Murals: Public art form that often celebrates the life of common people, depicts political struggle, or expresses the cultural heritage of minority groups. Many American murals were inspired by an artistic style that rose to popularity in Mexico and elsewhere in the 1920's and 1930's from the international recognition accorded the Mexican artists, José Clemente Orozco (1883-1949), Diego María Rivera (1886-1957), and their followers. Orozco studied painting informally in Mexico before moving to the United States. His first mural to achieve international acclaim was *Prometheus,* commissioned by Pomona College in Claremont, California. He became politicized during his residency in New York City, where he became obsessed by revolutionaries as diverse as Vladimir Ilich Lenin and Mahatma Gandhi. His passion is reflected in the murals featuring these leaders at the New School for Social Research in New York (1931). Following Orozco's return to Mexico, he formed the nucleus of the "postrevolutionary muralists," who, along with Rivera, became the inspiration and source of the impassioned Chicano muralist movement of the 1970's.

Rivera studied art in Mexico, Spain, and Paris, then returned to Mexico in 1921, where he painted his first revolutionary mural at the National Preparatory School. Following his enrollment in the COMMUNIST PARTY, he painted a series of murals devoted to the social and political history of Mexico.

The revolutionary zeal of the social realist school of Mexican art fueled the fires of the awakened Chicano consciousness of the 1970's. Deriving many of its themes and a bold visual style from the postrevo-

Drawing on the social consciousness expressed in the murals of Mexican artist Diego Rivera, this Chicano mural in San Francisco's Mission District celebrates the cultural heritage of influential guitarist Carlos Santana. (Robert Fried)

lutionary Mexican muralists, Chicano muralism tends to be anonymous, reflective of its community, and done by amateur or student artists rather than professionals. It can be seen on the outer walls of stores and public buildings, in parks, and along highways in cities of the Southwest. Such murals served as a model for the expression of community identity for other racial and ethnic groups in inner city neighborhoods throughout the United States.

California provides a wealth of examples of American mural styles. San Francisco is the site of several murals in public buildings commissioned by the Works Progress Administration during the NEW DEAL of the 1930's; they are notable for their vibrant colors and heroic depictions of working Americans. Los Angeles is home to hundreds of murals, ranging from humble images of the Virgin of Guadalupe on a garage in East Los Angeles to the celebrated African American murals of St. Elmo's Village to the impressive Great Wall of Los Angeles on the sides of an artificial river basin in the San Fernando Valley. During the 1970's and 1980's, many California cities and organizations commissioned professional artists to work with teams of young people to design and create ambitious historical murals on multicultural themes. By the 1990's, the community mural project was rare, but murals were increasingly common vehicles for solo artists and advertisers.

SUGGESTED READINGS. *The Mexican Muralists in the United States* (1989) by Laurance P. Hurlburt discusses the work of Orozco, Rivera, and David Alfaro Siqueiros. More recent developments in the art of the mural are examined in Alan W. Barnett's *Community Murals: The People's Art* (1984), Eva Cockcroft's *Toward a People's Art: The Contemporary Mural Movement* (1977), and *Signs from the Heart: California Chicano Murals* (1990), edited by Eva Cockcroft.

Murayama, Milton: Japanese American writer. The son of a Hawaiian plantation laborer, Murayama is known for his *All I Asking for Is My Body* (1975). A coming-of-age narrative told from the perspective of Kiyoshi Oyama, the novel chronicles Oyama's Depression-era experiences living on a Hawaiian plantation in a segregated camp for Japanese American laborers. The narrative concluded during the immediate aftermath of Pearl Harbor. The first portion of the novel was published in a slightly different version in *Arizona Quarterly* in 1959 and was reprinted in *The Spell of Hawaii* in 1968.

Museums and research centers: The great age of museum building began in the United States following the Civil War. Artifacts and archival materials pertaining to the founding of the nation had been collected in a wide variety of historical repositories outside of Washington, D.C., before the nineteenth century through public and private contributions, bequests, and endowments. As ethnic loyalties and differences began to be seen in a positive light as important characteristics to study and preserve, private ethnic research centers began to be established as early as the last decades of the nineteenth century. They increased following the great waves of immigration from eastern Europe in the early twentieth century. The multicultural awakening of the 1960's and 1970's, stimulated by the CIVIL RIGHTS MOVEMENT and the ethnic heritage revival, led to the establishment of a wealth of multicultural museums and resource centers across the United States that continue to proliferate.

This essay can only describe a small number of both well-known and obscure institutions, which are listed here by region. Some are oriented to the general pub-

Los Angeles' Olvera Street is home to this cultural institute (right) that documents the influence of Mexican culture in early California history. (Valerie Marie)

lic, while others serve mainly scholars. Some have been established by members of the cultural groups they document, while others are government or university facilities.

Northeastern United States. The American Museum of Immigration on Liberty Island in New York City was founded in 1954 as part of the National Park Service. It is a major source of national immigration records and photographs and runs continuing exhibits on immigration history.

The ANTI-DEFAMATION LEAGUE of B'NAI B'RITH in NEW YORK CITY maintains a library and archival repository founded in 1913. It is an important source for personal records, correspondence, printed materials and photographs of the early history of JEWISH IMMIGRATION from Eastern Europe. The center's purpose is to promote intergroup and interreligious understanding through education and public awareness.

The Balch Institute of Ethnic Studies, founded in 1971 in Philadelphia, Pennsylvania, contains a library, archive, and gallery. Its collections cover artifacts traditionally used by various ethnic cultures in America as well as manuscripts, books, and visual media related to American immigrant and ethnic history.

The Center for Migration Studies of New York in New York City maintains a library and archival center founded in 1964. The purpose of the collection is to serve as a center for materials documenting the history of immigration and to study the forces affecting human migration and intergroup relations. It also provides speakers, sponsors public performances, and supports work in film and television to projects falling within its areas of interest.

The Ellis Island Immigration Museum, located on Ellis Island in New York City is one of the newest multicultural museums, founded in 1989. Its galleries devoted to the history of nineteenth and twentieth century immigration to the United States are notable for their inclusion of personal oral histories and their use of computer technology to aid in genealogical research.

The Moorland-Springarn Research Center of HOWARD UNIVERSITY in Washington, D.C., houses one of the world's largest collections of documents on the history and culture of peoples of African descent in the Americas, Africa, and Europe. It sponsors programs, performances, and research into African heritage.

The National Folklife Center in Lowell, Massachusetts, is a repository and dissemination center for in-

formation related to ethnic folk cultures in the United States and is located within The National Heritage Park, which is also operated by the National Park Service. A complex of museums, libraries, galleries, and archives is situated in former textile mills and corporate boarding houses along the canals and waterways of the Merrimack River. It sponsors free public performances and is the site of the annual National Folk Festival. It is an invaluable source for materials relating to the early industrial history of the United States and immigration from the 1830's to the early 1900's.

The Smithsonian Institution in Washington, D.C. was founded with the proceeds of a $500,000 bequest made by British scientist James Smithson. Originally planned to include a library, art gallery, museum, and scientific research facilities, the Smithsonian eventually expanded beyond its original 1854 structure known as "the Castle." Two galleries devoted to African American and Native American Indian art and culture were opened in 1992. Its Museum of Natural History and Museum of History and Technology have frequent exhibits on multicultural themes. The institute sponsors an annual outdoor Festival of American Folklife highlighting different American cultures and subcultures each year. It also supports considerable multicultural scholarship through its departments and fellowships.

South and South Central United States. The Amistad Research Center of Tulane University in New Or-

Established in Philadelphia in 1976, the Afro-American Historical and Cultural Museum was one of the first modern museums to house a permanent collection of materials related to black culture in North America. (Afro-American Historical and Cultural Museum, Philadelphia, Pa.)

leans, Louisiana, maintains a library and archival center founded in 1966 by the United Church Board for Homeland Ministries. It holds an important collection of primary source materials from the early 1700's to the present on the history of the ethnic history and civil rights legacy of the United States, including material on American Indians, African Americans, Asian Americans, and Latinos, as well as Acadian, French, and European American documents.

ring and Alonzo J. Aden's efforts as director of the Barnett-Aden Gallery in Washington, D.C.

Central United States. The Arms Museum of the Mahoning Valley Historical Society in Youngstown, Ohio, was founded in 1875 by the Mahoning Valley Historical Society. It houses a small collection of foreign language materials, pioneer artifacts and pictorial, photographic, and oral historical records of Americans of Hungarian, Italian, German, and Slovak heritage.

Located in Michigan on the campus of Suomi College, the Finnish Americans Heritage Center contains historical archives, a museum, an art gallery, and a theater dedicated to preserving Finnish culture in the United States. (Suomi College Finnish Americans Heritage Center, Hancock, Mich.)

The Federal Archives and Records Center in East Point, Georgia, was founded in 1969 by the National Archives and Records Service. It contains audiovisual materials and local archival material in addition to the official federal records of the BUREAU OF INDIAN AFFAIRS; microfilms of the records of the Bureau of Refugees; naturalization records; records pertaining to Freedmen and Abandoned Lands; and census records. A published guide to the collection exists and materials are available through interlibrary loan as well as on site. The AFRICAN AMERICAN Museum of Tampa, Florida, was founded in the 1980's. It houses one of the most significant collections of African American art in the nation from the collection of James V. Her-

The Du Sable Museum of African American History in Chicago, Illinois, was founded in 1961 by cultural activist Margaret T. Burroughs. In addition to telling the story of key periods in black history, it houses important collections of African American art. The Greater Cleveland Ethnographic Museum, founded in 1975, serves as a repository for artifacts, audiovisual productions, photographs, and oral histories of the immigration experience of all ethnic and racial groups in the Ohio River Valley. Its services include lectures, public performances, resource persons for school projects, and an advisory bureau.

The Immigration History Research Center of the University of Minnesota in Saint Paul, Minnesota was founded in 1964 by the University of Minnesota. It contains a vast collection of original source materials that document the origins of migration and subsequent histories of more than thirty ethnic groups. It provides loans of its materials to schools, operates a speakers bureau, and engages in the microfilming of ethnic archives.

The Jesse Besser Museum, located in Alpens, Michigan, is a center devoted to preserving the artifacts, records, and works of art of European immigration to the central states. Its archives occupy over 15,000 cubic feet and consist of personal papers, correspondence and printed and photographic materials. Its collections include examples of the decorative arts and crafts of European pioneers as well as American Indians and African Americans.

Southwest United States. The Colorado Springs Fine Arts Center, located in Colorado Springs, Colorado, maintains a museum, library, and art gallery. Founded in 1936, its collections contain artifacts, works of art, printed and photographic materials pertaining to the art, archaeology, anthropology, and ethnology of the Southwest. The Taylor Museum houses American Indian and Latino arts of the Southwest, the Plains, the Northwest Coast, Mexico, and Guatemala.

The Museum of International Folk Art in Santa Fe, New Mexico, was founded by the Museum of New Mexico in 1953. It collects, preserves, and displays folk art from all parts of the world. It specializes in folk costumes, Spanish colonial arts, textiles, pottery, and Alpine art, and conducts research and public programs on contemporary folk art of the Southwest.

The Museum of the Great Plains in Lawton, Oklahoma, maintains a center founded by the Institute of the Great Plains and the City of Lawton in 1960. The stated purpose of its collections, which include over 200,000 primary documents, artifacts, personal papers, correspondence, and unpublished materials, is to interpret culture on the Plains from prehistoric times to the present. It conducts tours, sponsors historical and archaeological research, and runs educational programs. Among its artifacts are examples of Spanish armor, stone age weapons of the Paleo tribe, objects related to other Plains tribes, and relics of European and Anglo-American exploration and settlement.

The Hubbell Trading Post National Historic Site, located at Ganado, Arizona, was founded by the National Park Service in 1967. It houses a vast repository of archival material, including personal papers, correspondence, pictorial materials, oral histories, and trading post records pertaining to the history of the NAVAJOS, as well as Mexican and European American settlers.

West Coast and Extra-Continental United States. The Alaska Historical Library is part of the Alaska Division of State Libraries and Museums in Juneau, Alaska. It houses more than eighteen thousand books, 250 periodicals, and a large collection of audiovisual materials. Its archives contain personal papers, correspondence, unpublished records, photographs, manuscripts and oral history pertaining to the history and development of Alaska, including the history of Alaska natives and Russians.

Lyman House Memorial Museum, located on the island of Hilo in Hawaii, maintains a museum and library founded in 1932. The library contains over three thousand books and periodicals as well as artifacts, works of art, volcanological, geological, and mineralogical materials. Archival materials focus on the seven main national groups living in Hawaii.

Los Angeles contains two multicultural museums which opened in the early 1990's. One of the most unusual multicultural museums in the country is the Simon Wiesenthal Center's Museum of Tolerance, which opened in Los Angeles in 1993. Its striking, interactive exhibits document the HOLOCAUST and highlight other, less obvious manifestations of racism and intolerance in American and world history. Los Angeles' Little Tokyo neighborhood is the home of the JAPANESE AMERICAN National Museum, which opened in 1992. The museum is the first in the United States to focus solely on the Japanese American experience.

Other notable multicultural museums in the West include the California Afro-American Museum, the Southwest Museum, and the Craft and Folk Art Museum in Los Angeles; the Mexican Museum and Judah L. Magnes Memorial Museum of Jewish Culture in the San Francisco Bay Area; the Wing Luke Memorial Museum in Seattle's International District; and the Makah Museum run by the Makah Indians in Washington's Olympic Peninsula.

SUGGESTED READINGS. Many guides and directories with inclusive lists of multicultural museums and centers are available. The most helpful are *The Official Museum Directory* by the American Association of Museums and National Register (1986), Joseph Graham's *Hispanic-American Material Culture: An Annotated Directory of Collections, Sites, Archives, and Festivals in the United States*, (vol. 24, 1989), *Profile of Black Museums: A Survey Commissioned by the African Museums Association* (1988) by the American Association of State and Local History. Valuable guides to the history and function of ethnological museums and resources can be found in Gaynor Kavanagh's *History Curatorship* (1990), as well as in journals such as *Americana, Smithsonian, Oral History Review, American Heritage,* and *El Palacio.*—Barbara Langell Miliaras

Music: Music in the United States has been characterized by the boundary crossing between sacred and secular contexts; black and white styles and forms; written and oral traditions; and popular, art, and folk genres. Formed during four centuries of intense culture contact, migration, and technological change, and underpinned by the most powerful entertainment industry in the world, American music has served to express changing cultural ideas and values for diverse groups of people within and outside the United States.

Americans listen to and perform music for aesthetic pleasure, dancing, recreation, worship, ceremony, education, therapy, advertising, and dramatic effect, as well as background in stores, restaurants, airplanes, and daily life. Music is a pervasive element of American culture, but relatively few Americans participate as music performers. A well-developed music industry and broadcast media system enable Americans to hear a broad array of musical styles without extensive personal contact with musicians.

Religious Music. Religious themes and occasions underlie much of the music practiced in the United States. AMERICAN INDIANS utilize complex musical ceremonies in worship in traditions believed to date back centuries. The Pilgrims brought Protestant church music to the United States in the 1600's, consisting of psalms sung in loose unison without instrumental accompaniment. These were collected in the first book printed in the British North American colonies, the *Bay Psalm Book* (1640). As American congregations distanced themselves from European practice, many abandoned written texts and music in their psalm singing and utilized instead a system called "lining out" in which the leader sang each line for the congregation to repeat. This simple, democratic singing style conformed with austere PURITAN values.

African slaves in the United States were forbidden their traditional religions, and most converted to Protestant faiths. Applying African music styles to Protestant hymns, AFRICAN AMERICANS developed a new church music that included harmony; rhythmic accompaniment with hand claps and foot stamps; and a new freedom in musical improvisation, calling and shouting, body posture, and movement. They utilized fuller voices and slightly different scales, and devised lyrics that promised emancipation through religious metaphor. These adaptations resulted in a more exuberant and emotional style of religious music than that of white congregations.

The late 1700's brought a drive to increase musical literacy in the white Christian church, and musicians began to compose and arrange hymns for performance in a more formal, harmonized style. Many composers wrote both sacred and secular music in the European style, and the line between religious and art music began to blur. Counter to this trend were southern interracial camp meetings, where blacks and whites shared music and worship in the folk style.

After the CIVIL WAR, European influence extended toward African American music. Groups such as the Fisk Jubilee Singers from FISK UNIVERSITY went on extensive concert tours to perform African American hymns, now called SPIRITUALS, in the controlled, formal fashion of European choir music. While these tours raised international awareness of African American music, the formal European style was not embraced by all branches of the church. PENTECOSTAL-style sects retained a vigorous musical style, developing a repertoire of "shout" and "holy roller" songs. In the 1920's, BLUES musician Thomas Dorsey embarked upon a campaign to inject new life into African American church music by introducing the blues inflections and instrumental accompaniments of secular music to spirituals, and GOSPEL music was born. Since then, gospel has followed trends in secular music by adopting electric instruments and amplification, and it is often performed in secular concert settings.

Contemporary Christian churches utilize a variety of musics in worship, including traditional hymns and gospel, the sung CATHOLIC mass, sacred and secular art music, and popular devotional music. Some charismatic churches with youthful congregations emphasize composition, performance, and recording of original devotional songs, featuring lead vocalists accompanied by electrified ensembles. Popular musicians such as the hard rock band Stryper and vocalist Amy Grant perform rock-influenced religious music for listening outside the church. Many other forms of religious music are practiced by numerous faiths and ethnic groups in the United States in the contexts of worship, concerts, and community events.

Art Music. Art music in the United States generally refers to concert compositions following the tradition of European composers such as Bach, Mozart, and Beethoven. These works employ European orchestral instruments and operatic voices. Musicians perform from written notation with little or no improvisation, so that a composition theoretically sounds the same over the course of centuries. The members of the ensemble are dictated by tradition and the composer; it is rarely acceptable, for instance, for an oboe to play a violin part. Art music is generally performed for aesthetic achievement and enjoyment, though it is deployed in a variety of contexts, such as advertising. Art music forms the core of most music education curricula.

Avant-garde composer John Cage incorporated silence and environmental sounds into his musical pieces. (AP/Wide World Photos)

The earliest American art compositions were vocal, mostly religious compositions of the "New England School" during the late 1700's and early 1800's. A move to return folk-style Protestant music to European art practice, supported by an immigration wave of European professional musicians, encouraged American composers to write more complex music for the church. Fugues, set pieces, and anthems for four-part vocal ensembles began to replace simple, unison hymns. Groups in eastern cities formed concert societies to sponsor art music performance, establishing the basis for modern-day metropolitan orchestras.

During the 1800's, American composers embraced themes of Romantic nationalism, popular among European musicians and artists of the time. The idea that creative vitality lay in the folk roots of the nation inspired instrumental works utilizing "American" themes, folk tunes, and references to American Indians and African Americans. Ironically, the most famous work in this style was written by the Czech composer Antonín Dvorák. Visiting the United States as director of New York's National Conservatory from 1892 to 1895, Dvorák wrote the "New World" symphony, including themes the composer attributed to Indian and African American music. Other important composers in the American nationalist style were Anthony Philip Heinrich, whose compositions included *The Negro Banjo's Quickstep* and *The Indian's Festival of Dreams*, and Louis Moreau Gottschalk of Louisiana, who utilized African and Latin American melodies and rhythms in his work. Aaron Copland continued the nationalist movement in the 1900's with several symphonic works based on British American folk song, including *Billy the Kid, Rodeo,* and *Appalachian Spring.*

With the turn of the century, the American popular music industry grew vigorously, supporting a great variety of sheet music publications and exerting a new presence in the prevailing art/folk music dialogue. In the 1920's, the national fascination with jazz pervaded art music. While art composers such as Aaron Copland drew on JAZZ styles, popular composers such as George Gershwin began to write jazz-influenced music for the symphony orchestra. During the 1930's both black and white big band jazz groups began to employ symphonic techniques in scoring and arrangement, and during the 1940's, black composer and band leader Duke ELLINGTON pioneered true symphonic jazz. African American art composer William Grant Still used the sounds of jazz in his works, including the 1937 ballet *Lenox Avenue,* about life in New York City's Harlem. The mingling of concert and jazz music, named "Third Stream" music in the 1950's, continues to the present day. Many people consider jazz itself to be an art music, because it is musically complex, technically demanding, and is often performed in formal concert settings.

Another development in the first half of the twentieth century was "ultra-modern music," an avantgarde movement led by composers such as Alan Hovhaness, Henry Cowell, and Edgard Varèse. These composers shared an interest in various world musics and a willingness to experiment with atonality, new compositional forms, and electronic instruments. Improvisation and performance options lessened the authority of the written composition. John Cage, a West Coast follower of this movement, composed pieces such as *Music of Changes* (1951), in which the musician uses the Chinese philosophy of *I Ching* to decide what to play, and *4'33".* (1952), consisting entirely of audience and environmental sounds. Philip Glass continues this experimental tradition, composing large, multimedia theatrical pieces that draw on musical styles of many cultures and utilize nontraditional sounds and forms.

Though many contemporary American composers continue to experiment with the art tradition, the repertoire of eighteenth and nineteenth century European composers dominates concert performance in the United States. Supported mostly by government and private foundations, supplemented by individual contributions, and ticket and record sales, most concert musicians and organizations remain committed to the maintenance and development of European tradition.

Popular and Folk Music. Folk and popular music have interacted significantly over the course of American music history. Both styles are generally recreational, for personal expression, social enjoyment, and dancing. Popular music is distinguished by being part of a commercial music industry. Often, musicians make folk music popular by adding new sounds and stylistic changes that express current concerns and values. Though such musicians might not be motivated by money, profit is the goal of the industry that markets music for mass consumption in the form of sheet music, records, tapes, compact discs, videos, or broadcast media.

In 1790, the first American copyright law was established, resulting in the formation of publishing companies and the founding of an industry deriving its revenues from music. The most popular style of the time was the light art music performed in British "pleasure gardens," which was transplanted overseas by way of sheet music. Americans adapted the frivolous, love-oriented texts to the moralistic social values of the newly-founded republic, resulting in songs such as "Home Sweet Home" (1823), the highest-selling sheet music publication of the nineteenth century.

During the early 1800's, white Americans became aware of the exotic-sounding folk music of African American slaves, which provided material for both romance and parody in white popular music. In minstrel shows, white musicians wore black face make-up and performed satiric renditions of slave songs, sung in dialect with lively rhythms and simple choral refrains. Many minstrel songs were composed by northern white musicians who knew little of the South. Stephen Foster, born in Pittsburgh, wrote minstrel songs for commercial publication such as "Oh! Susannah!" and "Camptown Races" that are now considered American folk songs. Foster also wrote "plantation songs," such as "Old Folks at Home," that romanticized slave life.

This musical exchange served to both break down and reinforce racial barriers; while white awareness of black culture increased, many of the images portrayed in minstrel music and plantation songs were stereotyped and condescending.

After the Civil War, freed African Americans in the South faced expanded opportunities for music making, and three new genres emerged: the folk BLUES, ragtime, and jazz. Folk blues was a solo song form that musicians performed mostly for themselves or local friends. The song texts expressed the financial and emotional pressures of post-Emancipation life, travel themes, and messages of personal independence. The blues spread throughout the South, eventually developing into a standardized, AAB verse form with set, repeated chords, but performed without written music. Ragtime was much more formal than the blues. These written compositions for piano utilized strict European forms along with the "ragged" rhythms of African American folk music.

Early jazz was a rhythmically and melodically complex music based on improvised versions of European

Blues and jazz musician Thomas Dorsey, shown here in 1923 at the piano, devoted himself exclusively to composing and promoting gospel music. (AP/Wide World Photos)

Irving Berlin, a first-generation Jewish immigrant to America, earned musical fame for his witty Tin Pan Alley songs, musical scores for film and Broadway theater, and the patriotic anthem, "God Bless America." (AP/Wide World Photos)

brass band marches. New Orleans musicians such as trumpeters Joe "King" Oliver and Louis ARMSTRONG, trombonist Edward "Kid" Ory, and pianist Ferdinand "Jelly Roll" Morton led bands of five or more musicians, improvising interwoven melodies without written sheet music. Blues, ragtime, and jazz influenced each other, trading tunes and styles, but each retained its unique instrumentation.

Meanwhile, in New York, the multiethnic immigrant population created a new style of musical theater. Tin Pan Alley was the name given to 28th Street, where composers "plugged" their latest songs to potential publishers by playing them on cheap pianos that were said to sound like tin pans. These songs reflected the experience of New York's migrants and immigrants—Jews, Irish, Italians, Germans, Poles, and African Americans—while emphasizing themes of patriotism and Americana. Written for performance in short cabaret skits or full-length musical plays, Tin Pan Alley songs were lively, witty, and built upon a memorable, singable chorus. A song formula eventually developed, in which a long introductory verse was followed by a repeated chorus with an AABA phrase structure. The consistent use of this formula enabled listeners to know what to "expect," establishing one of the important tenets of American popular music. The most famous and prolific Tin Pan Alley songwriter was Irving Berlin, a first-generation Jewish immigrant who wrote songs ranging from "God Bless America" to "White Christmas."

During the 1910's, phonograph records began to be commercially released for home playback. While the main initial recording activity was in big cities, soon every American genre—from blues, ragtime, and jazz, to Anglo American folk, or "hillbilly" music, Tin Pan Alley, classical, and religious music—was available on record. In the 1920's, broadcast radio brought a wide variety of recorded music into American homes.

Records, radio, and the increasing popularity of jazz contributed to a national dance craze. Jazz bands expanded in size, turning to Tin Pan Alley and blues songs for melodies upon which to improvise. As jazz song forms regularized into AAB and AABA structures, musicians began to make written arrangements in the style of orchestral music. Meanwhile, Tin Pan Alley songs borrowed the rhythms and instrumentation of jazz for incorporation into theater music, such as Berlin's "Alexander's Ragtime Band." Music performances in northern cities became increasingly interracial as musical theater featured both black and white performers, and mixed audiences attended nightclubs to hear African American performers such as blues singer Bessie Smith.

Though the GREAT DEPRESSION hurt the music industry, the national love of big band jazz, the new recording and radio technology, and escapist films stimulated continued musical growth and new genres. In African American music, jazz became increasingly sophisticated, and new forms such as GOSPEL, jump blues, and RHYTHM AND BLUES emerged. Anglo American folk traditions led to the Nashville sound of COUNTRY-WESTERN MUSIC, as well as bluegrass and western swing. Latin American styles such as the mambo became popular for dancing. The first musical "stars," such as Bing Crosby and Rudee Vallee, became famous via radio and films. The variety of popular music was unprecedented.

WORLD WAR II and the conservative suburbanism of the 1950's created a rebellious white youth culture that sought musical expression of youthful ideals. Black rhythm and blues, an up-tempo dance style, provided that expression, and white southern musicians such as Elvis Presley, Carl Perkins, and Jerry Lee Lewis began to perform rhythm and blues with a country and western flavor. Elvis Presley's 1956 recording "Hound Dog" was the first record to be number one on all three Billboard charts: popular, country-western, and rhythm and blues. The music industry dubbed the new crossover style ROCK AND ROLL.

Paul Simon, who began his career as a folk-rock musician, later incorporated elements from world music traditions into his work. (AP/Wide World Photos)

Since the inception of rock and roll, much of the innovation in American popular music has been instigated by young musicians. SOUL MUSIC, MOTOWN, acid rock, folk rock, glam and arena rock, country rock, disco, punk and new wave, RAP and HIP-HOP, heavy metal, industrial rock, and grunge rock have all reflected youth values seeking a new form of expression. Older listeners tend to favor the musical genres popular when they were younger. Popular music, however, is not always a youth-driven march forward. Many young musicians consciously perform in older popular genres. For example, trumpet player Wynton Marsalis has made recordings of early Dixieland jazz, and the group Take Six performs in the a cappella gospel quartet style popular during the 1940's.

Contemporary popular music often serves as a forum for blurring ethnic, gender, and class boundaries. Many ethnic groups in the United States incorporate elements of rock into their own music traditions, creating hew hybrid, or "syncretic" music styles. Likewise, American popular musicians such as Paul Simon and David Byrne have drawn upon various world musics in their work. New Age music fuses art, popular, and jazz music with many world music traditions and the meditative aesthetic of Eastern religions and philosophies. Musicians such as Michael Jackson and Madonna mix black and white, male and female imagery and styles in their music performances.

Institutions: The Music Industry, Education, and Government. The music industry has served to both segment and integrate American musics. By dividing musical genres into "charts" and employing separate sales forces and marketing strategies for each, executives have established musical boundaries by ethnicity, age, and socioeconomic status. On the other hand, the widespread availability of all music styles in recordings and broadcast media has encouraged mutual awareness and influence across these boundaries. Some record companies have actively encouraged musical crossovers; for example, Atlantic Records introduced black rhythm and blues artists such as Joe Turner and Ruth Brown to white audiences in the 1950's, helping to form the audience for rock and roll.

Other effects of the music industry include the addition of arrangers and producers to the music making context; a tendency toward short, standard song forms and "hit" formulas; and a constant quest for technological sophistication. Periodic rebellions against these ideals, such as punk and grunge rock, do not appear to have significantly altered the direction of the

American music industry.

Most publicly sponsored music education emphasizes the European art tradition by teaching orchestral instrumental technique, music notation, and theory. The culmination of American music education is a music conservatory, such as Juilliard in New York, or university music departments, that prepare musicians for professional performance, composition, or teaching in the art music tradition.

Many popular and folk musicians are not trained in the music education system. As popular music becomes increasingly pervasive, however, schools and departments that teach popular instrumental techniques and recording arts are becoming more common. The Guitar Institute of Technology in Los Angeles, part of the Musicians Institute, for example, specializes in rock and jazz guitar techniques. Many musicologists and ethnomusicologists discuss popular music in their scholarly writings and university classes.

The U.S. government sponsors music through programs such as the National Endowment for the Arts, which favors folk and art music projects. This funding is under close scrutiny for its cost, and for the cultural, aesthetic, and social content of sponsored projects.

SUGGESTED READINGS. Two broad surveys of American music are Charles Hamm's *Music in the New World* (1980) and Gilbert Chase's *America's Music: From the Pilgrims to the Present* (1955, rev. 1977). *The New Grove Dictionary of Music and Musicians* (1980), edited by Stanley Sadie, is an extensive twenty-volume reference work focusing on Western art music but covering many other genres. Henry Kingsbury's *Music, Talent and Performance: A Conservatory Cultural System* (1988) examines American music conservatories, proposing that they might foster a notion of musical "talent" with no corollary in many non-Western music cultures.—*Elizabeth J. Miles.*

Music—African American: Perhaps the most important broad category of ethnic music in the United States because of its interaction with and great influence on other musical styles. Indeed, much of what has come to be known as American popular music in the rest of the world in the twentieth century is essentially African American music.

African American styles have shown great variety across time, regions, and musical genres. Despite this prodigious diversity, African American musical forms share many common aesthetic and stylistic characteristics. Many employ an African-derived antiphonal technique known as call and response (either in literal, modified, or derivative form). Many use various types of improvisation to some degree. They may also incorporate African-derived vocal devices such as shouts, moans, "blue" notes, multiphonics, falsetto, and special timbres or effects to heighten the emotionalism of the music. Virtually all African American styles are strongly rhythmic, drawing on syncopation, complex polyrhythms, and distinctive use of percussion. These musical features are among the most obvious AFRICAN CULTURAL SURVIVALS in the New World.

Musical Roots Before 1900. Despite restrictions on their musical activity during the era of SLAVERY, early AFRICAN AMERICANS developed an impressive array of musical forms on plantations in the South. These included field hollers and work songs, game songs, and SPIRITUALS, each of which played a function in the work life, recreation, and religious experience of the slaves. African Americans also developed instruments such as the banjo based on African models, while taking up other instruments such as the fiddle and guitar. These early styles were the folk heritage of later forms such as country blues.

The music and dance of the enslaved population had long been a source of entertainment for and exploitation by the white slave masters. By the 1800's, white and black GOSPEL singing traditions were borrowing from each other. White minstrel show entertainers put on black face and imitated crude STEREO-TYPES of African American styles in performances that became highly popular. With the creation of highly syncopated ragtime music by eminent black composers and musicians such as Scott JOPLIN in the 1890's, African Americans gained a foothold of influence in American popular music that would only grow stronger in the ensuing years.

Blues. One of the oldest and most influential of black American music styles is the BLUES. It may be more accurate to think of the blues as a form or principle, rather than a style, since the blues has found a home in virtually every major African American musical style of the twentieth century.

The blues as a highly expressive form of music grew directly out of the experiences of African Americans and spoke of the hardships, loss, and heartache they faced. Blues lyrics typically follow an AAB pattern and employ Black English. The earliest form of vocal blues was country or downhome blues, accompanied by guitar or piano, which began in the Mississippi Delta and east Texas in the early 1900's with artists such as Blind Lemon Jefferson. The 1920's saw the development of classic blues bands with female vocalists such as Bessie Smith. Urban blues, a post-World War II development in Chicago, featured amplified electronic instruments and male singers.

The blues has a melodic structure in which the first phrase is immediately repeated and subsequently followed by a contrasting phrase. Each of the three phrases are of equal length, traditionally four bars or measures. In most vocal blues, and many instrumental blues, only half of each phrase constitutes the principal melody. The other half constitutes an antiphonal response and is usually given by one or more contrasting instruments.

Jazz. The most technically sophisticated of all African American styles is JAZZ. It came into existence sometime between 1900 and 1910 as a style independent of ragtime and syncopated dance band music in New Orleans, Louisiana.

The pioneering New Orleans jazz style was played by a small ensemble containing a rhythm section and a front line. The front line was an improvisational unit consisting principally of a trumpet, clarinet, and trombone that each played independent, yet related, lines. Ideally, the trumpet improvised the main melody, the clarinet provided a faster countermelody accompaniment, and the trombone completed the combination with a slower, polyphonic accompaniment. The harmonies of the New Orleans style were basically simple and diatonic in meters based on groupings of two beats.

The jazz style that followed was called swing. Though it was rooted in the big band experimentations of Fletcher Henderson and Don Redman in the mid-1920's, it did not become fully crystallized until the 1930's. The instrumentation of a typical swing ensemble consisted of sections of horns or wind instruments (such as saxophones, trumpets, and trombones) supported by an enlarged rhythm section that almost always included piano. Such an ensemble allowed for a much broader textural expression of melody, harmony, and rhythm. Improvisation was constrained within a more controlled framework, and consequently, was of greater structural import. The timbral dimension of jazz was expanded prodigiously with these new orchestrational possibilities. The swing style in its original form is still practiced by a few surviving personalities from the swing era, and/or their heirs. It

Legendary trumpet player Louis Armstrong transformed the simple harmonies of the New Orleans jazz style into a complex mainstream musical tradition. (AP/Wide World Photos)

is mainly preserved, however, through big bands and jazz orchestras at the music departments of educational institutions.

The two jazz styles that succeeded swing are bebop and cool successively. They, too, are occasionally heard today in their original forms. Though similar in instrumentation, they differ quite radically from swing in other ways. Bebop, for example, employs more melodic syncopation with a considerably expanded harmonic vocabulary. Bebop also brought attention back to improvisational virtuosity in a way that could not be accommodated in big band contexts. Thus, the

small ensemble resurfaced as the prominent bebop medium.

Bebop was marked by melodic, harmonic, and improvisational tension and diversity, mirroring the socio-economic asymmetries and radicalism of the age. The ethos of cool jazz, by contrast, was smoothness, color, control, and symmetry, all reflected in the musicians' technique.

Most of the mainstream jazz styles of the late 1900's were derived principally from the jazz styles succeeding cool. The "back to the roots movement" of the late 1950's, which emphasized popular musical

Quincy Jones, shown here with an armful of Grammy Awards in 1991, has popularized African American musical styles as a multitalented composer, producer, and performer. (AP/Wide World Photos)

influences, inevitably led to jazz rock and fusion movements. The "avante garde" movement of the 1960's, with its stress on rhythmic, harmonic, timbral, and improvisational experimentation, expanded the technical vocabulary of jazz so profoundly that it has yet to be transcended. The two broad stylistic directions of fusion and noncommercial progressive jazz, along with updated bop and prebop styles of the past, essentially shape the modern jazz scene. Jazz music is now played by musicians of diverse backgrounds all over the world; even within the United States, jazz has lost its black audience base and is mainly patronized by a small, loyal group of white fans. For most Americans, jazz is overshadowed by another vernacular tradition that is much more popular and stronger economically—the tradition of African American popular music.

African American Popular Music. Contemporary black popular music owes much to the traditions from which it emanates. From blues and gospel music it derived many of the vocal characteristics that make it so unique and emotionally powerful. From the black folk tradition and Tin Pan Alley, it derived much of its unique lyricism. Since 1950 it has existed in a number of different styles, such as RHYTHM AND BLUES, SOUL, FUNK, DISCO, RAP, and HIP HOP. While the stylistic lines of demarcation are not always clear, particularly among successive styles, virtually all types of black popular music share a number of important characteristics.

First, they employ the attributes of African vocality as the principal means of injecting emotion into the music. The proportion of these attributes, however, varies within each style. Second, the lead vocalist generally relates to his/her background vocal unit in a manner that is valued just as much for its rhythmic interplay as for its lyrical import. Third, repeated bass patterns are a standard element of African American popular music, contributing significantly to the identification of each style.

African American popular music has been imitated, redefined, and marketed in the United States in a manner that has more to do with the economic and aesthetic interests of the entertainment industry and its mass clientele than with the cultural interests of its black creators. This may change as increasing numbers of African Americans such as Quincy JONES become producers and other leaders in the industry.

Sacred and Folk Music. African American sacred music is mainly represented by two vernacular tradi-

tions: gospel music and spirituals. Though both are expressive of the religiosity of the people, they differ in several important ways. Black gospel music grew out of an urban religious setting, and has historically borrowed more from nonsacred vernacular traditions such as rhythm and blues. By contrast, spirituals are much older than gospel music, dating back to prototypes in the early nineteenth century. Though the earliest spirituals were improvised songs, they have since become a formal body of literature. In fact, they are the definitive form of notated African American folk song. Large contemporary gospel choirs at African American churches are one of the key ways of maintaining community bonds and passing on the culture to the young.

African American folk traditions in the late nineteenth century have been largely eclipsed by popular music. The exceptions are regional styles such as the children's game songs of the GULLAH people of the Georgia Sea Islands or the zydeco music of Louisiana and the Gulf coast. Zydeco is an indigenous American music that grew out of the Creole culture of African Americans in French-speaking parts of Louisiana. It represents the coalescence of French or ACADIAN AMERICAN musical influences with the blues as well as rhythm and blues. The style is characterized by simple dance rhythms, diatonic harmonies, blues-derived vocal style, and the accordion as lead instrument in an amplified band.

SUGGESTED READINGS. A historical overview of African American music is provided in Eileen Southern's *The Music of Black Americans: A History* (2d. ed., 1983). Other useful sources include John Storm Roberts' *Black Music of Two Worlds* (1972); LeRoi Jones' *Blues People: Negro Music in White America* (1963); and Dena Epstein's *Sinful Tunes and Spirituals; Black-Folk Music to the Civil War* (1977).—*Earl L. Stewart*

Music—American Indian: Music of the native peoples of the Americas. Vocal songs accompanied by drums and rattles form the core of most North American Indian musical repertoires. Stylistic characteristics vary widely by region and tribe, but share many musical and functional attributes.

Social and Ceremonial Function. American Indian music is an integral part of religious, social, and healing ceremonies, ritual gambling games, yearly and life cycle events such as rites of passage and harvest, and social dances and gatherings. Many American Indians believe that music has supernatural power with useful applications in the natural world. The Plains people, for instance, go on individual vision quests, during which they receive songs from spirits. The individual owns any song received in this way and can use the song for personal success in war or other endeavors. The Navajos believe that music heals and restores the harmony between people, nature, and gods. They practice six different types of healing rituals that employ a complicated sequence of songs, lasting from two to nine days.

Contemporary American Indian women are increasingly active as musicians in the wake of media influence and gender equality movements in the United States.

Vocal, Instrumental, and Dance Music. The voice is the most important element of American Indian music. The singing often employs a tense, high-pitched vocal style, using both lyrics and nonmeaningful syllables, or "vocables." Musicians sometimes replace lyrics with vocables when singing sacred songs for outsiders, to protect the secrecy of the sacred texts.

This American Indian musician shares the ceremonial traditions of his heritage as he teaches schoolchildren how to play and sing with a tribal drum. (James L. Shaffer)

Musicians are generally participants rather than professionals, but ceremonial specialists sometimes lead musical events. Scholars suggest that most American Indian musicians are men, who appear to wield the most power in ceremony and ritual. Yet there is evidence that women in some tribes played important ceremonial and musical roles before European contact.

The most important instruments in the repertoire are drums, rattles, scrapers, and bells. They are rarely played alone, but accompany singing with rhythmic patterns that can be quite complex. The many different types of drums and rattles vary by tribe and by their ceremonial use. Other important musical instruments include several types of flute, which are used to play the melody along with the singer.

Music and dance are closely intertwined, and many songs accompany ceremonial or social dances. Usually performing in a closely coordinated group in circle or line formations, the dancers might contribute to the music with the rhythmic sounds made by bells, beads, or jingles on their costumes.

Regional and Tribal styles. The native musics of the United States can be quite different, varying with traditional lifestyles and values. Historically agricultural, stationary peoples such as the Eastern Woodlands tribes and the PUEBLO Indians of the Southwest share a relaxed vocal style, long, complex song forms, and texts that give thanks to the natural and spiritual worlds for providing rain and fertility. The Plains peoples, traditionally warriors, use a very high, tense voice marked by pulsations, cries, and special effects. The salmon fishers of the Pacific Northwest employ an intense, emotional song style, including a "crying" sound. Alaskan natives are known for vocal games, or *katajait,* which include a game in which the players sing into each other's mouth. The great variety of native musics reflect differences between tribal cultures across the continent.

Documentation. Studies of American Indian music figured prominently in early American anthropology and ethnomusicology. In the early 1900's, native culture was considered both accessible and "authentic," unspoiled by European influence, and many music scholars strove to investigate and preserve traditional musics before they were altered by the presence of foreign musical styles. The first such scholars included Alice Fletcher, working at the beginning of the twentieth century, and Frances Densmore, who collected thousands of transcriptions by writing down native songs in Western music notation. Since then, scholars have contributed transcriptions, recordings, articles, and books that study and document many aspects of native music culture, from specific ceremonies to regional and tribal styles. Native musicians have become increasingly active in documenting and explaining their art.

Influences and Recent Developments. The European invasion and contemporary mass media have resulted in musical mixing among tribes, and between Indian, European, and African American styles. An early intertribal style was GHOST DANCE music of the late 1800's, which was believed by its practitioners to have the power to drive away white soldiers and settlers. Today, the most important forum for intertribal music and dance is the POWWOW, a festival of singing, dancing, competition, food, and American Indian arts and crafts, lasting one or more days. The Plains style of music and dance is widely performed at powwows throughout the United States as a commonly understood style in which many different tribes can participate.

Many types of American Indian music are now sung with English texts and performed in concerts instead of their traditional ceremonial or social contexts. Indian musicians are also influenced by ROCK, COUNTRY-WESTERN, and European or American FOLK MUSIC. Classical choral arrangements and country gospel styles have been adopted by some Christian American Indian musicians.

In the face of these changes, community members and scholars often try to preserve traditional music and dance by making archival audio and video recordings and instituting educational programs to teach and perpetuate traditional arts. In Alaska, regional native-owned corporations sponsor traditional music and dance groups, allowing them to preserve traditional styles, and perform for each other and tourists. Despite such preservational efforts, there is still a widespread belief that traditional musical repertoires are shrinking over time.

SUGGESTED READINGS. For a general overview of native musics of all the Americas, see Paul Collaer's *Music of the Americas* (1973). David P. McAllester provides a summary of North American styles, including song transcriptions and texts, in "North American Native Music," published in *Musics of Many Cultures* (1980), edited by Elizabeth May. *Women in North American Indian Music* (1989), edited by Richard Keeling, contains six essays that examine historical and contemporary gender roles in various native musics—*Elizabeth J. Miles*

Music—Asian American: Asian Americans participate fully in musical life in the United States as musicians and composers. For example, many immigrants from Korea and Japan have been well-trained in European classical music and can be found in American music conservatories and concert halls, while other Americans of Asian background are active in jazz music. Music that is unique to the Asian American community, however, generally consists of forms that have been preserved or adapted from their origins in various Asian countries. This music exhibits a diversity as great as the diversity of the Asian American population itself, with scales, rhythmic patterns, musical structures, instrumentation, and vocal styles that are often unfamiliar to Western ears. Generally, Asian music in the United States is classical, folk, or popular forms that are associated with new immigrants, strongly identified older immigrant communities, ethnic organizations, and third-generation Asian Americans discovering their roots.

Asian classical musical forms often derive from ancient court traditions that are linked to the aristocratic classes. For example, in China, the long *ch'in* zither was traditionally a scholar's instrument; in Korea, certain types of Confucian ritual music were heard only in the palace. These classical traditions take many years to master, as Asian Americans who were trained in fine arts academies in Seoul, Bangkok, or Tokyo can attest. Once transplanted to the United States, it is difficult for Asian classical musicians to maintain their former level of professionalism. A small number find teaching positions at American universities with ethnomusicology (world music) programs; others lead community-based ensembles and give private lessons; a greater number, however, take jobs as housepainters or accountants, keeping their music only as a hobby. Capitalizing on the strong interest in Asian Indian music in the United States that developed in the 1970's, some Indian musicians have opened academies that train Americans in instruments such as the lush, stringed sitar, or tabla drum. Likewise, INDONESIAN AMERICANS may act as teachers but probably constitute a minority of the people in gamelan, the complexly layered gong ensemble of Bali and Java that has fascinated musicians and composers around the world for generations.

Among CHINESE AMERICANS, Cantonese opera and Peking opera are popular with older Cantonese-speaking and new Mandarin-speaking communities, respectively. Most Chinatowns have as least one opera club in which dedicated amateurs socialize around rehearsals of the demanding multifaceted art form, which involves singing, acting, and some choreography. The clubs stage elaborate productions complete with stylized costumes and makeup for their enthusiastic fans. This tradition generally remains within the community, a nostalgic form of musical recreation that links participants with their homeland.

Asian folk music in its traditional form remains strong in closely knit, somewhat isolated communities, such as that of HMONG AMERICANS of Fresno, California, where a number of men play a long bamboo mouth organ while executing acrobatic dance steps at events such as New Year celebrations. Other groups have revived folk traditions, such as the *kulintang* gong and drum ensemble of the Philippines, the newer high-energy taiko drumming tradition of Japan, or the folk lute music of Tibet as part of their quest for ethnic identity. Nearly every major Asian American community has a performing group that presents folk and sometimes classical dance at Asian events as well as multicultural festivals, but live folk music is not heard nearly so often outside the community. Like traditional classical forms, Asian folk music is undergoing change in its new context.

Asian popular music is perhaps the most thriving

This Hmong-American musician performs on a traditional bamboo mouth organ called a gaeng *at a funeral in Merced, Calif.* (Eric Crystal)

of the three genres in the United States, particularly when famous pop stars have been part of the immigrant wave or when there are large numbers of young new immigrants. For example, THAI, CAMBODIAN, and VIETNAMESE AMERICAN rock bands can be found at many community celebrations as the entertainment portion of the program after traditional chanting by BUDDHIST priests.

Some Asian Americans have promoted the development of a distinctively Asian American sound, rather than one preserved from Asian tradition. An instance of this is the hybrid blend of the multicultural Los Angeles-based band Hiroshima, which uses the Japanese *koto* and other special effects to mix JAZZ, popular, and Asian idioms. American composers of various backgrounds have increasingly incorporated Asian instruments and timbres into their work, from the low drone of the chanting of Tibetan monks to the ethereal sound of the wooden shakuhachi flute of Japan.

SUGGESTED READINGS. For an introduction to the wide spectrum of Asian musics, see William Malm's *Music Cultures of the Pacific, the Near East, and Asia* (2d ed., 1977). Among scholarly studies of Asian music in the United States is Ron W. Riddle's *Flying Dragons, Flowing Streams: Music in the Life of San Francisco's Chinese Community* (1983). The journals *Ethnomusicology* and *Asian Music* also publish articles and bibliographies on Asian American music.

Music—Latino: Latin music in the twentieth century has played an important role in shaping popular music in the United States. Rooted in folk and popular forms, Latin music exported north has brought the nation a blend of European, African, and American Indian influences. Though only a handful of Latin American styles garnered wide popularity in the United States, they became part of a diverse multicultural musical mix that persists.

Latin Musical Roots. The four areas of Latin America and the Caribbean that have exerted the greatest influence on modern popular music in the United States are Cuba, Brazil, Argentina, and Mexico.

In Cuba, the presence of European and African rhythms, melodies, and harmonic forms eventually blended in distinct folk and popular music forms, especially for dancing. The most important type was the habañera, which evolved for the *contradanza*, a French seventeenth century line dance. The habañera was born when the traditional European choreography and instrumentation of the *contradanza* were syncopated with African rhythms, an innovation that came to be known as *ritmo de tango*. By the late nineteenth century, the habañera became known as the *danzón*. Another important style was the *son*, a classic Afro-Cuban form emerging in Havana around the time of

World War I. Originating as an Afro-Cuban rural form accompanied by percussion, the son was played by string-percussion quartets and *septetos* (trumpet-led string groups).

Popular in the 1930's, the folkloric rumba incorporated percussion, dancing, and commentary on everyday life. It was largely street music performed in working-class neighborhoods. This was followed by the mambo, a form that came out of Congolese religious cults and was based on the *danzón*. The mambo-mix emerged when African rhythmic elements in the form of forceful percussion was added to the *charanga* (a Cuban dance orchestra), by Antonio Arcaño and Israel Lopez. The chachacha, another dance form, was developed around 1953 among *charanga* orchestras, and is assumed to have derived from the *danzón* or the mambo.

Another country with a strong African-European musical mix, in this case fed by the Portuguese language, is Brazil. Its influence has not been as widespread as that of Cuba but was no less important as two forms were exported to the United States: the samba and the bossa nova. Brought to Rio de Janiero as part of Carnival (MARDI GRAS) in 1877, the samba, then known as the *lundu*, was a dance and song of Congolese-Angolan derivation. A variation of the traditional *lundu* was the *maxixe*, considered a predecessor to the urban samba that was eventually brought to American ballrooms and dance clubs. The Bossa nova was not related to folk or popular forms but was created by Brazilian jazz musicians during the 1950's, particularly João Gilberto.

The tango developed in Argentina in the early twentieth century and took its rhythmic base from the Cuban habañera and the Argentinean *milonga*. It began strictly as a dance form with instrumentation of violin, flute, guitar, and accordion; the vocal tango developed in 1917, with Carlos Gardel as its leading exponent. Unlike the African-influenced music of Cuba and Brazil, the tango is, for the most part, European.

Mexico, like Argentina, saw its music evolve from various European elements combined with local folk-popular forms. Mexican folk styles such as the CORRIDO and *ranchera* (ranch song) and ensembles such as the mariachi influenced folk music and country and western music in the United States, as in some songs by Woody Guthrie or in the Texas swing style. The *orquesta típica*, first formed in 1884 to play popular Mexican dance styles utilizing string and wind instrumentation, evolved from military bands. Such ensem-

Latino percussionist Tito Puente is known as the "king" of salsa music. (AP/Wide World Photos)

bles toured the United States at the beginning of the twentieth century.

Early Latin Musical Influences in the United States. The hybridization of Latin music in the United States occurred through the popularity of dance forms, popular vocal music, film, Broadway, and JAZZ music. Performances of this music by Latino and non-Latino musicians, and the publication of sheet music, likewise contributed to its accessibility.

Latin dance forms became crucial parts of the ball room dance craze of the first half of the twentieth century. The tango was brought to the United States by Vernon and Irene Castle in 1912 via Paris. It was soon heard in urban dance clubs and remained popular through the 1920's. The same happened with the rhumba in the 1930's as Cuban big bands popularized it while touring the United States. The popularity of the American rhumba led to numerous recordings and made entertainers such as Xavier Cugat and Desi Arnaz famous. The mambo followed in the late 1930's, with a success that extended to the early 1950's. Latino audiences could listen to Machito, Tito Puente, Tito Rodriguez, Xavier Cugat, and Perez Prado. By 1951, the cha-cha emerged from the mambo.

Tin Pan Alley became fully involved with Latin music through the publication of popular Latin standards or Latin-inspired music. Songs such as "Mexicali Rose" (1923) owed much to Mexican music in the Southwest. Mexican folksongs such as "Cielito Lindo," "Alla en el Rancho Grande," and "La Cucaracha" were also very popular. A number of songs were published or recorded in the International Latin Style, which relied on guitar trios and the slow, sentimental *bolero* from Cuba. For example, "Maria Elena," "Brazil," and "Frenesi" were recorded in English, and "Cuando Vuelva a tu Lado," composed by Maria Grever in 1934, was released as "What a Difference a Day Made," in 1944.

Increasingly, Broadway and Hollywood came to rely on Latin music. Broadway musicals used Latin music in ways that were often humorous, romantic, or satirical, while films used the music in its scores, but they rarely dealt with Latin themes.

One of the most important developments of the early period was Cubop, an experiment combining jazz bebop with Cuban rhythms. Its exponents and practitioners included Dizzy Gillespie, Stan Kenton, Machito, Charlie PARKER, Miles Davis, and Thelonius Monk. Though outcomes were mixed, Cubop was important because jazz players learned about Latin rhythms, and Latin musicians began to incorporate jazz into their performances. This set the stage for innovations in the 1950's.

Regional Developments. As the early Latin music forms matured, they became integrated into popular American culture. Several regions played a major role in shaping the Latinization of American music: they were centered in New Orleans, New York, California, Texas, and Miami. Musical activity in these cities reflected the make-up of the Latino population in the region, such as Chicanos in the West and Cuban Americans in Florida.

RHYTHM AND BLUES drew much of its influence from New Orleans piano styles rooted in ragtime, which in turn was influenced by the *ritmo do tango* heard in the Cuban habañera. One need only listen to the recordings of Professor Longhair, Doctor John, and Antoine "Fats" Domino or songs such as "Mambo Baby" by Ruth Brown, "Bo Diddley" and "I'm a Man" by Bo Diddley, or "Tweedle Dee" by Laverne

Cuban American pop sensation Gloria Estefan. (AP/Wide World Photos)

Some Latino musicians, like the drummer from New York City shown above, make or repair their own instruments. (Hazel Hankin)

Baker to hear Cuban rhythmic influences.

In New York, Latin jazz matured. Perhaps the most successful jazz artist utilizing Latin-jazz rhythms at the time was Gato Barbieri. For example, his album *Chapter 3* was arranged by Chico O'Farrill, a Cuban musician who worked with Machito, Stan Kenton, and Dizzy Gillespie in the early days of Cubop. By the 1980's, Latin jazz musicians could be found in other major cities, for example Poncho Sanchez in Los Angeles. Another jazz form, the bossa nova, hit the United States in 1964. The song "Girl from Ipanema" by Stan Getz, João Gilberto, and Antonio Carlos Jobim won a Grammy Award for best song. Moreover, the bossa nova phenomenon encouraged younger Bra-

zilian jazz musicians to come to the United States.

The *bugalú*, which blended mambo with rhythm and blues, was developed by young PUERTO RICAN musicians who were not interested in playing jazz or traditional Cuban music. Percussionist Mongo Santamaria, as an example, merged traditional Cuban rhythms, jazz, and rhythm and blues. His music influenced other percussionists as well as artists such as Curtis Mayfield; Bobby Bland; the Drifters; Earth, Wind and Fire; War; and Mandrill. The strongest New York development, however, was SALSA MUSIC, played largely by Puerto Rican musicians. It became so popular that an entire industry grew up around it including recording companies and dance clubs.

Popular music on the West Coast was affected by Latin music, with California its crossover center. Herb Albert and the Tijuana Brass with its MARIACHI-inspired horns had a number of hits beginning with "The Lonely Bull." Trini Lopez merged urban folk styles with Mexican elements for Frank Sinatra's Reprise label. Mexican Americans Lil' Julian Herrera and Ritchie VALENS each scored hits with ROCK AND ROLL audiences in "Lonely, Lonely Nights" and "Lá Bamba," respectively. The emergence of the band SANTANA saw the merging of Latin and African rhythms, as in the recording "Jingo" composed by Nigerian percussionist Olantunji, and "Evil Ways," a rendition of jazz musician Willie Bobo's earlier recording. In the 1970's and 1980's, Chicano bands such as LOS LOBOS combined a rock sensibility with gestures to their Mexican folk musical roots.

In Texas, Mexican influences were evident in a number of areas. Traditional TEX-MEX MUSIC was popular in both Mexican and non-Mexican communities. Country music was influenced by the likes of Freddy Fender, whose hits "Wasted Days and Wasted Nights" and "Before the Next Teardrop Falls" have become classics. In rock, Doug Sahm's group, the Sir Douglas Quintet, utilized Tex-Mex rhythms in songs such as "She's About a Mover" and "Mendocino." Other bands with Tex-Mex influences included Sam the Sham and the Pharaohs.

Since the 1960's Miami had boasted a strong Cuban music scene, which—unlike Latino music elsewhere in the United States—remained relatively isolated from the homeland for political reasons. CUBAN AMERICANS quickly took their place as the wealthiest, best educated Latino population and built Miami as the country's strongest Latino music industry center by the late 1980's. Their success was fueled by the enormous popularity of singers such as GLORIA ESTEFAN.

Throughout the twentieth century, and indeed since the annexation of Mexican territory in the 1800's, Latinos have played and enjoyed their folk and popular music in their own communities. Puerto Rican New Yorkers have maintained the folkloric *bomba* and *plena* dance rhythms, passing them on to a younger generation rediscovering its heritage. Recent Mexican immigrants request their favorite *ranchera* song in a local *cantina*, singing along with tearful nostalgia, while fourth-generation Mexican Americans play trumpet in a mariachi group in an EAST LOS ANGELES parade for Mexican Independence Day. Central American refugees join forces with others to perform *nueva cancion*, songs of social protest in both popular and folkloric idioms, or the traditional marimba music of Guatemala. Brazilian Americans teach their musical heritage through *escolas de samba* and classes in the Afro-Brazilian martial art form called *capoeira*, which is performed to musical accompaniment. Whether a large community at a public fiesta or a small one at a family gathering, Latinos of all backgrounds make music a center of their holidays and festivals.

SUGGESTED READINGS. For more information on the impact of Latin music, consult *The Latin Tinge* by John Storm Roberts (1979); *Salsa!: The Rhythm of Latin Music* by Charley Gerard with Marty Sheller (1989); and *The Story of Jazz* by Marshall Sterns (1956).—*Carlos F. Ortega*

Music—women's: Gender-specific movement originating in the 1970's expressing the cultural and political views of LESBIAN and FEMINIST communities. Since its inception,the movement has become less issue-oriented, but remains women-identified.

The emergence in the 1970's of a unified feminist movement found a natural medium for cultural activism in women's music. The *Ladyslipper Catalog and Resource Guide and Catalog of Records and Tapes by Women* defines the term as "music springing from a feminist consciousness, utilizing women's talent . . . with production, presentation and finances controlled by women." Women musicians self-consciously sought to emphasize the significance of sexual codes in a political (and musical) context, while exploring the interrelated roles of women as performers and as audience.

The women's music movement was established as a genre with the emergence of singers such as Holly Near, Chris Williamson, and Meg Christian. Their music, a combination of FOLK, ballad, pop, and COUNTRY, was strictly women-identified, imbued with a feminist and lesbian perspective. Anchored by women-run record companies such as Olivia and Redwood, which specialized in women's music, Near, Williamson, and Christian produced some of the best-selling independently issued records ever. Though they never achieved prominent commercial success, they are ranked among the most influential voices in the movement, playing venues from coffee houses and pop festivals to performances at Carnegie Hall.

Throughout the 1970's, the movement was most effectively promoted by festivals and concerts of music by female composers. The first National Women's Music Festival was held in 1974 at the University of Illinois, Urbana. The first Women's Jazz Festival followed in Kansas City in 1978.

women artists such as Tracy Chapman, the Indigo Girls, and k. d. lang gained cross-cultural acceptance, mixing gender-specific and lesbian perspectives with a liberal, humanist motifs.

Singer Holly Near was one of the influential leaders of the women's music movement in the 1970's. (AP/Wide World Photos)

Women's music in the 1980's tended to soften its advocacy edge without blunting its message, creating a women-identified music often more accessible to a larger audience, which was therefore more popular and commercially successful than the original 1970's music. While many foremothers of women's music reject the mainstream turn, the stylized sounds of

The shift from feminist and lesbian activism in women's music to a music emphasizing a broader range of women's roles reflects a cultural shift from the isolation of activists in the 1970's to the diverse integration of women in the 1980's. Susan McClary, in her book *Feminine Endings: Music, Gender, and Sexuality*, points out that to be comprehensive, women's music must create "musical and visual narratives that celebrate multiple rather than unitary identities." Regardless of the mutations and variations inherent in any musical genre, women's music insists on challenging existing cultural norms, providing alternative voices exploring female identities.

SUGGESTED READINGS. For a discussion of the relation between popular female vocalists and feminist musical activists, see Susan McClary's *Feminine Endings: Music, Gender, and Sexuality* (1991). Susan Watrous and Bob Blanchard's interview with Holly Near in the *Progressive* 54 (March, 1990), p. 34, reviews her role in the 1970's women's music movement, as does Alanna Nash's insightful profile "Holly Near" in *Stereo Review* 53 (January, 1988), pp. 86-87. Another perspective on the subject may be found in V. J. Beauchamp's "Music—Not Just Women's Music" in *Visibilities* 5 (September, 1991), p. 22.

Musicians and composers: American musicians and composers earn their living by performing, teaching, making recordings or videos, and composing for commission and royalties. In addition to those who have achieved high public profiles in art and popular music, such as classical cellist Yo-Yo MA or popular vocalist Whitney Houston, there are many who compose and perform music for film, theater, television, advertising, local clubs and restaurants, private celebrations, and religious events, without great public recognition. Though there are many professional career paths for musicians and composers, access can be difficult and financial rewards limited.

Background and Education. Professional musicians and composers in the United States come from a variety of social and occupational backgrounds. Some follow parents or other family members into the profession. For instance, the Work family of Nashville, Tennessee, was very influential in turn-of-the-century African American religious and FOLK MUSIC. Composer, conductor, and vocalist John Wesley Work conducted the Fisk Jubilee Singers, one of the first ensembles to bring international attention to African American SPIRITUALS, in the early 1900's. His wife Agnes Haines was a vocalist; his brother Frederick was a composer and scholar of African American folk music; and his son John Wesley, a composer of choral folk song arrangements, also directed the Jubilee Singers. Drummer Mickey Hart of the ROCK band the Grateful Dead inherited his musical interest from his mother and father, both champion, but amateur, military drummers. JAZZ trumpeter Miles Davis, in contrast, was the son of a well-to-do dentist. While family influence seems to encourage prospective musicians in their careers, the wide availability of music and musical role models encourages many to pursue music outside of family tradition.

There is no single standardized education or training required to become a composer or musician. Universities and music conservatories offer degrees in music performance, composition, and theory that emphasize the technique and notation of the European art music tradition. Most musicians and composers who seek a profession in that tradition pursue such a degree. Many popular musicians, however, learn their craft from a teacher or mentor outside of academia; by ear, listening to and imitating live and recorded music; and from books and private instruction programs. Despite these various backgrounds, most professional musicians and composers share a common understanding of basic musical concepts and terminology based upon the European tradition. In addition, a specialized jargon has developed referring to musical technology and the recording studio, which most musicians learn only through professional experience.

Women and Minorities. Historically, performance careers in American popular and art music alike have presented obstacles to women and minorities, though perhaps fewer than other professions. Social and economic conditions often discouraged women and minorities from pursuing the formal training required for a career in art music. Though socioeconomic constraints on obtaining art music education remain, most contemporary performance ensembles and audiences support diversity. The first symphony composed by a black American to be performed by a major orchestra was William Grant Still's *Afro-American Symphony* (1930). Over the ensuing decades, many AFRICAN AMERICANS, Asian Americans, and women have pursued successful performance careers in art music, with decreasing, if still apparent obstacles.

In popular music, public censure and white male music industry executives precluded opportunities for minorities and women in the past. Some of the first important female popular musicians of the twentieth century were BLUES singers during the 1920's, such as Bessie Smith, who dominated the nightclub performance of "classic" blues and established the social and commercial acceptability of female vocalists singing lyrics of sexual connotation. Though this period provided professional access for female popular vo-

Known as the "Father of the Blues," W. C. Handy was the legendary composer of songs such as "St. Louis Blues" and "Memphis Blues." (AP/Wide World Photos)

calists, women instrumentalists remained rare. Many women played piano in the home. The pioneering female jazz instrumentalists included pianist Lil Hardin Armstrong in the 1910's and 1920's, and pianist, composer, and arranger Mary Lou Williams in the swing era of the 1930's and 1940's. In contemporary popular music practice, many women play piano, synthesizer, and guitar, but less commonly perform on wind or percussion instruments. Few women specialize in instrumental session work, instead utilizing their instrumental skills in a performing ensemble or to accompany their own vocals.

African American musicians have been extremely influential in popular music since the Civil War, but have often encountered DISCRIMINATION and unfair business practices in the entertainment industry. Black musicians were previously required to perform to SEG-REGATED audiences, and many were cheated out of royalties and performance fees by record companies and concert promoters. Since the CIVIL RIGHTS MOVE-MENT and social changes of the 1960's, however, performance situations and legal arrangements have been improved by the efforts of musicians, audiences, and the music industry. Mainstream popular music has become increasingly multiethnic and open to women, LESBIANS, and gays. There are also many popular genres expressing the values and aesthetics of subgroups within American culture, including Chicano rock, hard-core RAP, and WOMEN'S MUSIC.

Multicultural aesthetics influence the work of contemporary American composers and musicians. Art music composers such as Philip Glass draw on the musical styles of many cultures, as well as popular and African American musics. Many popular music groups are made up of diverse musicians, and song lyrics refer to mutual tolerance and the advantages of

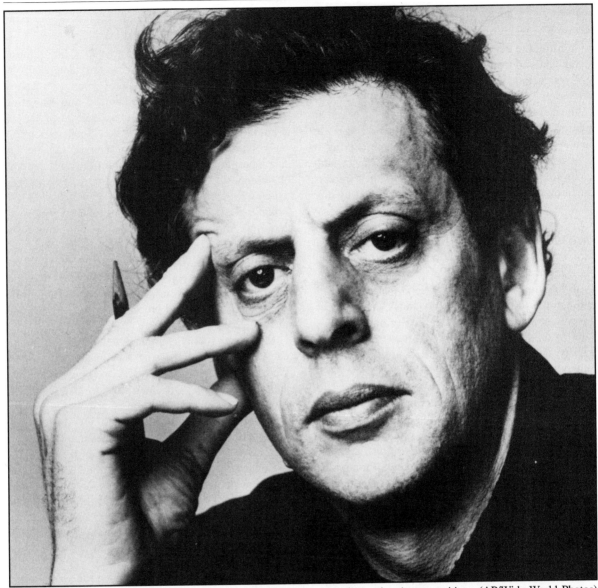

Philip Glass incorporates multicultural musical styles into his minimalist art/music compositions. (AP/Wide World Photos)

diversity. Musicians such as Paul Simon and David Byrne have spotlighted musicians and styles of other cultures in their work. The degree to which these practices provide financial and social empowerment to traditionally oppressed groups remains unclear, but musicians and composers have been at the forefront in the expression of American diversity.

Professional Careers and Lifestyles. Art musicians derive most of their income and professional recognition from concert performance in orchestras, wind ensembles, opera and choral groups, chamber ensembles, and solo recitals. Musicians might change jobs and relocate many times in pursuit of the best position in the most prestigious performing organization, gradually building their reputation and enhancing their professional status. In addition to relocating for career development, solo performers and members of major metropolitan orchestras travel on national and international concert tours on an annual basis. While at home, most ensembles follow regular rehearsal, recording, and performance schedules, but overall, the musician's lifestyle requires flexibility and endurance.

Art composers create works on commission for performance groups and earn royalties on publication and performance of their compositions. Because concert artists perform a great deal of previously existing repertoire, the demand for new compositions is relatively low, and many composers also work as performers, conductors, professors, or composers for film and television.

Popular musicians generally achieve fame and financial reward with "hit" recordings that achieve top national sales and radio play. Musicians striving to establish an individual sound and musical identity often tour extensively at the outset of their careers, performing concerts to encourage listeners to buy their recordings. Successful, well-known musicians may tour less frequently, pursuing recording projects from their home base and relying on their established reputation and record company marketing efforts to sell their musical product.

In addition to pop music "stars," many musicians work as touring, studio, or session musicians, who perform with different groups in a variety of styles. Session or touring musicians rely on their technical virtuosity, network of contacts, and ability to work with others to obtain and successfully complete jobs. Though such musicians exercise less artistic and logistical control over their careers than stars, they rely less on public popularity for their success.

Many popular musicians compose some or all of their own material, and their compositional style becomes part of their individual sound. Professional songwriters compose much of the American popular repertoire, selling the rights to their songs or collecting royalties on publication and performance. Successful popular composers often have ongoing relationships with performers and producers, writing songs tailored to an artist's strengths and aesthetics. Because the demand for new popular music is high, established composers generally enjoy busy and lucrative careers. Yet it is very difficult for an unknown composer to sell or publish songs.

The process of creating music for commercial release or performance involves many other creative roles that blur the distinction between musician and composer. One such position is that of musical director, who oversees the musical content, style, and arrangement of live music performances. He or she employs a staff of arrangers who prepare compositions for performance, using different musical styles and instruments to achieve the desired effect. Arrangers may in turn use the support of orchestrators, who assign individual parts to instruments, and copyists, who write out the instrumental parts from the composer's score.

In the recording studio, the producer, like a music director, works with musicians and technicians to achieve a certain musical sound, and must have a knowledge of the playing technique and acoustical properties of each instrument, as well as of the recording technology of the studio. Often responsible for contributing arrangements or musical sequences to a composition, producers generally have a background in composing, arranging, or record engineering. Quincy JONES, for instance, worked as a musician and composer-arranger for Count Basie's jazz band, and has since produced many successful pop recordings, including U.S.A. for Africa's *We Are the World* and several songs by Michael Jackson. Producers work closely with engineers, who operate the recording console, and make decisions regarding microphone techniques and audio signal processing to achieve the producer's goals.

Most professional musicians belong to the American Federation of Musicians, a national union that establishes minimum pay scales, working conditions, and contract terms for performance and recording. Most major performance venues and record companies engage only union musicians, but many small, local performances and private or demonstration recording sessions are conducted outside the union.

Composers generally belong to one of two organizations that collect and distribute royalties and fees. The American Society of Composers, Authors, and Publishers (ASCAP) and Broadcast Music, Inc. (BMI) monitor the commercial broadcast and use of musical compositions to determine the moneys due to composers.

Despite the vast amount of music performed and recorded in the United States, opportunities to work in the upper echelons of commercial or art music are relatively limited, and many musicians instead perform locally, in small concerts, clubs, festivals, parties, and churches. These "gigging" musicians are generally paid per performance, at a relatively low rate. There is little job security, and some musicians derive their main income from other employment.

Some of the most influential American musicians have crossed the lines between musician and composer, as well as art and popular music. Leonard Bernstein (1918-1992), for instance, was a pianist, conductor, and composer. Trained at Harvard and conductor of the New York Philharmonic Orchestra, the Israel

Philharmonic Orchestra, and the Boston Symphony Orchestra, Bernstein composed orchestral, choral, chamber, and solo vocal music, opera, ballets, and a film score. He also wrote in the popular style of musical theater, including the musical *West Side Story*, that incorporated the sounds of popular, jazz, and symphonic music in a story addressing ethnic tensions in New York.

Duke ELLINGTON, an African American pianist, composer, arranger, and band leader, also crossed

Panamanian American musician and composer Rubén Blades has combined his musical career with a successful acting career. (AP/Wide World Photos)

many of the boundaries of American music. Ellington began as a jazz pianist and became famous as leader of a big band performing at New York's COTTON CLUB. In addition to composing numerous jazz standards and pioneering complex, symphonic-style jazz arrangement techniques, Ellington wrote symphonic jazz concert music such as *Black, Brown and Beige* (1943), and also composed suites and religious music drawing on jazz and art music styles and forms. He was perhaps the first to earn consideration of jazz as a "serious" concert music, and was, along with Louis ARMSTRONG among the first African American musical heroes with equal appeal to blacks and whites.

SUGGESTED READINGS. For brief biographies of many concert musicians, see *Baker's Biographical Dictionary of Musicians* (5th ed., 1971), edited by Nicolas Slonimsky. Two books examining the role of gender in Western music composition and performance are Susan McClary's *Feminine Endings: Music, Gender, and Sexuality* (1991), and *Women Making Music: The Western Art Tradition, 1150-1950* (1986), edited by Jane Bowers and Judith Tick. See also *Women and Music: A History* (1991), edited by Karin Pendle, *Blacks in Classical Music* (1977), by Raoul Abdul, and *Black Popular Music in America* (1986), by Arnold Shaw.—*Elizabeth J. Miles*

Muslims: Adherents of Islam. Muslims are divided into two main traditions, the Sunni and the Shiite, which differ principally over religious authority. In most matters of faith, ritual, and ethical practice, however, there is little to differentiate them. For both, the prophet Muhammad (570?-632) is believed to be the last and greatest of the prophets. Both hold that Allah's purpose for humanity is revealed in the Koran, the scripture of Islam. Both consider Muhammad a model of the true Muslim and look to his example as authoritative for religious practice. Both traditions observe the "five pillars": the confession of the unity of Allah, ritual prayer five times daily, fasting during the month of Ramadan, almsgiving, and pilgrimage to Mecca.

Though Islam originated in the Middle East, it is found today in nearly every country of the world. Not only are Muslims the dominant religious group among countries of the Arabic-speaking world, Turkey, and Iran, they are majorities as well in countries such as Pakistan, Bangladesh, Indonesia, and other Asian nations as well as in many nations of sub-Saharan Africa. Significant Muslim populations are also found in China, India, parts of Europe, and the former Soviet

Muslims in the United States aspire to fulfilling one of the "five pillars" of their faith—a pilgrimage to Mecca and the Grand Mosque pictured here. (AP/Wide World Photos)

Union. In the twentieth century immigrant peoples from nearly sixty countries have made Islam an important and uniquely diverse religious community in North America.

In the United States, where some demographers estimate that Islam will overtake Judaism as the second-largest religion in the twenty-first century, Islam has shown itself to be an ethnic religion with the challenges that face such communities. The challenge of overcoming the national and religious tensions that have historically divided Muslims has been particularly urgent for many Muslims in the United States. Also important has been the need to preserve Muslim religious identity within the context of modern American society. Local mosques and Islamic centers such as that of Toledo, Ohio, offer models for bringing Muslims from diverse national and religious backgrounds together for worship and prayer, religious education, and spiritual direction. Beginning in 1952 with the organization of the Federation of Islamic Associations, American Muslims have promoted cooperation among their diverse communities. The Muslim Student Association (1963) today encourages the preservation of Muslim identity among university students, and the Islamic Society of North America (1981) is dedicated to the unity of diverse ethnic Muslim communities. Muslim organizations have also played an increasingly visible role in educating the American public about the Arab world and taking a stand on conflicts such as the Persian Gulf War in the Middle East and the Bosnian civil war in the former Yugoslavia.

The overwhelming number of converts to Islam in the United States have been AFRICAN AMERICANS, who number approximately one million of the six million orthodox Muslims in the United States. Some of these converts came to Islam through the influence of Elijah MUHAMMAD and the NATION OF ISLAM. MALCOLM X, a prominent member of that movement, did much to move blacks closer to normative Islam, and Wallace D. Muhammad completed the transition to orthodoxy, adopting in 1980 the name American Muslim Mission for the movement. The old Nation of Islam was revived by LOUIS FARRAKHAN with an estimated twenty thousand members.

SUGGESTED READINGS. A brief overview with an interesting section on Islam in the United States is found in Frederick M. Denny's *Islam and the Muslim Community* (1987). For greater detail, see Yvonne Haddad's and Adair Lummis' *Islamic Values in the United States* (1987), Haddad's *The Muslims of America* (1991), and *The Muslim Community in North America* (1983) by Earle Waugh and others. On Islam among African Americans, see Charles Eric Lincoln's *The Black Muslims in America* (1961).

Mutual aid societies and organizations: Associations formed by ethnic groups for economic and social benefit. In the United States during the nineteenth and twentieth centuries, thousands of mutual aid societies were begun by free people of color, emancipated slaves, and immigrants of virtually every nationality. Individuals who shared a common plight created organizations designed to meet their needs and mitigate their problems.

Mutual aid societies represent a strategy for group, rather than individual, adaptation to a market economy and competitive political context. By pooling money and mobilizing cooperative effort, members hoped to overcome shared disadvantages. By reinforcing group identities, mutual aid societies helped shape the landscape of ethnic relations and contributed significantly to the economic well-being of low-income wage earners.

These were largely secular organizations in which members paid dues in exchange for a range of financial benefits. Although they existed across a wide spectrum of ethnic groups in the United States, they took on highly similar structures and functions. Typically they began as burial societies, formed out of the basic need to ensure loved ones a proper funeral and internment. When a community is composed mainly of young people, as is typical for migrant groups, death is less frequent and benefit claims are few. Thus, many small premiums amass over time into sizable amounts of capital. This often allowed burial societies to invest and expand into other cooperative ventures.

Members invested in meeting halls and recreational equipment, creating community centers where they could reinforce social ties and nourish national pride. Meeting halls generated additional revenues from private rentals and admission charges to social and cultural events. Members pooled their capital to fund such things as medical care, loans for houses and businesses, and student scholarships. The development of American mutual aid societies reveals both similarities and differences among ethnic groups adjusting to urban industrial conditions.

AFRICAN AMERICANS, European Americans, and Latinos formed mutual benefit societies in the United States that closely paralleled one another. They drew from a common European tradition of guilds, brotherhoods, and friendly societies. West African tribal associations and secret societies may have also influenced the African American societies. Early Asian immigrants also created formal associations modeled on Chinese cultural traditions. Mutual aid among States were formed by Africans. The Free African Society was founded in 1778 in Philadelphia by veterans of the revolutionary war, among others. In the pre-emancipation period, hundreds of African American mutual benefit societies were formed in cities in the Northeast. Free people of color also established socie-

Southeast Asian mutual assistance associations are the modern successors to mutual aid societies. Here a Laotian refugee practices English skills in a Merced, Calif., training program. (L. Gubb/UNHCR)

American Indians has operated mainly within family, clan, and tribe, without voluntary associations comparable to those of other ethnic groups.

African American Mutual Aid Societies. Some of the earliest mutual benefit societies in the United ties in several southern cities, notably Charleston, South Carolina; Richmond, Virginia; and New Orleans. Whether in the North or the South, free Africans confronted many social barriers and economic disadvantages. Mutual aid societies eased those problems by offering alternative social opportunities and a means of raising capital. They affirmed social and cultural ties while providing sick pay, survivors benefits, educational assistance, support for the elderly, and in a few cases, help with emigration back to Africa.

After the CIVIL WAR, mutual aid societies established by freed slaves proliferated. These societies tended to be small and localized, drawn from the members of a church or group of churches in the same community. Many societies sponsored annual celebrations of the EMANCIPATION PROCLAMATION, reflecting a common sense of ethnic and political identity. In the late 1800's, several African American mutual aid societies grew quite large, spawning local chapters in other cities and states.

Dues payments across broad geographic regions created large bases of capital, which in turn seeded the development of banking, insurance, and business investment in many African American communities. For example, the True Reformers, a religious mutual benefit society, began in 1883 in Richmond, Virginia, with one hundred members and $150. In less than twenty years, they had built a multistate enterprise with more than fifty thousand subscribers whose dues premiums underwrote the creation of a bank, a home for the elderly, a communal farm, and a string of member-operated businesses. Although the True Reformers did not survive past WORLD WAR I, other such enterprises did manage to endure. Many contemporary African American banks and insurance companies had their origins in mutual benefit societies. Some insurance companies, however, were paradoxically weakened by the loss of a captive SEGREGATED market after the passage of civil rights laws.

Immigrant Societies. Immigrants in the nineteenth and early twentieth centuries typically formed mutual aid societies in the United States within a short time after arrival. NEW YORK CITY, the major port of entry, was also the cradle of immigrant mutual aid. Irish, Swedes, and Germans had mutual aid societies there in the mid-1800's. After the Civil War, and especially after the beginning of the twentieth century, immigrant lodges could be found in nearly all large American cities and towns. Italians, Poles, Yugoslavs, Jews, Mexicans, Bohemians, Cubans, Greeks, and dozens of other groups formed local organizations to help themselves adapt to places like Omaha, Nebraska; Sioux Falls, South Dakota; Denver, Colorado; Tampa, Florida; Cleveland, Ohio; and Pittsburgh, Pennsylvania.

Literally thousands of these organizations were es-

tablished in the early 1900's. In CHICAGO, several nationality groups had societies numbering in the hundreds. Membership in immigrant societies was often based on origins in a particular region or village, rather than national identity. This, combined with religious and political factions, produced a highly segmented system of very similar institutions. For example, Cleveland in 1900 had thirty-five different Italian societies, twenty-five of which restricted membership to persons from a particular village.

Immigrant lodges helped both to shape and to define ethnic diversity in urban communities. Local culture was in large measure centered on the meeting halls of lodges. Dances, picnics, musical performances, holiday observances, and community meetings combined with an increasingly sophisticated system of social welfare benefits. Groups with similar origins and interests often joined together in multiethnic labor organizations.

As immigration increased, groups set up ethnic associations at the state and national levels which offered greater advantages of scale and coordination of benefits. Organizations such as the Polish National Alliance, the Sons of Italy, and the Croatian Fraternal Union provided a national voice for ethnic interests and the corporate capacity to establish systems of mortgage lending, scholarships, and publishing. These broader ethnic organizations helped overcome regional divisions and forged a more unified sense of identity, conditioned in part by the ongoing interest of exiles in nationalist issues in their homelands.

The early twentieth century immigrant mutual aid societies are to some extent relics of the past, although they have by no means disappeared. In many cities, local lodge halls still serve as gathering points for social and cultural activities. National ethnic organizations that began in the early 1900's still influence aspects of U.S. foreign policy.

Industrial dislocations in the 1930's and radical transformation of cities in the 1950's and 1960's eroded the common base of work and neighborhood that had nurtured the early organizations. Aging members drew more heavily on the benefit plans. Commercial and employer group insurance became more popular, although ethnic insurance still claims millions of subscribers. Several of the national organizations continue to have large and complex operations, although membership has been declining steadily.

Early Asian immigrants in the United States also created mutual aid societies. Chinese and Japanese immigrants on the West Coast joined organizations based on origins in a particular district in China or prefecture in Japan. These locality-based organizations were allied into large federations. In San Francisco, the Chinese federation known as the "Six Companies" exerted considerable power in Chinatown. Japanese federations called Japanese Associations of America existed in four western cities (Los Angeles, San Francisco, Portland, and Seattle). The associations were licensed by Japan to secure documents needed by immigrants from the Japanese government. The federations and local associations provided varied types of assistance to newcomers and tried to shield them from the severe DISCRIMINATION faced by early Asian immigrants on the West Coast. Within these organizations, lines of extended family offered extremely important networks of mutual assistance.

In 1965, U.S. immigration laws that had discriminated against Asians in particular, and non-Europeans in general, were reformed. The flow of immigrants since then has accelerated, dominated by arrivals from Asia and Latin America. These newer immigrants have formed various kinds of associations in cities where numbers are sufficient to support them. Such organizations generally focus on social, cultural, and educational activities; some pursue exile political interests or help settle the newest arrivals within the group. For example, Southeast Asians have developed a network of hundreds of mutual assistance associations (MAAs) since the mid-1970's which use government funds and private donations to offer housing assistance, job training, and English classes to needy refugees. Other new immigrants continue to find mutual aid in a traditional type of organization set up to offer rotating credit to its members.

Rotating Credit Associations. In addition to formal immigrant associations, both CHINESE and JAPANESE AMERICANS historically operated rotating credit associations. This institution, called *hui* in Chinese and *tanomashi* in Japanese, was invented at least eight hundred years ago in China. Groups of up to one hundred immigrants established common funds based on individual donations made on a weekly basis. Each week, one member would receive the lump sum, with the process continuing for as many weeks as there were participants. Those who collected early in the cycle received an interest-free loan; those who collected later engaged in forced savings. Many variations are found in particular arrangements: For example, some involved weekly feasts given by the organizer, who made no contribution to the fund, while others had variable rates of interest or lotteries to decide the sequence of collection.

Rotating credit associations offered access to capital in a commercial lending environment that was extremely hostile to Asian immigrants. This form of capitalization gave rise to many Asian businesses and helped underwrite the costs of HIGHER EDUCATION for many families.

Rotating credit associations play an important role in economic adjustment for new immigrants including not only those from China, Japan, and Korea, but also those from the West Indies and Mexico. Such associations, called *esusu* in Yoruba, had long been popular in West Africa. Africans in Jamaica, Trinidad, and other parts of the Caribbean transported this tradition first to the islands as slaves, and much later to the United States as immigrants. Among Mexican immigrants, rotating credit associations or *tandas* are also common, especially among women. Trust and mutual responsibility are crucial to the success of rotating credit in all groups that use this system.

SUGGESTED READINGS. See Susan Greenbaum's review essay, "Comparison of African American and Euro-American Mutual Aid Societies in Nineteenth Century America," in *Journal of Ethnic Studies* 19 (Fall, 1991), pp. 95-121. Other sources for European mutual aid include *Self-Help in Urban America* (1980), edited by Scott Cummings, and the Immigration History Research Center, University of Minnesota's *Records of Ethnic Fraternal Benefit Association in the United States* (1981). Latino mutual aid is discussed in Jose Rivera's "Self Help as Mutual Protection: The Development of Hispanic Fraternal Benefit Societies," in *Journal of Applied Behavioral Sciences* 23, no. 3 (1987), pp. 387-396. Asian societies and rotating credit associations are covered in Ivan Light's *Ethnic Enterprise in America* (1972). Jamaican and Mexican revolving credit associations are discussed in Aubrey Bonnett's *Institutional Adaptation of West Indian Immigrants to America* (1981) and Carlos Velez-Ibanez's *Bonds of Mutual Trust* (1983), respectively.—*Susan Greenbaum*

Myrdal, Gunnar (Dec. 6, 1898, Gustafs, Dalecarlia, Sweden—May 17, 1987, Stockholm, Sweden): Swedish economist. Myrdal studied law and economics at the University of Stockholm, Sweden, and subsequently taught there from 1927 to 1950 and again from 1960 to 1967. He served as minister of trade and commerce for

Sweden (1945-1947) and as executive secretary of the United Nations Economic Commission for Europe (1947-1957). Myrdal is most recognized in the United States for his contribution to sociology in *An American Dilemma: The Negro Problem and Modern Democracy* (1944), a study of American race relations. His other works include *Beyond the Welfare State: Economic Planning and Its International Implications* (1960), and *The Challenge to Affluence* (1963). In 1974, he was awarded the Nobel Prize in Economic Sciences, jointly, with Friedrich A. von Hayek.

Mythology, American Indian. *See* **Religion and mythology—American Indian**